THE CUBAN REVOLUTION

THE CUBAN REVOLUTION

A Research-Study Guide (1959-1969)

BY

Nelson P. Valdés and Edwin Lieuwen

UNIVERSITY OF NEW MEXICO PRESS

Albuquerque

FOREWORD

Work on this bibliography began in 1959, the year of Castro's revolutionary triumph. At the time a Cuban Professor, Dr. Miguel Jorrín, Director of the Division of Latin American Affairs at the University of New Mexico, had the foresight to begin collecting all available materials on the developing Cuban social revolution. Professor Jorrín's untimely death in the spring of 1965 did not interrupt the collection process, for a Cuban student, Nelson P. Valdés, continued the work

In the fall of 1965, the University of New Mexico was awarded a five-year grant by the Ford Foundation to conduct training and research on the process of social revolution in Latin America. Under the grant Mr. Valdés was appointed a research assistant and a substantial portion of his energies have since been devoted to collecting bibliography on the Cuban revolution. In this work, the University of New Mexico has worked closely with the Hispanic Foundation of the Library of Congress, with the Hoover Library of Stanford University, with the University of Miami, as well as with the principal international dealers in Cuban books.

By the spring of 1970 about 12,000 bibliographical items dealing with the Cuban revolution (1959-1969) had been collected. During the summer of 1970, the selection and classification process took place. We have selected for this bibliography what we believe to be the 3839 most important items essential for humanities and social science scholars interested in pursuing research on various aspects of the Cuban revolution. Included are books, documents, pamphlets, and articles. If this research guide in any way contributes to scholarly research on the Cuban revolution, the authors will have achieved their purpose.

Edwin Lieuwen

CONTENTS

INTRODUCTION

The Cuban revolution, the most fundamental and thorough-going social upheaval that has affected Latin America in the modern era, has been underway now for more than a dozen years. In the process, the pre-revolutionary political organizations, economic systems, social structures, and institutions have been overturned and a new revolutionary order has taken form.

Despite the vast outpouring of literature and information on the revolution by journalists, travelers, scholars, exiles, revolutionary leaders, and by pro- and anti-Cuban governments around the world, more heat than light has been shed on the nature of revolution itself. The great bulk of the material thus far published tends to be polemical. In fact the place of publication usually indicates the bias of the author. If the item in question is published in Havana, Moscow, Bucharest, Prague, or Leipzig it will invariably be pro-revolution, whereas if the place of publication is Miami, Washington, or Caracas, it will be anti-revolution. There is a reasonably good balance of pro- and anti-revolutionary works, and a generally more scholarly tone for works emanating from Western Europe, the United States (except for Washington and Miami), and Latin America (except for Caracas and Havana).

This vast outpouring of literature on the Cuban revolution is testimony to the worldwide interest and impact of this social unheaval. Although the domestic implications of the phenomenon affect less that nine million people, its foreign implications have reached the farthest corners of the world and have deeply involved not only the neighboring Latin American republics but all the major powers of the world. Hence the sudden growth of interest in contemporary Cuba by most foreign governments, followed by a new interest in Cuba in academic communities. In the United States, in Latin America, and in Western Europe, as well as in Cuba itself, government agencies, exile organizations, private research institutions, universities, and individual scholars and researchers continue to increase the flow of materials on the Cuban revolution.

Up until now there has been no systematic effort to collect, locate, select, classify, and judge the quality of this increasingly unmanageable flow of material.

The purpose of this Guide is to provide a useful bibliographical tool for all those interested in developing their interest, pursuing research, or teaching courses on the Cuban revolution. It is designed to save time—to lead the researcher quickly to the essential sources on any topic dealing with revolutionary Cuba. It attempts to open up the main themes of the Cuban revolution by citing the principal printed sources on all major subjects.

The present work includes bibliographical tools, guide books, documents (including collections), journalists' accounts, eyewitness reports, memoirs, mimeographed reports, dissertations, scholarly monographs, books of every nature on contemporary Cuba, and the most important periodical and newspaper articles. Approximately 40 per cent of the titles are in Spanish, 40 per cent in English, and the remaining 20 per cent in various East and West European languages. All items not printed in Roman script have been transliterated.

An effort has been made to make the references as brief as possible. Each item, wherever possible, includes the following: (1) Author (2) Title (3) Place of publication (4) Publisher (5) Date of publication and (6) Number of pages. Brief annotations have been added wherever the authors felt it necessary to reveal the subject matter, nature, bias, or quality of the item in question. Only when such matters are apparent from the author, title, or place of publication, have annotations been omitted.

The table of contents, broken down into a large variety of categories and sub-categories, should readily lead the researcher or teacher to the specific subject matter in which he is interested. The author index will quickly supply all the major items written by not only contemporary scholars and observers interested in the revolution but also the speeches and writings by key revolutionary personalities, such as Fidel Castro, Che Guevara, Blas Roca, Raúl Roa, Raúl Castro, Armando Hart, Carlos Rafael Rodríguez, Antonio Núñez Jiménez and others.

Particularly, care has been taken to include in this bibliography all the important background materials essential for a study of the various aspects of the revolution. Such materials will be found under the appropriate subject headings. A complete listing of revolutionary periodicals and newspapers, which are broad sources for information on many aspects of the revolution, are found under Research Tools.

Obviously all the materials cited in this bibliography cannot be found in a single location. To assist the researcher in finding the scarcer materials, the general section includes a listing and brief description of the principal United States libraries holding important collections of materials relating to the Cuban revolution. Also in this section is included the names and addresses of the principal international bookdealers that handle publications emanating from revolutionary Cuba as well as foreign publications on the Cuban revolution.

The uneven quantity of materials published under the various subject classifications clearly reveals the gaps in information and research on the Cuban revolution. International relations, quite understandably, has been the most heavily worked, but curiously, information on contemporary Cuban society (that is, on social change, on class structure, on demography, crime, race, etc.—all important concerns for students of social revolution) has been scarce.

Ideally, the most useful bibliography would carry abundant entries for all categories of subject matter of potential interest to the student of the Cuban revolution. As a practical matter, however, the authors could obviously include only those categories for which published information was available. For example, under Political Structure (Section III C), it would seem vital to include sub-sections on public administration and the bureaucracy, but few important studies have been done on these matters. Similarly, in Section IV C (Relations with Latin America) it might seem curious, in view of the importance of Cuba's current relationships with Bolivia, Peru, and Chile, that the bulk of the entries relate to Mexico, Venezuela, and the Dominican Republic, which were more important up to 1967. Again, it is a question of availability of materials. In Section V (The Economy), the absence of published materials precluded a separate sub-category on *Fisheries,* even though this industry is probably just as important in Revolutionary Cuba as the sub-category *Stockraising.*

Hopefully, this bibliography will prove useful in helping scholars not only to digest and analyze the existing materials, but also to point the way to important new studies in the future.

Edwin Lieuwen
Nelson P. Valdés
University of New Mexico
Albuquerque, New Mexico

I. RESEARCH TOOLS

A. BIBLIOGRAPHIES

1. Braginskaia, E. V., and L. A. Shur, Comps., *Kuba v sovetskoi pechati,* Moscow: Vses. biblioteka inostr. lit., 1963. 75 pp.
   Books and articles on contemporary Cuba appearing in the Soviet press.

2. Caribbean Commission, *Current Caribbean Bibliography, 1951-,* San Juan: Corporación de Desarrollo Económico del Caribe, 1951-. Irregular, 11 volumes through 1968.

3. Cuba, Academia de Ciencias, *Guía del Archivo Nacional,* Havana, 1967. 19 pp.

4. Cuba, Biblioteca Nacional José Martí, *Bibliografía Cubana, 1959-,* Havana: Consejo Nacional del Cultura, 6 vols., 1967, 1968-.
   Most comprehensive current bibliography of books and pamphlets published in Cuba. Compiled by Marta Dulzaides Serrate and Marta Bidot Pérez.

5. Cuba, Biblioteca Nacional José Martí, *Guía de la Biblioteca Nacional José Martí,* Havana, 1960. 12 pp.

6. Cuba, Consejo Nacional de Cultura, *Guía de bibliotecas de la República de Cuba,* Havana: Biblioteca Nacional José Martí, 1966. 107 pp.

7. Cuba, Ministerio de la Industria Azucarera, *Datos bibliográficos,* Havana. 72 pp.

8. Cuba, Ministerio de la Industria Azucarera, *Resúmenes, bibliografías, índices de publicaciones,* Havana, 1966. 70 pp.

9. Fort, Gilberto V., *The Cuban Revolution of Fidel Castro Viewed from Abroad,* Lawrence: Univ. of Kansas Libraries, 1969. 140 pp.
   Books and pamphlets. Annotated.

10. Institute of Caribbean Studies, University of Puerto Rico, *Caribbean Studies 1961-.*
    Quarterly providing good list of books and articles from or about Cuba.

11. Okinshevich, Leo, *Latin America in Soviet Writings,* Baltimore: Johns Hopkins Press, 1966. 2 vols.
    Extensive listings on Cuba.

12. Pariseau, Earl J., *Cuba; a Select List of Reference and Research Tools,* Washington: Library of Congress, Hispanic Foundation, 1966. 11 pp.

13. Peraza, Fermín, *Anuario bibliográfico cubano,* Havana, 1937-1959; Miami, 1960-1965. 25 vols.
    Books and pamphlets. Author died in 1968.

14. Peraza, Fermín, *Bibliografía cubana,* Washington: Hispanic Foundation, U.S. Library of Congress, 1945. 58 pp.

An annotated guide to bibliographies on Cuba.

15. Peraza, Fermín, "Bibliografía cubana de libros de texto de historia de Cuba (1902-1958)," *Revista de archivos bibliotecas y museos,* (Madrid), Jan.-June 1959. pp. 257-273.

16. Peraza, Fermín, *Diccionario biográfico cubano,* Havana: Ediciones Anuario Bibliográfico Cubano, 1951-1960. 11 vols.
   Vol. 12 (1966) Gainesville; vol. 13 (1968) Coral Gables.

17. Peraza, Fermín, *Personalidades cubanas,* Havana: Ediciones Anuario Bibliográfico Cubano, 1957-1959. 7 vols.
   Biography of influential citizens.

18. Peraza, Fermín, *Personalidades cubanas, Cuba en el exilio,* Gainesville, 1965. 99 pp.
   Biographical dictionary of Cubans living in exile.

19. Peraza, Fermín, *Revolutionary Cuba: a Bibliographical Guide, 1966, Coral Gables,* Florida: University of Miami Press, 1967. 188 pp.
   Superceding *Anuario bibliográfico cubano* (1937-1965), 695 items cited.

20. Quintero Mesa, Rosa, *Cuba,* Ann Arbor, Michigan: University Microfilms, 1969. 209 pp.
   2,000 Cuban serial titles available in 20 U.S. universities.

21. Reason, Barbara, et al., *Cuba Since Castro; a Bibliography of Relevant Literature,* Washington: Special Operations Research Office, American University, 1962. 25 pp.

22. Soto Acosta, Jesús, *Bibliografía*

"prensa clandestina revolucionaria" (1952-1958), Havana: Biblioteca Nacional José Martí, 1965. 25 pp.
   Lists 94 periodicals.

23. Suchlicki, Jaime, ed., *The Cuban Revolution: A Documentary Bibliography, 1952-1968,* Coral Gables: University of Miami, 1969. 83 pp.

24. Trelles, Carlos M., *Bibliografía cubana del siglo xx (1900-1916),* Matanzas: Imprenta de Quiros y Estrada, 1916-1917. 2 vols.

25. U.S. Library of Congress. Hispanic Foundation, *Cuba: a Select List of Reference and Research Tools,* Washington, 1966. 11 pp.
   Mimeographed.

B. DIRECTORIES

26. *Anglo-American Directory of Cuba,* Almendares, Marianao, Cuba, 1960. 226 pp.

27. Anónimo, *Nuestra Sociedad,* Havana, 1958. 890 pp.

28. *Anuario Cinematográfico y Radial Cubano,* Havana, 1940-1958. 18 vols.

29. *Anuario comercial e industrial de Cuba,* Havana, 1952-1959. 7 vols.

30. Cuba, Cámara de Comercio, *Directorio comercial e industrial cubano,* Havana, 1951-1959. 4 vols.

31. Cuba, Cámara de Comercio, *Directorio oficial de exportación e importación, producción y turismo,* Havana, 1941-1959.
   Yearly.

32. Cuba, Ministerio de Estado, *Lista del cuerpo diplomático extranjero,* Havana: P. Fernández, Seoane, Fernández, 1934-1959. 19 vols.

33. Cuba, Ministerio de Relaciones Exteriores, *Lista del cuerpo diplomático y consular extranjero*, Havana, 1964. 184 pp.

34. Cuba, Ministerio de Relaciones Exteriores, *Lista del cuerpo diplomático y consular extranjero*, Havana, 1967. 182 pp.

35. *Cuban Oil Directory*, Havana: Editorial Petróleo, 1958. 119 pp.

36. Cuban Telephone Company, *Directorio telefónico*, Havana, 1885-1960. 102 vols.

37. *Directorio de Abogados de Cuba, 1952-1960*, Havana, 1952-1960. 7 vols.

38. *Directorio Bancario de Cuba*, Havana: Editorial Lex, 1950-1957. 7 vols.

39. *Directorio de Contadores Públicos de Cuba*. Havana: La Milagrosa, 1957-59. 6 vols.

40. *Directorio de Ingenieros y Arquitectos de Cuba*, Havana, 1953-1960. 6 vols.

41. *Directorio Médico-Social de Cuba, 1951-1960*, Havana: La Milagrosa, 1951-1960. 10 vols.

42. *Directorio Odontológico Social de Cuba, 1952-1959*, Havana: La Milagrosa, 1959. 2 vols.

43. *Directorio Social de La Habana*, Havana, 1929-1960. 32 vols.

44. *Libro de Oro de la Sociedad Habanera, 1945-1958*, Havana: Editorial Lex, 1945-1958. 14 vols.

45. Peraza Fermín, *Directorio de revistas y periódicos de Cuba*, Gainesville, 1963. 21 pp.
    Guide of newspapers and magazines published in Cuba, their addresses, rates, names of directors, etc.

46. *Primer anuario comercial e industrial de Cuba*, Havana, 1953-1957. 4 vols.

47. *Registro Social de la Habana, 1950-1959*, Havana, 1950-1959. 10 vols.

C. ENCYCLOPEDIAS, GUIDES, ALMANACS

48. *Album cubano*, Havana: Talleres de Avance Revolucionario, 1960. 210 pp.

49. *Almanaque de la Caridad; directorio oficial de las diócesis de Cuba*, Havana, 1882-1960. 78 vols.

50. *Almanaque judicial, 1887-1960*, Havana: Tipografía de la Gaceta Oficial, 1887-1960. 10 vols.

51. *Almanaque popular cubano*, Havana: Ediciones de Luxe, 1961. 144 pp.

52. Alvarez y Correoso, Juan Arturo, *Guía práctica de la ciudad de La Habana*, Havana, 1946. 213 pp.

53. Bustamante, Luis J., *Enciclopedia popular cubana*, Havana: Cultural, 194(?)-1948. 3 vols.

54. Clark, Sydney Aylmer, *All the Best in Cuba*, New York: Dodd, Mead, 1954. 235 pp.
    Guide.

55. *Cuba '67 Image of a Country*, Havana: Book Institute, 1967. 443 pp.
    Almanac.

56. *Cuba en la mano; enciclopedia popular ilustrada*, Havana: Ministry of Education of Cuba, 1940. 1302 pp.
    Natural history, history, education, tourism, politics, commerce, sports and maps.

57. Cuba, Instituto Cubano del Turismo, *Cuba, 1958: Travel to*

Cuba, Playland of the Americas, Miami, 1958. 98 pp.

58. Cuba, Ministerio de Comercio, Depto. de Asuntos Judiciales, *Guía legal del comerciante; relaciones de precios y otras disposiciones oficiales dictadas por el Ministerio de Comercio hasta diciembre 31 de 1960,* Havana, 1961. 181 pp.

59. Cuba, Ministerio de Relaciones Exteriores, *La Habana monumental,* Havana, 1960. 29 pp. Photographs.

60. Cuba, Ministerio de Relaciones Exteriores, *Perfil de Cuba,* Havana, 1965. 327 pp. Handbook-Almanac.

61. Cuba, Partido Comunista, *Cuba: Territorio libre de América,* Havana: Comisión de Orientación Revolucionaria, 1966. 99 pp.

62. Le Febure, Roger, ed., *The Blue Guide to Cuba . . . 1926-1941, 1947-1956,* Havana, 1926-1956. 26 vols.

63. González, Raúl, *Clipper Guide to Cuba,* Havana: Editorial Clipper, 1947. 255 pp.

64. *Gran guía industrial y comercial de Cuba "Mercurio,"* Havana: Editora Newsland, 1956-1959. 2 vols.

65. *Guía de la Habana, Industria, Comercio, Profesión y Artes,* Havana, 1951. 72 pp.

66. *Guía de la Habana y Marianao; Graphic Tourist Guide for the City of Havana and Marianao,* Havana, 1951. 64 pp.

67. Havana, *Calendario del Arzobispado de la Habana . . . 1831-1953,* Havana, 1831-1953. 123 vols.

68. Iglesias, Ramiro E., *Guía de in-*formación y plano de La Habana, Havana: Impr. F. Solana y cía, 1947. 36 pp.

69. Leaf, Earl, *A Guide to Cuba,* New York: F. Farnam Associates, 1951. 32 pp.

70. *Libro de Cuba; una enciclopedia ilustrada,* Havana: Publicaciones Unidas, 1954. 556 pp.

71. *Nueva completa guía de La Habana; enciclopedia de información general,* Havana: Ediciones Luxe, 1961. 128 pp.

72. Oliarte, Esteban R., ed., *Cuba en la mano; enciclopedia popular ilustrada,* Havana: Imprenta Ucar, García y Cia, 1940. 1302 pp.

73. Suárez, Alex, *Guía informativa de la Habana y curiosidades . . . 1949,* Havana: Editorial Lex, 1949. 240 pp.

D. GEOGRAPHY

74. Anónimo, *Geografía económica de Cuba,* Havana: Instituto del Libro, 1967. 133 pp.

75. Boix Comas, Alberto, *Así es Cuba,* Havana: Cía. Petrolera Shell de Cuba, s. a., 1954. 160 pp. Geography.

76. Guardado, Juana María, *Geografía elemental de Cuba,* Havana: Impr. P. Fernández y cía, 1947. 216 pp.

77. *Mapa de la Isla de Cuba,* Havana: Editorial Cenit, 1956. 46 x 104 cm. color.

78. Marrero y Artiles, Levi, *Elementos de geografía de Cuba,* Havana: Editorial Minerva, 1946. 540 pp.

79. Marrero y Artiles, Levi, *Geografía de Cuba,* Havana: Talleres Tipográficos Alfa, 1951. 736 pp.

80. Marrero y Artiles, Levi, *Nueva geografía elemental de Cuba,* Havana: Impr. El Siglo XX, 1951. 160 pp.

81. Núñez Jiménez, Antonio, *Así es mi país,* Havana: Imprenta Nacional de Cuba, 1961. 174 pp. Geography. Description.

82. Núñez Jiménez, Antonio, *Cuba con la mochila al hombro,* Havana: Ediciones Unión, Reportajes, 1963. 405 pp.

83. Núñez Jímenez, Antonio, *Geografía de Cuba,* Havana: Editorial Lex, 1959. 642 pp. Valuable detailed work.

84. Torre y Huerta, Carlos de la, *Geografía de Cuba,* Havana. Cultural, s. a., 1955. 287 pp.

E. HISTORY
(See also Background to Revolution)

85. Aguirre, Sergio, *Lecciones de historia de Cuba,* Havana: MINFAR, 1963. 116 pp.

86. Breuil, Dolores, *Lecciones de historia de Cuba,* Havana: Ministerio de Educación, 1961. 95 pp.

87. Corbitt, Duvan C., "Cuban Revisionist Interpretations of Cuba's Struggle for Independence," *Hispanic American Historical Review,* Aug. 1963. pp. 395-404.

88. Cuba, Ministerio de Educación, *Historia de Cuba,* Havana: Editora Pedagógica, 1966. 2 vols.

89. Díaz, Emilio, *Essay of the Cuban History,* Coral Gables; Service Offset Printers, 1964. 427 pp. General history, last chapters on revolution.

90. Entralgo Vallina, Elias, *Lecciones de historia de Cuba,* Havana, 1960. 2 vols.

91. Fitzgibbon, Russell H., *Cuba and the United States, 1900-1935,* Menasha: The Collegiate Press, 1935. 311 pp.

92. Guerra y Sánchez, Ramiro, et al., eds., *Historia de la Nación Cubana,* Havana: Editorial Historia de la Nación Cubana, 1952. 10 vols. Comprehensive. Discovery to 1950.

93. Havana, Municipio, *Memoria anual . . . 1848-1959,* Havana, 1849-1959. 83 vols.

94. Jeréz Villarreal, Juan, *Oriente, biografía de una provincia,* Havana: El Siglo XX, 1960. 357 pp. Traced up to 1950's.

95. Johnson, Willis Fletcher, *The History of Cuba,* New York: B. F. Buck, 1920. 405 pp.

96. Márquez Sterling, Carlos, *Historia de Cuba, desde Colón hasta Castro,* New York: Las Américas Pub. Co., 1963. 496 pp. *Ortodoxo* historian.

97. Pardeiro, Francisco, *Geografía económica de Cuba,* Havana: Ed. López y Fraga, 1957. 3 vols.

98. Pérez Cabrera, José M., *Historiografía de Cuba,* Mexico: Instituto Panamericano de Geografía e Historia, 1962. 394 pp.

99. Pino-Santos, Oscar, *Historia de Cuba,* Havana: Editorial Nacional, 1964. 352 pp. Follows Marxist model.

100. Ponte Domínguez, Francisco J., *Matanzas; biografía de una provincia,* Havana: Imprenta El Siglo XX, 1959. 354 pp. Background study in regionalism.

101. Le Riverend, Julio, *La Habana,* (biografía de una provincia), Havana: Siglo XX, 1960. 507 pp.

102. Roig de Leuchsenring, Emilio, *Facetas de la vida de Cuba republicana, 1902-1952,* Havana: Oficina del Historiador de la Ciudad, 1954. 380 pp.

103. Roig de Leuchsenring, Emilio, *Historia de la Enmienda Platt; una interpretación de la realidad cubana,* Havana, 1961. 2 vols.

104. Roig de Leuchsenring, Emilio, *Introducción a la historia de Cuba Republicana: Los Estados Unidos contra Cuba libre,* Havana, 1959. 4 vols.

105. Roig de Leuchsenring, Emilio, *Tradición antimperialista de nuestra historia,* Havana, 1962. 87 pp.

106. Royal Institute of International Affairs, *Cuba: A Brief Political and Economic Survey,* London: Oxford University Press, 1958. 25 pp.

107. Santovenia, Emeterio, *Cuba y su historia,* Miami: Rema Press, 1965. 3 vols.
By former Batista official.

F. NEWSPAPERS

108. *América libre,* Los Angeles, 1965-.
Bi-weekly exile organ.

109. *Diario las Américas,* Miami, 1953-.
Daily. Mainly controlled by exiles.

110. *Diario de la Marina,* Havana, 1902-1959.
Reliable conservative daily.

111. *Diario de la Tarde,* Havana, 1961-1965.
Not official organ, although government-controlled daily. Ceased publication 21 October 1965.

112. Cuba, Partido Communista, *Granma,* Havana, Oct. 1965-.
Official organ of the Central Committee of the Communist Party. *Granma* was the result of the merging of *Revolución* and *Hoy.* Spanish version daily. English version weekly.

113. *Hoy,* Havana, 1934-1935; 1938-1953; 1959-1965.
Official organ of Partido Socialista Popular (communist). In 1965 it merged with *Revolución* giving rise to *Granma.*

114. *Juventud Rebelde,* Havana, 1965-.
Afternoon counterpart of *Granma.*

115. *El Mundo,* Havana, 1952-1968.
Most liberal daily in Havana. After 1960 it was government-controlled. Ended publication in 1968.

116. *Revolución,* Havana, 1957-1965.
Official organ of the Cuban revolutionary government.

117. *The Times of Havana,* Havana, Feb. 1957-Nov. 1960.
English language daily.

G. PERIODICALS

118. *Acción,* Miami, 1963-.
Organ of young Christian nationalists.

119. *Agro,* Havana, 1962-.
Bi-monthly bulletin.

120. *El amigo del pueblo,* New York, 1965-.
Irregular. Leftist exile publication.

121. Asociación de Hacendados de

Cuba, *Cubazúcar*, Havana, 1955-1960.
Monthly.

122. Asociación Judiciaria de Cuba en exilio, *Información judicial*, Miami, 1961.
Semi-monthly.

123. *El Avance criollo*, Miami, 1960-1962.
Weekly. Published by former staff of newspaper Avance.

124. *Bohemia*, Havana, 1908-.
Oldest and best privately owned newsweekly until taken over by the government in mid-1960. Illustrated.

125. Citizens Committee for a Free Cuba, *Cuba Policy Research Series*, Washington, 1964-.
Irregular.

126. Citizens Committee for a Free Cuba, *Free Cuba News*, Washington, 1963-.
Weekly. Irregular.

127. *Colina, revista universitaria cubana*, Rio Piedras, Puerto Rico, 1967-.
Irregular. Young leftist exiles.

128. Comité de Organizaciones Juveniles Cubanas en el Exilio, *Correo de la Juventud*, Miami, 1963-1965.
Monthly.

129. Consejo Revolucionario, *Cuba nueva*, Miami, 1961-1963.
Monthly. Exile publication.

130. *Correo de la Juventud*, Miami, 1963-1965.
Monthly. Organ of the Comité de Organizaciones Juveniles Cubanas in exiles.

131. Cuba, Academia de Ciencias, *Boletín de Geofísica*, Havana, 1965-.
Monthly.

132. Cuba, Academia de Ciencias, *Ciencias sociales contemporáneas*, Havana, 1965-.
Quarterly.

133. Cuba, Academia de Ciencias, Instituto de Etnología y Folklore, *Etnología y folklore*, Havana, 1966-.
Semi-annually.

134. Cuba, Academia de Ciencias, Instituto de Literatura y Lingüística, *Boletín, Havana*, 1967-.
Every two months.

135. Cuba, Academia de Ciencias, Instituto de Literatura y Lingüística, *L/L*, Havana, 1967-.
Quarterly

136. Cuba, Academia de Ciencias, *Revista de Agricultura*, Havana, 1967-.
Quarterly.

137. Cuba, Academia de Ciencias, *Revista Cubana de Ciencia Agrícola*, Havana, 1967-.
Irregular.

138. Cuba, Archivo Nacional, *Noticias y presencias*, Havana, Jan. 1960-.
Irregular.

139. Cuba, Asociación de Jóvenes Rebeldes, *Mella*, Havana, 1960-.
Monthly.

140. Cuba, Asociación Nacional de Agricultores Pequeños, *ANAP*, Havana, 1961-.
Monthly.

141. Cuba, Asociación de Técnicos Azucareros de Cuba, *Boletín oficial*, Havana, 1969-.
Quarterly.

142. Cuba, Banco Central, *Revista*, (Havana,) 1955-1960.
Monthly.

143. Cuba, Biblioteca Nacional, *Revista*, 1949-.
Havana, quarterly.

144. Cuba, Cámara de Comercio, *Cuba comercio exterior*, Havana, 1965-.
Bi-monthly.

145. Cuba, Cámara de Comercio, *Cuba; noticias económicas*, Havana, 1965-.
Monthly.

146. Cuba, Cámara de Comercio, *Industria y comercio*, Havana, 1901-.
Monthly, irregular.

147. Cuba, Casa de las Américas, *Casa de las Américas*, Havana, 1960-.
Monthly.

148. Cuba, Casa de las Américas, *Servicio de información*, Havana, 1960-.
Irregular.

149. Cuba, Centro de Documentación e Información Técnica de la Construcción, *Boletín informativo*, Havana, 1964-.
Irregular.

150. Cuba, Centro de Estudios Latinoamericanos, *Pensamiento crítico*, Havana, 1967-.
Monthly. Current political and social thought.

151. Cuba, Central de Trabajadores, *Orientación Sindical*, Havana, 1967-.
Monthly.

152. Cuba, Chamber of Commerce, *Cuba Foreign Trade*, Havana, 1964-.
Bi-monthly.

153. Cuba, Chamber of Commerce, *Economic News*, Havana, 1965-.
Monthly.

154. Cuba, Colegio Nacional de Arquitectos, *Arquitectura*, Havana, 1933-.
Monthly review on housing and city planning.

155. Cuba, Colegio Nacional de Arquitectos, *Cuba construye*, Havana, 1961-.
Monthly.

156. Cuba, Comisión de Orientación Revolucionaria, *Palante y Palante*, Havana, 1962-.
Weekly humor magazine.

157. Cuba, Comités de Defensa de la Revolución, *Con la Guardia en Alto*, Havana, 1961-.
Official organ of the CDR.
Weekly.

158. Cuba, Confederación de Trabajadores, *Boletín nacional*, Havana, 1959-.
Irregular.

159. Cuba, Confederación de Trabajadores, *C.T.C. Boletín*, Havana, 1951-1959.
Semi-monthly.

160. Cuba, Confederación de Trabajadores, *Vanguardia obrera*, Havana, 1963-1966.
Daily.

161. Cuba, Consejo Nacional de Cultura, *Boletín*, Havana, 1962-.
Monthly.

162. Cuba, Consejo Nacional de Cultura, *Cuba; Revolution et/and Culture*, Havana, 1965-.
Bi-monthly.

163. Cuba, Consejo Nacional de Cultura, *Culturales*, Havana, 1966-.
Monthly.

164. Cuba, Consejo Nacional de Cultura, *Información de actividades musicales*, Havana, 1963-.
Monthly.

165. Cuba, Consejo Nacional de Cultura, *Pueblo y Cultura*, Havana, 1962-.
Monthly.

166. Cuba, Consejo Nacional de Cuba, *Revolución y Cultura*, Havana, 1967-.
Bi-monthly.

167. Cuba, Comisión Nacional de la Unesco, *Boletín*, Havana, 1952-1958, 1962-.
Monthly.

168. Cuba, Comisión Nacional de la Unesco, *Cuadernos de ciencias sociales y económicas*, Havana, 1961-.
Irregular.

169. Cuba, Comisión Nacional de la Unesco, *Cuba en la Unesco*, Havana, 1960-.
Monthly.

170. Cuba, Comité de la Organización Latinoamericana de Solidaridad, *OLAS*, Havana, 1966-.
Monthly.

171. Cuba, Departamento de Asuntos Culturales, *Cuba*, 1960-.
Quarterly.

172. Cuba, Departamento de Asuntos Culturales. *Cultural bulletin*, Havana, 1961-.
Monthly.

173. Cuba, Departamento de Turismo, *Bulletin*, Havana, 1960-.
Bi-weekly.

174. Cuba, Dirección de Cultura, *Revista cubana*, Havana, 1935-1957. 31 vols.

175. Cuba, Dirección General de Cultura, *Artes plásticas*, Havana, 1960-.
Irregular.

176. Cuba, Dirección General de Cultura, *Nueva revista cubana*, Havana, 1959-.
Quarterly. Supersedes *Revista cubana*.

177. Cuba, Dirección General de Cultura, *Revista nacional de teatro*, Havana, 1961-.
Irregular.

178. Cuba, Escuelas de Instrucción Revolucionaria, *Teoría y práctica*, Havana, 1965-1967.
Monthly.

179. Cuba, Federación Estudiantil Universitaria de Oriente, *Mambí*, Santiago de Cuba, 1959-.
Pro-Revolution university thought. Bi-monthly

180. Cuba, Federación Filatélica, *Filatelia Cubana*, Havana, 1965-.
Quarterly.

181. Cuba, Federación de Mujeres Cubanas, *Mujeres*, Havana, 1960-.
Monthly.

182. Cuba, Federación de Mujeres Cubanas, *Vida nueva*, Havana, 1962-.
Irregular.

183. Cuba, Instituto de Ciencia Animal, *Revista Cubana de Ciencia Agrícola*, Havana, 1967-.
Quarterly.

184. Cuba, Instituto del Cine, *Cine cubano*, Havana, 1960-.
Monthly.

185. Cuba, Instituto Cubano del Petróleo, *ICP boletín estadístico*, Havana, 1961-.
Irregular.

186. Cuba, Instituto de Investigaciones de la Caña de Azúcar, *Boletín Informativo*, Havana, 1965-.
Irregular.

187. Cuba, Instituto Nacional de

Ahorro y Vivienda, *Cultura y divulgación,* Havana, 1964-.
Monthly.

188. Cuba, Instituto Nacional de Deportes, Educación Física y Recreación, *Boletín científico-técnico,* Havana, 1965-.
Irregular.

189. Cuba, Instituto Nacional de la Pesca, *Mar y Pesca; la revista del hombre de mar,* Havana, 1965-.
Monthly.

190. Cuba, Instituto Nacional de Reforma Agraria, *Avicultura,* Havana, 1966-.
Quarterly.

191. Cuba, Instituto Nacional de Reforma Agraria, *Boletín de divulgación,* Havana, 1960-.
Irregular.

192. Cuba, Instituto Nacional de Reforma Agraria, *Cuba,* Havana, 1962-1966.
Monthly.

193. Cuba, Instituto Nacional de Reforma Agraria, *Fruticuba,* Havana, 1965-.
Monthly.

194. Cuba, Instituto Nacional de Reforma Agraria, *INRA,* Havana, 1959-1962.
Best source on agrarian reform programs. Monthly. Illustrated. Superseded by *Cuba.*

195. Cuba, Instituto Nacional de Reforma Agraria, *Técnica Hidráulica,* Havana, 1967-.
Bi-monthly.

196. Cuba, Instituto de Neurofisiología y Psicología, *Boletín,* Havana, 1965-.
Quarterly.

197. Cuba, Instituto de Política In-

ternacional, *Política internacional,* Havana, 1963-.
Quarterly.

198. Cuba, Instituto de Radiodifusión, *Cuaderno de información ICR, Havana,* 1966.
Monthly.

199. Cuba, Junta Central de Planificación, *Investigación operacional,* Havana, 1966-.
Irregular.

200. Cuba, Junta Central de Salud y Maternidad, *Maternidad obrera,* Havana, 1959-.
Quarterly.

201. Cuba, Ministerio de Bienestar Social, *Metas,* Havana ,1959-.
Bi-monthly.

202. Cuba, Ministerio de Comercio, *Revista de economía,* Havana, 1951-1959.
Irregular.

203. Cuba, Ministerio de Comercio Exterior, *Alimentos,* Havana, 1965-.
Weekly.

204. Cuba, Ministerio de Comercio Exterior, *Azúcar-Tabaco,* Havana, 1965-.
Weekly.

205. Cuba, Ministerio del Comercio Exterior, *Boletín informativo,* Havana, 1964-.
Weekly.

206. Cuba, Ministerio de Comercio Exterior, *Comercio Exterior,* Havana, 1963-1966.
Quarterly.

207. Cuba, Ministerio de Comercio Exterior, *Equipos-Maquinarias,* Havana, 1965-.
Weekly.

208. Cuba, Ministerio de Comercio Exterior, *Información de países,*

boletín semanal del Mincex, Havana, 1966-.
Weekly.

209. Cuba, Ministerio de Comunicaciones, *C.I.C.; boletín de información técnica,* Havana, 1965-.
Monthly.

210. Cuba, Ministerio de Comunicaciones, *Comunicaciones,* Havana, 1965-.
Irregular.

211. Cuba, Ministerio de Educación, *Artes plásticas,* Havana, 1960-.
Monthly.

212. Cuba, Ministerio de Educación, *Boletín de información,* Havana, 1963-.
Irregular.

213. Cuba, Ministerio de Educación, *Boletín informativo educacional,* Havana, 1964-.
Monthly.

214. Cuba, Ministerio de Educación, *Educación en Cuba,* Havana, 1967-.
Bi-monthly.

215. Cuba, Ministerio de Educación, *Nueva revista cubana,* Havana, 1959-1961.
Spokesman for Pro-Revolution intellectuals. Quarterly.

216. Cuba, Ministerio de Estado, *DALA,* Havana, 1959-.
On Latin American developments. Semi-monthly.

217. Cuba, Ministerio de las Fuerzas Armadas Revolucionarias, *Verde Olivo,* Havana, 1959-.
Principal armed forces periodical. Weekly.

218. Cuba, Ministerio de Hacienda, *Trimestre,* Havana, 1962-.
Quarterly.

219. Cuba, Ministerio de Industrias,

Boletín informativo, Havana, 1965-.
Monthly.

220. Cuba, Ministerio de Industrias, *Nuestra industria,* Havana, 1961-.
Monthly.

221. Cuba, Ministerio de Industrias, *Nuestra industria, revista tecnológica,* Havana, 1962-.
Bi-monthly, irregular.

222. Cuba, Ministerio de la Industria Azucarera, *Boletín azucarero,* Havana, 1966-.
Monthly.

223. Cuba, Ministerio de la Industria Azucarera, *Cuba-Azúcar,* Havana, 1966-.
Bi-monthly.

224. Cuba, Ministerio de la Industria Azucarera, *Divulgaciones tecnológicas azucareras,* Havana, 1965-.
Fortnightly.

225. Cuba, Ministerio del Interior, *El Moncada,* Havana, May 1966-.
Political police monthly.

226. Cuba, Ministerio de Relaciones Exteriores, *Boletín,* Havana, 1960-.
Weekly.

227. Cuba, Ministerio de Relaciones Exteriores, *Boletín cultural,* Havana, 1959-.
Indispensable record of revolutionary culture. Also in English, 1961-.

228. Cuba, Ministerio de Relaciones Exteriores, *Cuba en la Unesco,* Havana, 1960-.
Irregular.

229. Cuba, Ministerio de Relaciones Exteriores, *News of the Week,* Havana, 1960-.
Weekly.

230. Cuba, Ministerio de Relaciones

Exteriores, *Revista mensual*, Havana, 1961-.
Monthly.

231. Cuba, Ministerio de Salud Pública, *Boletín mensual*, Havana, 1959-.
Monthly.

232. Cuba, Ministerio de Salud Pública, *Revista de resúmenes*, Havana, 1965-.
Monthly.

233. Cuba, Ministerio del Trabajo, *Boletín informativo*, Havana, 1967-.
Bi-monthly.

234. Cuba, Ministerio del Trabajo, *Trabajo*, Havana, 1960-1964.
Monthly.

235. Cuba, Ministerio de Transportes, *Ferrocarriles de Cuba*, Havana, 1965-.
Bi-monthly.

236. Cuba, Movimiento Nacional de las Brigadas Técnicas, *Juventud técnica*, Havana, 1965-.
Monthly.

237. Cuba, Movimiento Revolucionario 26 de Julio, *Razones del Movimiento Revolucionario 26 de Julio*, Havana, 1959-1960.
Irregular.

238. Cuba, Organización Continental Latinoamericana de Estudiantes, *OCLAE*, Havana, 1967-.
Monthly.

239. Cuba, Organizaciones Revolucionarias Integradas, *El Orientador Revolucionario*, Havana, 1962-1965.
Fortnightly. Contains major speeches by revolutionary figures.

240. Cuba, Organization of Solidarity with the Peoples of Africa, Asia, and Latin America, *Trincon-*

tinental Bulletin, Havana, 1966-.
Monthly.

241. Cuba, Organization of Solidarity with the Peoples of Africa, Asia, and Latin America, *Tricontinental*, Havana, 1967-.
Bi-monthly.

242. Cuba, Partido Comunista, Comisión de Orientación Revolucionaria, *Ediciones COR*, 1965-.
Fortnightly. Contains major speeches by revolutionary figures.

243. Cuba, Partido Comunista, *El Militante Comunista*, Havana, 1966-.
Monthly.

244. Cuba, Partido Comunista, *PCC Boletín Provincial*, Havana, 1966-.
Monthly.

245. Cuba, Prensa Latina, *CUBA Internacional*, Havana, 1968-.
Monthly magazine about accomplishments of the Revolution.

246. Cuba, Prensa Latina, *Panorama Económico Latinoamericano*, Havana, 1960-.
Weekly.

247. Cuba, Sindicato Nacional de Representates y Empleados Oficiales de Hoteles, Clubes y Cabarets, *Control*, Havana, 1952-1959.
Monthly.

248. Cuba, Sindicato de Trabajadores Gastronómicos, *Acción gastronómica*, Havana, 1960-1961.
Monthly.

249. Cuba, Tribunal de Cuentas, *Boletín oficial*, Havana, 1951-1959.
Monthly.

250. Cuba, Unión de Escritores y Artistas, *La Gaceta de Cuba*, Havana, 1962-.

Literary journal. Bi-monthly.
251. Cuba, Unión de Escritores y Artistas, *Unión*, Havana, 1962-. Bi-monthly.
252. Cuba, Unión Nacional de Jóvenes Presbiterianos, *JUPRECU*, Havana, 1960-. Every two months.
253. Cuba, Unión de Periodistas, *Boletín del Periodista*, Havana, 1967-. Bi-monthly.
254. Cuba, Universidad de La Habana, *Vida Universitaria*, Havana, 1950-. Valuable continous record of university thought and activities. Monthly.
255. Cuba, Universidad de Las Villas, *ISLAS*, Havana, 1958-. One of the leading Latin American reviews. Tri-annually.
256. *Cuba nueva*, Miami, 1961-1963. Organ of the Consejo Revolucionario de Cuba, Bay of Pigs organizers.
257. *Cuban Newsletter*, Miami, 1961-1962. Organ of the Frente Revolucionario Democrático.
258. *The Cuban Report*, Miami, 1963-1965. Monthly. Cuban Student Directorate in exile.
259. *Defensa institucional cubana*, Mexico, 1962-. Monthly. Reportedly backed by Batista.
260. *Economía*, Coral Gables, Fla., 1961-1965. By economists in exile.
261. Editorial del Caribe, *Bohemia Libre*, Caracas, Oct. 9, 1960-. Weekly. Title varies.

262. *Exilio*, New York, 1967-. Quarterly.
263. *Foto-impresiones*, Miami, 1967-. Edited by former staff of *Diario de la Marina*.
264. Frente Obrero Revalucionario Democrático, *Cuba laboral*, Miami, 1964-1968. Reportedly backed by the AFL-CIO.
265. Havana, Universidad de la Habana, Escuela de Ciencias Biológicas, *Boletín docente*, Havana, 1965-. Monthly.
266. *Humanismo*, Havana, 1959-1961. Pro-Revolution bi-monthly.
267. *Informe sobre Cuba*, Miami Beach, 1963-1966. Monthly. General economic and political developments. Moderate exiles.
268. *El león cubano*, Miami, 1962-. Irregular. Lions' Clubs.
269. *Lux*, Miami, 1967-. Monthly. Electric Workers Confederation in Exile.
270. *Mella*, Havana, Feb. 14, 1944-Oct. 18, 1965. Monthly journal of the youth section of the Communist Party. Irregular 1953-1958. Merged with *Diario de la Tarde* in Oct. 1965 to form *Juventud Rebelde*.
271. Movimiento Revolucionario del Pueblo, *El correo*, Miami, 1962-. Weekly.
272. *El nacionalista*, Miami, 1967-. Weekly. Organ of the Cuban Nationalist Movement.
273. *Nueva generación*, Miami, 1967-. Irregular. Published by young

Christian Democrats and Socialists.

274. *Obra revolucionaria,* Havana, 1960-1965.
Bi-weekly. Policy statements and major speeches.

275. Partido Socialista Popular, *Fundamentos,* Havana, 1941-1960.
Irregular.

276. *Patria,* Miami, 1960-.
Weekly. Reportedly Batista-backed newspaper.

277. *La Prensa de Los Angeles,* Hollywood, Calif., 1967-.
Fortnightly.

278. *La Quincena,* Havana, 1955-1960.
Catholic fortnightly.

279. *El Rebelde,* Miami, 1962-.
Irregular. Bulletin of former members of the Rebel Army.

280. *RECE,* Miami, 1965-.
Monthly. Reportedly backed by exiled industrialist.

281. *Regreso,* Miami, 1968-.
Monthly. Backed by exile-businessmen.

282. *Réplica,* Miami, 1967-.
Weekly. Moderately leftist exile group.

283. *Revista cubana,* New York, 1968-.
Twice a year. Scholarly emigré journal.

284. Sociedad Cultural Nuestro Tiempo, *Nuestro Tiempo,* Havana, 1954-1959.
An unofficial organ of the Communist Party. Bi-monthly.

285. *Tridente,* Central America (?), 1963-.
Weekly. Organ of the Movimiento de Recuperación Revolucionaria.

286. *Trinchera,* Miami, 1960-1965.
Organ of the Directorio Revolucionario Estudiantil.

287. *Unidad,* Miami, 1963-1968.
Every 2 weeks. Reportedly backed by the CIA.

288. *Unión de cubanos en el exillio,* Caracas, 1960-.
Monthly. By liberal clergymen in exile.

289. Universidad Católica de Santo Tomás de Villanueva, *Insula,* Havana, 1957-1960.
Three times a year.

290. Universidad de la Habana, Escuela de Arquitectura, *Boletín,* Havana, 1965-.
Monthly.

291. *La voz de la justicia,* Miami, 1967-.
Bulletin of the Cuban Lawyers Association in exile.

H. STATISTICS

292. American Chamber of Commerce of Cuba, *Cuba: Facts and Figures,* Havana, 1957. 242 pp.

293. *Anuario Azucarero de Cuba,* Havana: Económica y Financiera, 1938-1958. 21 vols.

294. Benítez, Antonio, "Nuestra estadística y sus problemas," *Trabajo,* Aug. 1964. pp. 70-75.

295. Cuba, Comisión Nacional de Propaganda y Defensa del Tabaco Habano, *Nuestro comercio de exportación de tabaco en rama y manufacturado, desde 1963 a 1958,* Havana, 1959. 124 pp.

296. Cuba, Dirección Central de Estadística, *Anuario demográfico de Cuba,* Havana, 1961-.

297. Cuba, Dirección Central de Estadística, *Boletín estadístico de Cuba*, Havana, 1964-.
Yearly.

298. Cuba, Dirección Central de Estadística, *Resumen de estadísticas de población*, Havana, 1965-.
Yearly.

299. Cuba, Dirección General del Censo, *Censo de 1931*, Havana: Carasa y Cía, 1932. 106 pp.

300. Cuba, Dirección General del Censo, *Censo de 1943*, Havana: P. Fernández y Cía, 1945. 1373 pp.

301. Cuba, Dirección General del Censo, *Census of the Republic of Cuba, 1919*, Havana: Maza, Arroyo y Caso, 1920. 968 pp.

302. Cuba, Dirección General de Estadística, *Anuario estadístico de la República de Cuba*, Havana, 1914-1959. 45 vols.

303. Cuba, Dirección General de Estadística, *Balanza comercial de Cuba, 1955-1956*, Havana: Impresores P. Fernández y Cía, 1956-1957. 2 vols.

304. Cuba, Dirección General de Estadística, *Boletín mensual de estadísticas*, Havana, 1945-1959.

305. Cuba, Dirección General de Estadística, *Censo de población, viviendas y electoral, enero 28 de 1953: informe general*, Havana: P. Fernández y Cía, 1955. 325 pp.

306. Cuba, Dirección General de Estadística, *Comercio exterior, 1902-1961*, Havana, 1903-1961. 48 vols.

307. Cuba, Dirección General de Estadística, *Compendio estadístico de Cuba, 1965*, Havana, 1965. 1 vol.

308. Cuba, Dirección General de Estadística, *Resúmenes estadísticos seleccionados*, Havana: Imprenta P. Fernández, 1959. 143 pp.

309. Cuba, Dirección General del Censo, *Censo de la República de Cuba*, Havana: Arroyo y Caso, 1920. 977 pp.

310. Cuba, Dirección General del Censo, *Censo de 1943*, Havana: P. Fernández y Cía, 1945. 1,373 pp.

311. Cuba, Dirección Nacional de Estadística, *Estadística y análisis económico*, Havana, 1963-.
Irregular.

312. Cuba, Instituto Nacional de la Pesca, Depto. de Estadística, *Anuario estadístico*, Havana, 1964-.
Annually.

313. Cuba, Junta Central de Planificación, *Anuario demográfico de Cuba, 1961*, Havana, 1965. 258 pp.

314. Cuba, Junta Central de Planificación, *Anuario estadístico de pesca*, Havana, 1965. 125 pp.

315. Cuba, Junta Central de Planificación, *Boletín estadístico de Cuba*, Havana, 1962-1967.
Irregular.

316. Cuba, Junta Central de Planificación, *Estadística de defunciones, según los certificados médicos año 1959, 1961, 1963*, Havana, 1965. 1 vol. +.

317. Cuba, Junta Central de Planificación, *Estimación de la tendencia de la población nacional: 1953-1975*, Havana, 1963. 9 pp.
Mimeographed.

318. Cuba, Junta Central de Planificación, *Población estimada por provincias parte urbana y rural*,

sexo y grupos de edad: 1962-1965,
Havana, 1963. 21 pp.
Mimeographed.

319. Cuba, Junta Central de Planificación, *Principales indicadores de la actividad económica,* Havana, 1963. 94 pp.

320. Cuba, Junta Central de Planificación, *Resumen de estadísticas de población,* Havana, 1965. 31 pp.

321. Cuba, Junta Central de Planificación, *Resúmenes estadísticos seleccionados. Síntesis cronológica,* Havana: Impr. P. Fernández, 1959. 143 pp.

322. Cuba, Ministerio de Agricultura, *Memoria del censo agrícola nacional de 1946,* Havana: P. Fernández, 1951. 1253 pp.

323. Cuba, Ministerio de Educación, *Estadísticas de la educación, 1962-1964,* Havana, 1965. 3 vols.

324. Cuba, Ministerio de Hacienda, *Comercio exterior de Cuba,* Havana, 1902-1958.
Yearly.

325. Cuba, Ministerio de Industrias, *Anuario estadístico 1964,* Havana, 1964. 159 pp.

326. Cuba, Ministerio de la Industria Azucarera, *Historia azucarera en cifras, 1951-1966, (Ingenios),* Havana, 1967. 10 vols.
Mimeographed.

327. Cuba, Ministerio de Salud Pública, *Estadística de Salud Pública,* Havana: Centro Nacional de Información de Ciencias Médicas, 1967, 53 pp.

328. Cuba, Oficina del Censo, *Cuba: Population, History and Resources, 1907,* Washington, 1909. 275 pp.

329. Cuba, Oficina de Coordinación de Estadísticas e Investigaciones, *Informe estadístico semestral,* Havana, 1959-1960. 3 vols.

330. Cuba, Oficina Nacional de los Censos Demográficos y Electoral, *Censos de población viviendas y electoral,* Havana: P. Fernández, 1955. 325 pp.
1953 census.

331. Editora Mercantil Cubana, *Cuba económica y financiera,* Havana, 1926-1960. 35 vols.
Deals with all economic aspects.

332. Mesa Lago, Carmelo, "Availability and Reliability of Statistics in Socialist Cuba," *Latin American Research Review,* Spring, 1969, pp. 53-91; Fall, 1969. pp. 47-81.

333. Neilubin, N. I., "Estadística de población," *Trimestre,* (Havana), Jan.-Mar. 1964. pp. 43-75.

334. Pérez de la Riva, Juan, *Población de Cuba,* Havana: Universidad de La Habana, 1964. 17 pp.
Mimeographed.

I. LAWS

335. Alvarez Tabío, Fernando, *Evolución constitucional de Cuba, 1928-1940,* Havana: Tall. Gráficos O'Reilly, 1953. 21 pp.

336. Alvarez Tabío, Fernando, *El recurso de inconstitucionalidad,* Havana: Editorial Librería Martí, 1960. 209 pp.

337. Alvarez Tabío, Fernando, *Teoría general de la constitución cubana,* Havana: J. Montero, 1946. 357 pp.

338. Barreras, Antonio, *Las constituciones de Cuba,* Havana: El Mundo, 1942. 666 pp.

339. Borges, Milo A., *Compilación ordenada y completa de la legislación cubana de 1899 a 1958*, Havana: Editorial Lex, 1952, 1960. 4 vols.

340. Consejo Revolucionario de Cuba, *Programa mínimo para el gobierno provisional*, Miami, 1962. 4 pp.
Exiles' program.

341. Cuba, Congreso, Cámara de Representantes, *Compendio legislativo, 1902 a 1950*, Havana, 1950. 312 pp.

342. Cuba, Congreso, Cámara de Representantes, *Informe anual*, Havana, 1913-1959.
Yearly.

343. Cuba, Congreso, Cámara de Representantes, *Memorias de los trabajos*, Havana, 1902-1959. Yearly.

344. Cuba, Constitution, *Constitución de la República de Cuba*, Havana: Imprenta de Rambla, Bouza y Compañía, 1928. 32 pp.

345. Cuba, Constitution, *Constitución de la República de Cuba*, Havana: Imprenta de Rambla, Bouza y Cía, 1935. 53 pp.

346. Cuba Constitution, *Constitución de la República de Cuba*, Havana: Cultural, 1940. 104 pp.

347. Cuba, Leyes, *Código civil*, Havana, 1959-1961. 4 vols.

348. Cuba, Leyes, *Código de defensa social*, Havana: J. Montero, 1959. 459 pp.

349. Cuba, Leyes, *Colección legislativa, 1902-1955*, Havana: Imprenta Rambla, Bouza, 1956. 25 vols.

350. Cuba, Leyes, *El colono; recopilación de la legislación vigente*, Havana: Impresores Ucar, García, 1958. 383 pp.

351. Cuba, Leyes, *Compilación ordenada y completa de la legislación cubana de 1951 a 1958*, Havana: Editorial Lex, 1960. 1 vol.

352. Cuba, Leyes, *Derecho electoral*, Manzanillo: Editorial El Arte, 1945. 642 pp.

353. Cuba, Leyes, *Diccionario de legislación cubana*, Havana: Editorial Librería Selecta, 1950. 1328 pp.

354. Cuba, Leyes, *Folletos de divulgación legislativa*, Havana, 1959-. Monthly.

355. Cuba, Leyes, *Fundamental Laws of Cuba, 1959*, Washington: Pan American Union, 1959. 86 pp.
1959 Constitution.

356. Cuba, *Gaceta Oficial*, Havana, 1902-.

357. Cuba, Leyes, *Indice anual de la legislación revolucionaria*, Havana: Finanzas al Día, 1959-.
Laws, decrees, presidential proclamations, resolutions, accords and notices. In both chronological and alphabetical order.

358. Cuba, Leyes, *Legislación cafetalera vigente*, Havana: Talleres de Cultura Militar y Naval, 1941. 162 pp.

359. Cuba, Leyes, *Legislación social de Cuba*, Havana: Editorial Librería Selecta, 1948-1951. 3 vols.

360. Cuba, Leyes, *Legislación penal de la revolución*, Havana: Editora Universitaria, 1966. 140 pp.

361. Cuba, Leyes, *Legislación político-administrativa*, Havana: Editorial Lex, 1943. 208 pp.

362. Cuba, Leyes, *Ley de accidentes del trabajo y su reglamento a la*

luz de la jurisprudencia, Havana: Editorial Librería Martí, 1959. 610 pp.

363. Cuba, Leyes, *Ley constitucional para la República de Cuba,* Havana: J. Montero, 1952. 105 pp.

364. Cuba, Leyes, *Ley fundamental,* Havana: J. Montero, 1959. 104 pp.

365. Cuba, Leyes, *Ley fundamental de la República de Cuba actualizada hasta mayo de 1963,* Havana, 1964. 2 vols.

366. Cuba, Leyes, *Ley orgánica de los municipios,* Havana: J. Montero, 1955. 275 pp.

367. Cuba, Leyes, *Ley del retiro civil con las modificaciones hasta el día 15 de julio de 1959,* Havana: J. Montero, 1959. 309 pp.

368. Cuba, Leyes, *Ley 881, seguros sociales del sector público. Texto completo,* Havana, 1960. 15 pp.

369. Cuba, Leyes, *Leyes civiles de Cuba y su jurisprudencia,* Havana: Editorial Lex, 1959. 4 vols.

370. Cuba, Leyes, *Leyes civiles de la República de Cuba,* Havana: Editorial Lex, 1940. 661 pp.

371. Cuba, Leyes, *Leyes, decretos, legislación municipal y provincial de Cuba,* Havana: Editorial Lex, 1955. 2 vols.

372. Cuba, Leyes, *Leyes, decretos, presupuesto general . . . 1857-1953,* Havana: Imprenta Nacional, 1857-1953. 65 vols.

373. Cuba, Leyes, *Leyes-decretos vigentes; recopilación de las promulgadas durante el período comprendido entre el día 10 de marzo de 1952 y el día 27 de enero de 1955,* Havana: Editorial Lex, 1956-1957. 2 vols.

374. Cuba, Leyes, *Leyes fiscales vigentes,* Havana: Editorial Lex, 1960. 588 pp. 1959-1960.

375. Cuba, Leyes, *Leyes del gobierno provisional de la revolución,* Havana: Editorial Lex, 1959. 15 vols.

376. Cuba, Leyes, *Leyes del gobierno revolucionario de Cuba,* Havana: Imprenta Nacional, 1959-. Irregular.

377. Cuba, Leyes, *Leyes de trabajo y su jurisprudencia,* Havana: Editorial Lex, 1942. 1283 pp.

378. Cuba, Leyes, *Nueva legislación del retiro civil,* Havana: Editorial Selecta, 1960. 493 pp.

379. Cuba, Leyes, *Nuevas leyes y resoluciones de 1961 del Banco Nacional de Cuba,* Havana, 1961, 24 pp.

380. Cuba, Leyes, *Nuevo ordenamiento tributario de la República: leyes fiscales vigentes; con los reglamentos adaptados a cada impuesto,* Havana: Editorial Lex, 1959. 376 pp.

381. Cuba, Tribunal Superior Electoral, *Jurisprudencia electoral,* Havana: P. Fernández y Cía, 1954-1957. 3 vols.

382. D'Estéfano Pisani, Miguel A., ed., *Ley fundamental de 7 de febrero de 1959; anotada y concordada con la Constitución de 1940, sus leyes complementarias y jurisprudencia fundamental,* Havana: J. Montero, 1959. 104 pp.

383. Estrada y Zayas, Edmundo, *Leyes-decretos,* Havana: Editorial Lex, 1956. 1971 pp. Compilation of governmental decrees from Mar. 10, 1952 to Jan. 27, 1955.

384. Hernández Corujo, Enrique, *Historia constitucional de Cuba*, Havana: Editora de Libros y Folletos, 1960. 2 vols.

385. Lancis, Antonio, *Elecciones y administración en la república, 1902-1952*, Havana, 1953. 32 pp.

386. Lazcano, Andrés, *Las constituciones de Cuba*, Madrid: Ediciones Cultura Hispánica, 1952. 1066 pp.

387. Sánchez Roca, Mariano, *Curso de legislación mercantil*, Havana: Editorial Lex, 1959. 1090 pp.

388. Sánchez Roca, Mariano, comp., *Primer índice anual de la legislación revolucionaria, 1 de enero a 31 de diciembre de 1959*, Havana: Ed. Lex, 1960. 305 pp.

389. Vega, Juan, *Legislación penal de la revolución*, Havana: Editora Universitaria, 1966. 140 pp.

390. Vilches, Isidro, *Derecho cubano del trabajo*, Havana: J. Montero, 1948. 757 pp.

J. BOOKDEALERS

391. *Boekhandel Marnix Pvba*, Ajuinlei 18, Ghent, Belgium.

392. *Boekhandel Pegasus*, Leidsestraat 25, Amsterdam C, Holland.

393. *Cartimex*, 3, rue 13 Decembrie, Bucharest, Romania.

394. *Central Books Ltd.*, 37 Grys Inn Road, London, W. C. 1, England.

395. *Collet's Holding Ltd.*, Denington State, Wellingborough, London Road, Northgate, England.

396. *Davis Book Company Ltd.*, 2220 Beaconsfield Avenue, Montreal 28, Quebec, Canada.

397. *Ediciones Amate S. A.*, Hamburgo 10, Mexico 6, Mexico.

398. *Editorial Siglo XXI*, Emilio Rubin 7, Madrid 16, Spain.

399. *Far Eastern Booksellers*, Kanda P. O. Box 72, Tokyo, Japan.

400. *Gustavo Rodríguez Villaba*, Juan María Pérez 2912, Montevideo, Uruguay.

401. *Instituto del Libro*, Depto. de Exportación 19 No. 1002, esquina a 10 Vedado, La Habana 6, Cuba. Best source for books published in Cuba.

402. *Jugoslovenska Knjika*, P. O. B. 36, Belgrade, Yugoslavia.

403. *Kultura*, P. O. B. 149, Budapest 62, Hungary.

404. *Librairie des Editions Espagnoles*, 72 Rue de Seine, Paris 6, France.

405. *Librería Delta*, Avenida Itallia 2817, Montevideo, Uruguay.

406. *Librería Puvil*, Barcelona 9, Spain.

407. *Librería Ruedo Ibérico*, 203 Avenue Pierie, Brossolette 92 Montrouge, France.

408. *Mezhdunarodnaja Kniga*, Moscow, G-200, USSR.

409. *Progress Books*, 487 Adelaide St. West, Toronto 2B, Ontario, Canada.

410. *Richard Handyside Libro Libre*, 21 Theobalds Road, London WC 1, England.

411. *RUCH*, UI, Wronia 23, Warsaw, Poland.

412. *Visor Libros*, Legantos 34-1, Madrid 13, Spain.

K. UNITED STATES LIBRARIES

413. *Bancroft Library*, University of California, Berkeley, California.

Particularly strong on background materials.

414. *Hoover Library*, Stanford University, Palo Alto, California.
Best Cuba Revolution collection west of the Mississippi. Fine general collection, extensive serials and exchange programs. Vigorous acquisitions program financed by large budget for Cuba Revolution materials. Microfilm program for major revolutionary periodicals.

415. *Library of Congress*, Washington, D.C.
The most extensive Cuba Revolution collection in the U.S. Most complete collection of general works. Currently receives 68 serials from 40 institutions in Cuba. 1938 Executive Agreement governing U.S.-Cuban exchanges not abrogated by 1961 break in diplomatic relations. Complete file of publications of Cuba Foreign Ministry.

416. *New York Public Library*.
One of the most comprehensive collections of materials prior to 1959. Has about 75% of all available Cuban periodicals and monographs published by the revolutionary government.

417. *Princeton University Library*, Princeton, New Jersey.
Good background materials. Good census materials. Sizable runs of government documents; 36 periodicals.

418. *University of Florida Library*, Gainesville, Florida.
One of the best general collections. Since 1952 designation by Assoc. of Research Libraries as Farmington Plan representative for the Caribbean, this library has attempted complete coverage of Cuban publications of research value. Excellent background materials. Staff of Cuban exile librarians. About 25 revolutionary periodicals plus the major newspapers on microfilm. Complete record of Castro's speeches.

419. *University of Kansas Library*, Lawrence, Kansas.
5000 Cuban volumes. Good collection of background materials and later strengths concentrated in economics and politics of the Castro era.

420. *University of Miami*, Miami, Florida.
Most complete collection of exile publications and one of the best collections of revolutionary periodicals. Cuban staff. Essential stop for the serious researcher.

421. *University of New Mexico Library*, Albuquerque, New Mexico.
Has most of the important serials and newspapers. One of the better collections of books published outside Cuba concerning the Revolution.

422. *University of Pittsburgh Library*, Pittsburgh, Pennsylvania.
Strong on documents and statistical materials from 1959 onward. Extensive collection of revolutionary periodicals.

423. *University of Texas Library*, Austin, Texas.
Over 300 titles on the Revolution. Good document collection and vigorous exchange program. *Catalogue of the Latin American Collection*, (Boston: G.K. Hall, 1969), 31 vols. is comprehensive

source for Cuban titles held by the U T Library.

424. *Widener Library,* Harvard University, Cambridge, Massachusetts.

One of the best for background materials. Good on international law, international relations, and economic aspects of the Revolution.

425. *Yale University Library,* New Haven, Connecticut.

Good general collection. Vigorous collection program in progress. About twenty-five revolutionary periodicals. Broad exchange program with government agencies and academic bodies and institutions. Unique Andrew St. George collection of early revolutionary documents and photographs (over 6000). Film collection.

II. REVOLUTION–GENERAL
(See also History, Background to Revolution)

A. GENERAL WORKS

1. By Cubans

426. Alfonso, Gustavo, ed., *Memoria 1959: 200 fotos para la historia, año de la revolución*, Havana: Gustavo Alfonso y Eduardo Ferrer, 1959. 98 pp.

427. Barbeito, José, *Realidad y masificación. Reflexiones sobre la revolución cubana.* Caracas: Ediciones "Nuevo Orden," 1964. 277 pp.
Role of 26th of July movement. Participant.

428. Batista, Fulgencio, *Cuba Betrayed*, New York: Vantage Press, 1962. 332 pp.
"Betrayed by the U.S."

429. Batista, Fulgencio, *Paradojismo: Cuba, víctima de las contradicciones internacionales*, Mexico: Eds. Botas, 1964. 341 pp.

430. Batista, Fulgencio, *Piedras y leyes*, Mexico: Ediciones Botas, 1961. 495 pp.
English edition *Growth and Decline of the Cuban Republic*, 1964.

431. Batista, Fulgencio, *Respuesta*, Mexico: "Manuel León Sánchez," 1960. 545 pp.
"Social revolution was unnecessary."

432. Bonachea, Rolando E. and Nelson P. Valdés, *Che: Selected Works of Ernesto Guevara*, Cambridge, Mass.: M.I.T. Press, 1969. 456 pp.

433. Cabús, José Domingo, *Castro ante la historia*, Mexico: Editores Mexicanos Unidos, 1963. 263 pp.
Apology for Batista.

434. Carbonell Vivé, Jaime, *La verdad de la revolución de Castro*, Barcelona, 1966. 182 pp.
By an "average man." Hostile.

435. Cardosa Arias, Santiago, *Ahora se acabó el chinchero*, Havana: Ediciones Revolución, 1963. 267 pp.

436. Castro, Fidel, "Entrevista con los directores de diarios en la Sociedad Norteamericana de Diarios," *Revolución*, (Havana), Apr. 18, 1959. pp. 10, 17.

437. Castro, Fidel, *Major Speeches*, London: Stage I, 1968. 305 pp.

438. Castro, Fidel, *Pensamiento político, económico y social de Fidel Castro*, Havana: Editorial Lex, 1959. 138 pp.
Also English edition.

439. Castro, Fidel, *Révolution cubaine*, Paris: François Maspero, 1968. 2 vols.
Twenty-eight basic items, 1953-1968.

440. Cuba, Ministerio de Educación, *Documentos históricos. La revolu-*

ción cubana, su carácter, sus fuerzas y sus enemigos. Conclusiones del pleno del PSP celebrado del 25 al 28 de mayo de 1959. Material para el estudio de la revolución cubana, Havana: Instituto Superior de Educación, 1962. 59 pp.

441. Cuba, Ministerio de las Fuerzas Armadas Revolucionarias, Hacia una sociedad comunista nos encaminamos, Havana: Ediciones Combatientes, 1965. 70 pp.
Several speeches by Castro and letters from Guevara.

442. Cuba, Ministerio de Relaciones Exteriores, Dirección de Información, Perfil de Cuba, Havana: Empresa Consolidada de Artes Gráficas, 1965. 327 pp.

443. Cuba, Ministry of Foreign Relations, Profile of Cuba, Havana, 1965. 320 pp.

444. Cuba, Partido Comunista, Cronología de la revolución 1959-1965, Havana: Editorial EIR, 1966. 321 pp.

445. Defensa Institucional Cubana, Tres años, Mexico: Ediciones Botas, 1962. 693 pp.
Pro-Batista.

446. Dorticós, Osvaldo, "La revolución cubana en su cuarto aniversario," Cuba Socialista, (Havana), Jan. 1963. pp. 1-19.

447. Editorial, "En el sexto aniversario de nuestra revolución," Cuba Socialista, (Havana), Jan. 1965. pp. 1-8.

448. Editorial, "Seis año de revolución," Cuba, (Havana), Jan. 1965. pp. 4-11.

449. Entenza Escobar, Pedro, "Cuba, 1959-1961," Horizontes, (Ponce), Apr. 1962. pp. 103-121.

450. Fernández Caubí, Luis, Cuba, sociedad cerrada, Miami: Aip, 1968. 47 pp.
Exiled journalist.

451. Fernández Santos, Francisco, ed., Cuba: una revolución en marcha, Paris: Cuadernos de Ruedo Ibérico, 1967. 512 pp.
Fairly comprehensive anthology.

452. Gerassi, John, ed., Venceremos! The Speeches and Writings of Che Guevara, New York: MacMillan, 1968. 442 pp.

453. Goldenberg, Boris, "The Cuban Revolution: An Analysis," Problems of Communism, (Washington), Sept.-Oct. 1963. pp. 1-9.

454. Goldenberg, Boris, The Cuban Revolution and Latin America, New York: Praeger, 1965. 376 pp.
One of the best.

455. Goldenberg, Boris, "Die kubanische Revolution—ein never Revolutionstyp," Europa-Archiv, (Bonn, West Germany), Dec. 10, 1962. pp. 805-814.

456. Goldenberg, Boris and Klaus Esser, Zehn Jahre kubanische Revolution, Hannover, Germany: Verl. für Literatur u. Zeitgeschehen, 1969, 106 pp.
Scholarly analysis.

457. González, Angel, Derrotismo y contradicciones de Fidel Castro Ruz, Mexico: Editorial Vasco de Quiroga, 1965. 156 pp.
By former Treasury Minister.

458. González, Justo, Apocalipsis de Cuba, Costa Rica: Talleres Gráficos del COVAC, 1963. 146 pp.
Chronology of events in Cuba following Castro's seizure of power.

459. Guevara, Ernesto, Obra revolu-

cionaria, Mexico: Ediciones Era, S.A., 1967. 663 pp.
Good, but incomplete, compilation.

460. Guevara, Ernesto, *Socialism and Man in Cuba, and Other Works*, London: Stage 1, 1968. 68 pp.

461. Guevara, Ernesto, et al., *Temas en torno a la revolución*, Havana: Editorial Tierra Nueva, 1959. 141 pp.
Agrarian reform, revolutionary front in South America, guerrilla warfare, the humanistic revolution.

462. Kenner, Martin and James Petras, eds., *Fidel Castro Speaks*, New York: Grove Press, 1969. 332 pp.

463. Lavan, George, ed., *Che Guevara Speaks; Selected Speeches and Writings*, New York: Merit Publishers, 1967. 159 pp.

464. Lorenso, Orlando, ed., *Cuba: el paraiso perdido*, Miami: Editorial Iberoamericana, 1963. 106 pp.

465. Pérez, Faustino, "A diez años del 'Granma,'" *Cuba Socialista*, (Havana), Dec. 1966. pp. 2-13.

466. Roca, Blas, "El desarrollo histórico de la revolución cubana," *Cuba Socialista*, (Havana), Jan. 1964. pp. 8-27.

467. Rumbaut, Rubén Darío, *La revolución traicionada*, Miami: Frente Revolucionario Democrático, 1962. 32 pp.
Exile Christian Democrat.

468. Sánchez Lalebret, Rafael, "Diez años después," *Bohemia*, (Havana), Jan. 2, 1969. pp. 4-29.

469. Sardiña y Sánchez, Ricardo Rafael, *Seis minutos de tragedia*

cubana, Miami: Ta-Cuba Printing, 1962. 345 pp.
Pep talks to Cuban exiles.

470. Suárez Rivas, Educardo, *La revolución es buena y necesaria*, Havana: Carlos Romero, 1959. 30 pp.

471. Valdespino, Andrés, "¿Cuál es la situación del régimen de Castro al iniciar su quinto año?" *Bohemia Libre Puertorriqueña*, (Caracas), Jan. 20, 1963. pp. 32-34+.

472. Varona, Manual A. de, *El drama de Cuba o la revolución traicionada*, Buenos Aires: Editorial Marymar, 1960. 123 pp.
Former auténtico leader.

473. Walsh, Rodolfo J., ed., *Crónicas de Cuba*, Buenos Aires: Jorge Alvarez Editores, 1969. 248 pp.
Anthology of sympathetic essays.

2. By Latin Americans

474. Acuña, J. A., *¿Cuba, revolución frustada? ¡Que el pueblo juzgue!*, Montevideo, 1960. 139 pp.
Anti-Castro.

475. Acuña, J. A., *Cuba: revolución traicionada; Fidel, hoy entregado al comunismo que fué aliado de Batista ayer. Documentos irrefutables de la alianza del comunismo con el tirano Batista y de la traición de Fidel Castro*, Montevideo, 1962. 168 pp.

476. Cuenca, Humberto, *La revolución cubana*, Caracas: Editorial Cultura Contemporánea, 1962. 162 pp.
Sympathetic.

477. Fabela, Isidro, *El caso de Cuba*, Mexico: Ediciones Cuadernos Americanos, 1960. 87 pp.
Defends revolution.

478. Machado, Nery, *Cuba, Vanguarda e farol da América*, São Paulo: Editôra Fulgor, 1963. 127 pp.

479. Masetti, Jorge Ricardo, *Los que luchan y los que lloran; el Fidel Castro que yo vi*, Buenos Aires: Editorial Freeland, 1958. 142 pp.

480. Olmedo, José, *Cuba: la revolución de América*, Bogotá: Ediciones Suramérica, 1963. 135 pp.
"The Cuban example should be followed by Latin America."

481. Ramírez Gómez, Ramón, *Cuba socialista; de la revolución democrático-burguesa a la revolución socialista*, Mexico, 1962. 35 pp.

482. Sierra, Dante, *Algo rojo cayó en el Caribe; notas sobre la revolu ción de Cuba*, Buenos Aires: Editorial Freeland, 1961. 80 pp.
Communist "beachhead" in Latin America.

483. Stagni, Pablo, *¿Qué es la Cuba comunista de hoy?*, Buenos Aires, 1963. 371 pp.
Conservative critique by Paraguayan colonel.

484. Terra, Juan Pablo, "Pérfil de la revolución cubana," *Cuadernos Latinoamericanos de Economía Humana*, (Montevideo), Jan.-Feb. 1960. pp. 27-41.

485. Torres Restrepo, Camilo, *Cuba, paraíso perdido*, Bogotá: Edita Editores, 196?. 160 pp.

486. Torriente, Leopoldo de la, "Realidad y esperanza en la política cubana," *Cuadernos Americanos*, (Mexico), Nov.-Dec. 1959. pp. 35-65.

487. Valencia, Luis E., "Cuba y la unidad popular," *Casa de las Américas*, (Havana), July-Aug. 1963. pp. 66-90.

488. Valencia, Luis E., *Realidad y perspectivas de la revolución cubana*, Havana: Casa de las Américas, 1961. 407 pp.

489. Varela, Alfredo, *Cuba con toda la barba*, Buenos Aires: Editorial Esfera, 1960. 254 pp.
Sympathetic to Castro.

490. Vera, Alfredo, *Cuba, un nuevo mundo*, Ecuador: Fondo Universitario de Cultura, 1962. 92 pp.

491. Wincour, Marcos, *Cuba a la hora de América*, Buenos Aires: Ediciones Procyon, 1963. 261 pp.
Favorable to revolution.

3. By U.S. Nationals

492. Archer, Jules, *Thorn in Our Flesh: Castro's Cuba*, New York: Cowles Book Co., Inc., 1970. 193 pp.
1956-1962. For young adults.

493. Barnett, Clifford R. and Wyatt MacGaffey, *Special Warfare Area Handbook for Cuba*, Washington: Special Operations Research Office, 1961. 657 pp.

494. Burks, David D., "Cuba Seven Years After," *Current History*, Jan. 1966. pp. 38-44.

495. Burks, David D., *Cuba Under Castro*, New York: Foreign Policy Association, June 20, 1964. 64 pp.
1959-1963.

496. Draper, Theodore, "Castro's Cuba: a Revolution Betrayed?" *Encounter*, Mar. 1961. pp. 6-23.
Background, ideology, mythology, effects on leftist thinking generally.

497. Draper, Theodore, *Castro's Revolution, Myths and Realities*, New York: Praeger, 1962. 211 pp.

"Middle class revolution betrayed."

498. Draper, Theodore, *Castroism: Theory and Practice*, New York: Praeger, 1965. 263 pp.
On the nature of Castroism, relations with communists and changing economic policies.

499. Draper, Theodore, "Five Years of Castro's Cuba," *Commentary*, Jan. 1964. pp. 25-37.

500. Draper, Theodore, "Runaway Revolution," *Reporter*, May 12, 1960. pp. 14-20.

501. Dubois, Jules, *Fidel Castro, Rebel-liberator or Dictator?*, Indianapolis: Bobbs Merrill, 1959. 391 pp.

502. Fagen, Richard R., "Mass Mobilization in Cuba: the Symbolism of Struggle," *Journal of International Affairs*, No. 2, 1966. pp. 254-271.

503. Gerber, William, "Cuba under Castro," *Editorial Research Reports*, July 3, 1968. pp. 487-504.

504. Gómez, Tana de, *Cuba! the Yoke and the Star*, New York: Belmont Books, 1968. 309 pp.
Novel. 1933-1959 period.

505. Halperin, Ernst, *Castro's Cuba, August 1963*, Cambridge: M.I.T., 1963. 25 pp.

506. Halperin, Ernst, "Castro Finds His Place," *Current*, (New York), Jan. 1962. pp. 14-17.

507. Halperin, Ernest, "The Castro Regime in Cuba," *Current History*, Dec. 1966. pp. 354-359.

508. Halperin, Ernst, "The Cuban Revolution in 1968," *Current History*, Jan. 1969. pp. 42-46+.

509. Huberman, Leo and Paul M. Sweezy, *Cuba: Anatomy of a Revolution*, New York: Monthly Review Press, 1961. 208 pp.

510. Huberman, Leo and Paul M. Sweezy, *Socialism in Cuba*, New York: Monthly Review Press, 1969. 221 pp.
Socio-economic analysis.

511. Lazo, Mario, *Dagger in the Heart; American Policy Failures in Cuba*, New York: Funk and Wagnalls, 1968. 426 pp.

512. Lens, Sidney, "Which Way Cuba?," *Fellowship*, (New York), Mar. 1961. pp. 9-27.

513. Matthews, Herbert Lionel, *The Cuban Story*, New York: G. Braziller, 1961. 318 pp.

514. Mills, Charles Wright, *Listen, Yankee; the Revolution in Cuba*, New York: McGraw-Hill, 1960. 192 pp.
Marxist viewpoint.

515. Morray, Joseph P., *The Second Revolution in Cuba*, New York: 1962. 173 pp.
Events from 1959-1962 from Marxist-Leninist viewpoint.

516. Murkland, Harry B., "Cuba: The Evolution of a Revolution," *Current History*, Mar. 1960. pp. 129-133.

517. North, Joseph, *Cuba's Revolution; I Saw the People's Victory*, New York, 1959. 23 pp.

518. O'Connor, James, "Complete Breakdown in Cuba," *New Republic*, Oct. 8, 1962. pp. 9-10.

519. O'Connor, James, "The Foundations of Cuban Socialism," *Studies on the Left*, Fall 1964. pp. 97-117.

520. O'Connor, James, "Political Change in Cuba, 1959-1965," *Social Research*, Summer 1968. pp. 312-347.

521. Ruiz, Ramón E., *Cuba: the Making of a Revolution*, Mass.: University of Massachusetts Press, 1968. 190 pp.
Roots of revolution.

522. Schneider, Ronald M., "Five Years of Cuban Revolution," *Current History*, Jan. 1964. pp. 26-33.

523. Stone, R. E., "The Revolution in Cuba," *Political Affairs*, (New York), Aug. 1963. pp. 54-65.

524. Wilkerson, Loree A., *Fidel Castro's Political Programs: from Reformism to Marxism Leninism*, Gainesville: University of Florida Press, 1965. 100 pp.

4. By Europeans

525. Bercoff, André, "Cuba révolution sans frontières," *Jeune Afrique International*, (Paris), Sept. 1967. pp. 32-39.

526. Bolton, Charles D., "Cuba, September 1961: force et faiblesse de la révolution cubaine," *Etudes*, (Paris), Nov. 1961. pp. 57-167.

527. Claude, H., "La révolution cubaine," *Économie et Politique*, (Paris), Dec. 1961. pp. 5-22.

528. Connell-Smith, Gordon, "Fidel Castro's Challenge: Ten Years On," *World Today*, Jan. 1969. pp. 11-18.

529. Constandse, Anton L., *Cuba, dictators en rebellen*, Meppel: J. A. Boom, 1964. 267 pp.

530. Dall'Ongaro, Giuseppe, *Compagna Cuba*, Bologna: Carroccio, 1967. 274 pp.
On "totalitarian character" of the revolution.

531. Demagny, René, *Cuba; l'éxil et la ferveur*, Paris: Buchet-Chastel, 1962. 222 pp.

532. Dumur, Jean A., *Cuba*, Lausanne: Rencontre, 1962. 260 pp.
General description.

533. Faux, Claude, *Cuba cubain*, Lausanne: La Guilde du livre, 1961. 95 pp.
Good photographs. General work.

534. Ferrer Gutiérrez, Virgilio, *Cuba: país calumniado*, Madrid, 1965. 192 pp.

535. Francos, Ania, *La fête cubaine*, Paris: R. Julliard, 1962. 310 pp.
Sympathetic. General.

536. Frayer, H., *Cuba*, Paris: Editions du Burin, 1968. 251 pp.

537. Grubbe, Peter, (Pseud. Volkmann, Klaus), *Im schatten des kubaners, das neue gesicht lateinamerikas*, Hamburg: Christian Wegner Verlag, 1961. 326 pp.

538. Guilbert, Ives, *La révolution de Fidel Castro*, Paris: Club des amis du livre, 1962. 284 pp.

539. Hell, Jurgen, *Kurze Geschichte de kubanischen Valkes*, Berlin: Dietz, 1966. 502 pp.

540. Hennessy, C.A.M., "Cuba: the Politics of Frustrated Nationalism," in Martin C. Needler, ed., *Political Systems of Latin America*, New Jersey: Van Nostrand, 1964. pp. 183-205.

541. Julien, Claude, *La revolución cubana*, Montevideo: Ediciones Marcha, 1961. 259 pp.
Background, general work on revolution. Also in French.

542. Karol, K. S., *Les guerrilleros au pouvoir*, Paris: Laffont, 1970. 608 pp.

543. Kempf, Roger, "L'itinéraire de la révolution cubaine 1959-1961," *Critique*, (Paris), Dec. 1963. pp. 1083-1105.

544. Košta, Vjekoslav, *Kuba*, Belgrade: Izd. Instituta za medunarodnu politiku i privredu, 1962. 166 pp.

545. Landovský, Vladimír, *Kuba*, Prague: Státní nakl. politické literatury, 1960. 111 pp.

546. Melotti, Umberto, *La rivoluzione cubana*, Milan: Dall'Oglio, 1967. 305 pp.
General background.

547. Oltmans, Willem L., "People's Republics Are Not Overthrown: Report on Cuba," *United Asia*, (Bombay, India), Sept. 1962. pp. 503-509.

548. Popiel, Gerald, "Pachanga sí!" *Dalhausie Review*, (Halifax, Nova Scotia), Summer 1961. pp. 139-158.
Eyewitness report.

549. Popovici, Titus, *Cuba, teritoriu liber al Americii*, Bucharest: Editura Tineretului, 1962. 333 pp.

550. Sauvage, Léo, *Autopsie de castrisme*, Paris: Flammarion, 1962. 348 pp.

551. Stillman, Günter and Heinz Rosenkranz, *Kuba; Insel der Barbudos*, Leipzig: F. A. Brockhaus, 1961. 212 pp.
Sympathetic.

552. Thomas, Hugh, *Cuba: the Pursuit of Freedom*, Harper and Row, 1971. 1696 pp.
Encyclopedic compendium of Cuban history since 1762 with emphasis on period 1959-1962. Critical of the revolution.

553. Thomas, Hugh, "Paradoxes of Castro's Cuba," *New Statesman*, (London), Aug. 26, 1966. pp. 283-285.

554. Trappen, Friedel, *Die kuba-nische Volks-revolution*, Berlin: Staatsverlag der Deutschen Demokratischen Republik, 1965. 210 pp.

5. By Russians

555. Andrianov, Vasilii V., *Svobodnaia Kuba*, [Free Cuba], Moscow: Sotsekgiz, 1960. 84 pp.

556. Borovik, Genrikh, *Kak eto bylo na Kuba; glavy iz dokumental'noi povesti*, [How it happened in Cuba; chapters from a documentary tale], Moscow: Pravda, 1961. 63 pp.

557. Borovskii, V., "How the Cuban Revolution Began," *New Times*, (Moscow), July 31, 1963. pp. 4-7.

558. Borovskii, V., *Znamia revoliutsii nad Kuboi*, [The banner of revolution over Cuba], Moscow: Gospolitizdat, 1968. 78 pp.

559. Chichkov, V. M., *Zaria nad Kubaĭ*, [Dawn over Cuba], Moscow: Izd-vo IMO, 1961. 144 pp.

560. Dunavets, Mikhail, *Biografiia na edna revoliutsiia*, Varna, Bulgaria, 1963. 225 pp.

561. Efimov, Aleksei V., ed., *Piat' let Kubinskoi revoliutsii*, [Five years of the Cuban Revolution], Moscow: Izd-vo Akod. nauk SSSR, 1963. 292 pp.

562. Gorbachev, B., and A. Kalinin, "Zhivaia Istoriia Kubinskoi Revolyutsii," [History of the revolutionary process], *Kommunist*, (Moscow), July 1963. pp. 110-113.

563. Kalinin, A. and M. Moklinachev, "The Voice of Revolutionary Cuba," *Kommunist* (Moscow), May 1962. pp. 113-115.

564. Košta, Vjekoslov, "Karakteristike društveno-ekonomskog razvo-

ja Kuba" [Characteristic features of the social and economic evaluation of Cuba], *Medunarodni Problemi*, (Belgrade), July-Sept. 1963. pp. 79-103.

565. Slezkin, Lev Iurevich, *Istoriia Kubinskoi respubliki*, Moscow: Izdatelbstvo "Nauka," 1966. 465 pp.
    Scholarly. One-half devoted to the revolution.

566. Vakrouhlicky, Zbynek, *Victorious Advance of Cuban Revolution*, Washington: Joint Publications Research Service, Sept. 29, 1961. 14 pp.

567. Vartanov, G. A., *Revolutsionaya Kuba*, Leningrad, 1963. 71 pp.

568. Vasilevskia, Vanda Lvovna, *Arjipelag svobodi*, [Archipelago of freedom], Moscow: Isdatelstvo Pravda, 1962. 94 pp.

B. FOREIGN OBSERVERS (EYE-WITNESSES)

1. North American

569. Bethel, Paul D., *The Losers: the Definitive Report, by an Eyewitness, of the Communist Conquest of Cuba and the Soviet Penetration in Latin America*, New Rochelle, N.Y.: Arlington House, 1969. 615 pp.
    By a former U.S. Information Officer. Critical of U.S. policy.

570. Castro, Fidel, "Interview with ABC-TV," *I. F. Stone's Bi-Weekly*, (Washington, D.C.), May 27, 1963. pp. 3-5.
    Interview of May 10, 1963.

571. Chartrand, Michel, et al., *The Real Cuba*, Toronto: Fair Play for Cuba Committee, June 1964. 36 pp.

572. Eder, Richard, "Cuba Lives by Castro's Moods," *New York Times Magazine*, July 26, 1964. pp. 12ff.

573. Frank, Waldo, *Cuba: Prophetic Island*, New York: Marzani and Munsell, 1961. 191 pp.
    Journalistic.

574. Frankel, Max, "Journey of Inquiry in Castro's Cuba," *New York Times Magazine*, Jan. 22, 1961. p. 8+.

575. Friedenberg, Daniel M., "A Cuban Dialogue," *Dissent*, Autumn 1962. pp. 332-341.
    Conversation with Castro.

576. Friedenberg, Daniel M., "A Journey to Cuba," *Dissent*, Summer 1960. pp. 279-285.
    Economic and political conditions.

577. Gilly, Adolfo, "Inside the Cuban Revolution," *Monthly Review*, Oct. 1964. pp 1-88.

578. Gómez, Tana de, "A Recent Look at the Cuban Revolution," *The Independent*, (New York), May 1964. pp. 1ff.

579. Grant, Donald, "Cuba Revisited," *Progressive*, (Madison, Wisconsin), Oct. 1963. pp. 15-19.

580. Halperin, Ernst, "Fidel Castro's Dilemma; Letter from Cuba," *Encounter*, (London), Feb. 1964. pp. 57-66.

581. Hilty, Hiram, *Report of a Visit to Cuba*, Philadelphia: American Friends Service Committee, 1960. 7 pp.

582. Huberman, Leo, "A Revolution Revisited," *The Nation*, (New York), Aug. 2, 1965. pp. 51-54.

583. Huberman, Leo, "The Truth about Cuba," *Monthly Review*, (New York), June 1961. pp. 61-79.

584. Kraus, Richard and Edward Friedman, "The Two Sides of Castro's Cuba: Analysis and Report by Two Young Students Who Visited Cuba," *Dissent*, Winter 1961. pp. 53-61.

585. Landau, Saul, "Cuba: the Present Reality," *New Left Review*, (London), May-June 1961. pp. 12-22.
Interview with observer.

586. Lavine, Harold, "Social Revolution in Cuba: the Future of the New Regime," *Commentary*, (New York), Oct. 1959. pp. 324-328.

587. Lockwood, Lee, *Castro's Cuba, Cuba's Fidel*, New York: Mac-Millan, 1967. 288 pp.
Interviews with Castro and his main followers. Photographs.

588. Mackay, John A., "Cuba Revisited," *Christian Century*, (Chicago), Feb. 12, 1964. pp. 200-203.

589. Matthews, Herbert L., *Cuba*, New York: Macmillan, 1964. 134 pp.
For high school readers.

590. Matthews, Herbert L., *The Cuban Story*, New York: Braziller, 1961. 318 pp.
By sympathetic journalist.

591. Matthews, Herbert L., "Fidel Castro Revisited," *War/Peace Report*, Dec. 1967. pp. 3-5.
USSR criticized.

592. Matthews, Herbert L., *Return to Cuba*, Stanford University, Hispanic American Report, 1964. 16 pp.

593. Matthews, Herbert L., and Hiram Hilty, *Understanding Cuba*, Philadelphia: American Friends Service Committee, 1961. 26 pp.
"Mass media has mis-represented the revolution."

594. Miller, Warren, *90 Miles from Home; the Face of Cuba Today*, Boston: Little, Brown, 1961. 279 pp.
Sympathetic description of 1959-1960 developments.

595. Morray, J. P., "Questions and Answers on Cuba," *Monthly Review*, Sept. 1962. pp. 236-242.

596. McClatchy, Charles K., "Castro's Cuba Today," *The Progressive*, Dec. 1965. pp. 13-18.

597. Nearing, Scott, *Cuba and Latin America*, New York: New Century Publishers, 1963. 36 pp.
Reporter at Continental Congress for Solidarity with Cuba held in Brazil.

598. North, Joseph, *Cuba; Hope of a Hemisphere*, New York: International Publishers, 1961. 95 pp.

599. North, Joseph, *Cuba's Revolution: I Saw the People's Victory*, New York: New Century Publications, 1959. 23 pp.

600. Phillips, Ruby H., *The Cuban Dilemma*, New York: F. Obolensky, 1963. 357 pp.
Sequel to her *Island of Paradox*.

601. Porter, Charles O., "An Interview with Fidel Castro," *Northwest Review*, (University of Oregon), Fall 1963. pp. 73-88.

602. Power, Jonathan, "Report from Havana," *Journal of World Business*, July-Aug. 1969. pp. 27-34.

603. Purdy, Al et al., *The Canadian Students' Work Tour to Cuba*,

Toronto: Fair Play for Cuba Committee, 1964. 20 pp.

604. Rauf, Mohammed A., *Cuban Journal: Castro's Cuba As it Really Is,* New York: Crowell, 1964. 231 pp.

605. *The Real Cuba As Three Canadians Saw It.* Toronto: Fair Play for Cuba Committee, June 1964. 36 pp.

606. *A Report by Four Canadians,* Toronto: Fair Play for Cuba Committee, 1963. 31 pp.

607. Schmid, Peter, "Letter from Havana," *Commentary,* Sept. 1965. pp. 56-63.

608. Schneider, Ronald M., "Five Years of Cuban Revolution," *Current History,* (Philadelphia), Jan. 1964. pp. 26-33.

609. Scott, Jack, *Second Look at Cuba,* Toronto: Fair Play for Cuba Committee, 1963. 28 pp.

610. Shapiro, Samuel, "Extract from a Cuban Diary," *New Politics,* (New York), Fall 1962. pp. 70-83.

611. Skelton, Barbara, "In the Streets of Havana," *Atlas,* (Ohio), Dec. 1962. pp. 434-442.

612. Stone, R. E., "The Revolution in Cuba," *Political Affairs,* (New York), Aug. 1963. pp. 54-65.

613. Stuart, Lyle, "Diary of a Visit to Cuba," *The Independent,* (New York), Sept. 1964. pp. 1-16.

614. Szulc, Tad, "Cuba: Profile of a Revolution," *New York Times Magazine,* Apr. 24, 1960. pp. 9-11.

615. Szulc, Tad, "Cuba: Anatomy of a Failure," *Look,* July 18, 1961. pp. 76-82.

616. Szulc, Tad, "Castro: How Strong? How Long?" *New York Times Magazine,* Sept. 23, 1962. pp. 25-27+.

617. Szulc, Tad, "As Castro Speaks: the Wall! the Wall!" *New York Times Magazine,* Dec. 13, 1959. p. 11+.

618. Tetlow, Edwin, "Cuba: Why Castro Is Feeling Stronger," *New Republic,* July 11, 1964. pp. 9-10.

619. Tetlow, Edwin, *Eye on Cuba,* New York: Hartcourt, Brace and World, Inc., 1966. 291 pp. Reporter.

620. Wheeler, George, "Notes on Cuba's Progress," *New World Review,* (New York), May 1964. pp. 32-36.

621. Yglesias, José, "Last Seven Years in Cuba," *Massachusetts Review,* Autumn 1967. pp. 731-746.

2. Latin American

622. Andrade, Ramiro, *Cuba, el vecino socialista,* Bogota, 1961. 316 pp. Foreign relations, 1933-59.

623. Arguedas, Sal, *Cuba no es una isla,* Mexico: Ediciones Era, 1961. 205 pp. "It is the vanguard of the Latin American revolution."

624. Arvelo, Perina, *Revolución de los barbudos,* Caracas, 1961. 187 pp. Sympathetic account by Venezuelan observer.

625. Baciú, Stefan, *Cortina de hierro sobre Cuba,* Buenos Aires: Editorial San Isidro, 1961. 210 pp. Also in Portuguese.

626. Benítez, Fernando, *La batalla de Cuba,* Mexico: Ediciones Era, 1960. 185 pp.

Friendly review of the revolution by a Mexican reporter.

627. Bernhard, Guillermo, *Reportaje a Cuba*, Montevideo: Ediciones América Nueva, 1961. 190 pp.

628. Cabieses Donoso, Manuel, "Cuba, año Diez," *Punto Final*, (Chile), Dec. 31, 1968. Suplemento pp. 8-16.

629. Canelas O., Amado, *Cuba, socialismo en español*, LaPaz: Empresa Industrial Gráfica E. Burillo, 1964. 184 pp.
Bolivian observer; sympathetic.

630. Carmona, Dario, *Prohibida la sombra; reportajes en Cuba*, Havana: UNRAC, 1965. 132 pp.

631. Cordovín, J. J., *Lo que yo ví en Cuba*, Buenos Aires: Ed. San Isidro, 1962. 112 pp.

632. Cortázar, Julio, et al., *Cuba por Argentinos*, Buenos Aires: Editorial Merlín, 1968. 124 pp.

633. Cuenca, Humberto, *La revolución cubana*, Caracas: Editorial Cultura Contemporánea, 1962. 108 pp.
Sympathetic observer.

634. Délano, Luis Enrique, *Cuba 66*, Santiago de Chile: Editora Austral, 1966. 191 pp.
Reporter.

635. Febrat, Luis Izrael, "Cuba, año 4," *Revista Brasiliense*, (Rio de Janeiro), Sept.-Oct. 1962. pp. 62-95.

636. Fernández, Luis Efrén, *Cuba: un pueblo de patria o muerte*, Bogotá: Impreso en Editorial Colombia Nueva, 1964. 126 pp.
Visiting journalist.

637. Finamour, Jurema, *Vais bem, Fidel!*, Sao Paulo: Editôra Brasiliense, 1962. 427 pp.

638. Franco, Luis, *Espartaco en Cuba*, Buenos Aires: C. Dávalos/ D. C. Hernández, 1965. 313 pp.
The Latin American left and Cuba.

639. Frondizi, Silvio, *La revolución cubana, su significación histórica*, Montevideo: Editorial Ciencias Políticas, 1960. 178 pp.
"Wave of the future."

640. Gaganova, Valentina, "Lo que he visto en Cuba," *Literatura Soviética*, (Moscow), 1962. pp. 153-158.

641. Gallardo, Carlos M., *Esto ví en Cuba*, Montevideo: Ed. Periódico Lucha, 1961. 20 pp.
Journalist.

642. Gilly, Adolfo, "La révolution cubaine aprés cinq ans," *Partisans*, (Paris), Dec. 1963-Jan. 1964, pp. 101-118; and Feb.-Mar. 1964. pp. 62-73.

643. González, Manuel Pedro, "Un testimonio honrado sobre la revolución cubana," *Cuadernos Americanos*, (Mexico), May-June 1967. pp. 50-56.

644. Izcaray, Jesús, *Reportaje en Cuba*, Havana: Ediciones Venceremos, 1962. 244 pp.

645. Ladrón de Guevara, Matilde, *Adiós al cañaveral: diario de una mujer en Cuba*, Buenos Aires: Editorial Goyanarte, 1962. 290 pp.
Anti-Castro. Chapter on political prisoners.

646. Lequerica Vélez, Fulgencio, *600 días con Fidel. Tres misiones en La Habana*, Bogotá: Ediciones Mito, 1961. 157 pp.
Journalistic. 1959-1960.

647. Lortsch, Lucy, *Dos chilenas en*

la Habana, Santiago de Chile: ABC Plastigraf, 1963. 34 pp.
Eyewitness.

648. Martínez Estrada, Ezequíel, *En Cuba y al servicio de la revolución cubana,* Havana: Unión de Escritores y Artistas de Cuba, 1963. 175 pp.
Argentine socialist sympathizer who resided in Cuba. 1965 edition entitled *Mi experiencia cabana.*

649. Matos, Almir, *Cuba a revolução na América,* Rio de Janeiro: Vitória, 1961. 213 pp.
Reporter.

650. Olmedo, José Joaquín, *Cuba, la revolución de América,* Bogotá: Ediciones Sudamérica, 1963. 135 pp.
Castro's Latin American impact. Sympathetic.

651. Otero, Rafael, *Reportaje a una revolución; de Batista a Fidel Castro,* Santiago de Chile: Editorial del Pacífico, 1959. 262 pp.

652. Palacios, Alfredo L., *Una revolución auténtica en nuestra América,* Mexico: Ed. Cultura, 1960. 48 pp.
By leader of Socialist Party of Argentina.

653. Portnoy, Marcos, *Testimonio sobre Cuba,* Santiago de Chile: Ediciones del Litoral, 1964. 167 pp.
Chilean journalist. Sympathetic.

654. Ramírez Gómez, Ramón, *Cuba, despertar de América; ensayo económico-social,* Mexico: Escuela Nacional de Economía, 1961. 267 pp.

655. Ramírez Gómez, Ramón, "Cuba Socialista," *Ciencias Políticas y Sociales,* (Mexico), Apr.-June 1962. pp. 175-207.

656. Saldarriaga Betancur, J. M., *De la dictadura al comunismo,* Medellín, 1962. 208 pp.

657. Souchy, Agustín, *Testimonios sobre la revolución Cubana,* Buenos Aires: Editorial Reconstruir, 1960. 68 pp.
Anarcho-syndicalist view.

658. Valencia, Luis Emiro, *Realidades y perspectivas de la revolución cubana,* Havana: Casa de las Américas, 1961. 407 pp.

659. Varela, Alfredo, *Cuba con toda la barba,* Buenos Aires: Editorial Esfera, 1960. 254 pp.
Sympathetic. Journalist. 1959-1960.

660. Vargas Echevarría, José María, *Revolución cubana, despertar latinoamericano; notes de un viaje a Cuba,* Bogotá: Comité Pro-Nacionalización del Petróleo, 1961. 152 pp.

3. European—General

661. Alleg, Henri, *Victorieus e Cuba, de la guérilla au socialisme,* Paris: Editions de minuit, 1963. 207 pp.

662. Camus, Marie Hélène, *Lune de miel chez Fidel Castro,* Paris: A Fayard, 1960. 202 pp.

663. Carrillo, Santiago, *Cuba, 68,* Paris: Librarie du Globe, 1968. 72 pp.
Spanish communist describes stay in Cuba.

664. Cloës, Marie N., *Vivre à Cuba,* Paris: Tournai, 1968. 205 pp.
Descriptive, travel.

665. Demagny, René, *Cuba; l'evil et*

la ferveur, Paris: Buchet/Chastel, 1962. 222 pp.
Descriptive essay by left-of-center journalist.

666. Dufour, Jean Marc, *Révolution: capitale Cuba,* Paris: La Table Ronde, 1964. 222 pp.
Sympathetic reporter.

667. Dumont, René, *Cuba, est-il socialiste?* Paris: Editions du Seuil, 1970. 236 pp.

668. Ehnmark, Anders, *Cuba cubana,* Stockholm: Ed. Bonniers, 1963. 202 pp.
Editor of Swedish periodical reports his experiences.

669. Faux, Claude, *Cuba, cubain,* Lausanne, Switzerland: Maoson Mayer et Sauter, 1961. 94 pp.
Photographs.

670. Franco, Victor, *The Morning After,* New York: Praeger, 1963. 248 pp.
French journalist's report on domestic resistance to Castro.

671. Giroud, Françoise, "Voyage a Cuba," *L'Express,* (Paris), Oct. 7-13, 1967. pp. 19-22.

672. Gosset, Pierre, *L'adieu aux barbus,* Paris: Julliard, 1966. 204 pp.
Sympathetic journalist.

673. Guilbert, Yves, *La poudriére cubaine; Castro L'infidéle,* Paris: Table Ronde, 1961. 252 pp.
Journalist "Revolution betrayed."

674. Hochman, Jiri, *Patria ó muerte,* Prague: Státní nakl. politické literatury, 1961. 73 pp.
Journalist.

675. Krober, Llaus Dieter, *Kuba: Patria o muerte,* Leipzig: Uranis-Verlag, 1962. 196 pp.

676. Lanzmann, Jacques, *Viva Castro, suivi de trois vivats au Mex-*

ique, Paris: Fasquelle Editeurs, 1959. 203 pp.

677. Lascu, Petre, *Cuba,* Bucharest: Editura Stiintifica, 1962. 237 pp.
Journalist.

678. Marquardt, Otto, *Report aus Havanna,* Leipzig: Veb Interdruck, 1968. 267 pp.
Journalist.

679. Melotti, Umberto, *La rivoluzione cubana,* Milan, Italy: Dall 'Oglio Editora, 1967. 305 pp.
Pro-Castro. 1962 observer.

680. Meneses, Enrique, *Fidel Castro,* London: Faber, 1969. 238 pp.
Spanish journalist's memoirs of late 1950's.

681. Meneses, Enrique, *Fidel Castro: siete años de poder,* Madrid: Afrodisio Aguado, S. A. Editores, 1966. 270 pp.
Journalistic account.

682. Mulisch, Harry, *Het woord bij de daad. Getuigenis van de revolutie op Cuba,* Amsterdam: De Bezige Bij, 1968. 252 pp.

683. Otto, Herbert, *Republik der leidenschaft,* Berlin: Verlag Volk und Welt, 1961. 175 pp.
"Republic of Passion."

684. Pritt, D. N., "Cuba Travel Notes," *Labour Monthly,* (London), Mar. 1962, pp. 131-136; Apr. 1962. pp. 185-190.

685. Robinson, Joan, "Cuba—1965," *Monthly Review,* (New York), Feb. 1966. pp. 10-18.
Sympathetic observer.

686. Sartre, Jean Paul, *Sartre on Cuba,* New York: Ballantine Books, 1961. 160 pp.

687. Sartre, Jean Paul, *Sartre visita a Cuba; ideología y revolución. Una entrevista con los escritores cu-*

banos y Huracán sobre el azúcar, Havana: Ediciones R., 1960. 244 pp.

688. Sauvage, Leo, *Autopsie du Castrisme,* Paris: Flammarion, 1962. 348 pp.
Also a Spanish edition.

689. Soria, Georges, *Cuba à l'heure Castro,* Paris: Del Duca, 1961. 274 pp.
French communist's appraisal.

690. Stillman, Gunter, *Kuba, insel der barbudos,* Leipzig: Veb F. A. Brokhaus Verlag, 1961. 212 pp.

691. Sylvester, Anthony, "Cuban Lessons for the Developing World: Recent Impressions of a Visitor," *Contemporary Review,* (London), Feb. 1966. pp. 69-76.

692. Teague, Michael, "Castro's Cuba," *Geographical Magazine,* (London), Nov. 1959. pp. 265-275.

693. Vermehren, Michael, "These Are Cubans . . . Why They Endure," *Atlas,* (New York), May 1968. pp. 52-56.

694. Veyrier, Marcel, *Prospects of Cuban Revolution,* Washington: Joint Publications Research Service, Jan. 30, 1962. 16 pp.

4. Russian

695. Chichkov, Vasilii M., *Zaria nad Kubai.* Moscow: IMO, 1960. 124 pp.
Pravda correspondent describes his experiences in Cuba.

696. Borovsky, V., "In Revolutionary Cuba," *New Times,* (Moscow), Nov. 28, 1962. pp. 26-28.

697. Kamynin, Leonid Ivanovich, *Zdravstvui, Kuba!,* [Hello, Cuba!], Moscow: Izvestiia, 1960. 78 pp.

698. Kovalkin, V., *13 Mecyatsev na Kuba,* [13 months in Cuba], Minsk: Belarus, 1964. 68 pp.

699. Razumovich, Nikolai N., *Gosudarstvennye preobrazovaniia, revoliutsionnoi Kuby,* [Governmental reforms in Revolutionary Cuba], Moscow: Mezhdunarodnye otnosheniia, 1964. 105 pp.

700. Smirnov, S. S., *Poesdka na Kuba,* [Excursion to Cuba], Moscow: Sovetskii Pisatel, 1962. 246 pp.

701. Talovov, Valentin P., *Kubinskii reportazn,* [News stories from Cuba], Leningrad: Lenizdat, 1964. 87 pp.

702. Tikhmenev, Vladimir Evgen'evich, *Kuba-da!,* Moscow, 1961. 174 pp.

703. Vasilevskia, Vanda Lvovna, *Desiat Dniv Na Kubi,* [Ten Days in Cuba], Kiev: Radianskii Piomennik, 1962. 137 pp.

704. Volodkin, Vladimir, *Cuba, 1961,* Moscow: Editorial Joven Guardia, 1961. 42 pp.
Reporter.

C. BIOGRAPHY

705. Agüero, Luis, *Che Comandante. Biografía de Ernesto Che Guevara,* Mexico: Editorial Diógenes, 1969. 165 pp.
Compilation of articles.

706. Alexandre, Marianne, ed., *¡Viva Che! Contributions in Tribute to Ernesto Che Guevara,* London: Lorrimer, 1968, 120 pp.

707. Anonymous, *Camilo Cienfuegos, People's Hero,* Havana: Min-

isterio de Industrias, 1962. 24 pp.

708. Arredondo, Alberto, *Crónicas de actualidad. El "Che" Guevara: un guerrillero sin patria; su vida, sus aventuras, sus crímenes, sus ambiciones, su desaparición*, Miami: AIP, 1965. 16 pp.

709. Atías, Guillermo, *Después de Guevara*, Santiago de Chile: Ediciones Plan, 1968. 111 pp.

710. Cabus, José D., *Castro ante la historia*, Mexico: Editores Mexicanos Unidos, 1963. 270 pp.
"Castro was a communist since his university years."

711. Castro, Fidel, *Discurso pronunciado por el Cmdte . . . en la velada solemne en memoria del comandante Ernesto Che Guevara*, Havana: Instituto del Libaro, 1967. 16 pp.
Oct. 18, 1967. "Che is dead, but guerrilla warfare will continue in Latin America."

712. Conte Agüero, Luis, *Los dos rostros de Fidel Castro*, Mexico: Editorial Jus, 1960. 356 pp.

713. Conte Agüero, Luis, *Fidel Castro: psiquiatría y política*, Mexico: Editorial Jus, 1968. 372 pp.
Former comrade in arms of Fidel.

714. Conte Agüero, Luis, *Fidel Castro; vida y obra*, Havana: Editorial Lex, 1959. 702 pp.
Comprehensive and sympathetic.

715. Cuba, Ministerio de Educación, *Nuestro recuerdo a Camilo Cienfuegos*, Havana, 1960. 23 pp.

716. Cuba, Partido Comunista, *Material de estudio sobre el pensamiento de Ernesto Guevara*, Havana: Comisión de Orientación Revolucionaria, 1967. 53 pp.
Fragments of essays and speeches.

717. Darío Roldán, Rubén, *¿Es Castro un hombre honrado?*, Caracas, 1961. 90 pp.
"No."

718. Ebon, Marton, *Che: the Making of a Legend*, New York: New American Library, 1969. 176 pp.
Sympathetic.

719. Ferrieri, Giuliano, *Fidel Castro*, Milan: Trevi, 1961. 97 pp.
Sympathetic.

720. Gambini, Hugo, *El Che Guevara*, Buenos Aires: Editorial Paidos, 1968. 513 pp.
Based on published materials and interviews.

721. Hermans, H., *Fidel Castro: de ontembore rebel*, The Hague: Leopolds, 1964. 196 pp.

722. Hoeck, Albert von, *Viva Che!*, Brugge, Antwerpen: De Galpe, 1968. 192 pp.

723. Inclán Lavastida, Fernando, *Juan Manuel Márquez, una vida en defensa del pueblo y sus libertades*, Marianao: El Sol, 1959. 24 pp.
Márquez was with Granma invasion.

724. James, Daniel, *Che Guevara: A Biography*, New York: Stein and Day, 1969. 380 pp.

725. Kozolchyk, Boris, *The Political Biographies of Three Castro Officials*, Santa Monica: Rand Corp., 1966. 95 pp.
Raúl Roa, René Anillo and Fabio Grobart.

726. Martínez, Hugo, *Antecedentes biográficos del Comandante Ernesto Che Guevara*, Santiago, Chile, 1968. 180 pp.

727. Matthews, Herbert Lionel, *Fidel Castro*, New York: Simon and Schuster, 1969. 382 pp.

728. Morton, Ward McKinnon, *Castro As Charismatic Hero*, Lawrence, Kansas: Center for Latin American Studies, 1965. 30 pp.

729. Nuiry Sánchez, Juan, "José Antonio a través de su testamento político," *Bohemia*, (Havana), Mar. 13, 1964. pp. 83-85.
A Directorio Revolucionario leader killed in 1957.

730. Perini, Franco, *Che Guevara*, Milan, Italy: Longanesi, 1968. 250 pp.

731. Rodríguez Morejón, Gerardo, *Fidel Castro, biografía*, Havana: P. Fernández, 1959. 259 pp.
Adulatory. In cooperation with Fidel's mother.

732. Rojo, Ricardo, *Mi amigo el Che*, Buenos Aires: Editorial J. Alvarez, 1968. 266 pp.
Dial press edition in English.

733. Rojo, Ricardo, *My Friend Che*, trans. by Julian Casart, New York: The Dial Press, 1968. 220 pp.

734. Simón, Luis, "Mis Relaciones con el 'Che' Guevara," *Cuadernos*, (Paris), May 1962. pp. 35-42.

735. Valdés, Nelson P., "Version of Che," *Dissent*, (New York), May-June 1968. pp. 275-276.

736. Wilkerson, Loree, *Fidel Castro's Political Programs from Reformism to Marxism-Leninism*, Gainesville: University of Florida Press, 1965. 100 pp.

D. REVOLUTIONARY THEORY

1. Guerrilla Warfare

737. Almeida, Juan, "Discurso del 1 de mayo de 1967," *Política*, (Mexico), May 1-14, 1967. pp.I-XIV.
Says violent revolution inevitable in Latin America.

738. Andrade, Marcelo de, "Considérations sur les thèses de Régis Debray," *Les Temps Modernes*, (Paris), May 1969. pp. 2009-2036.

739. Debray, Regis, "Latin America: the Long March," *New Left Review*, (London), Sept.-Oct. 1965. pp. 17-58.

740. Debray, Regis, *¿Revolución en la revolución?*, Havana: Casa de las Américas, 1967. 110 pp.

741. Debray, Regis, *Revolution in the Revolution? Armed Struggle and Political Struggle in Latin America*, New York: Monthly Review Press, 1967. 126 pp.

742. Editorial, "The Strategy of Armed Struggle," *Monthly Review*, Sept. 1966. pp. 1-15.

743. Guevara, Ernesto, "Cuba: Exceptional Case?" *Monthly Review*, (New York), July-Aug. 1961. pp. 56-71.

744. Huberman, Leo et al., "Regis Debray and the Latin American Revolution," *Monthly Review*, July-Aug. 1968. pp. 1-96. (special issue).

745. Mallin, Jay, ed., *"Che" Guevara on Revolution: A Documentary Overview*, Coral Gables: University of Miami Press, 1969. 255 pp.

746. Methol Ferré, Alberto, "La revolución verde oliva, Debray y

la OLAS," *Víspera*, (Montevideo), Oct. 1967. pp. 17-39.
Critical of Debray thesis. Scholarly.

747. Moreno, José A., "Che Guevara on Guerrilla Warfare: Doctrine, Practice and Evaluation," *Comparative Studies in Society and History*, Apr. 1970. pp. 114-133.

748. Niedergang, Marcel, "Le 'Che' au la révolte permanente . . .," *Le Monde*, (Paris), Oct. 12-18, 1967. p. 2.

749. Niedergang, Marcel, "Fidel Castro consacre le schisme entre partisans et adversaires de la lutte armeé," *Le Monde*, (Paris), Oct. 10-16, 1967. p. 1, 3.

750. Petit, Antoine G., *Castro, Debray; contre le marxisme-léninisme*, Paris: R. Laffont, 1968. 208 pp.

751. Reblitz, Irma von, *Fidel Castro, Ernesto Che Guevara, Regis Debray. Materialen zur Revolution in Reden*, Darmstadt, Germany: Melzer, 1968. 264 pp.
On theory of revolution and guerrilla war.

752. Slovo, Joe, " 'Che' in Bolivia," *The African Communist*, (London), No. 38, 1969. pp. 46-61.
Revolutionary theory.

753. Slovo, Joe, "Latin America and the Ideas of Regis Debray," *African Communist*, (London), No. 33, 1968. pp. 37-54.
Revolutionary theory.

2. Process of Revolution

754. Alba, Víctor, "Cuba: a Peasant Revolution," *World Today*, (London), May 1959. pp. 183-195.

755. Arnault, Jacques, *Cuba et le marxisme; essai sur la Révolution cubaine*, Paris: Editions sociales, 1963. 221 pp.

756. Baran, Paul, "Reflections on the Cuban Revolution," *Monthly Review*, Jan. 1961, pp. 459-470; Feb. 1961. pp. 518-529.

757. Blackburn, Robin, "Prologue to the Cuban revolution," *New Left Review*, (London), Oct. 1963. pp. 52-91.

758. Blasier, Cole, "Studies of Social Revolution: Origins in Mexico, Bolivia, and Cuba," *Latin American Research Review*, Summer 1967, pp. 28-64.

759. Burks, David, "The Future of Castroism," *Current History*, Feb. 1963. pp. 78-83+.

760. Díaz Versón, Salvador, *Cuando la razón se vuelve inútil*, 1st ed., Mexico: Ediciones Botas, 1962. 155 pp.
"Revolution was unnecessary."

761. Enos, J. L., *An Analytic Model of Political Allegiance and Its Application to the Cuban Revolution*, California: Rand Corporation, 1965. 34 pp.

762. Fagen, Richard, "Charismatic Authority and the Leadership of Fidel Castro," *Western Political Quarterly*, June 1965. pp. 275-284.

763. Gitano, Henry, "First Year of the Cuban Revolution," *International Socialist Review*, (New York), Spring 1960. pp. 38-42.
Troksyist view.

764. Goldenberg, Boris, *Cuba's Road to Communism*, Washington: Joint Publications Research Service, Apr. 21, 1961. 8 pp.

765. Goldenberg, Boris, "Notes on the Cuban Revolution," *New Politics*, (New York), Fall 1962. pp. 51-58.

766. Guevara, Ernesto, "La experiencia de la revolución cubana," *Monthly Review*, (Buenos Aires), Oct. 1963. pp. 29-39.

767. Hansen, Joseph, *In Defense of the Cuban Revolution; An Answer to the State Department and Theodore Draper*, New York, 1961. 30 pp.
Trotskyist.

768. Hansen, Joseph, "Ideology of the Cuban Revolution," *International Socialist Review*, (New York), Summer 1960. pp. 74-78.
Sartre and Guevara on revolutionary theory.

769. Hansen, Joseph, *The Theory of the Cuban Revolution*, New York: Pioneer Publishers, 1962. 30 pp.
Trotskyist.

770. Hansen, Joseph, *The Truth about Cuba*, New York: Pioneer Publishers, 1960. 48 pp.

771. Horowitz, Irving L., "Castrologists and Apologists: A Reply to Science in the Service of Sentiment," *New Politics*, (New York), Winter 1966. pp. 27-34.

772. Horowitz, Irving L., "The Stalinization of Castro," *New Politics*, (New York), Fall 1965. pp. 62-69.

773. Kahlmey, Gunther, "Kubas Wirtschaftaufban," *Einheit*, (Berlin), June 20, 1965. pp. 61-70.

774. Lumsden, Ian, "On Socialists and Stalinists: A Rejoinder to Irving Louis Horowitz," *New Politics*, (New York), Winter 1966. pp. 20-26.

775. Mills, C. W., *Listen Yankee; the Revolution in Cuba*, New York: Ballantine Books, 1960. 192 pp.
Neo-Marxist interpretation.

776. Morray, J. P., *The Second Revolution in Cuba*, New York: Monthly Review Press, 1962. 173 pp.
1959-1962.

777. Obyden, Konstantin M., *Kuba v borbe za svobodu i nezavisimost*, Moscow: Gospolitizdat, 1959. 93 pp.
"Peasants and Communist Party made the revolution. Revolution in Latin America will be agrarian."

778. O'Connor, James, "The Classless Revolution; The Origin of Castro's Cuba: A Necessary Reconsideration," *Second Coming Magazine*, (New York), July 1961. pp. 8-12.

779. O'Connor, James, "Cuba: Anatomy of a Revolution," *Nation*, Oct. 8, 1960. pp. 230-231.

780. O'Connor, James, "On Cuban Political Economy," *Political Science Quarterly*, (New York), June 1964. pp. 233-247.

781. Roca, Blas, "Sobre la revolución cubana," *Estudios Políticos*, (Montevideo), Sept. 1959. pp. 32-45.

782. Sartre, Jean-Paul, "Ideology and Revolution," *Studies on the Left*, No. 3, 1960. pp. 7-16.

783. Sartre, Jean Paul, *Sartre on Cuba*, New York: Ballantine Books, 1961. 160 pp.

784. Sartre, Jean Paul, *Sartre visita a Cuba: Ideología y revolución*, Havana: Ediciones R, 1960. 244 pp.

785. Tabares del Real, José A., *En-*

sayo de interpretación de la revolución cubana, La Paz: Talleres Gráficos "Gutenberg," 1960. 98 pp.

786. Thomas, Hugh, "Middle-Class Politics and the Cuban Revolution," in Claudio Véliz (ed.), *The Politics of Conformity in Latin America,* London: Oxford University Press, 1967. pp. 249-277.

787. Victoria, Nelson Amaro, *La revolución cubana ¿por que? Ensayo teórico empírico sobre las condiciones de la revolución,* Santiago de Chile: Universidad Catolica, 1967. 265 pp.

788. Vitalé, Luis, "Phases of the Cuban Revolution," *International Socialist Review,* (New York), Spring 1963. pp. 41-45.

E. COMMUNISM
(See also Politics, Relations with Soviet Russia).

789. Acción Constitucional, *Cuba. ¿Hacia donde vamos?,* Havana, 1960. 83 pp.
On communist doctrine.

790. Aguirre, Severo, "Revoliutsiia na Kube," [The revolution in Cuba], *Mir. ekon. i mezhdunar. otn.,* May 1959. pp. 22-27.

791. Alexandrov, A., "El partido comunista de Cuba," *Tiempos Nuevos,* (Moscow), Oct. 1965. pp. 19-20.

792. Angell, A., "Castro and the Cuban Communist Party," *Government and Opposition,* (London), Jan.-Apr. 1967. pp. 241-252.

793. Aptheker, Herbert, "The Cuban Revolution," *Political Affairs,* March 1961, pp. 47-52; April 1961. pp. 34-45.

794. Arnault, Jacques, "Cuban Communists and the Revolution," *Marxist Leninist Quarterly,* (NY), May 1963. pp. 78-91.

795. Arredondo, Alberto, *La historia secreta del comunismo cubano, y sus purgas,* Miami: Ed. AIP, 1965. 35 pp.

796. Baciú, Stefan, *Cortina de hierro sobre Cuba,* Buenos Aires: Ed. San Isidro, 1961. 210 pp.
By Brazilian head of the Congress for Cultural Freedom. Also in Portuguese.

797. Basaldua, Pedro de, *La garra comunista en América Latina,* Buenos Aires: Asociación Argentina por la Libertad de la Cultura, 1962. 377 pp.
Section on Cuban Communism (pp. 209-228).

798. Cameron, James, "Cuba's Fumbling Marxism," *The Atlantic Monthly,* (Boston), Sept. 1964. pp. 92-102.

799. Castro, Fidel, "Comparecencia en el programa Ante la Prensa," *Revolución,* (Havana), May 22, 1959. pp. 1-2, 8, 11, 14.
Attacks communism.

800. Castro, Fidel, "Yo no soy comunista," *Diario de la Marina,* (Havana), Jan. 24, 1959. pp. 1, 19A.

801. "Cuba Paints Its Own Shade of Red," *Business Week,* (New York), June 13, 1964. pp. 46-54.

802. Deadline Data on World Affairs, *Communism-Cuban Style,* Greenwich, Conn., 1968. 78 pp.

803. "Declaró Ernesto Guevara que es izquierdista, no comunista," *Diario de la Marina,* (Havana), Jan. 11, 1959. pp. 1, 2A.

804. Díaz Lanz, Pedro Luis, "El

comunismo en Cuba," *Estudios sobre el comunismo,* (Santiago de Chile), Jan.-Mar. 1960. pp. 88-109.

805. Díaz Versón, Salvador, *Cuando la razón se vuelve inútil,* Mexico: Ediciones Botas, 1962. 155 pp.
"Freedom destroyed by Communism." Former Batista military officer.

806. Díaz Versón, Salvador, *Historia de un archivo,* Miami, 1961. 16 pp.
Former Cuban chief of army's military intelligence on communism.

807. Draper, Theodore, "Castro and Communism," *The Reporter,* (New York), Jan. 17, 1963. pp. 35-48.

808. Draper, Theodore, "Castro's 'New' Communists: l'affaire Escalante," *New Leader,* Apr. 16, 1962. pp. 3-7.

809. Editorial, "Cuba Today," *World Marxist Review,* Apr. 1959. pp. 69-70.

810. Fernández, Francisco, "La propaganda comunista contra Batista," *Defensa Institucional Cubana,* (Mexico), Apr. 1965. pp. 17-23.

811. Fernández Núñez, Guillermo, *Comunismo ¡jamás!,* Miami: Tacuba, 1962. 104 pp.

812. Fernández Varela, Angel, *Cuba, país comunista en 18 meses,* Buenos Aires: Editorial Ciudad y Espíritu, 1961. 61 pp.

813. Fiorini, Mario, "El comunismo en Cuba," *Estudios sobre el Comunismo,* (Santiago de Chile), July-Sept. 1956. pp. 75-79.

814. Gibney, Frank, *Media vuelta a la izquierda,* Havana: Diario de la Marina, 1960. 345 pp.
On communist infiltration.

815. Gómez, Pablo, *Conjura comunista sobre las juventudes de América,* Miami, 1965. 19 pp.

816. Guiza, Jesús, "El comunismo y la auto-determinación en Cuba," *Lectura,* (Mexico), Dec. 1, 1962. pp. 67-70.

817. Habel, Janette, "La procès de Marcos Rodríguez et les problèmes de l'unité du mouvement révolutionnaire à Cuba," *Les Temps Modernes,* (Paris), Aug.-Sept. 1964. pp. 491-531.
Purges.

818. Kucsynski, Jurgen, "Sobre el camino cubano en la construcción del socialismo," *Casa de las Américas,* (Havana), July-Aug. 1965. pp. 110-117.

819. Masó, Fausto, "Cuando los comunistas atacaban a Fidel Castro," *Bohemia Libre,* (Caracas), July 7, 1963. pp. 20-21+.

820. Mooray, J. P., ed., *Cuba and Communism,* New York: Monthly Review Press, 1961. 94 pp.
Articles by Guevara, Paul Baran and Castro.

821. Par, Francis, "La signification des attaques de Fidel Castro contre les communistes de Cuba," *Est et Ouest,* (Paris), July 16-31, 1962. pp. 8-11.

822. Pares, Fco., "Estrategia comunista en la revolución cubana," *Bohemia,* (Havana), Feb. 8, 1959. pp. 66-67, 109.

823. Peña, Alcira de la, "Cuba and Marxism," *World Marxist Review,* (Prague), June 1963. pp. 78-82.

824. Pflaum, Irving P., *Tragic Island: How Communism Came to Cuba,* Englewood Cliffs: Prentice-Hall, 1961. 196 pp.

825. Roca, Blas, *Los fundamentos del socialismo en Cuba,* Havana: Impr. Nacional, 1961. 225 pp.
  Updating of 1943 work. Also in English.

826. Rowan, Richard W., *Cuba: the Big Red Lie,* New York: Quinn Publishing Co., 1963. 95 pp.

827. Santa Pinter, José, "Legislación comunista en Cuba," *Estudios sobre el comunismo,* (Santiago de Chile), July-Sept. 1962. pp. 100-103.

828. Shaffer, Harry G., ed., *The Communist World: Marxist and Non-Marxist Views,* New York: Appleton-Century-Crofts, 1967. 558 pp.
  Chapter 9, on Cuba, includes articles by Dudley Seers, Ernst Halperin, and Edward Boorstein.

829. Stein, E. C., *Cuba, Castro, and Communism,* New York: Mac-Fadden Bartell Corp., 1962. 175 pp.

830. Suárez, Andrés, *Cuba: Castroism and Communism, 1959-1966,* Cambridge, Mass.: MIT Press, 1967. 266 pp.
  Good scholarship.

831. Thomas, Hugh, "Castro and Communism," *The Listener,* (London), Jan. 16, 1964. pp. 104-106.

832. Thomas, Hugh, "Murder in Havana," *The New Statesman,* (London), May 29, 1964. pp. 838-840.
  Purges.

833. Todd, Carlos, *Cuban Communism on the Map; Speech at the Rotary Club of Miami,* Miami, 1961. 7 pp.
  By *Times of Havana* editor.

834. Zeitlin, Maurice, "Castro and Cuba's Communists," *The Nation,* Nov. 3, 1962. pp. 284-287.

III. POLITICS

A. BACKGROUND TO REVOLUTION
(See also Revolution General)

835. Acuña, Juan Antonio, *Cuba: revolución traicionada; Fidel, hoy entregado al comunismo que fué aliado de Batista ayer*, Montevideo, 1962. 168 pp.
Has documents.

836. Angier, Angel, "Raúl Roa en la alborada de Cuba," *Bohemia*, (Havana), Apr. 10, 1964. pp. 82-83.

837. Baeza Flores, Alberto, *Las cadenas vienen de lejos; Cuba, América Latina y la libertad*, Mexico: Ed. Letras, 1960. 748 pp.
Revolution betrayed.

838. Barnet, Miguel, "Tiene la palabra el camarada Roa," *CUBA Internacional*, (Havana), Oct. 1968. pp. 78-87.

839. Blackburn, Robin, "Prologue to the Cuban Revolution," *New Left Review*, (London), Oct. 1963. pp. 52-91.

840. Castro, Fidel, "A esta revolución nada podrá vencerla porque 52-91. este pueblo, igual que ha luchado cien años por su destino, es capaz de luchar otros cien años," *El Mundo* (Havana), Oct. 11, 1968. pp. 2-5.
Speech of Oct. 10 1968. Historical roots of revolution.

841. Casuso, Teresa, *Cuba and Castro*, New York: Random House, 1961. 249 pp .
Castro's former UN Ambassador. Defector.

842. Cuba, Ejército, *Boletín*, Havana, 1950-58.
Bi-monthly.

843. Cuba, Ejército, Estado mayor general, *Ejército, revista oficial*, Havana, 1936-1956.
Irregular monthly.

844. Cuba, Policía Nacional, *Revista de la policía*, Havana, 1944-1959.
Monthly.

845. Díaz Versón, Salvador, *La mentira se viste de historia*, Miami, 1961. 38 pp.
"Since 1943 Castro was a communist."

846. Duarte Oropesa, José A., *Historiología cubana*, Hollywood, Calif., 1969. 4 vols.
Vol. 4, eyewitness account of revolutionary politics (1934-1952) by participant.

847. Elizalde, L. P., *Difamación*, Mexico: Defensa Institucional Cubana, 1961. 110 pp.
Defense of Batista.

848. Elizalde, L. P., *La tragedia de Cuba*, Mexico: Ediciones del Caribe, 1959. 236 pp.
Pro-Batista.

849. Gil, Federico G., "Antecedents of the Cuban Revolution," *The Centennial Review*, (East Lan-

47

sing, Michigan), Summer 1962. pp. 373-393.

850. Gónzales, Manuel Pedro and Ivan A. Schulman, *José Martí; esquema ideológico*, Mexico: Publicaciones de la Editorial Cultura, 1961. 551 pp.

851. González Pedrero, Enrique, *La revolución cubana*, Mexico: UNAM, 1959. 156 pp.
Background. Sympathetic.

852. Gray, Richard B., "José Martí and Social Revolution in Cuba," *Journal of Inter-American Studies*, Apr. 1963. pp. 249-256.

853. Gray, Richard B., *José Martí: Cuban Patriot*, Gainesville: University of Florida Press, 1962. 307 pp.
Martí's influence in shaping contemporary nationalism.

854. Grinevich, E., "Cuba before the Revolution," *International Affairs*, (Moscow), July 1963. pp. 65-70.

855. Hell, Jürgen, *Kurze Geschichte des kubanischen Volkes*, Berlin: Dietz Verlag, 1966. 502 pp.
One third of book on Castro period.

856. Hennessy, C. A. M., "The Roots of Cuban Nationalism," *International Affairs*, (London), July 1963. pp. 345-359.

857. León, Rubén de, *El origen del mal, Cuba, un ejemplo*, Miami: Service Offset Printers, Inc., 1964. 411 pp.
Blames problems on Spanish colonialism.

858. Mañach, Jorge, "El triunfo de la revolución cubana," *Cuadernos*, (Paris), Mar.-Apr. 1959. pp. 3-9.

859. Martínez, Marcial, *Cuba, la ver-* *dad de su tragedia*, Mexico, 1958. 173 pp.
Exile condemns Batista.

860. Masó y Vásquez, Calixto, "La realidad cubana," *Combate*, (San José, Costa Rica), Jan.-Feb. 1959. pp. 69-75.

861. Masó y Vázquez, Calixto, "La revolución cubana," *Combate*, (San José, Costa Rica), July-Aug. 1959. pp. 51-61.

862. Merino, Adolfo G., *Nacimiento de un estado vasallo*, Mexico: B. Costa-Amic, 1966.
By exiled journalist.

863. Mier Febles, Juan, "Un siglo ideológico: para llegar: recorrer el camino," *CUBA Internacional*, (Havana), Oct. 1968. pp. 150-154.
Revolutionary precursors.

864. Otto, Herbert, *Republik der Leidenschaft; Erlebnisse auf Kuba*, Berlin: Die Buchgemeinde, 1961. 177 pp.
Background to revolution.

865. Pendle, George, "Batista, Fidel Castro und die Wachstumsprobleme Kubas," *Europa-Archiv*, (Bonn, West Germany), Dec. 1959. pp. 747-760.

866. Phillips, Ruby H., *Cuba: Island of Paradox*, New York: McDowell Obolensky, 1959. 434 pp.
By long-time resident N. Y. *Times* reporter. Background to revolution.

867. Riera Hernández, Mario, *Cuba política, 1899-1955*, Havana: Imprenta Modelo, 1955. 628 pp.
Excellent survey.

868. Le Riverend, Julio, *La República, dependencia y revolución*, Havana: Editora Universataria, 1966. 376 pp.

869. Roa, Raúl, *Retorno a la alborada*, Las Villas: Universidad Central, 1964. 2 vols., 1066 pp.
Selected articles since 1930's tracing origins and triumph of Cuban nationalism.

870. Roig de Leuchsenring, Emilio, *Males y vicios de Cuba republicana*, Havana: Oficina del Historia dar de la Ciudad, 1959. 354 pp.
U.S. also gets blamed.

871. San Martín, Rafael, *El grito de la Sierra Maestra*, Buenos Aires: Ediciones Gure, 1960. 190 pp.
Background, 1933-1958.

872. Smith, Robert F., ed., *Background to Revolution: the Development of Modern Cuba*, New York: Knopf, 1966. 240 pp.
Scholarly articles.

873. Suárez Núñez, José, *El gran culpable*, Caracas, 1963. 174 pp.
Batista blamed for rise of communism.

874. Thomas, Hugh, "The Origins of the Cuban Revolution," *World Today*, Oct. 1963. pp. 448-460.

875. Vega Cabiellas, Ulpiano, *Batista y Cuba; crónica política y realizaciones*, Havana: Publicitaria Cultural, 1955. 280 pp.

876. Villares, Ricardo, "Precursores de la revolución," *Bohemia*, (Havana), Oct. 11, 1968. pp.74-78.

877. Volman, Sacha, *Batista y la revolución comunista*, Havana: Impr. Económica en General, 1959. 8 pp.

878. Zalamea, Jorge, *Antecedentes históricos de la revolución cubana*, Bogotá: Ediciones Suramérica, 1961. 172 pp.
Sympathetic to Castro.

1. Documents

879. Castellanos, Raúl, "El asalto al Cuartel Moncada y sus consecuencias," *La Universidad*, (El Salvador), No. 1, Jan.-Feb. 1968. pp. 39-59.

880. Castro, Fidel, "El asalto al cuartel Moncada," *Humanismo*, (Havana), Jan.-Apr. 1959. pp. 303-326.

881. Castro, Fidel, "¡Basta ya de mentiras!," *Bohemia* (Havana), July 15, 1956. p. 84.
Article denying links with communists.

882. Castro, Fidel, "La batalla de El Cerro," in René Ray Rivero, ed., *Libertad y Revolución*, Havana, 1959. pp. 81-84.
Communique of Sept. 27, 1958 on military defeat of enemy forces in Oriente province.

883. Castro, Fidel, "Carta denuncia de la oposición pacífica a Batista," *Diario de la Marina* (Havana), Jan. 5, 1959. p. 1.

884. Castro, Fidel, "Carta al Comandante Camilo Cienfuegos," *Verde Olivo*, (Havana), Oct. 29, 1960. p. 24.
June 27, 1958. Describes the difficulties faced by the guerrillas during the military offensive of the Batista troops.

885. Castro, Fidel, "Carta al Comandante Juan Almeida," in Fidel Castro, *Declaraciones en el juicio contra el ex-Comandante Hubert Matos*, Havana: CTC-R, 1959, pp. 24-26.
Oct. 8, 1958. On strategy and tactics of the guerrilla movement.

886. Castro, Fidel, "Carta a Luis Conte Agüero," in Luis Conte

Agüero, ed., *Cartas del presidio, anticipo de una biografía,* Havana: Editorial Lex, 1959. pp. 13-25.
Written on Dec. 12, 1953 describing the massacre of young men after the Moncada attack.

887. Castro, Fidel, "Comunicado de Noviembre 9, 1958," *Verde Olivo,* (Havana), Jan. 9, 1969. pp. 6-11.
On political and military situation.

888. Castro, Fidel, "Con Fidel Castro na 'zona da norte,'" *O Cruzeiro,* May 3, 1958. pp. 40-45.
Interview with Uruguayan reporter on political and social goals of the 26th of July Movement.

889. Castro, Fidel, "Declaraciones al salir de prisión," *El Mundo* (Havana), May 17, 1955, p. A8.
May 15, 1955.

890. Castro, Fidel, "Este es un minuto extraordinario," *Verde Olivo,* (Havana) Jan. 5, 1969. p. 8.
Radio broadcast of Nov. 11, 1958 ordering all-out offensive.

891. Castro, Fidel, "Este movimiento triunfará," *Verde Olivo,* (Havana), July 26, 1964. p. 5.
Speech delivered to the men who were to attack the Moncada Barracks on July 26, 1953.

892. Castro, Fidel, "Fidel ordena el avance rebelde sobre Santiago y La Habana y proclama la huelga general," *Revolución,* (Havana), July 26, 1962. p. 8.
Jan. 1, 1959.

893. Castro, Fidel, "Fidel rechaza la componenda del Episcopado con Batista," *Revolución* (Havana), July 26, 1962. p. 9.
March 9, 1958 statement.

894. Castro, Fidel, "Guerra total contra la tiranía," in Gregorio Selser, ed., *La revolución cubana,* Buenos Aires: Editorial Palestra, 1960. pp. 141-146.
Manifesto issued to Mar. 12, 1958 from the Sierra Maestra.

895. Castro, Fidel, *History Will Absolve Me,* New York: L. Stuart, 1961. 79 pp.
Allegedly reproduces the defense plea made by Fidel Castro on Oct. 16, 1953. There are no transcripts of the trial in existence.

896. Castro, Fidel, "Interview With Andrew St. George," *Look,* Feb. 4, 1958.
American reporter. U.S.-Cuban relations.

897. Castro, Fidel, "Letter to Celia Sánchez," *Granma* (Havana) Aug. 27, 1967. p. 8.
June 5, 1958. Castro attests his desire to fight the United States after Batista is overthrown.

898. Castro, Fidel, "Llamado a una huelga general," in *13 documentos de la insurrección,* Havana: ONBAP, 1959. 59 pp ·
Message read on April 9, 1958 over Radio Rebelde.

899. Castro, Fidel, and Raúl Gómez García, "Manifesto del Moncada," *13 documentos de la insurrección,* Havana: ONBAP, 1959. pp. 19-21.
Calling for a popular revolution in order to implement the ideals of past generations. Issued July 23, 1953.

900. Castro, Fidel, "Manifesto No. 1 del 26 de Julio al pueblo de Cuba," *Pensamineto Crítico* (Ha-

vana), No. 21, 1968, pp. 207-220.
Issued on Aug. 8, 1955 from Mexico outlining his revolutionary goals.

901. Castro, Fidel, "Manifesto No. 2 del 26 de Julio al pueblo de Cuba," *Pensamiento Crítico* (Havana), No. 21, 1968. pp. 221-227.
Issued Dec. 10, 1955 describing his activities among exile circles in the United States, and defining the 26th of July Movement.

902. Castro, Fidel, "La ofensiva," in Antonio Núñez Jiménez, *Geografía de Cuba*, Havana: Editorial Lex, 1959. pp. 578-588.
Radio broadcast of Aug. 18, 1958.

903. Castro, Fidel, "Orden militar disponiendo que el Che Guevara inicie la invasión de Las Villas," in *13 documentos de la insurrección*, Havana: ONBAP, 1959. p. 62.

904. Castro, Fidel, "Las órdenes de Fidel Castro," *El Mundo*, (Havana), Oct. 28, 1965. p. 8.
Aug. 18, 1958 order to Major Camilo Cienfuegos to invade Pinar del Río province.

905. Castro, Fidel, "Pacto de México," *El País* (Havana), Sept. 3, 1956. p. 1.
Signed by Castro and the leader of the Directorio Revolucionario in Aug. 1956.

906. Castro, Fidel, "Proclama al pueblo de Santiago," *Bohemia*, (Havana), Jan. 2, 1969. p. 47.
Dec. 31, 1958. Announces the surrounding of Santiago.

907. Castro, Fidel, "Proclama a los soldados de Batista," *Verde Olivo* (Havana), Apr. 12, 1964, p. 77.
Sept. 15, 1958.

908. Castro, Fidel, Raúl Chibás y Felipe Pazos, "Al pueblo de Cuba," *Bohemia* (Havana) July 28, 1957. pp. 69, 96-97.
Manifesto of July 12, 1957 calling on the people to fight against tyranny.

909. Castro, Fidel, "Se cursan órdenes militares a los mandos de Camagüey y de las gloriosas columnas 2 y 8 de Las Villas," *Revolución*, (Havana), July 26, 1962. p. 8.
Dec. 31, 1958. "Continue struggle until the Armed Forces surrender."

910. Castro, Fidel, "Se debió la victoria a que los rebeldes no predicaron la lucha de clases," *Diario de la Marina*, (Havana), Apr. 21, 1959. pp. 1, 2A.

911. Castro, Fidel, "Al Tribunal de Urgencia," *Granma* (Havana), July 26, 1966. p. 5.
Brief presented on Mar. 24, 1952 to the Urgency Court calling for the punishment of those who participated in the military coup.

912. Castro, Fidel, "Unity Manifesto of the Sierra Maestra," in Jules Dubois, *Fidel Castro, Rebel-Liberator or Dictator?* Indianapolis: Bobbs Merrill, 1959 pp. 280-283.
July 20, 1958 broadcast from Radio Rebelde announcing the unification of all opposition groups.

913. Castro, Raúl, "Durante aquel amanecer del 26 de julio se inició el fin del capitalismo en Cuba," (fragmentos de un diario escrito en el presidio), *Bohemia*, (Havana) July 26, 1963. pp. 66-71.

914. Cienfuegos, Camilo, *Páginas del diario de campaña*, Havana: Min-

isterio de Educación, 1962. 17 pp. 1956-58.

915. Cuba, Partido Comunista, *Moncada. Realizaciones del programa del Moncada,* Havana: Comisión de Orientación Revolucionaria, 1966. 263 pp.

916. Cuba, Partido Unido de la Revolución Socialista, *Relatos del asalto al Moncada,* Havana, 1964. 166 pp.

917. Cuba, Organización de Bibliotecas Ambulantes y Populares, *Trece documentos de la insurrección,* Havana, 1959. 64 pp.

918. Chomón, Faure, "El asalto al Palacio," *Bohemia,* (Havana), Oct. 11, 1968. pp. 50-53.
Mar. 13, 1957 attack on Presidential Palace.

919. Chomón, Faure, "Cuando el Che llegó al Escambray," *Bohemia,* (Havana), Dec. 10, 1965. pp. 52-56.
1958.

920. Chomón, Faure, *La verdadera historia del asalto al Palacio Presidencial,* Havana: Prensa Estudiantil, 1959. 8 pp.
Mar. 13, 1957. By participant.

921. Desnoes, Edmundo, *La sierra y el llano,* Havana: Casa de las Américas, 1961. 306 pp.
Compilation of documents of the revolutionary struggle. Reveals factionalism among the revolucionaries.

922. Franqui, Carlos, ed., *El libro de los doce,* Havana: Instituto del Libro, 1967. 284 pp.
Insurrection of 1956-1959, by participants. English edition *The Twelve,* 1968.

923. Guevara, Ernesto, *Che Guevara on Guerrilla Warfare,* New York: Praeger, 1962. 85 pp.
Revolutionary theory.

924. Guevara, Ernesto, *La guerra de guerrillas,* Havana: Departamento de Instrucción del MINFAR, 1960. 211 pp.

925. Guevara, Ernesto, *Pasajes de la guerra revolucionaria,* Havana: Ediciones Unión, 1963. 128 pp.
18 "pasajes" (main stories); in chronological order, from Dec. 2, 1956 to Dec. 1958.

926. Guevara, Ernesto, *Reminiscences of the Cuban Revolutionary War,* New York: Monthly Review Press, 1968, 287 pp.

927. Llerena, Mario, *Reminiscences of Participation in the Cuban Revolution, 1956-1958,* Miami, 1966.
Typescript at Stanford University.

928. Macaulay, Neil, *A Rebel in Cuba: An American's Memoir,* Chicago: Quadrangle Books, 1970. 199 pp.
An American who fought in the Rebel Army relates his experiences.

929. Martínez Páez, Julio, *Médicos en la Sierra Maestra,* Havana: Editorial Neptuno, 1959. 72 pp.

930. Montané, Comandante Jesús, "Del 26 de Julio des 1953 al 15 de mayo de 1955," *Verde Olivo,* (Havana), July 26, 1963. pp. 19-23.
Castro in prison.

931. Montané, Jesús, "El Moncada," *CUBA Internacional,* (Havana), Oct. 1968. pp. 110-111.
By participant.

932. Pardo Llada, Jose, *Memorias de la Sierra Maestra,* Havana: Edi-

torial Tierra Nueva, 1960. 172 pp.

933. Reyes Tujo, Cap. A., "Del Moncada a las montañas," *Verde Olivo*, (Havana), July 23, 1967. pp. 35-66.

934. Rodríguez Loeches, Enrique, *Rumbo a Escambray*, Havana, 1960. 102 pp.
1957-1958.

935. Rosell Leyva, Florentino E., *La verdad*, Miami, 1960. 83 pp.
Account of military developments from 1952-58 by colonel of Batista's Corps of Engineers.

936. Sánchez Amaya, Fernando, *Diario del Granma*, Havana: Editorial Tierra Nueva, 1959. 141 pp.
By participant.

937. Valdés, Nelson P. and Rolando Bonachea, "Documento: una bibliografía de Fidel Castro (1948-1958)," *Aportes* (Paris), October 1970, pp. 120-130.

938. Ventura Novo, Esteban, *Memorias*, Mexico, 1961. 314 pp.
By Havana police official under Batista.

2. Commentaries

939. Aaron, Harold R., "Guerrilla War in Cuba," *Military Review*, (Kansas), May 1965. pp. 40-46.

940. Aaron, Harold R., *The Seizure of Political Power in Cuba, 1956-1959*, Washington, 1964. 282 pp.
Georgetown University Ph.D. Thesis.

941. Bayo, Alberto, *Ciento cincuenta preguntas a un guerrillero*, Havana, 1961. 146 pp.

942. Bayo, Alberto, *Fidel te espera en la sierra*, Havana, 1960. 236 pp.

943. Bayo, Alberto, *Mi aporte a la revolución cubana*, Havana: Ejército Rebelde, 1960. 169 pp.
Training of Castro's guerrilla fighters in Mexico.

944. Brennan, Ray, *Castro, Cuba and Justice*, New York: Doubleday, 1959. 282 pp.
Events, 1956-1958.

945. Chapelle, Dickey, "How Castro Won," *Marine Corps Gazette*, Vol. 44, No. 2. pp. 36-44.

946. Condit, Doris M., et al., *Challenge and Response in Internal Conflict. The Experience in Africa and Latin America*, Washington: American University, Center for Research in Social Systems, 1968. 538 pp.
Large section on Cuban insurgency, 1953-1959.

947. Cubelas Secades, Rolando, "Recuento histórico de la lucha estudiantil universitaria," *Bohemia*, (Havana), July 23, 1965. pp. 100-105+.
1952-1958.

948. Cubillas, Vicente, "Cienfuegos; un pueblo a la vanguardia de la revolución," *Bohemia*, (Havana), Sept. 3, 1965. pp. 31-39.
Sept. 1957 navy revolt.

949. Desnoes, Edmundo, "El tren blindado," *Cuba*, (Havana), Aug. 1965. pp. 52-54.
Battle of Santa Clara, Dec. 1958.

950. Gaviria, Rafael, *Fidel Castro; la revolución de los barbudos*, Havana: Ed. Tierra Nueva, 1959. 81 pp.

951. Gímenez, Armando, *Sierra Maestra, la revolución de Fidel*

Castro, Buenos Aires: Editorial Lautaro, 1959. 191 pp.

952. Gómez, Gabriel A., *De la dictadura a la liberación; interpretación política y social de la revolución cubana*, Havana, 1959. 180 pp.

953. Gutiérrez, Carlos María, *En la Sierra Maestra y otros reportajes*, Montevideo: Ediciones Tauro, 1967. 206 pp.
Journalist.

954. Hernández, Melba, "Fueron los atacantes del Moncada una magnífica selección de revolucionarios," *Juventud Rebelde*, (Havana), July 19, 1966. p. 1.

955. Karol, K. S. *Les guerrilleros au pouvoir*, Paris: Laffont, 1970. 608 pp.
Also English edition.

956. Kling, Merle, "Cuba: a Case Study of Unconventional Warfare (1956-58)," *Military Review*, Dec. 1962. pp. 11-22.

957. Lancis y Sánchez, Antonio, *El proceso electoral de 1954*, Havana: Editorial Lex, 1955. 150 pp.
Criticism of electoral laws and procedures under Batista.

958. Lorencez, Charles Ferdinand de *Cuba: témoignages vécus, 1953-1960*, Bordeaux: Bière, 1963. 195 pp.

959. Lazar, Jacques, *Memorias de un capitán rebelde*, Santiago de Chile: Editorial del Pacífico, 1964. 293 pp.
By early defector from Castro.

960. Llerena, Mario, "Revolución: la verdad y la leyenda," *Bohemia Libre*, (Miami), Jan. 20, 1963. pp. pp. 12, 13, 80, 82.

961. Macaulay, Neill, "Guevara: Man Behind Castro," *Marine Corps Gazette*, Apr. 1963. pp. 38-42.

962. Mallin, Jay, "Castro's Guerrilla Campaign," *Marine Corps Gazette*, Jan. 1967. pp. 30-34.

963. Martínez, Pablo, "La apasionante historia de la revolución cubana," *Revolución*, (Havana), Jan. 12, 1959. pp. 6-16. 1952-1959.

964. Masetti, Jorge Ricardo, *Los que luchan y los que lloran: el Fidel Castro que yo vi*, Havana: Editorial Madiedo, 1959. 147 pp.

965. Medina y Puig, M.M., *El Club Náutico y la revolución*, Santiago de Cuba, 1959. 8 pp.

966. Merle, Robert, *Moncada, premier combat de Fidel Castro (26 juillet 1953)*, Paris: R. Laffont, 1965. 354 pp.
Based on interviesws with participants.

967. Monreal, Manuel, *Bayo, España y la libertad*, Havana: Sección de Impresión Capitolio Nacional, Editorial Revolucionaria Bayo Libras, 1961. 221 pp.
Section on Alberto Bayo's role in training Castro's men in Mexico.

968. Nalevka, V., "Some Comments on the Relationship between the People's Socialist Party of Cuba and the Movement of July 26 during the Guerrilla War," *Acta Universitatis Carolinae*, (Prague), No. 1-2, 1966. pp. 145-160.

969. Ray Rivero, René, *Moncada, Sierra Maestra: libertad y revolución*, Havana, 1959. 143 pp.
Member 26 July Movement.

970. Le Riverend, Julio, "La crisis de 1952-58," *Bohemia*, (Havana), July 3, 1964. pp. 26-28.

971. Rivero, Arnaldo, "La disciplina revolucionaria en la Sierra Maestra," *Humanismo*, (Havana), Año 7, No. 53-54, Jan.-Apr. 1959. pp. 369-382.

972. Rodríguez, Pedro M., *El segundo asalto al Palacio Presidencial*, Havana: Delegación del Galierno, 1960. 291 pp.
Lists March 1957 *Batistianos*.

973. Rojas, Marta, *La generación del centenario del Moncada*, Havana: Ediciones R., 1964. 479 pp.
Narrative. Documents.

974. Rojas, Marta, *El juicio del Moncada*, Buenos Aires: Ediciones de Ambos Mundos, 1966. 270 pp.
Pro-Castro.

975. Rojas, Marta, ed., *Mártires del Moncada*, Havana: Ediciones Revolución, 1965. 493 pp.

976. Otero Echeverría, Rafael, *Reportaje a una revolución; de Batista a Fidel Castro*, Santiago de Chile: Editorial del Pacífico, 1959. 262 pp.
Journalistic account of period 1953-1958.

977. Smith, Earl E. T., *The Fourth Floor*, New York: Random House, 1962. 252 pp.
By ex-U.S. Ambassador. "Revolution was communist-inspired."

978. Stecchini, Livio C., "Cuba's Revolt—an Appraisal," *Dissent*, Spring 1959. pp. 129-133.

979. Taber, Robert, *The War of the Flea. A Study of Guerrilla Warfare: Theory and Practice*, New York: Lyle Stuart, 1965. 192 pp.
Chapter on Cuba.

980. Tutino, Saverio, *L'ottobre cubano. Lineamenti di una storia della revoluzione castrista*, Torino: G. Einaudi, 1968. 414 pp.
Good on the 1953-1958 revolutionary struggle.

981. Valdés Miranda, J., *Cuba revolucionaria*, Havana, 1960. 190 pp. 1953-1958.

982. Vázquez Candela, Euclides, "Como entró Fidel en Santiago; la ruta de la victoria," *Bohemia*, (Havana), Feb. 26, 1965. pp. 100-102.

983. Vega Cabiellas, Ulpiano, *El general Fulgencio Batista y la sucesión presidencial*, Havana: Editora Colegial, 1957. 190 pp.
Defense of Batista.

984. Youngblood, Jack, *The Devil to Pay*, New York: Coward McCann, 1961. 320 pp.
Self-styled gun runner for Castro.

985. Zalamea, Jorge, *Cuba oprimida y liberada*, Havana: Imprenta Nacional, 1962. 93 pp. 1952-1958.

B. POLITICAL REVOLUTION

1. Jan. 1, 1959—July 26, 1961

986. Artime, Manuel F., *¡Traición! Gritan 20,000 tumbas cubanas*, Mexico: Ed. Jus, 1960. 263 pp.
Early communist influence in the Revolution.

987. Arvelo, Perina, *Revolución de los barbudos*, Caracas, 1961. 187 pp.
Describes events in 1961.

988. Barreiro, Jesús, et al., *Cuba Avanza. Cuatro charlas de orientación revolucionaria*, Havana, 1960. 96 pp.

989. Castro, Fidel, "Comparecencia para explicar los motivos de su dimisión del cargo de Primer Ministro," *Revolución*, (Havana), July 18, 1959. pp. 1, 2, 4, 10, 14, 18.

990. Castro, Fidel, "Desmiente el Primer Ministro cubano haber recibido a su hermano para 'limar diferencias entre ambos' " *Diario de la Marina*, (Havana), Apr. 28, 1959. pp. 1, 2A.

991. Castro, Fidel, "Discurso al asumir al cargo de Primer Ministro del Gobierno Revolucionario, el 16 de febrero de 1959," in *Discursos del Dr. Fidel Castro Ruz*, Havana: Oficina del Historiador de la Ciudad, 1959. p. 201.

992. Castro, Fidel, *Discursos del Dr. Fidel Castro Ruz, Comandante en Jefe del Ejército Rebelde 26 de Julio y Primer Ministro del Gobierno Provisional*, Havana: Oficina del Historiador de la Ciudad, 1959. 201 pp.

993. Castro, Fidel, *Discurso de 1 de mayo, 1960*, Havana: Cooperativa Obrera de Publicidad, 1960. 44 pp.
On Cuba's destiny.

994. Castro, Fidel, "Discurso en el campamento de Columbia el 8 de enero de 1959," *Diario de la Marina*, (Havana), Jan. 9, 1959. pp. 10-B.
First speech in the capital.

995. Castro, Fidel, "Discurso en el Parque Central de New York," *Revolución*, (Havana), Apr. 25, 1959. pp. 2, 14.
Defines revolution as "humanist."

996. Castro, Fidel, "Discurso en la concentración del día 26 de julio, 1959, en la Plaza Cívica," *Revolución*, (Havana), July 28, 1959. pp. 5-7.
Announces return as Prime Minister.

997. Castro, Fidel, *Discursos para la historia*, Havana: Imprenta Emilio Gall, 1959. 151 pp.

998. Castro, Fidel, "Discurso pronunciado en el Palacio Presidencial el 22 de enero de 1959," in *Discursos para la historia*, Havana: Imprenta Emilio Gall, 1959. pp. 31-46.

999. Castro, Fidel, "Este es un régimen socialista," *Bohemia*, (Havana), May 7, 1961. pp. 63-65+.
May Day speech.

1000. Castro, Fidel, "Habrá elecciones cuando la obra de la revolución haya avanzado lo suficiente para su consolidación," *Diario de la Marina*, (Havana), Apr. 10, 1959. pp. 1A-2A.

1001. Castro, Fidel, "Leader of Cuba's Revolt Tells What's Coming Next; Interview with Fidel Castro," *U.S. News and World Report*, Mar. 16, 1959. pp. 68-70.

1002. Castro, Fidel, "No es posible una democracia pura hoy en Cuba," *Diario de la Marina*, (Havana), Apr. 26, 1959. pp. 1, 14B.
Statement in Boston.

1003. Castro, Fidel, "Renuncia Fidel," *Revolución*, (Havana), July 17, 1959. pp. 1.
Because of split with President Urrutia over communism.

1004. Castro, Fidel, "Se celebrarán los elecciones cuando termine la revolución, dentro de 3 ó 4 años," *Diario de la Marina*, (Havana), Apr. 18, 1959. pp. 1, 8B, 9B.

1005. Castro, Fidel, "Vamos a reno-

var nuestra energías para el segundo año de la revolución," *Revolución*, (Havana), Jan. 2, 1960. pp. 1, 2.
Summarizes 1959 achievements.

1006. Castro, Fidel, "¡Viva la revolución socialista!," *Revolución*, (Havana), Apr. 17, 1961. pp. 3, 6, 7, 12-13.
First such declaration.

1007. Chomón, Faure, "Somos partidarios de la unidad sincera de la revolución cubana," *Bohemia*, (Havana), Jan. 18, 1959. pp. 72-74.
Conciliatory speech by leader of revolutionary student group.

1008. Cuba, Directorio Revolucionario, "Manifiesto," *Diario de la Marina*, (Havana), Jan. 7, 1959. p. 6B.

1009. Cuba, Ministerio de Salud Pública, *Temas revolucionarios*, Havana: Dirección de Investigaciones, Docencia y Divulgación "Carlos J. Finlay," 1960. 343 pp.

1010. Darío Roldán, R., *¿Es Castro un hombre honrado?*, Caracas, 1961. 90 pp.
Compares contradictory speeches made by Castro, 1959 and 1961.

1011. Díaz Versón, Salvador, *Ya el mundo oscurece*, Mexico: Ediciones Botas, 1961. 228 pp.
On the revolution.

1012. González, Justo, *La revolución que falta*, Havana: Editorial Cenit, 1959. 126 pp.
Program for revolution by an independent.

1013. Grau San Martín, Ramón, "Combatir la revolución es abrir la puerta al desastre," *Diario de la Marina*, (Havana), Feb. 4, 1959. pp. 1, 2A.

1014. Horstman, Jorge A., "Prío está empeñado en consolidar la revolución," *El Mundo*, (Havana), Jan. 8, 1959. p. A7.

1015. Iglesias, Abelardo, *Revolución y dictadura en Cuba*, Buenos Aires: Editorial Reconstruir, 1963. 94 pp.
Anti-Castro. By an anarchist.

1016. López-Fresquet, Rufo, *My 14 Months with Castro*, Cleveland: The World Publishing Company, 1966. 223 pp.
Jan. 1959-Mar. 1960, by former Treasury Minister.

1017. Massó, José Luis, *¿Qué pasa en Cuba?*, Madrid: Delegación del Frente Revolucionario Democrático, 1961. 114 pp.

1018. Mellado, Raúl, "Cuba: realidad de un sueño," *Bohemia*, (Havana), June 18, 1961. pp. 10-11.

1019. "'Necesarias las ejecuciones,' dijo el doctor R. Agramonte," *Diario de la Marina*, (Havana), Jan. 14, 1959. pp. 1, 6A.

1020. O'Connor, James, "Cuba's Counter-Revolution," *The Progressive*, Vol. 24, No. 12, Dec. 1960. pp. 8-11.

1021. Pérez, Francisco, "Cómo y porqué cayo el presidente Manuel Urrutia," *Bohemia Libre*, (Caracas), Aug. 26, 1962. pp. 20-23+.

1022. Portilla, Angel de la, *Todos tenemos un tanto de culpa*, Miami, 1966. 43 pp.
On causes of communist takeover.

1023. Rasco, José I., *Cuba 1959: artículos de combate*, Buenos Aires: Eds. Diagrama, 1962. 125 pp.
By Christian democrat.

1024. Roca, Blas, *Cuba's Socialist Destiny*, New York: Fair Play for Cuba Committee, 1961. 18 pp.

1025. Ruiz, Leovigildo, *Diario de una traición*, Miami: Florida Typesetting, 1965. 272 pp.
Chronology, 1959 events.

1026. Silió, Antonio F., *Tres aspectos de la revolución cubana y un mensaje*, Miami: Veritas Publishing Inc., 1961. 93 pp.

1027. Szulc, Tad, "From Robin Hood to Revolutionary Oracle," *New York Times Magazine*, July 16, 1961. pp. 9+.

1028. Universidad Popular, Havana, *Cuarto ciclo. La libertad*, Havana, 1960. 251 pp.
Radio conference. 10 government officials.

1029. Universidad Popular, Havana, *Primer ciclo: La liberación económica de Cuba*, Havana, 1960. 95 pp.
Radio conference. 4 top officials, including Guevara and Núñez Jiménez.

1030. Universidad Popular, Havana, *Segundo ciclo: Defensa de Cuba*, Havana, 1960. 227 pp.
Radio conference. 7 officials, including Fidel Castro, Raúl Castro and Carlos Rafael Rodríguez.

1031. Universidad Popular, Havana. *Tercer ciclo: La revolución cubana ante el mundo*, Havana, 1960. 144 pp.
Radio conference. Roa, Dorticós and 3 other officials.

1032. Various, *Cuba 1961*, Paris: Cuadernos, 1961. 64 pp.

1033. Varona, Manuel Antonio de, *El drama de Cuba ante América*, Mexico: Organización Pro-Res-

cate Democrático Revolucionario, 1960. 48 pp.
By auténtico leader. Anti-Castro.

1034. Zamora, Juan Clemente, "La traición continuada," *Cuba Nueva*, (Coral Gables), Dec. 15, 1962. pp. 10-13.

a. 26 of July Movement

1035. Anónimo, "Principales acciones del Movimiento 26 de Julio," *Revolución*, (Havana), July 26, 1959. pp. 2-7.
Chronology, 1952-1958.

1036. Carrera, Antonio de la, "Castro's Counter-revolution," *New Politics*, (New York), Vol. 2, Fall 1962. pp. 84-97.
Former *ortodoxo* leader.

1037. Luis, Carlos M., "Notes of a Cuban Revolutionary in Exile," *New Politics*, Autumn 1963. pp. 143-147.

1038. Movimiento Revolucionario 26 de Julio, "Algunos aspectos del desarrollo económico de Cuba," *Humanismo*, (Mexico), Jan.-Feb. 1958. pp. 113-148.

1039. Prío, Carlos, "Está eliminando a los comunistas el 26 de Julio," *Diario de la Marina*, (Havana), Jan. 30, 1959. pp. 1, 2A.

1040. Taber, Robert, *M-26, Biography of a Revolution*, New York: Lyle Stuart, 1961. 348 pp.

1041. Urrutia Lleó, Manuel, *Fidel Castro and Company, Inc.: Communist Tyranny in Cuba*, New York: Praeger, 1964. 217 pp.
First Revolutionary President.

1042. Valdespino, Andrés, "26 de Julio: las raíces del mito," *Bohe-*

mia Libre, (Caracas), July 29, 1962. pp. 14-15.
Moderate exile.

1043. Vázquez Candela, Euclides, "Aclarando," *Revolución*, (Havana), Sept. 7, 1959. pp. 1, 4.
Differences between M-26-7 and communists.

1044. Vázquez Candela, Euclides, "En torno al movimiento 26 de Julio," *Lunes de Revolución*, (Havana), July 26, 1959. pp. 4-5.
History and structure of the M-26-7.

1045. Vázquez Candela, Euclides, "Respuesta al PSP," *Revolución*, (Havana), Sept. 10, 1959. pp. 1, 17.
Differences between M-26-7 and communists.

1046. Vázquez Candela, Euclides, "Saldo de una polémica," *Revolución*, (Havana), Sept. 14, 1959. pp. 1, 10.
Differences between M-26-7 and communists.

b. Partido Socialista Popular

1047. Escalante, Aníbal, *Un año de revolución*, Havana: Tipográfica Ideas, 1960. 30 pp.

1048. Marinello, Juan, *La soberanía nacional y la paz*, Havana: Imprenta Nacional, 1960. 45 pp.

1049. Partido Socialista Popular, "Apoyo de los marxistas cubanos a la revolución," *Cruz del Sur*, (Caracas), Feb.-Mar. 1960. pp. 85-88.

1050. Partido Socialista Popular, *Documentos históricos: la revolución cubana; su carácter, sus fuerzas y sus enemigos. Conclusiones del pleno del P.S.P. celebrado del*

25 *al 28 de mayo de 1959*, Havana, 1962. 59 pp.

1051. Partido Socialista Popular, *VIII Asamblea Nacional: Informes, resoluciones, programa y estatutos*, Havana: Eds. Populares, 1960. 749 pp.

1052. Partido Socialista Popular, "A Program for Cuba," *Political Affairs*, (New York), June 1959. pp. 25-33.

1053. Partido Socialista Popular, "Tesis sobre la situación actual," *Hoy*, (Havana), Jan. 11, 1959. pp. 2-3.

1054. Roca, Blas, *29 artículos sobre la revolución cubana*, Havana: Partido Socialista Popular, 1960. 234 pp.
Former Secretary General of the communist party.

1055. Roca, Blas, *Balance de la labor del partido desde la última Asamblea Nacional y el desarrollo de la revolución*, Havana, 1960. 105 pp.
8th PSP Assembly. Interpretation of the revolutionary process. Also English version.

1956. Roca, Blas, *Los comunistas no ocultan nada*, Havana: Editorial Doctrina, 1959. 39 pp.

1057. Roca, Blas, "The Cuban Revolution," *Marxism Today*, (London), June 1961. pp. 165-169.

1058. Roca, Blas, "The Cuban Revolution," *Political Affairs*, (New York), Oct. 1960. pp. 11-31.

1059. Roca, Blas, "The Cuban Revolution in Action," *World Marxist Review*, (Prague), Aug. 1959. pp. 16-22.

1060. Roca, Blas, *The Cuban Revolution; Report to the 8th Nation-*

al Congress of the Popular Socialist Party of Cuba, New York: New Century, 1961. 127 pp.

1061. Roca, Blas, En defensa de la revolución, Havana: Comisión de Propaganda del Partido Socialista Popular, 1961. 48 pp.

1062. Roca, Blas, Lo que determina y condiciona la actual situación de Cuba, son los exitos alcanzados por la revolución, Havana: Imprenta Nacional, 1961. 71 pp.
Report to the PSP National Committee.

1063. Roca, Blas, "Diez puntos contra la revolución cubana," Diario de la Marina, (Havana), May 13, 1959. p. 6B.

1064. Roca, Blas, "La Marina," la democracia, las elecciones y la revolución, Havana: Tip. Ideas, 1960. 31 pp.
Denunciation of call for elections.

1065. Roca, Blas, "New Stage in the Cuban Revolution," World Marxist Review, (Prague), Oct. 1961. pp. 3-10.

1066. Roca, Blas, "Nueva etapa de la revolución cubana," Cuba Socialista, (Havana), Jan. 1962. pp. 38-53.

1067. Roca, Blas, Los regímenes sociales y el concepto de libertad, Havana: Capitolio Nacional, 1961. 31 pp.

1068. Serviat, Pedro, 40 Aniversario de la fundación del Partido Comunista, Havana: Editorial EIR, 1965. 158 pp.

2. Organizaciones Revolucionarias Integradas, July 26, 1961-February 22, 1963

1069. Anónimo, "Aprobado el carnet provincial," Cuba Socialista, (Havana), Oct. 1962. pp. 121-122.

1070. Anónimo, "La Dirección Nacional de las ORI," Cuba, (Havana), Apr. 1962. p. 65.

1071. Anónimo, "Nombran las ORI su dirección nacional," Cuba Socialista, (Havana), Apr. 1962. pp. 136-138.

1072. Anónimo, "El núcleo de revolucionarios activos y algunos aspectos de su funcionamiento," Cuba Socialista, (Havana), Mar. 1962. pp. 123-126.

1073. Anónimo, "Vida de la Organización Revolucionaria," Cuba Socialista, (Havana), June 1962, pp. 123-126; July 1962, pp. 130-134; Aug. 1962, pp. 126-134; Dec. 1962. pp. 117-129.

1074. Castro, Fidel, "Algunos problemas de los métodos y formas de trabajo de las ORI," Obra Revolucionaria, (Havana), No. 10, 1962. pp. 7-32.
Mar. 26, 1962 speech criticizing old-line communists' influence.

1075. Castro, Fidel, "Cuba Socialista," Cuba Socialista, (Havana), Sept. 1961. pp. 1-7.
Editorial announcing creation and purpose of above theoretical organ of the ORI.

1076. Castro, Fidel, "Fidel Castro le habló al pueblo en Santiago de Cuba," Obra Revolucionaria, (Havana), No. 24, 1962. pp. 7-24.
July 26, 1962. On future plans.

1077. Castro, Fidel, "Hay que crear en la juventud un mayor espíritu comunista," Revolución, (Havana), Mar. 14, 1962. pp. 1, 6, 9, 10.
Mar. 13 speech criticizing "sec-

tarian attitudes" of old communists.

1078. Castro, Fidel, *The Role of Revolutionary Instructors,* Washington: Joint Publications Research Service, July 30, 1962. 9 pp.

1079. Castro, Fidel, "Todos los hombres y las mujeres de bien caben en el socialismo," *Revolución,* (Havana), July 28, 1961. pp. 6-9.
July 26, 1961, speech announcing creation of Organizaciones Revolucionarias Integradas.

1080. Castro, Fidel, "Tres años de revolución," *Cuba Socialista,* (Havana), Jan. 1962. pp. 1-15.
Summary of achievements.

1081. Castro, Fidel, *La unidad dentro de los principios: esa es nuestra línea,* Havana: Ediciones ORI, 1963. pp. 3-20.
Jan. 2, 1963 speech on four years of revolution and Cuba-U.S. relations. 1963 to be the "year of organization."

1082. Castro, Fidel, "Vamos a trabajar bien en la renovación de los núcleos para un partido limpio," *Revolución,* May 19, 1962. pp. 2, 3.
Reiterates necessity to reorganize ORI.

1083. *Cristicism of Party Methods in Cuba,* Washington: Joint Publications Research Service, Sept. 18, 1962. 16 pp.

1084. Cuba, Asociación de Jóvenes Rebeldes, *Plenaria nacional,* Havana: Imprenta Nacional, 1961. 39 pp.
Speeches of Joel Iglesias, Aníbal Escalante, Fidel Castro.

1085. Cuba, Presidencia, *Comprometidos con nuestros propios prin-*

cipios, Havana: Editorial en Marcha, 1961. 25 pp.
Dorticós speech of Sept. 2, 1961.

1086. Cuba, Presidencia, *Relación entre los cambios económicos y políticos en la sociedad cubana,* Havana: Instrucción MINFAR, 1961. 16 pp.
June 14, 1961 speech.

1087. Cuba, Presidencia, "La Revolución Cubana en su cuarto aniversario," *Cuba Socialista,* (Havana), Jan. 1963. pp. 1-19.

1088. Cuba, Organizaciones Revolucionarias Integradas, *Tesis sobre la situación actual,* Havana, 1961. 24 pp.

1089. Domenech, Joel, "Experiencias del trabajo de reestructuración y depuración de la ORI en La Habana," *Cuba Socialista,* (Havana), June 1962. pp. 30-39.

1090. Editorial, "Changes in the Work of Party Branches in Cuba," *World Marxist Review,* (Prague), Aug. 1962. pp. 70-71.

1091. Editorial, "Crítica de los métodos del partido," *Bohemia,* (Havana), June 15, 1962. pp. 34, 35, 90.
On "sectarianism."

1092. Escalante, Aníbal, "The New Stage of the Cuban Revolution," *Marxism Today,* (London), July 1961. pp. 221-223.

1093. "Establecida la categoria de aspirante a miembro del partido," *Cuba Socialista,* (Havana), Oct. 1962. pp. 122-123.

1094. Florez, Julián, "Radiografía del partido comunista de Cuba," *Bohemia Libre Puertorriqueña,* (Caracas), Dec. 2, 1962. pp. 26-29+.

1095. Fuertes Jiménez, José, "El tra-

bajo organizativo en Camagüey," *Cuba Socialista*, Nov. 1962. pp. 121-125.
Communist party.

1096. García Galló, Gaspar J., *El Partido del proletariado y del pueblo*, Havana: Ministerio de Educación, 1962. 29 pp.

1097. Guevara, Ernesto, "El cuadro, calumna vertebral de la Revolución," *Cuba Socialista*, (Havana), Sept. 1962. pp. 17-23.
On Communist party cadres.

1098. "Integración del Secretariado y de Comisiones de la Dirección Nacional de las ORI," *Cuba Socialista*, (Havana), Apr. 1962. pp. 136-137.

1099. Malmierca, Isidoro, "La marcha de la construcción del Partido en La Habana," *Cuba Socialista*, (Havana), Oct. 1962. pp. 109-120.

1100. Risquet Valdés, Jorge, "La construcción del partido en la provincia de Oriente," *Cuba Socialista*, (Havana), Nov. 1962. pp. 116-121.

1101. Roca, Blas, "Path of Development of Newly Emergent Countries: Cuba," *World Marxist Review*, (Prague), May 1962. pp. 66-68.

1102. Rodríguez, Carlos R., "Cuba on the Threshold of 1962," *New Times*, (Moscow), Jan. 1, 1962. pp. 18-20.

1103. Rodríguez, Carlos R., "La autoridad de Cuba es la de haber hecho y continuar haciendo una revolución," *Cuba Internacional*, July 1969. pp. 44-57.

1104. Soto, Lionel, "Las Escuelas de Instrucción Revolucionaria en el ciclo político-técnico," *Cuba Socialista*, (Havana), Jan. 1965. pp. 67-82.

1105. Soto, Lionel, "Las Escuelas de Instrucción Revolucionaria en una nueva fase," *Cuba Socialista*, (Havana), Feb. 1964. pp. 62-77.

1106. Soto, Lionel, "Las Escuelas de Instrucción Revolucionaria y la formación de cuadros," *Cuba Socialista*, (Havana), Nov. 1961. pp. 28-41.

1107. Soto, Lionel, *New Development of Cuban Revolutionary Training*, Washington: Joint Publications Research Service, Oct. 8, 1962. 16 pp.

1108. Soto, Lionel, "El nuevo desarrollo de la instrucción revolucionaria," *Cuba Socialista*, (Havana), Aug. 1962. pp. 32-45.

1109. Soto, Lionel, "El quinto aniversario de las Escuelas de Instrucción Revolucionaria," *Cuba Socialista*, (Havana), Jan. 1966. pp. 72-91.

1110. Soto, Lionel, *Revolutionary Training Schools and Training of Cadres*, Washington: Joint Publications Research Service, Feb. 8, 1962. 25 pp.

1111. Zeitlin, Maurice, "A Cuban Journal; an Interview with 'Che'," *Root and Branch*, (Berkeley), Winter 1962. pp. 36-56.

3. Partido Unido de Revolución Socialista Cubana, February 22, 1963-October 3, 1965

1112. Anillo, René, "Actividad de los núcleos del PURS en Las Villas," *Cuba Socialista*, (Havana), Nov. 1962. pp. 125-127.

1113. Anónimo, "Acuerdo sobre la construcción del Partido Unido de la Revolución Socialista," *Cuba Socialista*, (Havana), Apr. 1963. pp. 117-122.

1114. Anónimo, "A estudiar las tareas fijadas por Fidel en el Sexto Aniversario," *Cuba Socialista*, (Havana), Feb. 1965. pp. 104-115.

1115. Anónimo, "Nueva etapa en el desarrollo del Partido marxista leninista cubano," *Cuba Socialista*, (Havana), Nov. 1965. pp. 8-82.

1116. "Balance de la construcción del PURS," *Cuba Socialista*, (Havana), April 1964. pp. 132-133.

1117. Barrera, Hernán, "La construcción del Partido Unido de la Revolución Socialista en Cuba; leyendo la prensa del PURS," *Revista Internacional*, (Prague), Dec. 1963. pp. 62-64.

1118. Cameron, James, "Cuba's Fumbling Marxism," *Atlantic*, (Boston), Sept. 1964. pp. 92-102.

1119. Castro, Fidel, "Comunicado del comandante en jefe," *Revolución*, (Havana), Oct. 14, 1963. pp. 1, 2.
On devastation caused by hurricane "Flora."

1120. Castro, Fidel, *Discurso en el aniversario del ataque al Palacio Presidencial*, Havana: Editado por la Comisión de Orientación Revolucionaria, 1964. 24 pp.
Mar. 13, 1964. On conflict within the government.

1121. Castro, Fidel, "Juntos como hermanos todos los revolucionarios," *Obra Revolucionaria*, (Havana), No. 11, 1964. pp. 5-47.
Mar. 26, 1964 speech at the trial of Marcos A. Rodríguez. On con-

flict between old-line communists and new ones.

1122. Castro, Fidel, "Más aliento y más alegria en este quinto aniversario," *Bohemia*, (Havana), Jan. 10, 1964. pp. 28-43.
Jan. 2, 1964 speech reviewing five years of revolution. Also in English by Fair Play for Cuba Committee, 1964.

1123. Castro, Fidel, "El Partido Unido de la Revolución Socialista," *Obra Revolucionaria*, (Havana), No. 46, 1961. pp. 11-55.
Dec. 2, 1961 speech declaring himself a Marxist-Leninist. Also in English by Fair Play for Cuba Committee, 1962.

1124. Castro, Fidel, "La revolución es una fuerza más poderosa que la naturaleza," *Cuba Socialista*, (Havana), Nov. 1963. pp. 9-70.
Oct. 21, 1963 interview with Radio Havana.

1125. Castro, Fidel, "¡Viva el Partido Unido de la Revolución Socialista!," *Revolución*, (Havana), Feb. 23, 1963. pp. 3-5.
Feb. 22, 1963 address announcing creation of PURSC.

1126. Cuba, Partido Unido de la Revolución Socialista, *Burocratismo y productividad*, Havana: Frente Ideológico, 1964. 48 pp.
Articles from *Hoy*.

1127. Cuba, Partido Unido de la Revolución Socialista, *César Escalante, un comunista ejemplar*, Havana, 1965. 36 pp.

1128. Cuba, Partido Unido de la Revolución Socialista, *Conciencia marxista-leninista*, Havana, 1964. 37 pp.

1129. Cuba, Partido Unido de la Revolución Socialista, *El idealismo de los comunistas,* Havana, 1962. 61 pp.

1130. Cuba, Partido Unido de la Revolución Socialista, *Más sobre el carácter socialista de nuestra revolución,* Havana: Frente Ideológico, 1965. 59 pp.

1131. Cuba, Partido Unido de la Revolución Socialista, *Más sobre la conciencia,* Havana: Frente Ideológico, 1965. 52 pp. Selections from *Hoy.*

1132. Cuba, Partido Unido de la Revolución Socialista, *Núcleos del Partido,* Havana, 1964. vol. 1.

1133. Cuba, Partido Unido de la Revolución Socialista, *El Partido Marxista-Leninista,* Havana: Dirección Nacional del Partido Unido de la Revolución Socialista de Cuba, 1963. 32 pp.

1134. Cuba, Partido Unido de la Revolución Socialista, *Programa de estudios marxista,* Havana, 1965. 32 pp.

1135. Cuba, Partido Unido de la Revolución Socialista, *Sobre la defensa de la revolución cubana,* Havana: Frente Ideológico, 1964. 61 pp.

1136. Cuba, Partido Unido de la Revolución Socialista, *Sobre la política y la economía,* Havana: Comisión de Trabajo Ideológico, 1965. 65 pp.

1137. Cuba, Partido Unido de la Revolución Socialista, *Sobre las organizaciones,* Havana, 1965. 47 pp.

1138. Cuba, Partido Unido de la Revolución Socialista, *Sobre los cuadros,* Havana, 1962. 50 pp.

1139. Cuba, Partido Unido de la Revolución Socialista, *El trabajo del partido en el campo,* Havana, 1963. 63 pp.

1140. Cuba, Unión de Pioneros, *Manual para ser pionero,* Havana, 1964. 95 pp.

1141. Editorial, "El quinto aniversario de la victoriosa revolución cubana," *Cuba Socialista,* (Havana), Jan. 1964. pp. 1-7.

1142. Editorial, "Seis años de revolución," *Cuba,* (Havana), Jan. 1965. pp. 4-11.

1143. Escalante, César, *La propaganda revolucionaria, la producción y la emulación socialista,* Havana, 1964. 44 pp.

1144. Guevara, Ernesto, *Construir sobre una sociedad que se destruye,* Havana: PURSC, 1963. 15 pp.

1145. Guevara, Ernesto, *El socialismo y el hombre en Cuba,* Havana: Ediciones R, 1965. 62 pp. Ideology of the revolution.

1146. Habel, Janette, "La procès de Marcos Rodríguez et les problèmes de l'unité du mouvement révolutionnaire à Cuba," *Les Temps Modernes,* (Paris), Aug.-Sept. 1964. pp. 491-531.

1147. Méndez, Luis, "La asamblea provincial del PURS en Matanzas," *Cuba Socialista,* (Havana), Mar. 1964. pp. 134-137.

1148. Méndez, Luis, "El avance del Partido en Matanzas," *Cuba Socialista,* (Havana), Feb. 1964. pp. 144-147.

1149. Roca, Blas, *Aclaraciones,* Havana: Editora Política, 1964-1966. 3 vols. Articles published in newspaper *Hoy.*

1150. Roca, Blas, "En torno al juicio contra un delator," *Cuba Socialista*, (Havana), May 1964. pp. 42-65.
Purges.

1151. Rodríguez, Laura, "Fidel, líder y profeta," *Siempre*, (Mexico), Mar. 17, 1965. pp. 5, 81.

1152. Rodríguez, Mario, "Experiencias del trabajo de educación del PURSC en Matanzas," *Cuba Socialista*, Jan. 1965. pp. 132-136.

1153. Soto, Lionel, "Las escuelas de instrucción revolucionaria en el ciclo político-técnico," *Bohemia*, (Havana), Jan. 1965. pp. 67-82.

1154 Vázquez Candela, Euclides, "La nueva escuela de ciencias políticas," *Revolución*, (Havana), Nov. 9, 1964. pp. 1-2.
For communist cadres.

1155. Zenske, M., "Die Bildung des Partido Unido de la Revolución Socialista de Cuba," *Wissenschaftliche Zeitschrift der Karl Marx-Universität Leipzig*, (Leipzig), No. 3, 1963. pp. 81-107.

4. Partido Comunista, October 3, 1965-1969

1156. Anónimo, "Avanza construcción del PCC en el Ejército de Occidente," *Granma*, (Havana), Jan. 19, 1966. p. 3.

1157. Anónimo, "El cuadragésimo aniversario del primer partido marxista-leninista en Cuba," *Cuba Socialista*, (Havana), Aug. 1965. pp. 2-13.

1158. Anónimo, "Orientaciones sobre el ingreso al Partido," *El Militante Comunista*, (Havana), Aug. 1968. pp. 5-30.

1159. Carrera, Antonio de la, "Fidel Castro's New Phase: after Che Guevara's Departure," *New Leader*, Oct. 25, 1965. pp. 3-12.

1160. Castro, Fidel "Discurso de clausura del XII Congreso de la CTC," *El Mundo*, (Havana), Aug. 30, 1966.
On building communism in Cuba.

1161. Castro, Fidel, "Discurso en el acto de conmemoración del cuarto aniversario del Ministerio del Interior," *Política Internacional*, (Havana), No. 10, 1965. pp. 297-312.
June 16, 1965. Sums up revolution's achievements.

1162. Castro, Fidel, "Discurso en el acto de entrega de diplomas y premios a los 5,000 trabajadores que más de distinguieron en la V Zafra del Pueblo," *Política Internacional*, No. 11-12, 1965. pp. 159-179.
July 24, 1965. On moral and material incentives.

1163. Castro, Fidel, "Discurso en el acto de presentación del Comité Central del Partido Comunista de Cuba," *Cuba Socialista*, (Havana), Nov. 1965. pp. 61-82.
Oct. 3, 1965 announcing Che's departure. Also in English, Havana: Ediciones en Colores, 1965.

1164. Castro, Fidel, "Discurso en la despedida a becarios que realizaron diversas tareas en el regional Guane-Mantua, Pinar del Río," *Orientador Revolucionario*, (Havana), Apr. 29, 1967, No. 9, 29 pp.
"Communism is abundance without egoism."

1165. Castro, Fidel, *Discurso en la reunión con los secretarios generales de los 25 sindicatos nacionales, los presidentes de las comisiones provinciales de la zafra y las direcciones del INRA y del MINAZ*, Havana: Comisión de Orientación Revolucionaria, 1965. 33 pp.
Jan. 21, 1965. "Prizes to be given to best sugar workers."

1166. Castro, Fidel, "Discurso pronunciado en el acto conmemorativo del V aniversario de la victoria de Playa Girón," *Política Internacional*, (Havana), No. 14, 1966. pp. 173-191.
Apr. 19, 1966. On revolution's achievements.

1167. Castro, Fidel, "Discurso pronunciado en la Plaza de la Revolución en la celebración del Día Internacional de los Trabajadores," *Política Internacional*, (Havana), No. 14, 1966. pp. 193-209.
May 1, 1966. On the new socialist state.

1168. Castro, Fidel, "Discurso pronunciado en la primera reunión del Comité Central del Partido Comunista de Cuba," *Cuba Socialista*, (Havana), Nov. 1965. pp. 58-60.
Oct. 2, 1965. On party organization.

1169. Castro, Fidel, "Este país es la primera trinchera en la lucha contra el imperialismo," *Bohemia*, (Havana), July 30, 1965. pp. 56-73.
July 26, 1965 speech. Relation between Communist Party and Revolutionary Government.

1170. Castro, Fidel, "¡De liberalismo y reblandecimiento nada! Este es pueblo combativo," *El Mundo*, (Havana), Sept. 29, 1968. pp. 1-4.
28 Sept. 1968 speech. Denounces advocates wanting to liberalize Cuban revolution.

1171. Castro, Fidel, "El mejor aporte que puede hacer la ciudad al campo es darle técnicos," *El Mundo*, Sept. 27, 1966. pp. 5, 6.
Sept. 25, 1966 speech.

1172. Castro, Fidel, "No puede haber socialismo ni desarrollo de la economía sin conciencia revolucionaria," *Revolución*, Nov. 11, 1961. pp. 1, 6, 8-10.
Nov. 10, 1961 speech to the National Commission on Revolutionary Orientation.

1173. Castro, Fidel, "Our Society is Serious in its Drive to Work Toward a Communist System of Distribution," *Granma*, (Havana), Jan. 14, 1968. pp. 2, 3, 4.

1174. Castro, Fidel, "El revolucionario cree en el hombre, cree en el ser humano, y si no cree en el hombre no se es revolucionario," *Bohemia*, (Havana), Feb. 5, 1967. pp. 62-71.
Jan. 28 speech. On Cuba's own brand of communism.

1175. Castro, Fidel, "Sexto aniversario de la revolución," *Bohemia*, (Havana), Jan. 8, 1965. pp. 30-45.
Jan. 2, 1965 speech on Cuban road to Communism. Also in English, Havana: Ministry of Foreign Relations, 1965.

1176. Castro, Fidel, "Speech at the Commemoration of the Defeat of Yankee Imperialism at Playa Girón," *Granma*, (Havana), Apr. 28, 1968. pp. 2-6.

"Cuba is building its own version of communism."

1177. Castro, Fidel, "We Will Never Build a Communist Consciousness with a Dollar Sign in the Minds and Hearts of Men," *Granma,* (Havana), Oct. 2, 1966. pp. 4-7.
Sept. 28, 1966 speech.

1178. Castro, Raúl, *Informe,* Montevideo: Talleres Gráficos de Rusty, 1968. 134 pp.
On Communist Party purges.

1179. Clark, Joseph, "Thus Spake Fidel Castro," *Dissent,* Jan.-Feb. 1970. pp. 38-56.
Emphasizes contradictions.

1180. Cuba, Partido Comunista, *Algunas cuestiones fundamentales planteadas en 1966,* Havana: Editora Política, 1966. 47 pp.

1181. Cuba, Partido Comunista, *Consideraciones sobre el trabajo ideológico. Material de estudio,* Havana: Ediciones COR, 1968. vol. 1.

1182. Cuba, Partido Comunista, *Directrices del Partido para los planes de eficiencia,* Havana, 1966-s67. 7 vols.
Plans for various ministries.

1183. Cuba, Partido Comunista, *4 editoriales sobre la lucha contra el burocratismo,* Havana: Editora Política, 1967. 24 pp.

1184. Cuba, Partido Comunista, *Sobre los cuadros,* Havana, 1966. 60 pp.

1185. Cuba, Presidencia, *El fortalecimiento ideológico ante las tareas organizativas,* Havana, 1966. 15 pp.

1186. Cuba, Presidencia, "En un país en que triunfa una revolución socialista, nada hay más importante que el trabajo creador," *Bohemia,* (Havana), Oct. 15, 1965. pp. 44-47.

1187. Cuba, Presidencia, "El sentimiento revolucionario debe traducirse en trabajos prácticos," *Bohemia,* (Havana), Feb. 4, 1966. pp. 44-47.

1188. "Nueva etapa en el desarrollo del Partido Marxista-Leninista Cubano," *Cuba Socialista,* (Havana), Nov. 1965. pp. 8-82.
1965 documents.

1189. Roca, Blás, "Acerca de la libertad," *Cuba Socialista,* (Havana), Oct. 1965. pp. 18-37.

1190. Soto, Lionel, "Lo importante es que desarrollemos nuestro camino," *Cuba Socialista,* (Havana), Jan. 1967. pp. 37-61.

C. POLITICAL STRUCTURE
(See also Women, Communism, Youth, Labor, Agriculture)

1191. Barrego, Orlando, "La administración socialista en Cuba," *Granma,* (Havana), July 6, 1966, p. 2; July 7, 1966. p. 2.

1192. Castro, Fidel, "Conclusiones sobre el Poder Local," *Cuba Socialista,* (Havana), Nov. 1965. pp. 13-42.
Sept. 30, 1965 speech on local government.

1193. Castro, "Los errores de la burocracia," *Revolución,* (Havana), July 12, 1963. pp. 1, 2.

1194. Castro, Raúl, *Constitución de la JUCEI en La Habana,* Havana: Impr. Nacional, 1962. 32 pp.
On Junta de Coordinación, Ejecución e Inspección.

1195. Domínguez, Jorge, *The Politics of the Institutionalization of the Cuban Revolution: the Search for the Missing Links,* New Haven, 1968. Yale Ph.D. thesis.

1196. Dorticós, Osvaldo, "Los cambios institucionales y políticos de la revolución socialista," *Cuba Socialista,* (Havana), Sept. 1961. pp. 22-33.

1197. Garcés, Joan E., "Cuba: un enfoque de su sistema político," *Revista de Estudios Políticos,* (Madrid), Nov.-Dec. 1967. pp. 183-203.

1198. Lapova, R. A., *Abschestvennyi i gosudarstvennyi stroi Kubinskoi Respubliki,* [The Social and Political System of the Cuban Republic], Saratov: Izd-vo Sarat. un-ta, 1963. 44 pp.

1199. Padrón, Pedro L., "La autogestión local," *Granma,* (Havana), Apr. 15, 1966. p. 8.
Political administration.

1200. Padrón, Pedro Luis, "Experiencia del poder local en la montaña," *Granma,* (Havana), Jan. 19, 1966. pp. 8.
Political administration.

1201. Padrón, Pedro Luis, "Lograr lo imposible," *Granma,* (Havana), Jan. 15, 1966. pp. 8.
Political administration.

1202. Riera, Pepita, *Servicio de inteligencia de Cuba comunista,* Miami: Distribuidor Universal, 1966. 225 pp.

1203. Saladrigas, René, "Criterio para una reestructuración político-administrativa de Cuba," *Cuba Socialista,* (Havana), Jan. 1963. PP 40-57.

1. Comités de Defensa de la Revolución

1204. Anónimo, "El Comité de Defensa en nuestros campos," *Verde Olivo,* (Havana), Aug 27, 1961. pp. 73-75.

1205. Anónimo, "Los CDR, vehículos de unidad," *Revolución,* (Havana), Sept. 27, 1961. pp. 1, 4.

1206. Anónimo, "Sobre el papel de los CDR en el Año de la Economía," *Con la Guardia en Alto,* (Havana), Mar. 1965. pp. 24-25.

1207. Castro, Fidel, *Con la guardia en alto,* Havana: Imprenta Nacional, 1961. 24 pp.
Sept. 28, 1961 speech reviewing work of Committees for the Defense of the Revolution.

1208. Cuba, Comisión Nacional de la UNESCO, *Comités de Defensa de la Revolución, Cifras de 1963, instrucción revolucionaria,* Havana, 1964. 12 pp.

1209. Cuba, Comisión Nacional de la UNESCO, *Doce preguntas y respuestas sobre los Comités de Defensa de la Revolución,* Havana: Impr. C.T.C. Revolucionaria, 1960. 32 pp.

1210. Cuba, Comisión Nacional de la UNESCO, *El MINSAP y los CDR en las tareas de salud,* Havana, 1964. 140 pp.

1211. Cuba, Comités de Defensa de la Revolución, *Los CDR, en granjas y zonas rurales,* Havana: Ediciones con la Guardia en Alto, 1965. 243 pp.

1212. Cuba, Comités de Defensa de la Revolución, *Comunicado de la Dirección Nacional de los Comités de Defensa de la Revolución, con motivo de su cuarto an-*

iversario, Havana: Ediciones con la Guardia en Alto, 1964. 11 pp.

1213. Cuba, Comités de Defensa de la Revolución, *Defensa civil,* Havana: INAV, Depto. de Relaciones Públicas, 1961. 31 pp.

1214. Cuba, Comités de Defensa de la Revolución, *Guía de las sectoristas,* Havana, 1967. 29 pp.

1215. Cuba, Comités de Defensa de la Revolución, *Guía para la acción,* Havana: Ediciones con la Guardia en Alto, 1963-1966. 32 vols.+.

1216. Cuba, Comités de Defensa de la Revolución, *Instrucción y trabajo,* Havana: Ediciones con la Guardia en Alto, 1964-1965. 2 vols.

1217. Cuba, Comités de Defensa de la Revolución, *Memorias de 1962,* Havana: Ediciones con la Guardia en Alto, 1963. 250 pp.

1218. Cuba, Comités de Defensa de la Revolución, *Memorias de 1963,* Havana: Ediciones con la Guardia en Alto, 1964. 414 pp.

1219. Cuba, Comités de Defensa de la Revolución, *Pueblo organizado,* Havana, 1965. 269 pp.
Fourteen reports on CDR's at block level.

1220. Cuba, Comités de Defensa de la Revolución, *12 preguntas y respuestas,* Havana: Imprenta CTC-R, 1961. 32 pp.

1221. Cuba, Partido Comunista, *Comités de Defensa de la Revolución,* Havana: Ediciones Con la Guardia en Alto, 1965. 243 pp.
On rural activities.

1222. Editorial, "El frente de instruccion revolucionario, otro triunfo de los CDR," *Con la Guardia en Alto,* (Havana), Aug. 1963. pp. 29-32.

1223. Escalante, César, "Los Comités de Defensa de la Revolución," *Cuba Socialista,* (Havana), Sept. 1961. pp. 66-77.

1224. Fagen, Richard R., *The Transformation of Political Culture in Cuba,* Stanford: Stanford University Press, 1969. 271 pp.
Scholarly study of the Committees for the Defense of the Revolution, Schools of Revolutionary Instruction, and literacy campaign of 1961.

1225. Fernández Rubio, Francisco, "Los Comités de Defensa de la Revolución," *Bohemia,* (Havana), May 14, 1961. pp. 42-45+.

1226. Mancebo, Radamés, "El trabajo de organización en los CDR," *Con la Guardia en Alto,* (Havana), Sept. 1963. pp. 16-18.

1227. Matar, José, "Dos años de experiencia de los Comités de Defensa de la Revolución," *Cuba Socialista,* (Havana), Nov. 1962. pp. 28-37.

1228. Matar, José, "Tres años de lucha en defensa de la Revolución Cubana," *Con la Guardia en Alto,* (Havana), Sept. 1963. pp. 4-11.
By head of CDR.

1229. Navarro, Manuel, "Un buen Comité de Defensa de la Revolución," *Verde Olivo,* (Havana), July 2, 1961. pp. 60-63.

1230. Parras, Rigoberto, "Este es año de la organización y de la instrucción revolucionaria en los CDR," *Con la Guardia en Alto,* (Havana), Sept. 1963. pp. 40-41.

1231. Yasells, Eduardo, "2,100 Comités de Defensa de la revolución en el corazón de la Habana," *Verde Olivo,* (Havana), June 11, 1961. pp. 14-18.

2. Armed Forces

1232. Barclay, C. N., "Cuba: 1962," *Army Quarterly and Defense Journal,* (London), Apr. 1962. pp. 28-32.

1233. Castro, Fidel, "Camilo Cienfuegos cayó cumpliendo con su deber," *Revolución,* (Havana), Nov. 14, 1959. pp. 10, 11, 12, 13, 14.
Speech of Nov. 12, 1959 on plane crash of Armed Forces head.

1234. Castro, Fidel, *Declaraciones en el juicio contra el excomandante Hubert Matos,* Havana: Cooperativa Obrera de Publicidad, 1959. 95 pp.
Speech of Dec. 14, 1959 containing history of Rebel Army; demands punishment of Matos.

1235. Castro, Fidel, "Discurso en Camagüey en la concentración popular celebrada en apoyo al Gobierno Revolucionario," *Revolución,* (Havana), Nov. 28, 1959. pp. 1-2.
Speech of Nov. 27, 1959. Denounces mass resignation of military in Camagüey.

1236. Castro, Fidel, "Discurso en Camagüey en ocasión de la traición de Hubert Matos," *Revolución,* (Havana), Oct. 22, 1959. pp. 16, 18-19.
Speech of Oct. 21, 1959.

1237. Castro, Fidel, "Discurso en el acto de graduación del quinto curso de la Escuela Básica para Oficiales de Matanzas," *Política*

Internacional, (Havana), No. 10, 1965. pp. 241-258.
May 18, 1965. Review of Cuba's military status.

1238. Castro, Raúl, "Millón y medio de hombres al servicio militar obligatorio," *Bohemia,* (Havana), Nov. 15, 1963. pp. 36-47.

1239. Cienfuegos, Camilo, "Discurso pronunciado en el regimiento Agramonte con motivo de la traición de Huber Matos," *Revolución,* (Havana), Nov. 16, 1959. p. 27.

1240. Cienfuegos, Camilo, "Necesario reorganizar las Fuerzas Armadas," *Diario de la Marina,* (Havana), Jan. 8, 1959. pp. 1, 9B.

1241. Cienfuegos, Camilo, "No hay comunismo en las Fuerzas Revolucionarias," *Diario de la Marina,* (Havana), Jan. 10, 1959. pp. 1, 2A.

1242. Cuba, Ejército Rebelde, Departamento Nacional de Cultura, *Curso de orientación revolucionaria,* Havana, 1959. 94 pp.

1243. Cuba, Ministerio de las Fuerzas Armadas Revolucionarias, *Consejos al combatiente,* Havana, 1961. 47 pp.

1244. Cuba, Ministerio de las Fuerzas Armadas Revolucionarias, *Curso de instrucción revolucionaria de la FAR,* Havana, 1961. 7 vols.

1245. Cuba, Ministerio de las Fuerzas Armadas Revolucionarias, *En el ejército de Oriente: construyendo el PURSC,* Havana, 1964. 33 pp.

1246. Cuba, Ministerio de las Fuerzas Armadas Revolucionarias, *Manual de capacitación cívica*

"¡Que la conciencia revolucionaria se apodere del país!" Havana: Imprenta Nacional, 1960. 383 pp.
Communistoid document which split the Rebel Army.

1247. Cuba, Ministerio de las Fuerzas Armadas Revolucionarias, *Manual del instructor revolucionario*, Havana: Imprenta Nacional, 1961. 77 pp.

1248. Cuba, Ministerio de las Fuerzas Armadas Revolucionarias, *Nuevo curso de instrucción revolucionaria de las FAR*, Havana, 1963-1964. 3 vols.

1249. Cuba, Ministerio de las Fuerzas Armadas Revolucionarias, *Objectivos y problemas de la revolución cubana*, Havana: Imprenta Marina de Guerra Revolucionaria, 1959. 22 pp.

1250. Cuba, Ministerio de las Fuerzas Armadas Revolucionarias, *El Partido, destacamento de vanguardia de nuestras FAR*, Havana, 1964. 63 pp.

1251. Cuba, Ministerio de las Fuerzas Armadas Revolucionarias, *Reglamento de las milicias nacionales revolucionarias*, Havana: Capitolio Nacional, 1960. 8 pp.

1252. Cuba, Universidad Popular, *Defensa de Cuba*, Havana: Impr. Nacional, 1960. 223 pp.

1253. Frente Obrero Revolucionario Democrático Cubano, *Servicio militar obligatorio en Cuba roja*, Miami, 1964. 34 pp.

1254. Guevara, Ernesto, "Proyecciones sociales del ejército rebelde," *Humanismo*, (Havana), Jan.-Apr. 1959. pp. 346-357.

1255. Ivdanov, N., "Nadezhnyi strazh revoliutsionnoi Kuby" [Faithful guardian of revolutionary Cuba],

Kommunist Vooruzhennykh Sil, (Moscow), May 1961. pp. 88-92.
Cuban armed forces.

1256. Leante, César, *Con las milicias*, Havana: Ediciones Unión, 1962. 97 pp.
Reports by Cuban journalist.

1257. Mora, Martín, *Importancia del adoctrinamiento revolucionario. La milicia dentro del proceso revolucionario*, Havana: Escuela de Adoctrinamiento Revolucionario, 1960. 32 pp.

1258. Ossovskii, P. and V. Ivanov, "Soldaty revoliutsionnoi Kuby," [Soldiers of revolutionary Cuba], *Sovetskii voin*, (Moscow), Aug. 1961. pp. 37-40.

1259. Pérez, Luis, *The Rise and Fall of the Cuban Armed Forces, 1902-1959*, Albuquerque: University of New Mexico, 1970. Ph.D. dissertation.

1260. Ponizovskii, V. and I. Khuzemi, "Boitsy revoliutsii," [Soldiers of the revolution], *Smena*, Jan. 1964. pp. 14-15.

1261. Rivero Lucena, Rigoberto, "Professionalism in the Cuban Armed Forces," *Military Review*, (Fort Leavenworth, Kansas), Mar. 1966. pp. 13-19.

1262. Roa, Raúl, "Cuba se reserva el derecho de adquirir el tipo de arma que necesite para su defensa," *Bohemia*, (Havana), Oct. 22, 1965. pp. 40-44.

1263. Roca, Blas, *La disciplina y la conciencia en la MNR*, Havana: Ed. Prensa Libre, 1961. 7 pp.
On militia.

1264. Rood, Harold W., "Military Operations Against Cuba," *Claremont Quarterly*, (Pomona), Winter 1963. pp. 5-18.

1265. Schratz, Paul R., "Clausewitz, Cuba, and Command," *United States Naval Institute Proceedings*, (Maryland), Aug. 1964. pp. 24-33.

1266. Valdés, Ramiro, "El ejército rebelde y la Reforma Agraria," *Humanismo*, (Havana), Jan.-Apr. 1959. pp. 343-345.

1267. Viera Trejo, Bernardo, "7 preguntas fundamentales al comandante Camilo Cienfuegos," *Bohemia*, (Havana), Feb. 22, 1959. pp. 52-54.

D. COUNTER-REVOLUTIONARIES

1268. Anónimo, "No se puede jugar a la guerra con la revolución," *INRA*, (Havana), Nov. 1960. pp. 88-93.
Anti-government guerrillas in Escambray mountains.

1269. Anonymous, "New Guerrilla Groups Spring Up in Cuba," *Free Cuba News*, (Washington), June 15, 1963. pp. 1-3.

1270. Bethel, Paul D., *Terror and Resistance in Communist Cuba*, Washington: Citizens Committee for a Free Cuba, 1964. 53 pp.

1271. Bonnay, Charles, "Renace la rebelión en Cuba," *Life in Español*, (NY), Sept. 3, 1962. pp. 13-21.

1272. Castro, Fidel, "Cada traición se convierte en ejemplo patriótico del pueblo," Oct. 21, 1959, *Revolución*, (Havana), Oct. 22, 1959. pp. 16, 18, 19.
Response to alleged bombing of Havana.

1273. Castro, Fidel, "Comparecencia ante las cámaras de T.V. de C.M.Q. con motivo de la conspiración trujillista-batistiana," *Revolución*, (Havana), Aug. 15, 1959. pp. 1, 2, 6-7.

1274. Castro, Fidel, "La contrarrevolución en el punto culminante de su descomposición," *Revolución*, Apr. 11, 1963. pp. 1, 6, 7.
On exile politics.

1275. Castro, Fidel, "Frente al terror de los contrarevolucionarios, el terror revolucionario," *Revolución*, Nov. 30, 1961. pp. 7-9.

1276. Castro, Fidel, "Liquidaremos este año la contrarevolución," *Revolución*, (Havana), Jan. 3, 1961. pp. 2, 3, 6, 7, 10.

1277. Castro, Fidel, "Podriamos fusilar a espías y traidores," *Revolución*, (Havana), Sept. 30, 1960. pp. 1, 2.

1278. Castro, Fidel, "Primero vencerá una revolución en E.U. que la contrarevolución aquí," *Revolución*, (Havana), Mar. 14, 1961. pp. 2-6.
Mar. 13 speech. Also English edition.

1279. Castro, Fidel, "El pueblo será claro con ellos: vamos a exterminar a los terroristas," *Revolución*, (Havana), Apr. 8, 1961. pp. 10-11.

1280. Castro, Fidel, *A un pueblo así hay que respetarlo*, Havana: INRA, 1959. 33 pp.
Speech made on Oct. 26, 1959 dealing with counter-revolution. English edition: Havana: Editorial en Marcha, 1959.

1281. Castro, Fidel, "Speech at the Funeral Services for Five Brave Revolutionary Fighters Who Died Defending their Country," *Granma*, (Havana), Apr. 26, 1970. pp. 1-2.

1282. Cobas Reyes, Mario, *Mentiras fabulosas sobre Cuba*, Mexico: Ediciones Botas, 1966. 62 pp.

1283. Cuba, Partido Unido de la Revolución Socialista, *La contrarevolución y el imperialismo al desnudo*, Havana, 1963. 20 pp.
Chronology of aggressions.

1284. Díaz Versón, Salvador, *Cuando la razón se vuelve inútil*, Mexico: Ed. Botas, 1962. 155 pp.
"Freedom destroyed."

1285. Fernández, Francisco M., "La revolución de Castro," *Defensa Institucional Cubana*, (Mexico), May 1963. pp. 26-29.
Anti-Castro.

1286. Fuentes, Norberto, "Geschichten aus dem Escambray," *Kursbuch*, (Frankfurt), Oct. 1969. pp. 51-62.
Anti-Castro "bandits" in the mountains.

1287. Guevara, Ernesto, "Un pecado de la revolución," *Bohemia*, (Havana), Feb. 12, 1961. p. 59+.
On counter-revolutionaries.

1288. Iraci, Leone, *New Resistance in Cuba*, Washington: Joint Publications Research Service, Aug. 9, 1961. 8 pp.

1289. Núñez García, Ricardo, *La otra imagen de Cuba*, Miami: Talleres Litográficos "Trail Printing," 1965. 231 pp.

1290. O'Connor, James, "Cuba's Counter-revolution," *Progressive*, Dec. 1960, pp. 8-11; Jan.-Feb. 1961. pp. 19-22.

1291. Orta, Jesús, "Escambray," *INRA*, (Havana), Apr. 1961. pp. 18-25.
Anti-Castro guerillas.

1292. Pardo Llado, José, *Fidel: sacude la mata y . . . ¡adelante!*, Havana: Editorial de Cadena Oriental de Radio, 1959. 31 pp.
"Smash the counter-revolution," says *Ortodoxo* leader.

1293. Pérez Madrigal, Joaquín, "Fidel Castro no ha traicionado a la revolución," *Defensa Institucional Cubana*, (Mexico), Oct.-Dec. 1964. pp. 19-29.

1294. Pizzi de Porras, Enrique, *Mensaje a todos los que en Cuba, en América, en Europa y en el mundo se llaman Batista*, Mexico: Ed. Botas, 1962. 255 pp.
Batista considered a "great figure and statesman."

1295. *Profesores y estudiantes en pie contra la reacción*, Havana: Impr. Nacional, 1961. 48 pp.
Against counterrevolutionaries.

1296. Roca, Blas, *El pensamiento íntimo de la contrarevolución*, Havana, 1961. 8 pp.

1297. Silverio Sainz, Nicasio, *En la Cuba de Castro: apuntes de un testigo*, Miami: New House Publishers, 1967. 327 pp.

1298. Suárez Rivas, Eduardo, *Un pueblo crucificado*, Miami, 1964. 383 pp.

1299. Tanner, Hans, *Counter-revolutionary Agent; Diary of the Events which Occurred in Cuba between January and July, 1961*, London: G. T. Foulis, 1962. 161 pp.

IV. INTERNATIONAL RELATIONS

A. REVOLUTIONARY FOREIGN POLICY

1. Documents

1300. Anónimo, "Cuba y la conferencia de comercio y desarrollo," *Comercio Exterior,* (Havana), July-Sept. 1963. pp. 49-53.

1301. Castro, Fidel, "Declaración del Primer Ministro sobre los 5 puntos que constituyen las garantías contra la agresión a Cuba," *Cuba Socialista,* (Havana), Dec. 1962. pp. 130-131.

1302. Castro, Fidel, *Discursos pronunciados por el comandante Fidel Castro Ruz en tres capitales de América Latina: Buenos Aires, Montevideo y Rio de Janeiro,* Havana: MINFAR, 1959. 61 pp.

1303. Castro, Fidel, *Meet the Press: Guest, Dr. Fidel Castro, Prime Minister of Cuba,* Havana, 1959. 7 pp.
Radio and TV interview, Apr. 19, 1959.

1304. Castro, Fidel, "We Offer the People of Vietnam Our Unhesitating, Unconditional Solidarity at any Time or Place and Under any Circumstances," *Granma,* (Havana), Jan. 7, 1968. pp. 2, 3, 4, 5.
Ninth aniversary speech.

1305. Cuba, Ministerio de Relaciones Exteriores, *Cuba en la Segunda Conferencia de Países No Alineados,* Havana: Dirección de Información, 1964. 77 pp.
Useful documents. Also in English.

1306. Cuba, Ministerio de Relaciones Exteriores, *Cuba responde al documento de la OEA sobre la Tricontinental,* Havana, 1967. 29 pp.

1307. Cuba, Ministerio de Relaciones Exteriores, *Declaración de La Habana,* Havana: Oficina del Premierato, 1960. 14 pp.

1308. Cuba, Ministerio de Relaciones Exteriores, *El más grande acto celebrado en América: II Declaración de La Habana,* Havana, 1962. 41 pp.

1309. Cuba, Ministerio de Relaciones Exteriores, *News from Cuba,* London: Cuban Embassy, 1962-.
Irregular.

1310. Cuba, Ministerio de Relaciones Exteriores, *Panamericanismo, imperialismo y no-intervención,* Havana, 1966. 45 pp.

1311. Cuba, Ministerio de Relaciones Exteriores, *Política internacional de la revolución cubana,* Havana: Editora Política, 1966. 2 vols. 807 pp.
Foreign policy evolution.

1312. Cuba, Ministerio de Relaciones Exteriores, *Posición de Cuba ante la crisis del Medio Oriente,* Havana: Instituto del Libro, 1967. 14 pp.

1313. Cuba, Presidencia, *Committed to Our Own Principles,* Havana: Editorial en Marcha, 1962. 23 pp. Dorticós 1961 speech at Non-aligned Countries Conference in Belgrade.

1314. Cuba, Presidencia, *Checoeslo-vaquia, China y Cuba, países amigos; solidaria expresión,* Havana: Imprenta Nacional de Cuba, 1961. 31 pp.

1315. Cuba, Presidencia, *Cuba en el pleno ejercicio de su soberanía no conocbirá y admitirá política inter-vencionista alguna,* Havana: Ministerio de Relaciones Exteriores, 1960. 10 pp. Speech.

1316. Cuba, Presidencia, *Este pueblo no renuncia a ejercitar su sobera-nía en una sola pulgada de nuestro territorio,* Havana: Imprenta Na-cional, 1961. 24 pp.

1317. Cuba, Presidencia, *Misión de paz y solidaridad,* Havana: Edito-rial en Marcha, 1962. 54 pp. Late 1961 around-the-world trip by Dorticós, Raúl Roa and Blas Roca.

1318. Guevara, Ernesto, *Una aspira-ción común: la derrota del im-perialismo, une a Cuba con Africa y Asia,* Havana: Ministerio de Re-laciones Exteriores, 1965. 23 pp. Speech at the II Afro-Asian Seminar held in Algeria on Feb. 22-27, 1965. Also in English.

1319. Guevara, Ernesto, *Ha sonado la hora prostera del colonialismo,* Havana: Ministerio de Relaciones Exteriores, Dirección de Informa-ción, 1965. 38 pp.

Attacks both U.S. and the U.S.S.R. Also in English.

1320. Guevara, Ernesto, "Posición de Cuba frente a los problemas inter-nacionales," *Cuba Socialista,* (Ha-vana), Jan. 1965. pp. 8-25. Dec. 11, 1964 speech.

1321. Guevara, Ernesto, "La única solución correcta a los problemas de la humanidad en el momento actual es la supresión de la explo-tación de los países capitalistas de-sarrollados," *Bohemia,* (Havana), Apr. 3, 1964. pp. 78-83.

1322. Roa, Raúl, "Un año de revolu-ción cubana," *Cuadernos America-nos,* (Mexico), May-June 1960. pp. 42-52.

1323. Roa, Raúl, 'Balance y perspec-tivas de las actividades del Minis-terio de Relaciones Exteriores du-rante el año 1963," *Bohemia,* (Havana), Dec. 27, 1963. pp. 40-45.

1324. Roa, Raúl, *Cuba tiene la razón,* San José: Sociedad de Amigos de la Revolución Cubana, 1960. 38 pp.

1325. Roa, Raúl, *Discurso en la Asamblea General de las Naciones Unidas,* Havana, Sept. 25, 1959. 8 pp.

1326. Roa, Raúl, "Perspectivas de la revolución cubana," *Ciencias Po-líticas y Sociales,* (Mexico), Apr.-June 1960. pp. 243-251.

2. Commentaries

1327. Anónimo, "A nadie le está per-mitido violar la soberanía de Cuba; un artículo de "Izvestia," *Bohemia,* (Havana), May 1, 1964. pp. 42-44.

1328. Basler, W., "Die Aussenpolitik der revolutionären Kuba," [The foreign policy of revolutionary Cuba], *Deutsche Aussenpolitik*, (Berlin), No. 7, 1961. pp. 833-842.

1329. Clairmonte, Frederick F., "Cuba and Africa," *The Journal of Modern African Studies*, (London), Nov. 1964. pp. 419-430.

1330. Cline, Howard F., "Mexico, Fidelismo and the United States," *Orbis*, Summer 1961. pp. 152-165.

1331. "Comunicado conjunto cubano-argelino," *Cuba Socialista*, (Havana), Nov. 1962. pp. 140-142.

1332. Conte Agüero, Luis, *Doctrina de la contra intervención; sovietización de la economía cubana*, Montevideo: Eds. Cruz del Sur, 1962. 141 pp.

1333. Crane, Robert D., "The Sino-Soviet Dispute on War and the Cuban Crisis," *Orbis*, Fall 1964. pp. 537-49.

1334. "Cuba Crisis," *On Record*, No. 1, 1963. pp. 1-72.
Chronology for 1961-1963.

1335. D'Estéfano, Miguel A., *Derecho internacional público*, Havana: Editora Universitaria, 1965. 821 pp.
Revolutionary view by Cuban expert.

1336. D'Estéfano, Miguel A., "Las nacionalizaciones del gobierno revolucionario y el derecho internacional," *Política Internacional*, (Havana), July-Aug.-Sept. 1963. pp. 41-88.

1337. D'Estéfano, Miguel A., "Las violaciones norte-americanas de la soberanía del espacio aéreo cubano," *Política Internacional*, (Havana), No. 6, 1964. pp. 75-99.

1338. Draper, Theodore, "Castro, Khrushchev, and Mao," *The Reporter*, (New York), Aug. 15, 1963. pp. 27-31.

1339. Escalante, Aníbal, "Del Grito de Yara a la Declaración de la Habana," *Cuba Socialista*, (Havana), Oct. 1961. pp. 1-9.

1340. Facts on File, *Cuba, the U.S. and Russia, 1960-63*, New York, 1964. 138 pp.
Chronology.

1341. Ferraris, Agustín, *Cuba en la problemática internacional*, Buenos Aires: Editorial 30 Días, 1965. 93 pp.
1955-1965.

1342. *Foreign and Internal Affairs in Cuba*, Washington: Joint Publications Research Service, Aug. 8, 1962. 27 pp.

1343. Furtak, Robert K., *Kuba und der Weltkommunismus*, Köln: Westdeutscher Verlag, 1967. 194 pp.
Cuba between USSR and Red China. Scholarly.

1344. Garner, William R., "The Sino-Soviet Ideological Struggle in Latin America," *Journal of Inter-American Studies*, Apr. 1968. pp. 244-255.

1345. Gelman, P., "Die wirtschaftliche Umgestaltung in der Republik Kuba," *Sawjetwissenschaft. Gessellschafts - wissenschaftliche Abteilung*, (Berlin), 1964. pp. 364-376.

1346. Gilly, Adolfo, *Cuba: coexistencia o revolución*, Buenos Aires: Editorial Perspectivas, 1965. 140 pp.
Trotkyist. Critical of the revolution.

1347. González, Manuel Pedro, "Raúl Roa, ideología y estilo," *Cuadernos Americanos,* (Mexico), Jan.-Feb. 1968. pp. 75-94.
Adulatory.

1348. Hulsey, Raymond H., "The Cuban Revolution: Its Impact on American Foreign Policy," *Journal of International Affairs,* No. 2, 1960. pp. 158-174.

1349. Krakau, Knud, *Die kubanische Revolution und die Monroe Doktrin,* Frankfurt: Metzner, 1968. 220 pp.

1350. Lamberg, Robert F., "Fidel Castro dilemma: Lage und Perspektiven der kubanischen Wirtschaft," *Europa-Archiv,* (Frankfurt-am-Main), Jan. 20, Feb. 5, Mar. 10, 1965. pp. 175-184.

1351. Ljunglof, L., "Castro's Kuba, Latinamerika och USA," *Utrikespolitika,* (Stockholm), Apr.-May 1962. pp. 52-62.

1352. Lowenthal, Richard, "Los Estados Unidos, Cuba y la Unión Soviética," *Cuadernos,* (Paris), Jan. 1963. pp. 27-36.

1353. Lumsden, C. Ian, "Cuba," in Bromke, Adam, ed., *The Communist States at the Crossroads Between Moscow and Peking,* New York: Frederick A. Praeger, 1965. pp. 164-178.

1354. Martínez, A. A., *A Red Inferno in the Caribbean,* San Juan: Gente Pub., 1964. 310 pp.

1355. Maza Rodríguez, E., "Castro, la revolución cubana y la 'autodeterminación de los pueblos,'" *Revista de Estudios Políticos,* (Madrid), July-Aug. 1962. pp. 175-190.

1356. McNaught, Kenneth, "Canada, Cuba, and the U.S.," *Monthly Review,* Apr. 1961. pp. 616-625.

1357. Movimiento Venezolano por la Paz y la Liberación Nacional, *Kennedy, Betancourt y Cuba,* Caracas, 1962. 28 pp.

1358. Niedergang, Marcel, "Moscow, La Havane, Hanoi," *Le Monde,* (Paris), Nov. 9-15, 1967. p. 4.

1359. Niedergang, Marcel, "'La Révolution cubaine ne sera jamais le satellite de personne, déclare M. Fidel Castro,'" *Le Monde,* (Paris), Mar. 16-22, 1967. p. 4.

1360. Niedergang, Marcel, "La Voie Cubaine: ni Moscou, ni Pékin , , ,," *Le Monde,* (Paris), Apr. 6-21, 1967. pp. 1, 2.

1361. Nellesen, B., *Cold Route to Power: Notes on Castro's Cuba,* Washington: Joint Publications Research Service, Dec. 18, 1963. 7 pp.

1362. O'Connor, James, "Cuba's Economic Revolution," *Progressive,* Jan. 1961. pp. 19-22.

1363. Prellwitz, Jürgen, "Die internationalen Verhandlungen über den 'Fall Kuba,'" *Europa-Archiv,* (Frankfurt-am-Main), Dec. 20, 1960. pp. 741-754.

1364. Rafat, Amir, *Expropriation of the Private Property of Aliens in Recent International Law: Iran, Egypt, Indonesia and Cuba,* Minneapolis, Minn., 1964. 452 pp.
University of Minnesota Ph.D. Thesis.

1365. Riemens, H., "De Cubaanse Kwestie," *Internationale Spectator,* (The Hague), Nov. 8, 1960. pp. 435-449.

1366. Roig de Leuchsenring, Emilio,

Tradición anti-imperialista de nuestra historia, Havana: Oficina del Historiador de la Ciudad, 1962. 87 pp.

1367. Roucek, Joseph S., "The Geopolitics of Cuba," *Política,* (Caracas), Dec. 1963. pp. 870-893.

1368. Semidei, M., "La crise cubaine," *Revue Française de Science Politique,* (Paris), Dec. 1965. pp. 1153-1169.

1369. United States, Congress, Senate, Committee on Armed Services, *Investigation of the Preparedness Program,* Washington, 1963. 18 pp.
On Cuban military build-up.

1370. Wohlstetter, Roberta, *Controlling the Risks in Cuba,* [Adelphi Paper No. 17], London: The Institute for Strategic Studies, 1965. 23 pp.

B. RELATIONS WITH THE UNITED STATES

1. Cuban Documents

1371. Castro, Fidel, "Acusa Fidel a E. U. por ataque pirata a otro barco de URSS," *Revolución,* Mar. 28, 1963. pp. 1, 4.
Attack by exiles.

1372. Castro, Fidel, "Afirma Fidel Castro que las relaciones con los E. U. deben ser cada días mejores," *Diario de la Marina,* (Havana), Apr. 17, 1959. pp. 1, 2A.

1373. Castro, Fidel, "Cambiaremos cuota por inversiones," *Revolución,* (Havana), June 25, 1960. pp. 1, 2, 18.
"If the U.S. cuts the sugar quota."

1374. Castro, Fidel, *Creen que la revolución va a fracasar porque el gobierno americano quiere,* Havana: Imprenta Nacional, 1960. 31 pp.
June 11, 1960 speech.

1375. Castro, Fidel, "Cuba exige indemnización por daños causados," *Revolución,* (Havana), May 23, 1961. pp. 1, 5.

1376. Castro, Fidel, "Cuba ha ganado todas las batallas contra el imperialismo," *Revolución,* (Havana) Jan. 1961. p. 1.

1377. Castro, Fidel, "Cuba único país víctima de ataques desde el exterior," *Revolución,* (Havana), Feb. 19, 1960. pp. 1, 14A, 15.
Exile air attacks from U.S.

1378. Castro, Fidel, "Culpable de la muerte de Fajardo el gobierno de los E.U. que lanza armas sobre el Escambray," *Revolución,* (Havana), Dec. 2, 1960. pp. 1, 12.

1379. Castro, Fidel, "Discurso en el acto conmemorativo del Día Internacional del Trabajo," *Política Internacional* (Havana), No. 6, 1964. pp. 133-152.
May 1, 1964. Denouncing "new U.S. provocations."

1380. Castro, Fidel, "Discurso en el acto conmemorativo del tercer aniversario de la victoria de Playa Girón," *Política Internacional,* (Havana), No. 6, 1964. pp. 99-111.
Apr. 19, 1964. "Cuba wants an honorable peace." Also in English, Havana: Ministry of Industries, 1964.

1381. Castro, Fidel, "Discurso en el IV aniversario de la victoria del Pueblo en Playa Girón," *Obra*

Revolucionaria, (Havana), No. 8, 1965. pp. 8-20.
"U.S. should be defeated in Vietnam."

1382. Castro, Fidel, "Discurso en el tercer aniversario de los Comités Defensa de la Revolución," *Obra Revolucionaria,* (Havana), No. 24, 1963. pp. 5-16.
Sept. 28, 1963 speech on "consistent anti-imperialism."

1383. Castro, Fidel, *Discursos memorables en una hora decisiva,* Havana: Imprenta Nacional, 1960. 62 pp.
July 6 and 8 speeches in response to U.S. cutting of Cuban sugar quotas.

1384. Castro, Fidel, "Discurso sobre el atentado a John F. Kennedy," *Revolución,* (Havana), Nov. 25, 1963. pp. 2-4.
Nov. 23, 1963.

1385. Castro, Fidel, *Discursos pronunciados en los Estados Unidos de Norteamérica,* Havana: MINFAR, 1959. 64 pp.

1386. Castro, Fidel, "Entrevista sobre relaciones cubano-norteamericanas," *Revolución,* (Havana), Feb. 16, 1961. p. 1.

1387. Castro, Fidel, "Espero lograr del pueblo de E. U. más comprensión para nuestro programa," *Diario de la Marina,* (Havana), Apr. 16, 1959. pp. 1, 6B.

1388. Castro, Fidel, "Los Estados Unidos dejan venir las avionetas o están muy mal preparados militarmente," *Revolución,* (Havana), May 14, 1960. pp. 1, 10, 20.

1389. Castro, Fidel, "EE. UU. prepara una agresión a Cuba a través de Guatemala," *Revolución* (Havana) May 2, 1960. pp. 2, 4, 6, 7, 10.

1390. Castro, Fidel, "Discurso en la Plaza Cívica," *Revolución,* (Havana), May 9, 1959. pp. 1-2, 13, 19.
On relations with the U.S.

1391. Castro, Fidel, "Fue un acto de piratería de E.U. arrebatarnos la cuota," *Obra Revoluconaria,* (Havana), No. 14, 1960. pp. 5-29.
July 18 speech.

1392. Castro, Fidel, "Hostigan a Cuba desde bases aéreas en EE. UU.," *Revolución* (Havana), Mar. 6, 1961. pp. 4, 5, 6, 7.

1393. Castro, Fidel, *Informe del Primer Ministro del Gobierno Revolucionario y Primer Secretario del PURSC,* Havana: Comisión de Orientación Revolucionaria, 1963. 32 pp.
Oct. 30, 1963 speech on U.S. subversion.

1394. Castro, Fidel, "La maniobra del petróleo: la primera gran zancadilla contra nuestra revolución," *Revolución,* (Havana), June 11, 1960. pp. 1, 8, 20.

1395. Castro, Fidel, "Mientras Estados Unidos no demuestre con hechos su amistad a Cuba nuestro embajador no regresará," *Revolución* (Havana), Mar. 29, 1960. pp. 6, 12, 17.

1396. Castro, Fidel, "Promueve el gobierno de E.U. agresión a nuestro país," *Revolución,* (Havana), Apr. 23, 1960. pp. 1, 2, 10.

1397. Castro, Fidel, "Resumen de la historia del azúcar en relación con los Estados Unidos," *Obra Revolucionaria,* (Havana), No. 12, 1960. pp. 3-39.
June 24, 1960 speech.

1398. Castro, Fidel, ¡Sabotaje!, Havana: CTC-R, 1960. 29 pp.
Mar. 5 speech charges U.S. complicity in explosion of munitions ship "La Coubre."

1399. Castro, Fidel, Si va a ocurrir algo en Cuba ¿por que la Embajada Americana está enterada? Havana: Imprenta Nacional, 1960. 32 pp.
May 14, 1960 speech.

1400. Castro, Fidel, "Sobre el rompimiento de relaciones entre los Estados Unidos y Cuba," Revolución, (Havana), Jan. 3, 1961. p. 6.

1401. Castro, Fidel, "El único camino que les queda a los yankis es respetar la soberanía de este país," Bohemia, (Havana), Mar. 22, 1963. pp. 4-11.
Mar. 18, 1963 speech.

1402. Cuba, Ministerio del Interior, "Nota sobre la frustrada infiltración de agentes de la CIA," Granma, (Havana), May 31, 1966. p. 3.

1403. Cuba, Ministerio del Interior, Presentation before Foreign Delegates and Journalists Attending the First Conference of OLAS of Two Agents of the United States Central Intelligence Agency (CIA) Who Tried to Penetrate through Pinar del Río Province, Havana, 1967. 71 pp.

1404. Cuba, Ministerio de Relaciones Exteriores, La base naval yanki en Guantánamo, un puñal clavado en el corazón del pueblo cubano, Havana: Editorial en Marcha, 1963. 56 pp.
Official statements and chronology of violations.

1405. Cuba, Ministerio de Relaciones Exteriores, Agresión económica, Havana, 1964. 31 pp.
Based on headlines from the principal U.S. newspapers.

1406. Cuba, Ministerio de Relaciones Exteriores, Cuba responde a la nota de EE. UU. en defensa de la soberanía nacional, Havana, 1960. 29 pp.
Nov. 13, 1959. Also in English.

1407. Cuba, Ministerio de Relaciones Exteriores, "Definición de la política y actitud del Gobierno y del pueblo cubano hacia el Gobierno y el pueblo de los Estados Unidos," El Mundo, (Havana), Nov. 14, 1959. p. A6.

1408. Cuba, Ministerio de Relaciones Exteriores, Frente a las agresiones imperialistas un solo grito en América: ¡Venceremos! ¡Cuba es la que acusa!, Havana: Impr. Nacional, 1964. 106 pp.

1409. Cuba, Ministerio de Relaciones Exteriores, "Nota de la cancillería de los Estados Unidos. Respuesta de Cuba," Bohemia, (Havana), June 21, 1959. pp. 76-77.
On application of Agrarian Reform law.

1410. Cuba, Ministerio de Relaciones Exteriores, Una nueva diplomacia, Havana, 1959. 35 pp.

1411. Cuba, Partido Comunista, Además de asesinos . . . Mentirosos!, Havana, 1966. 100 pp.
Conflict with U.S. at Guantánamo.

1412. Cuba, Presidencia, "Discurso en el acto inicio del 'Año de la Preparación Combativa,'" El Mundo, (Havana), June 5, 1966. pp. 5-6.
May 21, 1966 speech on the

death of Cuban soldier at Guantánamo Base.

1413. Cuba, Presidencia, *Reply to U.S.A.: Cuba Is a Sovereign Nation by Its Own Right, Not by Any Grant*, Havana: Ministry of Foreign Relations, 1960. 10 pp.
Jan. 27 in reply to President Eisenhower's Jan. 26 charges.

1414. Cuba, Presidencia, *The U.S. Naval Base at Guantánamo; Imperialist Outpost in the Heart of Cuba*, Havana: Editorial en Marcha, 1962. 52 pp.

1415. Cuba, United Nations, "Cuba Charges 'Economic Aggression' by United States; Security Council Defers Question Pending Report from OAS," *United Nations Review*, Sept. 1960. pp. 32-33+.
Document.

1416. Dorticós, Osvaldo, "Culpable Estados Unidos si surge una situación peligrosa," *Bohemia*, (Havana), Apr. 24, 1964. pp. 56-57.

1417. Guevara, Ernesto, "Cuba and the 'Kennedy Plan,'" *World Marxist Review*, Feb. 1962. pp. 33-39.

1418. Guevara, Ernesto, "En nuestra marcha hacia el futuro nos une una aspiración común: la derrota del imperialismo," *Bohemia*, (Havana), Mar. 5, 1965. pp. 30-35.

1419. Roa, Raúl, "Cuba denuncia; carta del Canciller al Secretario General de las Naciones Unidas, U Thant," *Bohemia*, (Havana), Mar. 1963. pp. 47-49+.

1420. Roa, Raúl, "Cuba denuncia; carta de U-Thant, Secretario General de la ONU," *Bohemia*, (Havana), May 1, 1964. pp. 28-35.

1421. Roa, Raúl, *Cuba responde a la nota de EE. UU., en defensa de la soberanía nacional*, Havana: Talleres Gráficos del Ministerio de Estado, 1959. 22 pp.

1422. Roa, Raúl, "Dos notas de protesta al Gobierno de los E. U.," *Política Internacional*, (Havana), No. 2, 1964, pp. 113-117.

1423. Roa, Raúl, "Es el Gobierno de Estados Unidos y no el de Cuba el que transgrede las leyes internacionales," *Bohemia*, (Havana), Mar. 1, 1963. pp. 64-65.

1424. Roa, Raúl, "Nota al Gobierno de los Estados Unidos," *Política Internacional*, (Havana), July-Sept. 1964. pp. 135-136.
May 18, 1964. On U.S. prohibition of export of medicine to Cuba.

1425. Roa, Raúl, "Nota al Gobierno de los Estados Unidos de la América del Norte," *Política Internacional*, (Havana), July-Sept. 1964. pp. 141-142.
June 10, 1964. "US Marines are shooting from Guatánamo at Cuban soldiers."

1426. Roca, Blas, "Los planteamientos de Fidel Castro sobre las relaciones Cuba-Estados Unidos," *Cuba Socialista* (Havana), Aug. 1964. pp. 1-17.

2. United States Documents

1427. Anonymous, "U.S. and the Situation in Cuba," *Congressional Digest*, Nov. 1962. pp. 257-267+.

1428. Ball, George W., *U.S. Policy toward Cuba*, Washington, 1964. 22 pp.
By Undersecretary of State.

1429. Dodd, Thomas J., "What Can We Do about Cuba?" *Congressional Record,* June 1963. pp. 9875-9883.

1430. Herter, Christian A., "News Conference of April 8, 1960," *Department of State Bulletin,* Apr. 25, 1960. pp. 644-646.

1431. Hilsman, Roger, "The Cuban Crisis: How Close are We to War," *Look,* Aug. 25, 1964. pp. pp. 17-21.

1432. Kennedy, John F., "Arms Quarantine of Cuba; The Soviet Military Build-up," *Vital Speeches,* Nov. 15, 1962. pp. 66-68.

1433. Kennedy, John F., "The Lesson of Cuba," *Department of State Bulletin,* May 8, 1961. pp. 659-661.
Speech of April 20, 1961.

1434. Kennedy, John F., "Senator John F. Kennedy on the Cuban Situation; Presidential Campaign of 1960," *Inter-American Economic Affairs,* Winter 1961. pp. 79-95.

1435. Martin, Edwin M., *Cuba, Latin America, and Communism,* Washington: Government Printing Office, 1963. 20 pp.
By Ass't. Sec. of State for L.A. Affairs.

1436. Martin, Edwin M., "U.S. Outlines Policy toward Cuban Refugees," *Department of State Bulletin,* June 24, 1963. pp. 983-990.

1437. McGovern, George, "Is Castro an Obsession with Us?" *New York Times Magazine,* May 19, 1963. p. 9ff.

1438. Morrison, Delesseps S., "U.S. Rebuts Cuban Charges in OAS of Intervention in Dominican Affairs," *Department of State Bulletin,* Dec. 18, 1961. pp. 1000-1003.
By OAS Ambassador.

1439. Rusk, Dean and Richard N. Gardner, "U.S. Position on U.N. Special Fund Project in Cuba," *Department of State Bulletin,* (Washington, D.C.), Mar. 11, 1963. pp. 357-360.

1440. Stevenson, Adlai E., "United States Replies to Charges Made by President of Cuba," *Department of State Bulletin,* Nov. 5, 1962. pp. 706-708.

1441. Stevenson, Adlai E., "U.N. Security Council Hears U.S. Charges of Soviet Military Build-up in Cuba," *Department of State Bulletin,* Nov. 12, 1962. pp. 723-740.

1442. United States, Congress, House, Committee on Foreign Affairs, *Claims of U.S. Nationals Against the Government of Cuba,* Washington, 1964, 176 pp.; 1965. 42 pp.

1443. United States, Congress, House, Committee on Foreign Affairs, *Special Study Mission to Cuba; Report by Albert P. Marano, Connecticut,* Washington, 1955. 16 pp.

1444. United States, Congress, Senate Committee on Foreign Relations, *Events in United States-Cuban Relations, Chronology, 1957-63,* Washington, 1963. 28 pp.

1445. United States, Congress, Senate, Committee on Foreign Relations, *Situation in Cuba, Hearings,* Washington, 1962. 117 pp.

1446. United States, Congress, Senate, Judiciary Committee, *Communist Threat to the United States through the Caribbean,*

Hearings, Washington, 1960, 323 pp.; 1966. 1046 pp.

1447. United States, Department of State, *Cuba,* Washington, 1961. 36 pp.
Schlesinger White Paper censuring Castro regime.

1448. United States, Department of State, *United States Policy toward Cuba,* Washington, 1964. 22 pp.

1449. United States, Treasury Department, *Cuban Assets Control,* Washington, 1964. 18 pp.
On Cuban property in the U.S.

3. Commentaries

1450. Alvarez Ríos, René, "Cuba: desarrollo interno y relaciones con los Estados Unidos de Norteamérica," *Política Internacional,* (Havana), 1964. pp. 59-136.

1451. Aguirre, Gustavo, "El dominio imperialista en Cuba," *INRA,* (Havana), Nov. 1960. pp. 70-73. U.S. control of economy.

1452. Alvarez Tabio, Fernando, "El principio de la no-intervención," *Cuba Socialista,* (Havana), Oct. 1963. pp. 83-103.

1453. Alexandrova, N., "American Imperialism and the Cuban Revolution," *International Affairs,* (Moscow), Nov. 1963. pp. 87-88.

1454. Andrade, Ramiro, *Cuba, el vecino socialista,* Bogotá: Talleres de Antares, 1961. 316 pp.
U.S.-Cuban relations and socialism in the island.

1455. Anónimo, "Cuba emplaza al imperialismo," *Bohemia,* (Havana), Oct. 8, 1965. pp. 58-62.

1456. Anónimo, "El fracaso de la política imperialista contra Cuba,"

Cuba Socialista, (Havana), May 1963. pp. 94-103.

1457. Anónimo, "La respuesta del pueblo a los actos vandálicos del imperialismo," *Cuba Socialista* (Havana), Oct. 1963. pp. 104-111.

1458. Anonymous, "Tax Effects on Cuban Expropriations," *Taxes,* (Chicago), Apr. 1961. pp. 309-313.

1459. Anonymous, "Treasury Rules on Cuban Expropriations," *Taxes,* (Chicago), Feb. 1963. pp. 93-97.

1460. Barrero Pérez, Juan, *La cubanía aniquilada por la enmienda Platt,* Sancti Spíritus, Cuba: Imprenta Iris, 1958. 245 pp.

1461. Bayer, Hermann - Wilfried, "Die Enteignungen auf Kuba vor den Gerichten der Vereinigten Staaten," *Zeitschrift für ausländdisches öffentliches Recht und Völkerrecht,* (Stuttgart), No. 1, 1965. pp. 30-49.

1462. Benítez, F., *La batalla de Cuba,* Mexico: Eds. Era, 1960. 185 pp.

1463. Benítez, Jaime, "Los Estados Unidos, Cuba y la América Latina," *La Torre,* (Rio Piedras), July-Sept. 1963. pp. 11-29.

1464. Benítez, Jaime, *The U. S., Cuba and Latin America,* Santa Barbara: Center for the Study of Democratic Institutions, 1961. 11 pp.
Advocates U.S. support of social revolution.

1465. Berle, Adolf A., "The Cuban Crisis Failure of American Foreign Policy," *Foreign Affairs,* Oct. 1960. pp. 40-55.

1466. Bethel, Paul, *Cuba and U.S. Policy,* Miami: Citizens Com-

mittee for a Free Cuba, Inc., 1966. 69 pp.
By former U.S. press attaché in Havana embassy.

1467. Bonsal, Philip W., "Cuba, Castro and the United States," *Foreign Affairs*, Jan. 1967. pp. 260-276.

1468. Brookings Institution, *The Cuban Problem and U.S. Policy*, Washington, 1967. 9 pp.

1469. Cosío Villegas, Daniel, "The United States and Cuba: A Latin-American View," *The Malahat Review*, (Victoria, British Columbia), Oct. 4, 1967. pp. 25-38.
Critical view of U.S. behavior.

1470. Cruse, Harold W., "Cuba y el negro norte-americano," *Casa de las Américas*, (Havana), Aug.-Sept. 1960. pp. 65-67.

1471. Daniel, Jean, "Boycotting Cuba: Whose Interests Does It Serve?" *New Republic*, Dec. 28, 1963. pp. 19-22.

1472. Daniel, Jean, "Further clarification—Interviews with Kennedy and Castro," *New Republic*, Dec. 21, 1963. pp. 6-7.

1473. Daniel, Jean, "Unofficial Envoy, an Historic Report from Two Capitals," *New Republic*, Dec. 14, 1963. pp. 15-20.

1474. Daniel, Jean, "When Castro Heard the News," *New Republic*, Dec. 7, 1963. pp. 7-9.
Reaction to Kennedy assassination.

1475. Dean, Vera Michaels, "Cuba Dilemma," *Foreign Policy Bulletin*, Feb. 1, 1961. p. 76+.

1476. D'Estéfano Pisani, Miguel A., "El arreglo de las disputas en el derecho internacional y el defer-

endo cubano-norteamericano," *Política Internacional*, (Havana), Oct.-Dec. 1964. pp. 37-57.

1477. Draper, Theodore, "Cubans and Americans: a Report from New York," *Encounter*, (London), July 1961. pp. 59-77.

1478. Editorial, "Las condiciones de Cuba," *CUBA Internacional*, (Havana), Oct. 1969. p. 8.
Relations U. S.

1479. Editorial, "Cuba: respuesta a la agresión," *Política*, (Mexico), May 15-31, 1967. pp. 41-43.

1480. Editorial, "Fidel Castro and John Kennedy," *New Times*, (Moscow), May 1961. pp. 12-14.

1481. Editorial, "Interrogatorio a agentes de la CIA," *Revolución*, (Havana), Nov. 4, 1963. pp. 1, 4-6, 7.

1482. Editorial, "Nueva derrota del imperialismo en su acto de piratería contra Cuba," *Cuba Socialista*, (Havana), Mar. 1964. pp. 108-113.

1483. Editorial, "United States, Cuba, and the Monroe Doctrine," *World Today*, (London), Nov. 1960. pp. 457-459.

1484. Eisenhower, Milton S., *The Wine is Bitter; The United States in Latin America*, New York: Doubleday, 1963. 342 pp.
Chapter on Cuba.

1485. Ekman, P., et al., "Coping with Cuba: Divergent Policy Preferences of State Political Leaders," *Journal of Conflict Resolution*, June 1966. pp. 180-197.

1486. Fagen, Richard R., "Calculation and Emotion in Foreign Policy: The Cuban Case," *Jour-*

nal of Conflict Resolution, Sept. 1962. pp. 214-227.

1487. Fair Play for Cuba Committee, *Russell Assails U.S. Threats against Cuba*, Toronto, 1962. 30 pp.

1488. Falk, Richard, "Cuba: Our Cold-Shoulder Policy," *The Nation*, (New York), Sept. 14, 1964. pp. 113-117.

1489. Freeman, Thomas, (pseud.), *The Crisis in Cuba*, Derby, Conn.: Monarch Books, 1963. 159 pp.
"U.S. should intervene."

1490. Freidberg, Sidney, "The Measure of Damages in Claims against Cuba," *Inter-American Economic Affairs*, Summer 1969. pp. 67-86.

1491. Fulbright, J. W., "Let's Talk Sense about Cuba," *Saturday Evening Post*, May 16, 1964. pp. 8-10.

1492. García Menocal, Serafín, *The Lesson the United States Can Learn from Cuba*, Princeton: M. M. Wilson. 1965. 23 pp.
By former Batista official.

1493. Gardner, Richard N., *In Pursuit of World Order: U.S. Foreign Policy and International Organizations*, New York: Praeger, 1964. 263 pp.
Chapter on Cuba.

1494. Gill, Mario (pseud.), *Nuestros buenos vecinos*, Havana: Editora Popular, 1960. 300 pp.

1495. Gómez, Juan G., et al., *La lucha anti-imperialista en Cuba*, Havana: Editora Popular de Cuba, 1960. 2 vols.
Essays by long-time nationalist intellectuals.

1496. González, Bermijo, "Guantánamo, una cerca entre dos mun-

dos," *Cuba*, (Havana), No. 12, 1963. pp. 66-82.

1497. González, Manuel Pedro, "Why Cubans Resent the U. S.," *Monthly Review*, May 1960. pp. 18-23.

1498. Grossman, M. P., "The Cuban Blockade and the Cold War," *Contemporary Issues*, June-July 1963. pp. 3-7.

1499. Halsey, Ramón H., "The Cuban Revolution: Its Impact on American Foreign Policy," *Journal of International Affairs*, No. 2, 1960. pp. 158-174.

1500. Hudson, Richard, "Cuba: Test Case for Coexistence," *War/Peace Report*, Sept. 1964. pp. 3-6.

1501. Krakau, Knud, *Die Kubanishe Revolution und die Monroe Doktrin*, Frankfurt: Metzner, 1968. 220 pp.

1502. Langley, Lester D., *The Cuban Policy of the United States: A Brief History*, New York: John Wiley and Sons, 1968. 203 pp.

1503. Lazo, Mario, *Dagger in the Heart; American Policy Failures in Cuba*, New York: Funk and Wagnalls, 1968. 426 pp.
By corporation lawyer. Blames U.S. liberals for Castro's rise to power.

1504. Manrara, Luis V., *Betrayal Opened the Door to Russian Missiles in Red Cuba*, Miami: Truth about Cuba Committee, 1968. 168 pp.
"U.S. betrayal."

1505. Maris, Gary Leroy, *Some Aspects of International Law in United States-Cuban Relations, 1898-1964*, Durham, N. C., 1965. 404 pp.

Duke University Ph.D. Thesis.

1506. Mella, Julio Antonio, *La lucha revolucionaria contra el imperialismo,* Havana: Editora Popular de Cuba 1960. 106 pp.
By founder of Communist Party.

1507. Mezerik, Avrahm G., ed., *Cuba and the United States,* New York: International Review Service, 1960-1963. 3 vols.
Chronology, 1959-1963.

1508. Nearing, Scott, "Aggressing on Cuba," *Monthly Review,* (New York), Jan. 1964. pp. 518-521.

1509. Neely, Frances E., *Controversy over Cuba,* Washington: Friends Committee on National Legislation, 1961. 26 pp.
Critical of U.S. policy.

1510. Pardo Llada, José, *El Maine y La Coubre: 1898-1960,* Havana: Editorial Tierra Nueva, 1960. 32 pp.
Charges "both blown up by the U.S."

1511. Pazos, Javier, "Cuba—Was a Deal Possible in '59?" *The New Republic,* Jan. 12, 1963. pp. 10-11.

1512. Peinado, Fermín, *Beware Yankee, the Revolution in Cuba,* Miami, 1961. 46 pp.

1513. Pino Santos, Oscar, *El imperialismo norteamericano en la economía de Cuba,* Havana: Editorial Lex, 1960. 97 pp.
Has statistics.

1514. Plank, John, ed., *Cuba and the United States: Long Range Perspectives,* Brookings Institution, 1967. 265 pp.

1515. Ramírez Novoa, Ezequiel, *El proceso de una gran epopeya; la revolución cubana y el imperialismo yanqui,* Lima: Ediciones "28 de Julio," 1960. 142 pp.

1516. Rivero Hernández, Nicolás, *Castro's Cuba, An American Dilemma,* Washington: Luce, 1962. 239 pp.
Moderate exile view.

1517. Rubin, Morris H., "The Tragedy of Cuba," *Progressive,* June 1961. pp. 9-26.
Recommends rapprochment.

1518. Samuels, Gertrude, "James Donovan and Castro," *The Nation,* (New York), Apr. 13, 1963. pp. 299-302.
Donovan negotiated release of Bay of Pigs prisoners.

1519. Sarabia, Nydia, "El pensamiento anti-imperialista de Frank País," *El Mundo,* (Havana), July 30, 1966. pp. 1, 8.

1520. Scheer, Robert and Maurice Zeitlin, *Cuba: an American Tragedy,* New York: Penguin Books, 1964. 368 pp.
"U.S. pushed Castro into the Soviet orbit."

1521. Sciaky, Albert et al., "U.S. Policy Toward Cuba," *New University Thought,* (Chicago), Summer 1961. pp. 42-61.

1522. Semidei, Manuela, *Les Etats-Unis et la Révolution cubaine, 1959-1964,* Paris: Librairie Armand Colin, 1968. 207 pp.

1523. Smith, Earl E. T., "How U.S. Helped Castro: Interview," *U.S. News and World Report,* Oct. 8, 1962. pp. 47-48.
Former U.S. Ambassador.

1524. Smith, Robert F., *The United States and Cuba; Business and Diplomacy, 1917-1960,* New York: Bookman, 1961. 256 pp.

1525. Smith, Robert F., ed., *What Happened in Cuba? A Documentary History*, New York: Twayne Publishers, 1963. 360 pp.
U.S.-Cuban relations since 1783.

1526. Taylor, Hal, "U.S. Closing Vise on Cuba," *Journal of Commerce*, Oct. 20, 1960. pp. 1+.

1527. Teison, Herbert J., "Cuba's Man-on-the-street," *New Leader*, Feb. 6, 1961. pp. 5-6.
Attitude towards U.S.

1528. Torras, Jacinto, "Las relaciones comerciales y económicas entre Cuba y los Estados Unidos, *Comercio Exterior*, (Havana), July-Sept. 1963. pp. 5-12.

1529. Torras, Pelegrin, "Cuba, Estados Unidos y la desnuclearización de América Latina," *Cuba Socialista*, (Havana), Oct. 1965. pp. 7-17.
Cuba opposes idea.

1530. "U.S.-Cuban Problems: Four [American] Views," *Foreign Policy Bulletin*, Sept. 15, 1960. pp. 5-8.

1531. Valcárcel, Gustavo, *¡Cuba sí; yanquis no!*, Lima: Universidad Nacional Mayor de San Marcos, 1961. 123 pp.

1532. Wilkins, John R., "Legal Norms and International Economic Development: The Case of Cuba Shipping Restriction in the United States Foreign Assistance Act," *California Law Review*, Oct. 1967. pp. 977-1019.

1533. Williams, William Appleman, "Cuba: Issues and Alternatives," *Annals of the American Academy*, Jan. 1964. pp. 72-80.
On U.S. policy.

1534. Williams, William Appleman, *The United States, Cuba, and Castro*, New York: Monthly Review Press, 1962. 179 pp.

1535. Wilson, L. C., "Monroe Doctrine, Cold War Anachronism: Cuba and the Dominican Republic," *Journal of Politics*, May 1966. pp. 322-346.

1536. Wright, Theodore P., Jr., "United States Electoral Intervention in Cuba," *Inter-American Economic Affairs*, (Washington, D.C.), Winter 1959. pp. 50-71.

4. Guantánamo Naval Base

1537. Alvarez Tabío, Fernando, "La base naval de Guantánamo y el derecho internacional," *Cuba Socialista*, (Havana), July 1962. pp. 9-34.

1538. Anónimo, "Guantánamo," *Cuba*, (Havana), May 1964. pp. 14-19.

1539. Bermejo González, Ernesto, "Guantánamo, una cerca entre dos mundos," *Cuba*, (Havana), No. 12, 1963. pp. 66-82.

1540. Castillo, Emilio, *Conjura contra Cuba en Caimanera*, Havana: Editorial en Marcha, 1961. 31 pp.
"CIA uses Guantánamo base to aid counterrevolutionaries."

1541. Castillo Ramos, Rubén, "Guantánamo," *Bohemia*, (Havana), Mar. 6, 1964. pp. 24-31.

1542. Castro, Fidel, "Declaración emitida en la noche del 27 de mayo de 1966 por el Primer Ministro del Gobierno Revolucionario," *Política Internacional*, No. 14, 1966. pp. 219-220.
On alleged clash between U.S. and Cuban soldiers at Guantánamo.

1543. Díaz, Manuel, "La historia de

Caimanera," *El Mundo*, (Havana), June 5, 1966. p. 9. (supplement).

1544. Editorial, "U.S. Breaks Ties with Cuba, Maintains Treaty Rights in Guantánamo Base," *Current History*, Apr. 1961. pp. 243-244.

1545. Lazar, J., "Cession in Lease of the Guantanamo Bay Naval Station and Cuba's Ultimate Sovereignty," *American Journal of International Law*, Jan. 1969. pp. 116-118.

1546. Mencer, Gejza, "Problèmes juridiques relatifs à la base de Guantánamo et au blocus de Cuba," *Revue de Droit Contemporain*, (Paris), No. 1, 1963. pp. 27-41.

1547. Moris, G. L., "Guantánamo: No Rights of Occupancy," *American Journal of International Law*, Jan. 1969. pp. 114-116.

1548. Olan, A., "Guantánamo—Voenno—morskaia baza SSha no Kube," [Guantánamo, the U.S. naval base in Cuba], *Mezhdunarodnaia zhizn'*, (Moscow), May 1961. pp. 112-115.

1549. Rosengren, Roswell P., "The Value of Guantanamo," *Army*, (Washington), Dec. 1962. pp. 26-28.

1550. Wilcox, Arthur M., "Cuba's Place in U.S. Naval Strategy," *U.S. Naval Institute Proceedings*, Dec. 1962. pp. 38-42.

5. Bay of Pigs—April 1961

1551. Acasuso, Rubén, *Playa Girón, hora 17 y 30; el pez empantanado*, Montevideo: Ediciones Estrella, 1961. 60 pp.

1552. Álvarez, Justina, *Héroes eternos de la patria*, Havana: Ediciones Venceremos, 1964. 582 pp.
Biography of defenders who died in April 1961 invasion.

1553. Álvarez Rios, Baldomero, "América Latina definde autodeterminación de Cuba," *Bohemia*, (Havana), July 30, 1961, pp. 100-103.

1554. Anónimo, "Derrotada la invasión," *INRA*, (Havana), May 1961. pp. 16-31.

1555. Anónimo, *Playa Girón, tumba de la invasión mercenaria; 339, el heroico batallón de Cienfuegos*, Havana: Pubs. Zitros, 1961. 113 pp.

1556. Baeza Flores, Alberto, "Cuba, centro de la guerra fría," *Cuadernos*, (Paris), July 1961. pp. 67-71.

1557. Baran, Paul A., "Cuba Invaded," *Monthly Review*, (New York), July-Aug. 1961. pp. 84-91.

1558. Blanco, Enrique José, *De Playa Girón a Punta del Este*, Buenos Aires, 1962. 94 pp.
OAS.

1559. Brigada de Asalto 2506, *Historia de una agresión; declaraciones y documentos del juicio seguido a la brigada mercenaria organizada por los imperialistas yanquis que invadió a Cuba el 17 de abril de 1961*, Havana: Ediciones Venceremos, 1962. 504 pp.

1560. Castro, Fidel, "Declaración de estado de alerta," *Revolución*, (Havana), Apr. 18, 1961. p. 4.
Response to Apr. 17 Bay of Pigs invasion.

1561. Castro, Fidel, "Fidel interrogó a los mercenarios," *Revolución*, (Havana), Apr. 27, 1961. pp. 1, 7.

1562. Castro, Fidel, *The FAR Airport is Bombed and Havana Woke up under the Imperialist Air Attack,* Havana: Editorial en Marcha, 1962. 31 pp.
Apr. 16, 1961 speech.

1563. Castro, Fidel, "Historia de una invasión," *Lunes de Revolución,* (Havana), May 8, 1961. pp. 17-27.

1564. Castro, Fidel, "Morir por la Patria es vivir," *Bohemia,* (Havana), Apr. 23, 1961. pp. 39-43+.
TV broadcast on Bay of Pigs victory. English edition, *Playa Girón,* Havana: Editorial en Marcha, 1961. 79 pp.

1565. Cuba, Comisión Nacional de los Caídos en Playa Girón, *Playa Girón,* Havana: Imprenta Nacional, 1961. 127 pp.

1566. Cuba, Embajada, Great Britain, *The Invaders of Cuba; Their Supporters, Their Illegality and Their Future Plans,* London, 1961. 15 pp.

1567. Cuba, Ministerio de Justicia, *Historia de una agresión: declaraciones y documentos del juicio seguido a la brigada mercenaria organizada por los imperialistas yanquis que invadió a Cuba el 17 de abril de 1961,* Havana: Ediciones Venceremos, 1962. 504 pp.
Also in English.

1568. Cuba, Ministerio de Justicia, *La sentencia, Brigada de Asalto 2605,* Havana, 1962. 83 pp.
Mimeographed.

1569. Cuba, Ministerio de Relaciones Exteriores, *Cuba demandó indemnización,* Havana: Imprenta Nacional de Cuba, 1961. 84 pp.
Bay of Pigs prisoners.

1570. Cuba, Partido Socialista Popu-

lar, *Héroes de Girón,* Havana: Empresa Consolidada de Artes Gráficas, 1963. 48 pp.

1571. Cuba, Presidencia, *No se apoderaron del aire, porque no había manera de apoderarse de él,* Havana: Imprenta Nacional, 1961. 39 pp.

1572. "Diálogo presidencial con los patriotas cubanos," *Bohemia Libre,* (Miami), Jan. 20, 1963. pp. 44-50, 63.
Kennedy and Bay of Pigs prisoners.

1573. Díaz Versón, Salvador, *Caníbales del siglo XX,* Miami: Editora Libertad, 1962. 123 pp.
Maltreatment of Bay of Pigs prisoners.

1574. Dulles, Allen, *The Craft of Intelligence,* New York: Harper and Row, 1963. 277 pp.
Section on Bay of Pigs.

1575. Dwiggins, D., "Guatemala's Secret Airstrip: Retalhuleu Base," *Nation,* Jan. 7, 1961. pp. 7-9.

1576. Gaja, Filippo, *L'invasione di Cuba,* Firenze, Italy: Parenti Editore, 1961. 326 pp.
Interviews with the prisoners.

1577. González, Raúl, *Gente de Playa Girón,* Havana: Casa de las Américas, 1962. 110 pp.

1578. González Lalondry, Luis, *Sangre en Bahía de Cochinos,* New York, 1965. 154 pp.
Exile version.

1579. Gordon, Jesse, and Hugh B. Hester, "A New Look at Cuba—the Challenge to Kennedy," *New World Review,* Apr. 1961. pp. 12-20.

1580. Johnson, Haynes Bonner, *The*

Bay of Pigs, New York: Norton, 1964. 368 pp.
Exiles' version.

1581. Lamont, Corliss, *The Crime Against Cuba,* New York: Basic Pamphlets, 1961. 39 pp.

1582. Larson, Arthur, "Cuba Incident and the Rule of Law," *Saturday Review,* May 13, 1961. pp. 28, 34-38.

1583. Light, Robert E. and Carl Marzani, *Cuba Versus CIA,* New York: Marzani and Munsell Publishers, 1961. 72 pp.
Bay of Pigs. Pro-Castro.

1584. Massó, José Luis, *Cuba: 17 de abril,* Mexico: Ed. Diana, 1962. 170 pp.
"U.S. betrayed the exiles."

1585. Meluza, Pedro, "Ocultó el New York Times la participación de la CIA en la invasión de Playa Girón," *Granma,* (Havana), June 20, 1966. p. 2.

1586. Meyer, Karl Ernest and Tad Szulc, *The Cuban Invasion,* New York: Praeger, 1962. 160 pp.
CIA and Bay of Pigs.

1587. Miró Cardona, José, "El libro blanco," *Boricua,* (San Juan), May 1963. pp. 52-57+.

1588. Murphy, Charles J., "Cuba: The Record Set Straight," *Fortune,* Sept. 1961. pp. 92-97.

1589. Otero, Lisandro, *Historia de una agresión,* Havana: Ediciones Venceremos, 1962. 504 pp.
Bay of Pigs speeches, documents, articles.

1590. Otero, Lisandro, et al., *Playa Girón, derrota del imperialismo,* Havana: Ediciones R., 1961-1962. 4 vols.

1591. Rozitchner, León, "Ensayo sobre la moral burguesa: a propósito de Playa Girón," *Universidad de la Habana,* (Havana), Mar.-Apr. 1963. pp. 7-141.
Ideology of the Bay of Pigs invaders.

1592. Schumacher, Günter, *Operation Pluto. Die Geschichte einer Invasion,* Berlin: Deutscher Militärverlag, 1966. 276 pp.

1593. Smith, Jean Edward, "The Unanswered Questions; Bay of Pigs," *The Nation,* (New York), Apr. 13, 1964. pp. 360-363.

1594. Stern, Daniel J., "El anticomunista norteamericano y la invasión a Cuba," *Casa de las Américas,* (Havana), Nov. 1962-Feb. 1963. pp. 92-106.

1595. Szulc, Tad and Karl E. Meyer, *The Cuban Invasion,* New York: Praeger, 1962. 156 pp.

1596. Taber, Robert, "Requiem al imperialismo," *Casa de las Américas,* (Havana), May-June 1961. pp. 76-81.

1597. "United States and Soviet Union Exchange Messages in Regard to Events in Cuba; Texts of Three Messages," *Department of State Bulletin,* May 8, 1961. pp. 661-667.

1598. Vera, Aldo, "Fracasó nuestro plan para eliminar a Castro," *Avance Criollo,* (Miami), Mar. 30, 1962. pp. 13, 47.

1599. Walzer, Michael, *Cuba: The Invasion and the Consequences,* New York: Dissent, 1961. 15 pp.

1600. Wheeler, K., "Hell of a Beating in Cuba," *Life,* Apr. 28, 1961. pp. 16-25.

1601. Wright, Quincy, "Intervention and Cuba in 1961," *Proceedings of the American Society of International Law,* (Washington, D.C.), 1961. pp. 2-19.

1602. Zhukov, V. and V. Listov, "The Events of Playa Girón," *International Affairs,* (Moscow), Apr. 1966. pp. 63-70.

6. Missile Crisis—October 1962

a. Documents

1603. Castro, Fidel, *A las armas,* Havana: Gobierno Municipal Revolucionario, 1962. 26 pp.
Reviews missile crisis and conversations with U Thant.

1604. Castro, Fidel, "El bloqueo lo resistiremos; la agresión directa la rechazaremos," *Revolución,* (Havana), Oct. 24, 1962. pp. 1, 7, 8.
Oct. 23, 1962 reply to Kennedy's address the previous day.

1605. Castro, Fidel, "Cuba está lista para librar la batalla decisiva," *Bohemia,* (Havana), Sept. 7, 1962. pp. 58-59.
Reply to J. F. Kennedy's Sept. 4, 1962 statement on Russian military build-up in Cuba.

1606. Castro, Fidel, "Discurso a los Comités de Defensa de la Revolución," *Obra Revolucionaria,* (Havana), No. 27, 1962. pp. 5-12.
Sept. 28, 1962 on Cuba's right to have any weapon it wants.

1607. Castro, Fidel, "Fidel a U Thant: nueva carta," *Revolución,* Nov. 20, 1962. pp. 1.
"No inspection on Cuban territory."

1608. Castro, Fidel, "Fidel Castro en la Universidad," *Revolución,* Nov. 6, 1962. p. 1.

Denounces Soviet withdrawal.

1609. Castro, Fidel, "Fija Fidel las 5 garantías contra la agresión a Cuba," *Revolución,* Oct. 29, 1962. pp. 1, 2.
Five conditions to end missile crisis.

1610. Castro, Fidel, "Fijó Cuba claramente sus puntos de vista a U-Thant," *Revolución,* Oct. 31, 1962. pp. 1, 4.

1611. Castro, Fidel, "Hay un idioma que nosotros no comprenderemos jamás; el idioma de la amenaza," *Bohemia,* (Havana), Sept. 14, 1962. pp. 58-62.
Sept. 10, 1962 speech defying U.S.

1612. Castro, Fidel, "Ordena el Primer Ministro Fidel Castro la nación en pie de guerra," *Revolución,* Oct. 23, 1962. p. 1.

1613. Castro, Fidel, "Queremos soluciones de paz con dignidad," *Bohemia,* (Havana), Nov. 9, 1962. pp. 30-39.
"Soviet withdrawal was a mistake."

1614. Castro, Fidel, "Responde Fidel a 'nota' Yanqui," *Revolución,* Sept. 1, 1967. pp. 1, 2.
Refutes charges of USSR military build-up in Cuba.

1615. Castro, Fidel, "La respuesta de Cuba a Kennedy," *Revolución,* Nov. 26, 1962. p. 1.
About U.S. on-the-spot inspection.

1616. Castro, Fidel, "Se evitó la guerra pero no se ganó la paz," *Revolución,* Jan. 16, 1963. pp. 1, 8-10.
Jan. 15, 1963 speech.

1617. Cuba, Organizaciones Revolucionarias Integradas, *Cuba responde al imperialismo,* Havana: MINFAR, 1963. 14 pp.

1618. Cuba, Organizaciones Revolucionarias Integradas, *Posición de Cuba ante la crisis del Caribe,* Havana: MININD, 1962. 95 pp.

1619. "Declaración del Gobierno Revolucionario del Cuba, del 29 de septiembre de 1962, sobre la Resolución Conjunta del Congreso de los Estados Unidos," *Cuba Socialista,* (Havana), Nov. 1962. pp. 132-139.

1620. Foreign Policy Association, *The Cuban Crisis: A Documentary Record,* New York: Headline Series, 1963. 84 pp.

1621. Kennedy, John F. and Nikita Khrushchev, "United States and Soviet Union Exchange Messages in Regard to Events in Cuba," *Department of State Bulletin,* May 8, 1961. pp. 661-667.

1622. Kennedy, Robert F., *Thirteen Days: A Memoir of the Cuban Missile Crisis,* New York: Norton, 1969. 224 pp.

1623. Rico Galán, Víctor, "Habla Dorticós . . .," *Siempre!,* (Mexico City), Dec. 5, 1962. pp. 6-9. Interview with Cuban president.

1624. Rusk, Dean, "Missile Sites in Cuba; Offensive Purpose Against the Hemisphere," *Vital Speeches,* Nov. 15, 1962. pp. 68-70.

1625. Stevenson, Adlai E., "The Cuban Crisis; a Base for Communist Aggression," *Vital Speeches,* Nov. 15, 1962. pp. 70-76.

1626. Stevenson, Adlai and Valerin A. Zorin, "Has the U.S.S.R. Missiles in Cuba?; United Nations Debate," *Vital Speeches,* Nov. 15, 1962. pp. 77-83.

1627. Thant, U, "The Cuban Affair; Negotiation and Compromise the Only Course," *Vital Speeches,* Nov. 15, 1962. pp. 76-77.

1628. "The U.S. and the Situation in Cuba," *Congressional Digest,* (Washington, D.C.), Nov. 1962. pp. 257+.

1629. United States, Department of State, *U.S. Charges of Soviet Military Build-up in Cuba,* Washington, Nov. 1962. 36 pp. Adlai Stevenson's U.N. statements.

1630. United States, President, *U.S. Response to Soviet Military Build-up in Cuba,* Washington, Oct. 1962. 12 pp. President Kennedy's report to the people.

b. Commentaries

1631. Abel, Elie, *The Missile Crisis,* New York: J. B. Lippincott, 1965. 220 pp. Journalist.

1632. Alba, Víctor, "Bombas Atómicas en Cuba," *Combate,* (San José, Costa Rica), Nov.-Dec. 1962. pp. 59-72.

1633. Alberto Monge, Luis, "Unas lecciones del bloqueo a Cuba," *Combate,* (San José, Costa Rica), Nov.-Dec. 1962. pp. 57-59.

1634. Alexander, Robert J., "Why President Kennedy Was Right in the Cuban Crisis," *New Politics,* (New York), Fall 1962. pp. 41-50.

1635. Allison, Graham T., *Conceptual Models and the Cuban Missile Crisis: National Policy, Organization Process, and Bureau-*

cratic *Politics,* Santa Monica, Calif.: Rand Corporation, 1968. 69 pp.

1636. Altschul, Frank, "Cuba: a Turning Point in World History?" *Looking Ahead,* (Washington, D.C.), Feb. 1963. pp. 1-14+.

1637. Anónimo, "El histórico mensaje de Kruschov, en defensa de la paz mundial y de la independencia de Cuba," *Nueva Era,* (Buenos Aires), Oct. 1962. pp. 1-12.

1638. Anonymous, "Castro Disarmed; Resolution of the Cuban Crisis," *The Round Table,* (London), Dec. 1962. pp. 3-6.

1639. Ascoli, Max, "Escalation from the Bay of Pigs," *The Reporter,* 27, Nov. 8, 1962. pp. 24-25.

1640. Beedham, B., "Cuba and the balance of power," *World Today,* (London), Jan. 1963. pp. 36-41.

1641. Chase, S., "Political Missiles to Cuba," *War/Peace Report,* (New York), Feb. 1963. pp. 9-10.

1642. Chayes, Abram, "Law and the Quarantine of Cuba," *Foreign Affairs,* (New York), Apr. 1963. pp. 550-557.

1643. Chayes, Abram, "The Legal Case for U.S. Action on Cuba," *Department of State Bulletin,* Nov. 19, 1962. pp. 763-765.

1644. Christol, Carl Q. and Charles R. Davis, "The Naval Interdiction of Offensive Weapons and Associated Material to Cuba, 1962," *American Journal of International Law,* July 1963. pp. 525-545.

1645. Crane, Robert D., "The Cuban Crisis: a Strategic Analysis of American and Soviet Policy," *Orbis,* (Philadelphia), Winter 1963. pp. 528-563.

1646. Cuba, Colegio de Abogados, *El bloqueo de Cuba por los piratas yanquis, su total ilegalidad conforme al derecho internacional vigente,* Havana, 1962. 14 pp.

1647. Daniel, James and John G. Hubbell, *Strike in the West, the Complete Story of the Cuban Crisis,* New York: Holt, Rinehart and Winston, 1963. 180 pp. Spanish version also.

1648. Dewart, Leslie, "The Cuban Crisis Revisited," *Studies on the Left,* (Chicago), Spring 1965. pp. 15-40.

1649. Doress, Irvin, "Seven Days from October," *Fact,* (New York), May June 1964. pp. 37-43. Missile crisis.

1650. Draper, Theodore, "Castro and Communism: a Detailed Account of the Background and Consequences of the Missiles Crisis in Cuba," *Reporter,* (New York), Jan. 17, 1963. pp. 35-40+.

1651. Editorial, "The Cuban Crisis in Perspective," *Monthly Review,* (New York), Dec. 1962. pp. 401-413.

1652. Editorial, "Comunicado sobre la orden de alarma de combate data por el comandante Fidel Castro ante las medidas agresivas del imperialismo norteamericano contra Cuba," *Cuba Socialista,* (Havana), Dec. 1962. p. 130. Oct. 23, 1962.

1653. Editorial, "El imperialismo norteamericano está advertido," *Cuba Socialista,* (Havana), Oct. 1962. pp. 87-98.

1654. Editorial, "Respuesta de Cuba al Presidente Kennedy," *Cuba Socialista,* (Havana), Dec. 1962. pp. 1-6.

1655. Editorial, "Le tappe fondamentali del problema di Cuba," *Relazioni Internazionali*, (Milan), Nov. 1962. pp. 1261-1265.

1656. Espín, Vilma, "In the Face of Any Imperialist Aggression, Our People Are and Always Will Be by the Side of the Korean People," *Granma*, June 29, 1969. p. 3.

1657. Franco, Cid, *Bloqueio de Cuba e guerra nuclear*, São Paulo: Editôra Fulgar, 1963. 68 pp.

1658. Freeman, Thomas, (pseud.), *The Crisis in Cuba*, Derby, Conn.: Monarch Books Inc., 1963. 159 pp.
Rightwing interpretation.

1659. Garelli Farias, Miguel José, *La crisis internacional de 1962 y el bloqueo de Cuba*, Mexico: UNAM, 1967. 154 pp.
Legal analysis.

1660. Gelbert, Lionel, "Bases and Blockade in the Caribbean: a Twentieth Century Precedent," *Contemporary Review*, (London), Feb. 1963. pp. 81-83.

1661. González Pedrero, Enrique, *Anatomía de un conflicto*, Xalapa: Universidad Veracruzana, 1963. 136 pp.

1662. Haerdter, Robert, "Monroe-Doktrin und Kuba-Krise," *Aussenpolitik*, (Stuttgart), Nov. 1962. pp. 735-741.

1663. Hagan, Roger, and Bart Bernstein, "Military Value of Missiles in Cuba," *Bulletin of Atomic Scientists*, Feb. 1963. pp. 8-13.

1664. Halsti, Ole R. and R. A. Brody, "Measuring Affect and Action in International Reaction Models. Empirical Materials from the 1962 Cuban Crisis," *Journal of*

Peace Research, (Oslo), No. 3-4, 1964. pp. 17-19.

1665. Harmel, Claude, "Cronología comentada de la crisis cubana," *Este y Oeste*, (Paris), Dec. 15-30, 1962. pp. 3-6.

1666. Horelick, Arnold Lawrence, *The Cuban Missile Crisis; An Analysis of Soviet Calculations and Behavior*, Santa Monica, Calif.: Rand Corp., 1963. 60 pp.

1667. Illán, José M., "La verdad sobre el bloqueo económico de Cuba," *Cuba Nueva*, (Coral Gables), Aug. 1, 1962. pp. 22-24.

1668. Izakov, Boris, "Aspects of the 'Cuban Crisis'," *New Times*, (Moscow), Nov. 7, 1962. pp. 19-21.

1669. Izakov, Boris, "The Negotiations Continue," *New Times*, (Moscow), Nov. 14, 1962. pp. 9-11.
U.S.-Cuban relations.

1670. Kalodkin, A. L., "Morskaia blokada i sovremennol mezhdunarodnol pravo," [the naval blockade and present day international law], *Sov. gas. i. provo.*, (Moscow), Apr. 1963. pp. 92-103.

1671. Kenworthy, E. W., "Cuba Air Photos Started Crisis," *The New York Times*, Nov. 3, 1962. pp. 1ff.

1672. Khrushchev, Nikita S., "Present International Situation and Soviet Foreign Policy," *Political Affairs*, (New York), Jan. 1963. pp. 30-40.
Describes missile crisis.

1673. Knebel, Fletcher, "Washington Crisis: 154 Hours on the Brink of War," *Look*, (New York), Dec. 18, 1962. pp. 42-54.

1674. Knorr, Klaus, "Failure in National Intelligence Estimates, the Case of the Cuban Missiles," *World Politics,* Vol. 16, No. 3, Apr. 1964. pp. 455-467.

1675. Kristol, Irving, "The Case for Intervention in Cuba," *The New Leader,* Oct. 15, 1962. pp. 10-11.

1676. Larson, David L., ed., *The Cuban Crisis of 1962,* Boston: Houghton-Mifflin, 1963. 333 pp. Documents and chronology.

1677. Lavergne, B., "L'affaire de Cuba, l'action du Président Kennedy, le rôle de l'ONU," *Année Politique et Économique,* (Paris), Dec. 1962. pp. 315-338.

1678. Levin, Vitaly, "Tension in the Caribbean," *New Times,* (Moscow), No. 14, Apr. 4, 1962. pp. 13-15.

1679. Manera, Regueyra, E., "Reflexiones sobre la crisis internacional cubana," *Revista de Política Internacional,* (Madrid), Nov.-Dec. 1962. pp. 85-93.

1680. Martel, Benjamín, "Cuba— plaza sitiada," *Cuba Nueva,* (Coral Gables), Sept. 1, 1962. pp. 11-15.

1681. Matteson, Robert E., "Die amerikanische Abriistungspolitik nach der Kuba-Krise," *Europa-Archiv,* (Frankfurt-am-Main), No. 2, 1963. pp. 67-71.

1682. Maza Rodríguez, E., "La crisis del Caribe y la 'promesa de no-invasión'," *Revista de Política Internacional,* (Madrid), Jan.-Feb. 1963. pp. 51-62.

1683. McWhinney, E., " 'Coexistence,' the Cuban Crisis, and Cold War International Law," *International Journal,* (Toronto), Winter 1962-1963. pp. 67-74.

1684. Meeker, L. C., "Defensive Quarantine and the Law," *American Journal of International Law,* July 1963. pp. 512-524.

1685. Monge, Luis Alberto, "Unas lecciones del bloqueo a Cuba," *Combate,* (San José, Costa Rica), Nov.-Dec. 1962. pp. 57-58.

1686. Morgenthau, Hans J., "Cuba— the Wake of Isolation," *Commentary,* (New York), Nov. 1962. pp. 427-429.

1687. Pachter, Henry M., *Collision Course: the Cuban Missile Crisis and Coexistence,* New York: Praeger, 1963, 261 pp. Includes documents.

1688. Pagés, Pedro, "Bombas atómicas en Cuba," *Combate,* (San José, Costa Rica), Nov.-Dec. 1962. pp. 59-71.

1689. Panatela (pseud.), "Some Misunderstanding! a Report from Cuba on How Khrushchev's Tactics Look to Castro," *Reporter,* (New York), Dec. 6, 1962. pp. 33-35.

1690. Partan, Daniel G., "The Cuban Quarantine: Some Implications for Self Defense," *Duke Law Journal,* 1963, no. 4. pp. 696-721.

1691. Pazos, Javier Felipe, "Cuba— 'Long Live the Revolution!'; a Foe of Castro Counsels against Invasion," *The New Republic,* (Washington, D.C.), Nov. 3, 1962. pp. 15-19.

1692. Plank, John N., "Monroe's Doctrine, and Castro's," *New York Times Magazine,* Oct. 7, 1962. p. 30+.

1693. Rego, José, *Ianques contra Cuba: David enfrenta Golias,* São

Paulo: Editôra Fulgor, 1963. 110 pp.
Anti-U.S.

1694. Rodríguez, Manuel L., "A crise cubana, Kruchtchev e o regime de Fidel Castro," *Rumo*, (Lisbon), Nov. 1962. pp. 316-320.

1695. Russell, Bertrand Russell, *Unarmed Victory*, New York: Simon and Schuster, 1963. 155 pp.

1696. Sandiford, R., "La crisi e il bloco d Cuba," *Storia e Politica*, (Milan), Vol. 1, No. 4, Oct. 1962. pp. 642-678.

1697. Schick, F. B., "Cuba y el imperio de la ley," *Cuadernos Americanos*, (Mexico), July-Aug. 1963. pp. 113-127.
Missile crisis.

1698. Steinicke, Dietrich, *Quellenindex zur Cubakrise*, Hamburg: Metzner in Kommission, 1969. 400 pp.

1699. Stone, I. F., "Castro's Startling New Account of Why He Asked for Nuclear Missiles," *I. F. Stone's Bi-Weekly*, (Washington), Dec. 23, 1963. p. 2.

1700. Strange, Susan, "Cuba and After," *The Yearbook of World Affairs*, (London), 1963. pp. 1-28.

1701. Smolansky, Oles M., "Moscow and the Cuban Missile Crisis: Reflections on Khrushchev's Brinkmanship," *Politico*, (Pavia, Italy), Sept. 1968. pp. 509-526.

1702. Thomas, Norman, et al., "Cuba Blockade Crisis: a Symposium," *New Politics*, Fall 1963. pp. 18-97.
9 articles: radical and socialist thought.

1703. Wilson, L. C., "International Law and the United States Cuban Quarantine of 1962," *Journal of Inter-American Studies*, Oct. 1965. pp. 485-493.

1704. Wohlstetter, Roberta, "Cuba and Pearl Harbor: Hindsight and Foresight," *Foreign Affairs*, July 1965. pp. 691-707.

1705. Wrong, Dennis H., "After the Cuban Crisis," *Commentary*, Jan. 1963. pp. 28-33.
U.S. policy.

7. Exiles

1706. Agencia de Informaciones Periodísticas, *Éxodo; un pueblo en fuga del terror*, Miami, 1965. 8 pp.

1707. Agencia de Informaciones Periodísticas, *Un pueblo que huye hacia la libertad y reveses del sistema comunista*, Miami, 1965. 7 pp.

1708. American Council for Nationalities Service, *Cuban Refugee Problems*, New York, 1962. 110 pp.

1709. Anónimo, "Polémica del más bajo nivel: la contrarrevolución en crisis," *Bohemia*, (Havana), Apr. 26, 1963. pp. 38-46.

1710. Anónimo, ¿Por qué luchan los cubanos . . . ? Por la libertad: un derecho y un deber; justificación, Miami: "Cuba," 1968. 22 pp.

1711. Anonymous, "Cuban Refugee Agreement—Whose Victory?," *Communist Affairs*, (Los Angeles), Jan.-Feb. 1966. pp. 13-14.

1712. Baggs, W. C., "Other Miami, city of intrigue," *New York Times Magazine*, Mar. 13, 1960. p. 25+.

1713. Bernard, William S., "The Integration of Immigrants in the

United States," *International Migration Review*, Spring 1967. pp. 23-32.
On Cuban refugee program.

1714. Bracker, Milton, "Cuba's Refugees Live in Hope and Despair," *New York Times Magazine*, Sept. 30, 1962. pp. 21-22, 85-87.

1715. Carrera, Antonio de al, "Cuba: What Now?," *The New Leader*, May 13, 1963. pp. 3-6.
U.S. policy toward the exiles.

1716. Castro, Fidel, "Atacado el litoral habanero," *Revolución*, Aug. 25, 1962. p. 1.
Exile attack on hotel housing Soviet "technicians."

1717. Castro, Fidel, "Discurso pronunciado resumiendo los actos del V Aniversario de los Comités de Defensa de la Revolución," *Política Internacional*, (Havana), No. 11-12, 1965. pp. 225-238.
Sept. 28, 1965. "Cubans can leave island without restrictions."

1718. Castro, Fidel, "Declaraciones del Primer Ministro en respuesta a ciertas manifestaciones del Departamento de Estados de los EE. UU.," *Política Internacional*, No. 11-12, 1965. p. 239.
Sept. 30, 1965 statement on how U.S. should help Cubans become exiles.

1719. Castro, Juana, "My Brother Is a Tyrant and He Must Go," *Life*, (New York), Aug. 28, 1964. pp. 22-23.

1720. Chibás, Raúl, "What Next for Cuba—An Exile's View," *New Republic*, Nov. 10, 1962. p. 9.

1721. Conte Agüero, Luis, *América contra el comunismo*, Miami: Frente Anticomunista Cristiano, 1961. 197 pp.
By helping Cuban exiles Latin American governments will defeat communism.

1722. "Cuba-U.S. Agreement on Refugees," *International Legal Materials*, Nov. 1965. pp. 1118-27.
Document.

1723. Cubillas, Vicente, "De Miami a Cuba, tres años después," *Bohemia*, (Havana), June 4, 1965. pp. 42-44+.
Returned exiles.

1724. Fagen, Richard R., Richard A. Brody and Thomas J. O'Leary, *Cubans in Exile: Disaffection and the Revolution*, Stanford, Calif.: Stanford University Press, 1968. 161 pp.
Useful study.

1725. Fagen, Richard R., and Richard A. Brody, "Cubans in Exile: A Demographic Analysis," *Social Problems*, Spring 1964. pp. 389-401.

1726. González, Marta A., *Bajo palabra*, Havana: Ediciones Venceremos, 1965. 220 pp.
On exiles by returned refugee.

1727. Landau, Saul, "Reflexiones sobre los exilados cubanos," *Casa de las Américas*, (Havana), Sept.-Dec. 1963. pp. 87-92.

1728. Lee, V. T., *Cuban Counterrevolutionaries in the United States: Who Are They?*, New York: Fair Play for Cuba Committee, 1962. 11 pp.

1729. Llerena, Mario, "Razones y dificultades de un gobierno en el exilio," *Bohemia Libre*, (Miami), Oct. 28, 1962. pp. 24-25, 66.

1730. Manrara, Luis V., *El único camino para liberar a Cuba*, Miami, 1967. 20 pp.

1731. Martínez, José A., *El derecho de asilo y el regimen internacional de refugiados,* Mexico: Ediciones Botas, 1961. 174 pp.
Chapters on Cuban refugees.

1732. Martínez Márquez, Guillermo, "Cuba: los exilados y el regreso," *Bohemia Libre Puertoriqueña,* (Caracas), Jan. 13, 1963. pp. 42-43+.

1733. Medrano, Humberto, *Sin patria pero sin amo,* Coral Gables: Service Offset Printers, 1963. 462 pp.
Series of articles by exile commentator.

1734. Micocci, A. A., "New Life for Cuban Exiles," *American Education,* Mar. 1965. pp. 29-33.

1735. Miró Cardona, José, "Anti-Castro War Already Is Under Way," *U.S. News,* Jan. 23, 1961. pp. 79-81.
Former prime minister and head of anti-Castro movement.

1736. Mitchell, William L., "The Cuban Refugee Program," *Social Security Bulletin,* (Washington, D.C.), Mar. 1962. pp. 3-8.

1737. Oettinger, Katherine Brownell, "Services to Unaccompanied Cuban Refugee Children in the United States," *The Social Service Review,* (Chicago), Dec. 1962. pp. 377-384.

1738. Prío Socarrás, Carlos, "Esta es una guerra de independencia; habla el presidente," *Bohemia Libre Puertorriqueña,* (Caracas), Oct. 1963. pp. 26-28+.

1739. Quintana, Jorge, "Cuba's Fight for Freedom," *Vital Speeches of the Day,* (New York), June 15, 1961. pp. 527-530.

1740. Ray, Manuel, "Hay factores internos suficientes para derrocar al comunismo en Cuba," *Bohemia Libre* (New York), Dec. 16, 1962. pp. 31-33, 67.

1741. Senior, Clarence Ollson, *Our Citizens from the Caribbean,* St. Louis: Webster Division, McGraw-Hill, 1965. 122 pp.
Has chapter on Cuban exiles.

1742. St. George, Andrew, "Hit and Run to Cuba with Alpha 66," *Life,* (New York), Nov. 16, 1962. pp. 55-58.
Raids by exiles.

1743. St. George, Andrew, "Vamos! the Buccaneers Attack the Soviet Prey," *Life,* (New York), Apr. 12, 1963. pp. 18-25.
Raids by exiles.

1744. Szulc, Tad, "Guerra—Still the Word in Miami," *New York Times Magazine,* July 5, 1964. pp. 9ff.

1745. Tamargo, Augustín, "Camarioca: un pueblo huye hacia la libertad," *Bohemia,* (Puerto Rico), Nov. 14, 1965. pp. 33-94.
Refugees.

1746. Thomas, John F., "Cuban Refugees in the United States," *International Migration Review,* (New York), Spring 1967. pp. 46-57.

1747. Unidad Nacional Revolucionaria, *Manifiesto programa; Cuba 1961,* Hollywood, Calif., 1961. 66 pp.

1748. United States, Department of State, *Movement of Cuban Refugees to the United States,* Washington: GPO, 1966. 19 pp.
Nov. 6, 1965 Cuba-U.S. agreement arranged via Swiss Em-

bassy in Havana. Also Spanish edition.

1749. United States, Congress, Senate, Judiciary Committee, *Cuban Refugee Problems, Hearings,* Washington, 1962, 304 pp.; 1963, 399 pp.; 1966. 304 pp.

1750. United States, President, *Report to President of United States on Cuban Refugee Problem,* Washington, 1961. 15 pp.
By Tracy S. Voorhees.

1751. Vila, José Jorge and Guillermo Zalamea, *Exilio,* Miami: AIP, 1967. 416 pp.

1752. Yearly, C. K., "Cubans in Miami," *Commonweal,* (New York), Nov. 19, 1965. pp. 210-211.

C. RELATIONS WITH LATIN AMERICA

1. Exporting the Revolution

1753. Anónimo, "Acciones e ingerencias del Castrismo en América Latina," *Este & Oeste,* (Paris), July 30, 1963. pp. 8-17.

1754. Arguedas, Sol, "¿Dónde está el Che Guevara?" *Cuadernos Americanos,* (Mexico), May-June 1966. pp. 67-89.
Che's influence on Fidel and their disputes.

1755. Asencio Suárez, Lázaro, "Lo que significa la muerte de Ernesto Che Guevara," *Bohemia Libre,* (Caracas), Nov. 5, 1967. pp. 27-32; 65-69.

1756. Braña Chansuolme, Manuel, *El aparato,* Coral Gables: Service Offset Printers, 1964. 22 pp.
Cuba's espionage network in Latin America.

1757. Braña, Manuel, *La diplomacia de Fidel Castro en la América Latina,* Miami: Distribuidor Fermín Peraza, 1964. 577 pp.
Cuba's infiltration through its embassies.

1758. Calas, Raúl, "La révolution cubaine et les luttes libératrices des peuples de l'Amérique latine," *Cashiers du Communisme,* (Paris), Oct. 1962. pp. 111-121.

1759. Castro, Fidel, "Clamó el Dr. F. Castro en New York por la unión de todos los pueblos de la América Latina," *Diario de la Marina,* (Havana), Apr. 22, 1959. pp. 1, 2A.

1760. Castro, Fidel, "Discurso en la concentración en conmemoración del XI aniversario del 26 de Julio," *Bohemia,* (Havana), July 31, 1964. pp. 40-54.
On relations with hemisphere.

1761. Castro, Fidel, "Discurso en la conmemoración del Día Internacional del Trabajo," *Política Internacional,* (Havana), No. 10, 1965. pp. 189-206.
On U.S. invasion of Dominican Republic. Calls for worldwide revolutionary offensive.

1762. Castro, Fidel, *Discurso pronunciado con motivo de conmemorarse el X aniversario del asalto a Palacio.* Havana: Editora Política, 1967. 38 pp.
Condemns Latin American communist parties.

1763. Castro, Fidel, *Discurso pronunciado por el Cmdte . . . en el desfile militar con motivo del octavo aniversario de la revolución,* Havana: Editora Política, 1967. 30 pp.
Attacks Latin American communist parties.

1764. Castro, Fidel, "Introducción necesaria al diario del Che," *Bohemia,* (Havana), July 5, 1968. pp. 50-54.
Denounces orthodox communist parties of Latin America for not supporting Che.

1765. Castro, Fidel, "Las condiciones objectivas las hace la historia, pero las subjectivas los hombres," *Granma,* (Havana), July 27, 1966. pp. 2-7.
July 26, 1966 speech on necessity of revolutionary war in Latin America.

1766. Castro, Fidel, "Servirá la experiencia chilena para justificar más el camino de Cuba," *El Mundo,* (Havana), Mar. 20, 1966. pp. 1, 5.
Mar. 19, 1966 statement replying to comment made by Chilean president.

1767. Castro, Fidel, "VI aniversario de la victoria de Girón," *Ediciones el Orientador Revolucionario,* (Havana), No. 8, 1967. 23 pp.
Apr. 19 speech. On revolutionary strategy for Latin America.

1768. Castro, Raúl, *Nosotros sabemos donde tiene su talón de Aquiles el Imperialismo!,* Havana: Comisión de Orientación Revolucionaria del Comité Central del Partido Comunista de Cuba, 1966. 31 pp.
Fomenting Latin American revolutions.

1769. "Comunicado de la conferencia de los Partidos Comunistas de América Latina," *Cuba Socialista,* (Havana), Feb. 1965. pp. 140-142. Met in Havana, Nov. 1964.

1770. Conte Agüero, Luis, *América contra el comunismo,* Miami: Cuba Printing, 1961. 197 pp.
Domino theory.

1771. *Cuban Embassies to Aid in Infiltrating Spies Among Workers,* Washington: Joint Publications Research Service, Nov. 14, 1962. 3 pp.

1772. Donovan, James B., "Castro, Cuba, and Latin America," *National Catholic Education Association Bulletin,* Aug. 1964. pp. 308-14.

1773. Donovan, John, *Red Machete; Communist Infiltration in the Americas,* Indianapolis: Bobbs-Merrill, 1962. 310 pp.
By journalist.

1774. Dubois, Jules, *Operation America; the Communist Conspiracy in Latin America,* New York: Walker, 1963. 361 pp.
Veteran journalist.

1775. Faleroni, Alberto D., *Penetración comunista en el continente a través del castrismo,* Buenos Aires: Frente Americano de la Libertad, 1963. 27 pp.

1776. Galeano,, Eduardo, "'Che' Guevara—the Bolívar of Our Time?" *Monthly Review,* Mar. 1966. pp. 34-42.

1777. Gilly, Adolfo, "'Che' Left Cuba As a Hero—Why?" *Atlas,* Jan. 1966. pp. 39-41.

1778. Guevara, Ernesto, *El diario del Che en Bolivia: noviembre 7, 1966 a octubre 7, 1967,* Havana: Instituto del Libro, 1968. 346 pp.

1779. Halperin, Ernst, *Castro and Latin American Communism,* Cambridge: M.I.T., 1963. 14 pp.

1780. Halperin, Ernst, *Sino-Cuban*

Trends: The Case of Chile, Cambridge: M.I.T., 1963. 163 pp.

1781. Hart, Armando, "En la mayoría de los países de América Latina hay condiciones para la lucha armada," *Granma,* (Havana), Aug. 14, 1966. pp. 6-7.

1782. James, Daniel, ed., *The Complete Bolivian Diaries of 'Che' Guevara and Other Captured Documents,* New York: Stein and Day, 1968. 330 pp.

1783. Macaulay, Neil, 1st Lt., USAR, "Castro's Threat to the Hemisphere," *Marine Corps Gazette,* Feb. 1961. pp. 21-27.
Guerrilla warfare.

1784. Maldonado Denis, Manuel, "Efectos de la revolución cubana en la política puertorriqueña," *Revista de Ciencias Sociales,* (Puerto Rico), Sept. 1964. pp. 271-279.

1785. Mallin, Jay, *Caribbean Crisis,* New York: Doubleday, 1965. 192 pp.
"Castro started the Dominican revolution."

1786. Murkland, H. B., "Fidelism for Export," *Current History,* Apr. 1961. pp. 219-224.

1787. Nearing, Scott, "Cuba y la América Latina; informe de un testigo presencial acerca del Congreso Continental de Solidaridad con Cuba," *Paz y Soberanía,* (Havana), Jan.-Mar. 1964. pp. 13-35.

1788. Nierdergang, Marcel, "La guérrilla revolutionnaire en Amérique Latine," *Le Monde,* (Paris), Feb. 10-16, 1966. p. 4; Feb. 17-23, 1966, p. 3.

1789. Poppino, Rollie E., *International Communism in Latin America: A History of the Move-* *ment, 1917-1963,* New York: Free Press, 1964. 247 pp.
Chapter on Cuban-Latin American Communists relations.

1790. Roig Ortega, P. L., *Como trabajan los espías de Castro,* Miami: Duplex Paper Products, 1964. 95 pp.

1791. Rubottom, Roy R., *International Communism in Latin America,* Washington, 1960. 11 pp.

1792. United States, Congress, House, Committee on Foreign Affairs, *Castro-Communist Subversion in the Western Hemisphere, Hearings,* Washington, 1963. 295 pp.

1793. United States, Congress, House, Committee on Foreign Affairs, *The Communist Threat in Latin America, Hearings,* Washington, 1960. 81 pp.

1794. United States, Congress, House, Committee on Foreign Affairs, *Communism in Latin America, Hearings,* Washington, 1965. 123 pp.

1795. United States, Congress, Senate, Judiciary Committee, *Cuba as a Base for Subversion in America; a Study Presented to the Sub-committee to Investigate the Administration of the Internal Security Act and Other Internal Security Laws,* Washington, 1963. 23 pp.

1796. United States, Department of State, "Department Reports on Cuban Threats to the Western Hemisphere," *Department of State Bulletin,* Jan. 22, 1962. pp. 129-130.
Summary document.

1797. United States, Department of State, "Responsibility of Cuban

Government for Increased International Tensions in the Hemisphere," *Department of State Bulletin,* Aug. 29, 1960. pp. 318-346.

1798. Viera, Eduardo, *El discurso de Fidel y la revolución latinoamericana,* Montevideo: Ediciones de la Comisión Nacional de Propaganda del Partido Comunista, 1962. 52 pp.

2. Impact of Revolution

1799. Adams, Mildred, "Latin America Takes Another Look at Castro," *New York Times Magazine,* Jan. 21, 1961. pp. 73-74.

1800. Alvarez Ríos, Baldomero, "América Latina defiende autodeterminación de Cuba frente al intervencionismo de los Estados Unidos," *Bohemia,* (Havana), July 30, 1961. pp. 100-103.

1801. Arredondo, Alberto, et al., *Conflictos económicos: Cuba comunista y el panorama económico latinoamericano,* Miami: AIP, 1965. 5 pp.

1802. Azicri-Levy, Max, "Cuba: desafío y crisis para Latinoamérica," *Estudios sobre el Comunismo,* (Santiago de Chile), Jan/Mar 1962. pp. 34-42.

1803. Calo, Vincenzo, *Cuba non è una eccezione,* Milan: Longanesi, 1963. 213 pp.
Cuba an example for Latin America.

1804. Baraibar, Carlos de, "La revolución cubana amenaza gravemente el desarrollo común latinoamericano," *Estudios sobre el Comunismo,* (Santiago de Chile), Oct.-Dec. 1960. pp. 1-12.

1805. Castro, Fidel, "Discurso en el décimo aniversario del 26 de Julio," *Obra Revolucionaria,* (Havana), No. 20, 1963. pp. 9-31.
The road to revolution in Latin America.

1806. Castro, Fidel, "El imperialismo no podrá impedir las revoluciones," *Bohemia,* (Havana), Aug. 7, 1964. pp. 80-89.
July 26, 1964 conference with foreign press.

1807. Castro, Fidel, "Séptimo aniversario del 26 de julio," *Obra Revolucionaria,* (Havana), No. 16, 1960. pp. 5-13.
Cuba's revolutionary model for Latin America.

1808. Claude, A., et al., *Eveil aux Ameriques-Cuba,* Paris: Editions Sociales, 1962. 275 pp.
French communists' comment on revolution's impact.

1809. Duch, Juan, *Visión de Cuba, reportaje sobre una realidad,* Mérida, Venezuela: Escritores y Artistas de Yucatán Asociados, 1961. 43 pp.
Reporter.

1810. Ferguson, J. H., "The Cuban Revolution and Latin America," *International Affairs,* (London), No. 3, July 1961. pp. 285-292.

1811. Fitzgibbon, Russell H., "The Revolution Next Door," *The Annals of the American Academy,* Mar. 1961. pp. 113-122.
Impact of Cuba on Latin America.

1812. González, Alfonso, "Castro's Economic Effects on Latin America," *Journal of Inter-American Studies,* Apr. 1969. pp. 286-309.

1813. Gutiérrez Girardot, Rafael, "Lateinamerika un die cubanische

Revolution," *Merkur,* (Stuttgart), No. 3, 1965. pp. 272-284.

1814. Halperin, Ernst, "Castroism—Challenge to the Latin American Communists," *Problems of Communism,* (Washington), Sept.-Oct. 1963. pp. 9-18.

1815. Halperin, Ernst, "What Castro Wants in Latin America," *Current,* (New York), Aug. 1963. pp. 49-53.

1816. Mikhailov, S., "The Cuban Revolution and Latin America," *International Affairs,* (Moscow), Dec. 1963. pp. 44-49.

1817. Núñez, Carlos, *Crónicas de este mundo,* Montevideo: Ediciones Tauro, 1969. 239 pp.

1818. Peréz, Victorino, "Barómetro internacional: Castro y América," *Foro Internacional,* (Mexico), July-Sept. 1961. pp. 7-11.

1819. Ramírez Gómez, R., "Cuba; despertar de América," *Investigación Económica,* (Mexico), 3rd trimester, 1961. pp. 1-267.

1820. Rodríguez, Enrique, "Kuba i revoliutsiia v Latinskoi Amerike," [Cuba and the revolution in Latin America], *Kommunist* (Moscow), Nov. 1963. pp. 100-106.

1821. Salazar Bondy, Sebastián, *Cuba, nuestra revolución,* Lima: Ediciones de la Patria Libre, 1962. 30 pp.

1822. Silvert, Kalman H., "The Island and the Continent: Latin American Development and the Challenge of Cuba," *American Universities Field Staff Reports,* 1961. VIII:1.

1823. Taboada Terán, Nestor, *Cuba, paloma de vuelo popular,* Bolivia:

Editorial Aniversitaria, 1964. 233 pp.
Declarations of Havana. Also in Quechua.

1824. Teichert, Peter C. M., "A América Latina e o impacto socio-economico de revolução cubana," *Revista Brasileira de Política Internacional, (Rio de Janeiro),* Mar. 1962. pp. 89-115.

1825. Timossi, Jorge, *El desafío cubano,* Montevideo: Aportes, 1969. 107 pp.

1826. Various, "Cuba et le Castrisme en Amérique Latine," *Partisans,* (Paris), Apr.-June 1967. 151 pp. Special issue on Castro influence in Latin America with general statements on several of the other Latin American republics.

3. Organization of American States

1827. "American Foreign Ministers Condemn Sino-Soviet Intervention in American States: Seventh Meeting of Consultation of the American Foreign Ministers at San José, Costa Rica," *Department of State Bulletin,* Sept. 12, 1960. pp. 395-409.

1828. Anónimo, "Dos asambleas y dos declaraciones," *INRA,* (Havana), Oct. 1960. pp. 24-35. On San José Declaration and Cuban reply.

1829. Anónimo, "La farsa de la OEA en Punta del Este," *Cuba Socialista,* (Havana), Mar. 1962. pp. 91-102.

1830. Azicri, Max, "The OAS and the Communist Challenge [Concerning Cuba-Based Communist Activity in Latin America]," *Com-*

munist Affairs, July/Aug. 1964. pp. 8-11.

1831. Castro, Fidel, "Cuba llevará al imperialismo al banquillo de los acusados," *Revolución,* Jan. 24, 1962. pp. 2, 8, 9.
Jan. 22, 1962 speech on Punta del Este conference.

1832. Castro, Fidel, *Declaration of Santiago,* Toronto, 1964. 36 pp.
July 26, 1964 reply to OAS approval of Rio Treaty measures against Cuba.

1833. Castro, Fidel, "Discurso ante los 21 en Montevideo," *Revolución,* May 4, 1959. pp. 2, 12.
May 2 speech at OAS-ECOSOC. English translation, Havana: Imprenta Nacional, 1959.

1834. Castro, Fidel, "Esos bandidos que se reunen en la OEA para juzgar y condenar a Cuba," *Política,* (Mexico), Sept. 15-Oct. 14, 1967. pp. I-IV.
Speech of Sept. 28, 1967 to the CDR.

1835. Castro, Fidel, *Second Declaration of Havana,* Havana: Imprenta Nacional, 1962. 41 pp.
Reply to ouster of Cuba from OAS.

1836. Conte Agüero, Luis, *América contra el comunismo,* Miami: Frente Anticomunista Cristiano, 1961. 197 pp.
Advocates collective intervention.

1837. Corominas, Enrique Ventura, *Cuba en Punta del Este,* Buenos Aires: Ediciones Finanzas, 1962. 236 pp.
Includes documents.

1838. "Cuba Eludes Boycott," *Christian Science Monitor,* (Boston), Jan. 30, 1964. p. 1.

1839. Cuba, Ministerio de Relacio-

nes Exteriores, *Cuba en la OEA,* Havana: Imprenta Nacional, 1960. 164 pp.
Cuba's position at Aug. 1960 San José, Costa Rica meeting of OAS Foreign Ministers. Text of the first Declaration of Havana (Sept. 2, 1960).

1840. Cuba, Ministerio de Relaciones Exteriores, *Cuba responde al documento de la OEA sobre la Tricontinental,* Havana, 1967. 29 pp.

1841. Cuba, Ministerio de Relaciones Exteriores, *Declaraciones de La Habana y de Santiago,* Havana: Editora Política, 1965. 164 pp.
Replies to OAS charges.

1842. Cuba, Ministerio de Relaciones Exteriores, *What is the OAS?* Havana, 1968. 46 pp.

1843. Cuba, Presidencia, *Cuba acusa; discursos y conferencia de prensa en Punta del Este,* Havana: Imprenta Nacional, 1962. 40 pp.
Dorticós' speech.

1844. Cuba, Reunión de Consulta de los Ministros de Relaciones Exteriores del Hemisferio, *Cuba en la OEA,* Havana: Imprenta Nacional, 1960. 164 pp.
Held at San José, Costa Rica.

1845. De Santis, Sergio, "Vers la troisième agression contre Cuba," *Partisans,* (Paris), Dec. 1963-Jan. 1964. pp. 87-100.

1846. Drier, John C., "The OAS and the Cuban Crisis," *SAIS Review,* (Washington), Winter 1961. pp. 3-8.

1847. Fabela, Isidro, *El caso de Cuba,* Mexico: Ediciones Cuadernos Americanos, 1960. 87 pp.
Cuba and OAS.

1848. Falcón-Briceño, Marcos, *Reunión de Consulta en Punta del Este: posición de Venezuela*, Caracas: Imprenta Nacional, 1962. 48 pp.
Diplomat opposes Castro.

1849. Fenwick, Charles G., "The Issues at Punta del Este: Non Intervention vs Collective Security," *The American Journal of International Law*, Apr. 1962. pp. 469-474.

1850. Godoy, G., *El caso cubano y la Organización de Estados Americanos*, Madrid: Aldus, 1961. 110 pp.
Calls for OAS intervention.

1851. Guevara, Ernesto, *Cuba en Punta del Este*, Havana: Editorial en Marcha, 1961. 68 pp.

1852. Guevara, Ernesto, *Discurso en la Conferencia del CIES en Punta del Este, Montevideo*, Havana: Ediciones Prensa Libre, 1961. 7 pp.

1853. Guevara, Ernesto, *Interpreta Che Guevara la conferencia de Uruguay*, Havana: Imprenta Nacional, 1961. 16 pp.

1854. Guevara, Ernesto, "Texto del discurso pronunciado en la Reunión del Consejo Interamericano Económico y Social celebrada en Punta del Este," *Ciencias Políticas y Sociales*, (Mexico), July-Sept. 1961. pp. 445-477.

1855. Lechuga, Carlos, "Intervención en la O.E.A.," *Islas*, (Santa Clara), Jan.-June 1962. pp. 29-41.

1856. Listov, V., "Punta del Este— Defeat for Washington," *New Times*, (Moscow), Feb. 14, 1962. pp. 8-10.

1857. Meek, G., "Eighth Meeting of Consultation," *Américas*, (Washington), Mar. 1962. pp. 2-7.

1858. Morrison, De Lessepes, "OAS Foreign Ministers to Consider Extra Continental Intervention," *Department of State Bulletin*, Dec. 25, 1961. pp. 1069-1071.

1859. "Ninth Meeting of Consultation: OAS Foreign Ministers Vote Measures against Cuba," *Américas*, (Washington), Sept. 1964. pp. 1-10.

1860. Oliver, Covey, *The Inter-American Security System and the Cuban Crisis*, Dobbs Ferry, New York: Oceana Publications, 1964. 96 pp.
Assistant Secretary of State for Latin America.

1861. Organización de Estados Americanos, Comisión Interamericana de los Derechos Humanos, *Informe sobre la situación de los derechos humanos en la República de Cuba*, Washington, 1962. 9 pp.

1862. Píriz, Hernán, ed., *La "culpa" la tiene Cuba*, Montevideo: Ediciones Estrella, 1962. 75 pp.
Six newspapermen "expose" the Punta del Este conference.

1863. "OAS Approves Rio Treaty Measures Against Castro Regime," *Department of State Bulletin*, (Washington), Aug. 10, 1964. pp. 174-184.

1864. Organization of American States, *Ninth Meeting of Consultation of Ministers of Foreign Affairs Serving As Organ of Consultation in Application of the Inter-American Treaty of Reciprocal Assistance*, Washington, 1964. 18 pp.
Resolutions condemning Cuba for aggression and intervention in the affairs of Venezuela.

1865. Organization of American States, "Resolutions of OAS Condemning Cuba in OAS Official Records," *Current History*, Jan. 1965. pp. 40-44.

1866. Organization of American States, Inter-American Commission on Human Rights, *Report of the Situation of Political Prisoners and Their Relatives in Cuba*, Washington: Pan American Union, 1961, 8 pp.; 1963. 64 pp.

1867. Organization of American States, Inter-American Economic and Social Council, Delegation from Cuba, *Cuba at Punta del Este*, Havana: Editorial en Marcha, 1962. 67 pp.
1961 meeting.

1868. Organization of American States, Inter-American Peace Committee, *Report to the Eighth Meeting of Consultation of Ministers of Foreign Affairs, 1962*, Washington: Pan American Union, 1962. Variously paged.

1869. Organization of American States, Special Consultative Committee on Security, *Cuba as a Base for Subversion in the Americas*, Washington, 1963. 23 pp.

1870. Organization of American States, Special Consultative Committee on Security, *The First Tricontinental Conference: Another Threat to the Security of the Inter-American System*, Washington, 1966. 79 pp.

1871. "Las sanciones a Cuba," *Finis Terrae*, (Santiago de Chile), Vol. 11, No. 44, July-Aug. 1964. pp. 42-46.

1872. "San José Doctrine: an Anticommunist Declaration by the Organization of American States,"

Economist, (London), Sept. 3, 1960. pp. 869-870.

1873. Scheyven, Raymond, *De Punta del Este a la Habana; América y el Mundo*, Santiago de Chile: Ed. del Pacífico, 1962. 223 pp.

1874. Selser, Gregorio, *Punta del Este contra Sierra Maestra*, Buenos Aires: Editorial Hernández, 1968. 222 pp.

1875. Seltzer, Steve, "Cuban Blockade and the Cold War," *Contemporary Issues*, (New York), Spring 1964. pp. 16-17.

1876. Stillman, Pedro, "Una voz de la revolución cubana en la Conferencia de la OEA," *Marcha*, (Montevideo), Aug. 21, 1959. p. 7.

1877. "Los sucesos en Punta del Este," *Cuadernos Americanos*, (Mexico), Mar.-Apr. 1962. pp. 7-78.
Text of speeches by Manuel Tello, Dean Rusk and Osvaldo Dorticós.

1878. Tondell, Lyman M., ed., *The Inter-American Security System and the Cuban Crisis: Background Papers and Proceedings of the Third Hammarskjöld Forum*, Dobbs Ferry, New York: Oceana, 1964. 96 pp.

1879. Travis, Helen, "Cuba Answers the OAS," *New World Review*, (New York), Apr. 1962. pp. 11-15.

1880. Torras, Pelegrín, "La conferencia de Punta del Este," *Cuba Socialista*, (Havana), Oct. 1961. pp. 53-68.

1881. United States, Department of State, "Responsibility of Cuban Government for Increased International Tensions in the Hemisphere," *Department of State Bul-*

letin, Aug. 29, 1960. pp. 317-346. Memorandum submitted to Inter-American Peace Committee.

1882. United States, Department of State, "United States Submits [June 27, 1960] to Inter-American Peace Committee, Memorandum on Provocative Actions of Cuban Government," *Department of State Bulletin,* July 18, 1960. pp. 79-87.

4. Organización Latinoamericana de Solidaridad

1883. Castro, Fidel, *Discurso en la conmemoración del XIV aniversario del asalto al cuartel Moncada,* Havana: Instituto del Libro, 1967. 36 pp.
July 26, 1967. On OLAS.

1884. Castro, Fidel, *Revolución, revolución, OLAS, solidaridad,* Havana: Instituto del Libro, 1967. 59 pp.
Aug. 10, 1967. Closing session of OLAS condemns conservatism of orthodox communist parties in Latin America.

1885. Cuba, Presidencia, *Discurso en el acto de inauguración de la Primera Conferencia de la Organización Latinoamericana de Solidaridad (OLAS),* Havana: Instituto del Libro, 1967. 17 pp.

1886. Devlin, Kevin, "Permanent Revolutionism of Fidel Castro," *Problems of Communism,* (Washington, D. C.), Jan. 1968. pp. 1-11.
OLAS Conference.

1887. Organización Latinoamericana de Solidaridad, *Actuación de la OEA: Guatemala (1954), República Dominicana (1965), Cuba*

(1959-1967). Intervencionismo y fuerza interamericana de paz, Havana: Instituto del Libro, 1967. 28 pp.

1888. Organización Latinoamericana de Solidaridad, *América Latina y la educación,* Havana: Instituto del Libro, 1967. 63 pp.

1889. Organización Latinoamericana de Solidaridad, *Declaración general,* Havana: Dirección Nacional de los CDR, 1967. 14 pp.

1890. Organización Latinoamericana de Solidaridad, (OLAS), *Documentos aprobados,* Havana, 1967. 79 pp.

1891. Organización Latinoamericana de Solidaridad, *El imperialismo, deformador de nuestra tradición histórica,* Havana: Instituto del Libro, 1967. 31 pp.

1892. Organización Latinoamericana de Solidaridad, *Informe de la delegación cubana a la primera conferencia de la OLAS,* Havana, 1967. 159 pp.

1893. Organización Latinoamericana de Solidaridad, *La penetración imperialista en: literatura, arquitectura, artes plásticas, cinematografía,* Havana: Instituto del Libro, 1967. 15 pp.

1894. Organización Latinoamericana de Solidaridad, *Penetración y expoliación del imperialismo en la cultura latinoamericana,* Havana: Instituto del Libro, 1967. 35 pp.

1895. Organización Latinoamericana de Solidaridad, *Primera conferencia,* Havana: Instituto del Libro, 1967. 140 pp.

1896. Organization of American States, Consultative Committee on Security, *First Conference of the Latin American Solidarity Organization (LASO)*, Washington, 1968. 24 pp.

1897. "Primera conferencia de solidaridad de los pueblos de América Latina," *Política*, (Mexico), July 15-31, 1967. pp. XVI-XVIII, Sept. 1-30, 1967. pp. XL-LXIII, Oct. 1-14, 1967. pp. V-XLI.
Documents.

1898. U.S., Congress, Senate, Judiciary Committee, Subcommittee to Investigate the Administration of the Internal Security Act, *The First Conference of the Latin American Solidarity Organization, July 28-August 5, 1967; a Staff Study*, Washington, 1967. 124 pp.

5. Relations With Individual Countries

1899. Anónimo, "Trujillo, verdadero jefe de la contrarevolución," *Revolución*, (Havana), Aug. 20, 1959. p. 16.

1900. Betancourt, Rómulo, "That Man in Cuba," *Atlas*, (New York), March 1965. pp. 164-166.

1901. Bremauntz, Alberto, *Mexico y la revolución socialista cubana*, Morelia, Michoacán, Mexico: Fímex, 1966. 88 pp.

1902. Carpio Castello, Rubén, *México, Cuba y Venezuela*, Caracas: Imp. Nac., 1961. 226 pp.

1903. Castro, Fidel, "Conferenció con el Presidente electo de Venezuela, Dr. Rómulo Betancourt," *Diario de la Marina*, (Havana), Jan. 27, 1959. pp. 1, 8B.

1904. Castro, Fidel, "Estamos armados hasta los dientes porque el país capitalista mas poderoso nos

amenaza," *Revolución*, Nov. 18, 1961. pp. 1-6.
Attack on Rómulo Betancourt.

1905. Communist Party of Venezuela, "Le bureau politique du P. C. vénézuélien rejette avec violence les accusations de M. Fidel Castro," *Le Monde*, (Paris), Mar. 16-22, 1967. p. 5.

1906. Domingo, Alberto, "Cuba, Venezuela, la O.E.A.," *Política*, (Mexico), Mar. 14, 1964. p. 15.

1907. Dorticós Torrado, Osvaldo, "Cuba y México," *Cuadernos Americanos* (Mexico), July-Aug. 1960. pp. 11-12.

1908. Fenn, Peggy, "Non-intervention and Self-determination as Cornerstones of Mexican Foreign Policy; Their Application to the Cuban Crisis," *Topic*, (Washington, D.C.), Fall 1962. pp. 39-53.

1909. Fernández, Jesse, "Tres días con Fidel en Trinidad," *Revolución*, (Havana), Aug. 15, 1959. p. 18.
Trujillo's attacks on Cuba.

1910. Granma, *El insólito caso del espía de la CIA*, Havana: Instituto del Libro, 1969. 164 pp.

1911. López Mateos, Adolfo, "México y Cuba," *Cuadernos Americanos*, (Mexico), July-Aug. 1960. pp. 9-10.

1912. Martínez Suárez, F., *Tres años de Castro-comunismo; Venezuela ante la agresión totalitaria*, Caracas, 1962. 135 pp.

1913. Organization of American States, Council, *Report of the Investigating Committee*, Washington: Pan American Union, Feb. 18, 1964. 112 pp.
On Venezuelan charges of aggression against Cuba.

1914. Vázquez Candela, Euclides, "Historia de la conspiración," *Revolución*, Aug. 17, 1959. pp. 17-19; 22-25.
Trujillo and counterrevolution.

1915. Venezuela, Ministerio de Relaciones Exteriores, *Seis años de agresión*, Caracas: Imprenta Nacional, 1966. 95 pp.
On Cuba-supported guerrillas in Venezuela.

1916. Venezuela, Oficina Central de Información, *Six Years of Aggression*, Caracas, 1967. 95 pp.

1917. Venezuela, Presidencia, *Venezuela y Cuba; rompimiento de relaciones, respaldo nacional*, Caracas: Impr. Nacional, 1961. 124 pp.

1918. Whitaker, Arthur P., "Cuba's Intervention in Venezuela: a Test of OAS," *Orbis*, Fall 1964. pp. 511-536.
1963 incident.

D. RELATIONS WITH SOVIET RUSSIA
(See also Missile Crisis)

1919. Andrianov, Vasilii Vasilevich, *Nach drug Kuba*, [Our Friend Cuba], Moscow: Izdatelstvo Instituta Meshdunarodnij otnoschenii, 1963. 102 pp.

1920. Baeza Flores, Alberto, "La URSS en Cuba; historia y crítica de la táctica del Partido Comunista Cubano," *Estudios sobre la Unión Sovietica*, (Munich), Dec. 1963. pp. 3-87.

1921. Bhattacharya, Sauridapa, "Cuban-Soviet relations under Castro, 1959-1964," *Studies on the Soviet Union*, (Munich), No. 3, 1965. pp. 27-36.

1922. Bolgarov, N. P., *Joint Russian-Cuban Oceanographic Studies*, Washington: Joint Publications Research Service, Sept. 30, 1966. 7 pp.

1923. Castro, Fidel, "Comunicado conjunto soviético-cubano," *Revolución*, May 25, 1963. pp. 2, 3.
From Moscow.

1924. Castro, Fidel, "Cordial reunión de Fidel con la familia Jruschov," *Revolución*, May 2, 1963. p. 7.

1925. Castro, Fidel, "Joint Soviet-Cuban Communiqué on Stay of Fidel Castro in the Soviet Union," *Current Soviet Documents*, (New York), Feb. 10, 1964. pp. 19-26.
Translated from Soviet press of Jan. 23, 1964.

1926. Cepero Bonilla, Raúl, *El convenio cubano-soviético*, Havana: Editorial Echevarría, 1960. 45 pp.
Also in English.

1927. "Comunicado cubano-soviético del 3 de septiembre de 1962," *Cuba Socialista*, (Havana), Oct. 1962. pp. 129-131.

1928. Cuba, Tratados, "Comunicado conjunto cubano-soviético sobre la estancia del Primer Ministro de la República de Cuba, Fidel Castro, en la Unión Soviética," *Cuba Socialista*, (Havana), Feb. 1964. pp. 157-164.

1929. Cuba, Tratados, "Texto del convenio a largo plazo sobre suministro de azúcar a la URSS por parte de la República de Cuba," *Cuba Socialista*, (Havana), Feb. 1964. p. 165.

1930. "Declaración conjunta soviética cubana," *Cuba Socialista*, (Havana), June 1963. pp. 17-18.
Document.

1931. "Druzhba i edinstovo," [Friendship and Unity], *Novoe Vremia*, (Moscow), Feb. 1964. pp. 1-2.
USSR-Cuban relations.

1932. Erven, L., "The Khrushchev-Castro Talks," *Review of International Affairs*, (Belgrade), Feb. 5, 1964. pp. 8-9.

1933. Ferraris, Agustín, *Cuba en la problemática internacional*, Buenos Aires: Editorial Treinta Días, 1965. 93 pp.
Traces Cuban gravitation toward USSR.

1934. González, Edward, "Castro's Revolution, Cuban Communist Appeals and the Soviet Response," *World Politics*, (Princeton), Oct. 1968. pp. 39-68.

1935. González, Edward, *The Cuban Revolution and the Soviet Union, 1959-1960*, Los Angeles: University of California, Ph.D. dissertation, 1966.

1936. Halperin, Ernst, *Cuba on Kremlin Path*, Washington: G.P.O., 1962. 37 pp.

1937. Jackson, D. Bruce, *Castro, the Kremlin, and Communism in Latin America*, Baltimore: Johns Hopkins Press, 1969. 163 pp.

1938. "Joint Soviet-Cuban Communique on Stay of Fidel Castro in the Soviet Union," *Current Soviet Documents*, (New York), Feb. 10, 1964. pp. 19-26.
Translated from *Pravda* of Jan. 23.

1939. Julien, Claude, "Les relations tumultueuses de Moscou et de La Havane," *Le Monde*, (Paris), June 22-28, 1967. pp. 1, 4.

1940. Khrushchev, Nikita S., and Fidel Castro, "Friendship Rally Speeches," *Current Digest of the Soviet Press*, (Ann Arbor), June 19, 1963. pp. 3-8.
Speeches of May 23, 1963.

1941. Lukovets, A., ed., *Narodi SSSR i Kubi naveki vmeste*, [The Peoples of the USSR and Cuba Will Always March Together], Moscow: Pravda, 1963. 446 pp.
Documents. Also Spanish version.

1942. Ostroverkhyi, I. I., *Krepnut' nashei druzhbe*, [Our friendly ties will grow stronger], Kiev: Zanannia, 1964. 48 pp.

1943. Pravda, *Los pueblos de la URSS y Cuba marcharán siempre juntos; documentos sobre la amistad soviético-cubana*, Moscow: Ediciones Pravda, 1963. 438 pp.

1944. Pravda, *¡Viva Cuba! Visita de Fidel Castro Ruz a la Unión Soviética*, Moscow: Ediciones Pravda, 1963. 191 pp.

1945. Suárez, Andrés, "Castro Between Moscow and Peking," *Problems of Communism*, (Washington), Sept.-Oct. 1963. pp. 18-26.

1946. Torras, Jacinto, "Dos años de relaciones fraternales entre Cuba y la Unión Soviética," *Cuba Socialista*, (Havana), June 1962. pp. 1-7.

1947. Tretiak, Daniel, "Cuba and the Soviet Union: the Growing Accommodation, 1964-65," *Orbis*, Summer 1967. pp. 439-458.

1948. U.S.S.R., "Texto completo del comunicado de la URSS en apoya a Cuba," *Revolución*, Feb. 19, 1962. p. 2.

1949. Wordemann, Franz, "Fiederinsel Kuba. Fidel Castro und der Kommunismus," *Der Monat*, (Frankfurt-Main), No. 134, 1959-1960. pp. 12-21.

1. Cuban Policy

1950. Castro, Fidel, "An Eternal 'Viva!' to the Immortal Lenin!" *Granma*, (Havana), May 3, 1970. pp. 1-4.

1951. Castro, Fidel, "Castro in Red Square," *New World Review*, (New York), June 1963. pp. 14-17.

1952. Castro, Fidel, "Comunicado de Fidel Castro al Gobierno de la URSS," *Revolución*, Feb. 26, 1962. p. 5.

1953. Castro, Fidel, "La declaración soviética ha sido formulada de manera espontánea," *Revolución*, July 11, 1960. pp. 2, 21.
On USSR pledge to purchase Cuban sugar.

1954. Castro, Fidel, *La división frente al enemigo no fue nunca una estrategia revolucionaria ni inteligente*, Havana: Comisión de Orientación Revolucionaria, 1965. 15 pp.
Mar. 13, 1965 speech against Sino-Soviet conflict. Also in English.

1955. Castro, Fidel, "Discurso sobre su viaje a la Unión Soviética," *Obra Revolucionaria*, (Havana), No. 15, 1963. pp. 9-46.
June 4, 1963 speech.

1956. Castro, Fidel, "Ejemplar la amistad de Cuba y URSS," *Revolución*, May 9, 1963. pp. 1, 5.
Statement while in U.S.S.R.

1957. Castro, Fidel, "Fidel elogia el espíritu revolucionario de la Unión Soviética," *Revolución*, May 2, 1963. p. 16.

1958. Castro, Fidel, *El gobierno soviético siempre, espontáneamente*

nos ha ayudado, Havana: Ediciones Prensa Libre, 1961. 11 pp.
July 5, 1961 speech.

1959. Castro, Fidel, "Informe al pueblo sobre su reciente visita a la URSS," *Bohemia*, (Havana), Jan. 31, 1964. pp. 44-55.
Jan. 23, 1964 speech. "Soviet solidarity is firm and decisive."

1960. Castro, Fidel, "Interview With Richard Eder," *New York Times*, July 6, 1964. pp. 1, 12.
On peaceful coexistence.

1961. Castro, Fidel, "Mensaje de Fidel a Nikita Jruschov," *Revolución*, (Havana), June 5, 1963. p. 1.
Expresses solidarity with USSR.

1962. Castro, Fidel, "Lo que ha protegido esta revolución, lo que la hizo posible, fue la sangre de los hijos de este pueblo," *El Mundo*, (Havana), Aug. 24, 1968. pp. 2-5.
Speech of Aug. 23, 1968 supporting Soviet invasion of Czechoslovakia.

1963. Castro, Fidel, "Soviet-Cuban Solidarity," *Political Affairs*, (New York), July 1963. pp. 19-23.

1964. Castro, Fidel, "A Speech to Soviet Technicians on the Occasion of their Departure," *Political Affairs*, Nov. 1962. pp. 31-36.
June 29, 1962.

1965. Castro, Raúl, "Informe del comandante Raúl Castro," *Granma*, (Havana), Feb. 11, 1968. pp. 7, 8.
On Soviet intrigue.

1966. Cuba, Presidencia, *Cuba y la URSS, amistad y solidaridad*, Havana: Imprenta Nacional, 1961. 15 pp.

1967. Editorial, "Fidel Marches to

His Own Tune," *Economist*, (London), Feb. 3, 1968. p. 30.
Cuba-U.S.S.R. relations.

1968. "Joint Soviet-Cuban Communiqué on the Visit of President Osvaldo Dorticós Torrado of Cuba to the Soviet Union," *Current Digest of the Soviet Press*, (Ann Arbor), Nov. 11, 1964. pp. 23-24.
Oct. 14-17 visit.

1969. Ortega, Antonio, et al., "¿Qué significa el viaje de Fidel a Moscú?" *Bohemia Libre*, (Caracas), May 26, 1963. pp. 30-34+.

1970. Rodríguez, Carlos R., "Speech on Behalf of the Central Committee of the Communist Party of Cuba at the Moscow Conference," *Granma*, (Havana). June 15, 1969. p. 6.

2. Russian Policy

1971. Abdurazakov, B., "Kuba no odinoka," [Cuba is not alone], *Kommunist Uzbekistana*, Oct. 1964. pp. 85-92.

1972. Anonymous, "New Soviet Military Complex in Pinar del Rio," *Free Cuba News*, (Washington), Aug. 31, 1963.

1973. Bartos, Robert E., *The Soviet Penetration of Cuba*, Oberammergau, Germany, 1962. 59 pp.
U.S. Army Intelligence study.

1974. Berner, Wolfgang W., "Soviet Strategy Toward Cuba. Latin America and the Third World," *Institute for the Study of the USSR Bulletin*, (Germany), July 1968. pp. 3-12.

1975. Brzezinski, Zbigniew, "Cuba in Soviet Strategy," *New Republic*,

(Washington), Nov. 3, 1962. pp. 7-8.

1976. Burks, David, *Soviet Policy for Castro's Cuba*, Columbus: Ohio State University Press, 1964. 26 pp.

1977. "Communiqué on Mikoyan-Guevara Talks in Moscow," *Current Digest of the Soviet Press*, (Ann Arbor), Jan. 18, 1961. pp. 21-23.
Dec. 20, 1960 meeting.

1978. Goldenberg, Boris, "South of Cuba: Latin America in the Soviet Mirror," *Survey*, (London), July-Sept. 1961. pp. 12-17.

1979. Cruz Cobos, A., *La trampa china de Kruschev*, Caracas: Eds. del Exilio, 1964. 268 pp.

1980. "Cuba: from Protests to Removal of Soviet Missiles," *The Current Digest of the Soviet Press*, (Ann Arbor), Nov. 21, 1962. pp. 3-15.

1981. "Declaración del gobierno de la URSS el 11 de septiembre de 1962, en apoyo de Cuba, contra los planes agresivos norteamericanos," *Cuba Socialista*, (Havana), Oct. 1962. pp. 131-142.

1982. "Declaración del gobierno de la URSS en apoyo a Cuba hecha el 18 de Febrero de 1962," *Cuba Socialista*, (Havana), Mar. 1962. pp. 131-140.

1983. "Discurso de N. Jruschov en el acto de amistad soviético-cubana," *Cuba Socialista*, (Havana), July 1962. pp. 91-108.

1984. Hart, Armando, "Discurso en nombre del CC del PCC al XXIII Congreso del PCUS," *Granma*, (Havana), Apr. 1, 1966. p. 2.

1985. Hinterhaff, Eugene, "Sawjetische Wassen nach drei Kontinenten," *Aussenpolitik,* (Stuttgart), Nov. 1962. pp. 725-734.

1986. Khrushchev, Nikita S., *Druzhba-naveki,* [Eternal friendship], Moscow: Gospolitizdat, 1962. 19 pp.
June 2 speech to Cuban students in the USSR.

1987. Khrushchev, N. S., "Rockets Over Cuba a 'Symbolic' Declaration," *Current Digest of the Soviet Press,* (Ann Arbor), Nov. 30, 1960. pp. 6-7.

1988. Khrushchev, Nikita S., *Sovremennoe mezhdunarodnoe polozhenie i vneshniaia politika Sovetskogo Oviuzu, dokład na sessii Verkhovnogo Soveta SSSR 12 dekabria 1962 goda,* [The present day international situation and the foreign policy of the Soviet Union; a report to the session of the Supreme Soviet on December 12, 1962], Moscow: Gospolitizdat, 1962. 63 pp.

1989. *La URSS salvó la paz, solidaridad con Cuba,* Montevideo: Publicaciones de la revista URSS, 1963. 59 pp.

1990. Mikoyan, Anastas I., *Mikoyan in Cuba,* New York: Crosscurrents Press, 1960. 88 pp.

1991. Monahan, James and K. O. Gilmore, *The Great Deception: the Inside Story of How the Kremlin Took Over Cuba,* New York: Farrar, Strauss, 1963. 213 pp.

1992. Niedergang, Marcel, "Les attaques de la presse sovietique et communiste d'Europe centrale provoquent l'indignation des dirigeants cubains," *Le Monde,* (Paris), Oct. 3-9, 1967. p. 1.

1993. Roca, Blas, *El XXII Congreso del Partido Comunista de la URSS, y el desarrollo de la revolución cubana,* Havana, 1961. 62 pp.

1994. Synnestedt, Sig, "Red Drive in Cuba," *Current History,* Oct. 1963. pp. 216-222+.

1995. Tass, "Statement on Aid to Cuba and U.S. 'Provocations,'" *The Current Digest of the Soviet Press,* (Ann Arbor), Oct. 10, 1962. pp. 13-15+.

1996. Weyl, Nathaniel, *Red Star Over Cuba, the Russian Assault on the Western Hemisphere,* New York: Devin-Adair, 1960. 222 pp.

1997. Wilson, D. P., "Strategic Projections and Policy Options in the Soviet-Cuban Relationship," *Orbis,* Summer 1968. pp. 504-517.

3. Economic Aid

1998. Arkhipov, I., "Soviet-Cuban Economic Co-operation," *International Affairs,* (Moscow), Dec. 1963. pp. 50-53.

1999. Castro, Fidel, "Fidel en la firma del convenio con la URSS," *Revolución,* Aug. 4, 1962. pp. 1, 5.
Economic agreement.

2000. Castro, Fidel, "Nos sentimos capaces de resistir a los imperialistas y combatir contra ellos," *Bohemia,* (Havana), May 21, 1965. pp. 40-43.
May 14, 1965 speech on Soviet aid.

2001. Maldonado, R., "Cuban-Soviet Commercial Ties Strengthen and Develop," *Vneshmara Torgovlia,* (Moscow), Aug. 1962. pp. 24-25.

2002. Mikoyan, A. I., "On Cuba,"

New Times, (Moscow), Feb. 1960. pp. 16-17.
Feb. 16 press conference.

2003. Riccardi, Antonio, "La ayuda económica y la cooperación científica y técnica de los países socialistas a Cuba," *Bohemia,* (Havana), Aug. 17, 1962. pp. 100-102+.

2004. Roldán, Luisa, "El puente petrolero URSS-Cuba," *Cuba,* (Havana), May 1964. pp. 38-41.

2005. Walters, Robert, "Soviet Economic Aid to Cuba: 1959-1964," *International Affairs,* (London), Jan. 1966. pp. 74-86.

4. Military Aid

2006. Anónimo, "Amigos en el puerto," *Cuba Internacional,* (Havana), Oct. 1969. pp. 10-19.
Soviet warships in Cuba.

2007. Anónimo, "En Cuba el Ministro de Defensa de la URSS Mariscal Andrei A. Grechko," *Bohemia,* (Havana), Nov. 21, 1969. pp. 66-69.

2008. Anonymous, "Predosterezhenie agressoram," [A warning to aggressors], *Novoe vremia,* (Moscow), Sept. 1962. pp. 1-3.
Soviet military assistance.

2009. Editorial, "Extraordinaria ayuda militar y técnica de a URSS," *Bohemia,* (Havana), Sept. 7, 1962. p. 71.

2010. Mallin, Jay, *Fortress Cuba; Russia's American Base,* Chicago: H. Regnery Co., 1965. 192 pp.
Journalistic.

2011. Navarro, M., *An Analysis of Soviet Reasons for the Military Build-up in Cuba,* Maxwell Air Force Base, Alabama, 1964. 50 pp.

2012. Portell Vilá, Herminio, "Intervención militar soviética en América," *Bohemia Libre,* (Caracas), July 14, 1963. pp. 28-29+.

2013. "Sino-Soviet Bloc Military Aid to Cuba Summarized," *Department of State Bulletin,* Apr. 16, 1962. pp. 644-646.

2014. U.S. Department of State, *Charges of Soviet Military Build-up in Cuba,* Washington, 1962. 36 pp.

5. "Satellite?"

2015. Arana, Orlando A., "Cuba: First Communist State in America," *Ukrainian Quarterly,* Fall 1966. pp. 246-259.

2016. Aubry, Michel, *Cuba, naçao independente au satélite?,* Rio de Janeiro: Ed. GRD, 1963. 75 pp.
"Satellite."

2017. James, Daniel, *Cuba: the First Soviet Satellite in the Americas,* New York: Avon Books, 1961. 320 pp.
Communist conspiracy theory.

2018. Manrara, Luis V., "Cuba in Communist World Strategy; the 'Show Case' Theory," *Vital Speeches,* Feb. 1, 1963. pp. 236-240.

2019. Massó, José Luis, *Cuba R.S.S.,* Miami: Casablanca Printing Corp., 1964. 164 pp.
"Cuba is a satellite of the Soviet Union." Exile.

E. RELATIONS WITH THE REST OF THE WORLD

1. United Nations

2020. Anónimo, "Cuba derrota moral y políticamente al imperialismo norteamericano en la ONU," *Cuba Socialista*, (Havana), Nov. 1962. pp. 80-96.

2021. Castro, Fidel, *Discurso ante la Organización de los Naciones Unidas el 26 de septiembre de 1960,* Havana: Oficina del Historiador de la Ciudad, 1960. 70 pp.
Denounces imperialism. Advocates peace.

2022. Cuba, Ministerio de Relaciones Exteriores, *Apelación de Cuba al Consejo de Seguridad de las Naciones Unidas; denuncia formulada por la Gobierno Revolucionario contra el Gobierno de los Estados Unidos de Norteamérica,* Havana: Imprenta Nacional, 1960. 59 pp.

2023. Cuba, Ministerio de Relaciones Exteriores, *Cuban Protest to the United Nations,* Havana, 1963. 28 pp.

2024. Cuba, Presidencia, *Speech to the United Nations,* New York: Fair Play for Cuba Committee, 1962. 18 pp.
Oct. 8, 1962.

2025. "Efforts to Negotiate Agreement for Peaceful Settlement," *United Nations Review,* (New York), Nov. 1962. pp. 14-15.
U.S. relations.

2026. Glick, Edward B., "Cuba and the Fifteenth UN General Assembly: a Case Study in Regional Disassociation," *Journal of Inter-American Studies,* Apr. 1964. pp. 235-248.

2027. Goldenberg, Gregorio, *Misión a la ONU,* Havana: Editorial Vanguardia Obrera, 1960. 305 pp.
By Cuban delegate.

2028. Guevara, Ernesto, *Ha sonado la hora postrera del colonialismo,* Havana: Ministerio de Relaciones Exteriores, 1965. 38 pp.
Speech at U.N.

2029. "Khrushchev va al encuentro de Fidel," *Revolución,* (Havana), Sept. 21, 1960. pp. 1, 20.
At the UN.

2030. Lechuga Hevia, Carlos, "Cuba at the United Nations," *Revolution,* (Paris), Vol. 1, No. 7, Nov. 1963. pp. 59-61.
Interview with Cuban delegates.

2031. Lechuga, Carlos, *Cuba's Road to Peace,* Toronto: Fair Play for Cuba Committee, 1963. 12 pp.
Speech by UN delegate.

2032. Lodge, Henry Cabot, "Security Council Considers Cuban Complaint: Texts of Statements Made by U.S. and a Resolution Adopted on July 19, 1960," *Department of State Bulletin,* Aug. 8, 1960. pp. 199-205.

2033. Nizard, Lucien, "La question cubaine devant de Conseil de Securité," *Revue Generale De Droit International,* (Paris), July-Sept. 1962. pp. 486-545.

2034. "No Action on Cuba's Complaint against the United States," *United Nations Review,* Mar. 1962. pp. 13-15.

2035. Padilla Nervo, Luis, "Presencia de México en las Naciones Unidas. El caso de Cuba," *Cuadernos Americanos,* (Mexico), May-June 1963. pp. 72-87.

2036. Pardo Llada, José, *La delegación cubana ante la XV Asamblea General de la ONU,* Havana, 1960. 48 pp.

2037. Roa, Raúl, *Cuba denuncia al patrullaje yankee en el Caribe como actividad intervencionista*

del imperialismo, Havana: Imprenta Nacional, 1960. 15 pp.
Foreign Minister's UN speech.

2038. Stevenson, Adlai E., "UN General Assembly Debates Cuban Complaint," *Department of State Bulletin,* May 8, 1961. pp. 667-685.
Statements, texts of resolutions.

2039. Stevenson, Adlai E., "U.N. Security Council Rejects Cuban Call for Opinion of World Court on OAS Action," *Department of State Bulletin,* Apr. 23, 1962. pp. 684-694.

2040. United Nations, General Assembly, *Complaint by the Revolutionary Government of Cuba Regarding the Various Plans of Aggression and Acts of Intervention Being Executed by the Government of the United States,* New York: mimeograph, Mar. 17, 1960. 7 pp.

2041. United Nations, General Assembly, *Letter from the Representative of the United States of America,* New York, Oct. 13, 1960. 34 pp.
Reply to allegations made in the U.N. by Castro.

2042. United Nations, Security Council, *Provocative Actions of the Government of Cuba against the United States which Have Served to Increase Tensions in the Caribbean Area,* New York, July 15, 1960. 12 pp.

2. Europe

2043. Barbieri, Frane, "Yugoslavia, Cuba, la Tricontinental y Rico: conclusiones prefabricadas," *Granma,* (Havana), May 4, 1966. p. 2.
Cuban-Yugoslav disputes.

2044. Castro, Fidel, "Conferencia de prensa," *Revolución,* Jan. 21, 1960. pp. 1, 2, 6.
Expulsion of Spanish ambassador.

2045. "Comunicado conjunto polaco-cubano," *Cuba Socialista,* (Havana), July 1961. pp. 139-142.

2046. Cuba, Partido Comunista, *Respuesta a la prensa yugoslava,* Havana: Ediciones Granma, 1966. 93 pp.
Various articles.

2047. Editorial, "Ataques de la prensa yugoslava a las posiciones revolucionarias de Cuba," *Granma,* (Havana), May 4, 1966. p. 1.

2048. Editorial, "Britain Rejects Call for Cuba Boycott," *The Times Weekly Review,* (London), Oct. 11, 1962. p. 6.

2049. Editorial, "Nuestro agente en La Habana," *Marcha,* (Montevideo), Jan. 23, 1959. pp. 9-10.
British weapons to Batista.

2050. Rand Corp., *British Attitudes in the Cuban Crisis,* Santa Monica, 1963. 23 pp.

2051. Schaedler, Silvio, "Spain and Cuba," *Swiss Review of World Affairs,* (Chicago), Jan. 1963. pp. 5-6.

2052. Sylvester, Anthony, "East Europeans in Cuba," *East Europe,* (New York), Oct. 1965. pp. 2-8.
Block advisors condemn Castro's errors.

2053. "Tito and the Cuban Revolution," *Peking Review,* (Peking), Dec. 7, 1962. pp. 9-12.

2054. *West German Comments on Cuba,* Washington: Joint Publications Research Service, Nov. 22, 1961. 44 pp.

3. Red China

2055. "All Out Support for Cuba," *Peking Review,* (Peking), Nov. 9, 1962. p. 11.

2056. Castro, Fidel, "Discurso pronunciado en la conmemoración del IX aniversario del asalto al Palacio Presidencial, *Política Internacional,* (Havana), No. 13, 1966. pp. 227-2589.
Mar. 13, 1966. On relations with China and Chile.

2057. Castro, Fidel, "Respuesta de Fidel Castro a las declaraciones del gobierno chino," *Cuba Socialista,* (Havana), Mar. 1966. pp. 2-15
Feb. 5, 1966 note answering Chinese position on trade. Denounces Chinese efforts to infiltrate Cuban Armed Forces.

2058. Castro, Fidel, "Siete años de revolución," *Cuba Socialista,* (Havana), Feb. 1966. pp. 2-27.
Jan. 2, 1966 speech disclosing trade problems with China.

2059. Cartier, Raymond, "Fidel Castro reta con violencia a China Roja," *Blanco y negro,* (Madrid), Feb. 1966. pp. 52-55.

2060. "Chinese Government Statement Supporting Cuba and Opposing U. S. War Provocation," *Peking Review,* (Peking), Nov. 2, 1962. p. 5.

2061. "Defend Cuba, Defend the Cuban Revolution!" *Peking Review,* (Peking), Nov. 9, 1962. pp. 9-12.

2062. Gironella, José María, *On China and Cuba,* Notre Dame: Fides Publishers, 1963. 175 pp.

2063. Kuo, Mo-Jo, *La victoria del pueblo cubano es nuestra victoria,* Havana: Ediciones del Movimiento por la Paz y la Soberanía de los Pueblos, 1961. 15 pp.

2064. Li Hsi-pi, Yü Ch'u-ying, and Lu Hung-chi, "The Development of the Friendship between the Chinese and Cuban People," *Li-shih Yen-chiu,* (Peking), Feb. 15, 1964. pp. 47-62.

2065. MacDougall, Calina, "Cultivating Cuba," *Far Eastern Economic Review,* Dec. 22, 1960. p. 628.
Early Chinese interests.

2066. People's Republic of China, "Cuba, We Are With You!; Fraternal Unity," *Peking Review,* (Peking), Apr. 19, 1963. pp. 12-13.

2067. República Popular China, *En apoyo de la justa lucha del pueblo cubano y de los otros pueblos latinoamericanos contra el imperialismo de EE. UU.,* Peking, 1962. 191 pp.

2068. "President Dorticós in China," *Peking Review,* (Peking), Sept. 29, 1961. pp. 5-7.

2069. República Popular China, Embajada, Cuba, *El pueblo chino está siempre junto al pueblo cubano,* Havana: Embajada de la República China en Cuba, 1963. 74 pp.

2070. Tang, Peter S. H. and Joan Maloney, *The Chinese Communist Impact on Cuba,* Chestnut Hill, Mass.: Research Institute on the Sino-Soviet Bloc, 1962. 125 pp.

2071. Tse-Tung, Mao, *En apoyo de la justa lucha del pueblo cubano y de los otros pueblos latinoamericanos contra el imperialismo de EE. UU.,* Peking: Ediciones en

Lenguas Extranjeras, 1962. 192 pp.

2072. Wai wên ch'u pan shê, *Support the Cuban and Other Latin American People's Just Struggle Against U.S. Imperialism,* Peking: Foreign Languages Press, 1961. 184 pp.

2073. "We Stand by Cuba," *Peking Review,* (Peking), Nov. 2, 1962. pp. 3-4.

4. Tri-Continental Congress (See also Relations With Latin America)

2074. Alarcón, Ricardo, "América Latina y la Conferencia Tricontinental," *Casa de las Américas,* (Havana), Mar.-Apr. 1966. pp. 4-10.

2075. Alvarez Tabío, Fernando, "Primera conferencia de solidaridad de los pueblos de Africa, Asia y América Latina," *Política Internacional,* (Havana), No. 1, 1966. pp. 7-58.

2076. Anónimo, "Con la Tricontinental comienza el año de la solidaridad," *Bohemia,* (Havana), Jan. 7, 1966. pp. 52-55. (supplement).

2077. Barbieri, Frane, "Después de la Conferencia de La Habana," *Granma,* (Havana), May 3, 1966. p. 2.
Cuban-Yugoslav disputes.

2078. Bercoff, André, "La Havane, une nouvelle internationale?" *Jeune Afrique International,* (Paris), Aug. 27, 1967. pp. 12-15.

2079. Bethel, Paul D., "The Havana Conference," *The Reporter,* (New York), Mar. 24, 1966. pp. 25-29.

2080. Bochkarev, Iu. A., *Rukopozhatie trekh kontinentov. Konfer-*

entsiia solidarnosti narodov Azii, Afriki i Latin Ameriki v Gavane, Moscow: Politizdat, 1966. 56 pp.

2081. Castro, Fidel, "Carta al secretario general de las Naciones Unidas," *Política Internacional,* (Havana), No. 13, 1966. pp. 199-202.
On Tricontinental Conference. Also in English.

2082. Castro, Fidel, "Discurso en la clausura de la Conferencia Tricontinental," *Cuba Socialista,* (Havana), Feb. 1966. pp. 78-100. Jan. 15, 1966. On Cuba's revolutionary internationalism.

2083. Cienfuegos, Osmany, "Discurso en el acto de constitución oficial del ejecutivo de la OSPAAAL," *El Mundo,* (Havana), June 1, 1966. p. 5.
Secretary General of OSPAAAL.

2084. Cuba, Organización de Solidaridad de los Pueblos de Africa, Asia y América Latina, *Tres Continentes,* Havana: Ediciones Prensa Latina, 1966. 835 pp.
Worldwide struggle against imperialism.

2085. Cueto, Mario G., "Cuba preside: una entrevista especial al Canciller Raúl Roa, Presidente de la Conferencia Tricontinental," *Bohemia,* (Havana), Jan. 14, 1966. pp. 42-43.

2086. "Declaración general de la Primera Conferencia," *Tricontinental,* (Havana), November-December 1967. pp. 101-112.

2087. Dorticós, Osvaldo, "Discurso en la apertura de la Conferencia Tricontinental," *Cuba Socialista,* (Havana), Feb. 1966. pp. 29-39.

2088. "Dos años del secretariado de la OSPAAAL," *Tricontinental,*

(Havana), July-August 1967. pp. 147-148.

2089. Editorial, "The Tricontinental and After," *Monthly Review*, Apr. 1966. pp. 1-11.

2090. Fejto, François, "La conferencia de La Habana ¿y ahora que?" *Estudios*, (Buenos Aires), Mar.-Apr. 1966. pp. 132-134.

2091. Fejto, François, "La conferencia tricontinental de La Habana y la política soviética," *Estudios*, (Buenos Aires), Jan.-Feb. 1966. pp. 28-29.

2092. Gerassi, John, "Havana: A New International is Born," *Monthly Review*, Oct. 1967. pp. 22-35.

2093. Gilly, Adolfo, "A Conference Without Glory and Without Program," *Monthly Review*, Apr. 1966. pp. 21-34.
Tricontinental Congress.

2094. González, Enrique, "Constituido el Secretariado de la OSPAAAL," *El Mundo*, (Havana), June 1, 1966. pp. 1, 6.

2095. Guevara, Ernesto, *Mensaje a la Tricontinental*, Havana, 1967. 24 pp.

2096. Jackson, D. B., "Whose Men in Havana?" *Problems of Communism*, (Washington), May 1966. pp. 1-10.

2097. Lamberg, Roberto F., "La formación de la línea castrista desde la Conferencia Tricontinental," *Foro Internacional*, (Mexico), Jan.-Mar. 1968. pp. 278-301. 1966-1967.

2098. Lentin, Albert Paul, *La lutte tricontinentale: impérialisme et révolution après la conférence de La Havane*, Paris: François Maspero, 1966. 330 pp.

2099. Niedergang, Marcel, "La Conférence des Trois Continents a la Havane," *Le Monde*, (Paris), Dec. 30, 1965-Jan. 5, 1966. p. 1; Jan. 20-26, 1966, p. 5.

2100. Organización de Solidaridad de los Pueblos de Asia, Africa y América Latina, *Anti-imperialismo en Latinoamérica. Pensamiento y acción de sus libertadores*, Havana, 1967. 27 pp.

2101. Ratliff, William E., "First Conference of the Latin American Solidarity Organization," in Richard V. Allen, ed., *Yearbook on International Communist Affairs: 1968*, Stanford: Hoover Institution Press, 1969. pp. 758-763.

2102. "Tres años de una reunión histórica," *Tricontinental*, (Havana), January-February 1969. pp. 121-126.

2103. Various, "La Primera Conferencia de Solidaridad de los Pueblos de Africa, Asia y América Latina," *Cuba Socialista*, (Havana), Feb. 1966. pp. 1-216.
Documents.

2104. Various, "Significado de la Conferencia Tricontinental," *Tricontinental*, (Havana), January-February 1969. pp. 127-136.

2105. Vazeilles, José, "The Tricontinental: Concrete Internationalism and Revolution," *Monthly Review*, June 1966. pp. 28-34.

V. ECONOMY
(See also Statistics, Geography)

A. HISTORY

2106. Alienes, Julián, *Economía de la postguerra y desempleo*, Havana, 1949. 177 pp.

2107. Alienes, Julián, "Evolución de la economía cubana en la postguerra," *Trimestre Económico* (Mexico), Vol. 17, 1950. pp. 186-213.

2108. Alienes, Julián, *Características fundamentales de la economía cubana*, Havana: Banco Nacional, 1950. 405 pp.

2109. Arredondo y Gutiérrez, Alberto, *Cuba: tierra indefensa*, Havana: Editorial Lex, 1945. 500 pp.

2110. Cepero Bonilla, Raúl, *Obras históricas*, Havana: Instituto de Historia, 1963. 482 pp.
Economic history essays.

2111. Cuba, Banco Nacional, *La economía cubana en 1951-1957*, Havana, 1953-1958. 6 vols.

2112. Cuba, Banco Nacional, *Economic Development Program*, Havana, 1956. No. 1, 35 pp.; No. 2. 91 pp.
General study of Cuban economic development from 1952-1956 with particular emphasis on banking and finances.

2113. Cuba, Banco Nacional *Memoria, 1949-1957*, Havana: Editorial Lex, Editorial Cenit, 1949-1958. 10 vols.

2114. Cuba, Banco Nacional, *Programa de desarrollo económico*, Havana: Editorial Cenit, 1957. 145 pp.

2115. Cuba, Banco de Desarrollo Económico y Social, *Memoria, 1955-1957*, Havana: Editorial Cenit, 1957-1958. 2 vols.

2116. Cuba, Banco de Desarrollo Económico y Social, *Programa de desarrollo económico*, Havana, 1956-1958, 4 vols.
Also in English.

2117. Cuba, Banco de Fomento Agrícola e Industrial, *Memoria*, Havana: Editorial Lex, 1952-1958. 6 vols.

2118. Cuba, Consejo Nacional de Economía, *El programa económico de Cuba*, Havana, 1955. 84 pp.

2119. Cuba, Organización Latino-Americana de Solidaridad, *La economía de Cuba*, (1902-58; 1959-66), Havana: Instituto del Libro, 1967. 32 pp.

2120. Cuba, Tribunal de Cuentas, *Recopilación y análisis de los ingresos y presupuestos de Cuba*, Havana, 1953. 426 pp.

2121. Editora Mercantil Cubana, *Cuba económica y financiera*, Havana, 1926-1960.

Indispensable monthly. Statistics and summary articles.

2122. Friedlander, Heinrich, *Historia económica de Cuba,* Havana: J. Montero, 1944. 596 pp.
Standard work. Scholarly.

2123. Gímenez, Fernando, *The Economic Development of Cuba, 1952-1958,* Gainesville: University of Florida Press, 1963. 81 pp.

2124. Grupo Cubano de Investigaciones Económicas, *A Study on Cuba,* Coral Gables: University of Florida Press, 1965. 774 pp.
On economic structure, institutional developments, from 16th century to mid-1960's.

2125. Gutiérrez, Gustavo, *El desarrollo económico de Cuba,* Havana: Junta Nacional de Economía, 1952. 257 pp.

2126. Gutiérrez, Gustavo, *Presente y futuro de la economía cubana,* Havana: Junta Nacional de Economía, 1950. 84 pp.

2127. Havana, Municipio, *Presupuesto,* Havana, 1919-1960. 7 vols.

2128. International Bank for Reconstruction and Development, *Annual Report, 1945/1946-1958/1959,* Washington, 1946-1959. 14 vols.
Has data on Cuba.

2129. International Bank for Reconstruction and Development, *Report on Cuba: Findings and Recommendations of An Economic and Technical Mission,* Washington, 1951. 1049 pp.
Mission headed by Francis Adams Truslow.

2130. Lorenzo, Raúl, *El empleo en Cuba: azúcar, desarrollo, salarios, comercio exterior, finanzas públi-*cas, Havana: Seoane, Fernández impresores, 1955. 143 pp.
Useful pre-revolutionary statistics.

2131. Movimiento 26 de Julio, "Algunos aspectos del desarrollo económico de Cuba," *Revolución,* (Revolución) Jan. 22-27, 1959.

2132. Newman, Philip C., *Cuba Before Castro,* New Jersey: Foreign Studies Institute, 1965. 123 pp.
Economic appraisal.

2133. O'Connor, James, *The Political Economy of Pre-revolutionary Cuba,* New York: 1964. 199 pp.
Columbia University Ph.D. Thesis.

2134. Pinos, Óscar, "Terratenientes y monopolios: la oligarquía del poder en Cuba," *Carteles,* (Havana), Mar. 15, 1959. pp. 46-47, 69.

2135. Le Riverend Brusone, Julio, *Historia económica de Cuba,* Havana, 1963. 264 pp.

2136. Stephens, Peter Scott, *Cuba: Economic and Commercial Conditions,* London: H. M. Stationery Office, 1954. 117 pp.

B. DOCUMENTS

2137. Castro, Fidel, "Este es el año de la planificación," *Revolución,* Jan. 3, 1962. pp. 2-3, 4, 5, 8.
Jan. 2 speech.

2138. Cuba, Colegio de Ingenieros Agronómos y Azucareros, *Conferencias sobre reforma agraria, desarrollo industrial y el progreso de la economía nacional,* Havana: Banco Núñez, 1958. 177 pp.

2139. Cuba, Consejo Nacional de

Economía, *Programa nacional de acción económica,* Havana, 1951. 239 pp.

2140. Cuba, Leyes, *El impuesto sobre la renta,* Havana: Editorial Lex, 1951. 263 pp.

2141. Guevara, Ernesto, "Cuba hace oir en Ginebra la voz de los pueblos subdesarrollados y explolados," *Política,* (Mexico), Apr. 1, 1964. pp. A-H.

2142. Guevara, Ernesto, "Cuba, su economía, su comercio exterior, su significado en el mundo actual," *Económica,* (Havana), Dec. 1964. pp. 3-12.

2143. Naciones Unidas, Comisión Económica para América Latina, "La economía cubana en el período 1959-1963," *Comercio Exterior,* (Mexico), Feb. 1965. pp. 143-48.

2144. Noyola, Juan F., *Aspectos económicos de la revolución cubana,* Havana: Comisión Nacional Cubana de la Unesco, 1961. 24 pp.

2145. Núñez Jímenez, Antonio, *Economic and Sociological Advances of the Cuban Revolution,* Washington: Joint Publications Research Service, Dec. 17, 1962. 22 pp.

2146. Roca, Blas, "The Economics of the Cuban Revolution," *Political Affairs,* (New York) Jan. 1961. pp. 47-56.
Report to 8th National Assembly of PSP.

2147. U. S. Department of Commerce, Bureau of Foreign and Domestic Commerce, *Economic Developments in Cuba, 1960,* Washington, D.C., 1961. 6 pp.

C. COMMENTARIES

2148. Agencia de Informaciones Periodísticas, *La ruina económica en Cuba comunista: falsas promesas y desastrosas realidades,* Miami, 1965. 9 pp.

2149. Alvarez Díaz, José R., *La trayectoria de Castro: encumbramiento y derrumbe,* Miami: Ed. Aip, 1964. 38 pp.
Also in English.

2150. Anónimo, "Cuba: una economía en ruinas," *Este & Oeste,* (Paris), Jan. 15-30, 1966. pp. 1-8.

2151. Anónimo, "Economía cubana en el período 1959-1963," *Banco Nacional de Comercio Exterior,* (Mexico), Feb. 1965. pp. 143-148.

2152. Asociación de Economistas Cubanos, *Cuba: Geopolítica y pensamiento económico,* Miami: Duplex, 1964. 576 pp.

2153. Bank of London, "Cuba: an Economy in Crisis," *BOLSA,* (London), July 1967. pp. 368-371.

2154. Barba, Antonio, *Cuba el país que fué,* Barcelona: Editorial Maucci, 1964. 229 pp.
"Castro ruined a prosperous Cuba."

2155. Bellows, Irving, "Economic aspects of the Cuban revolution," *Political Affairs,* (New York), Jan. 1964, pp. 14-29, Feb. 1964. pp. 43-51.

2156. Boorstein, Edward, *The Economic Transformation of Cuba: A First-Hand Account,* New York: Monthly Review Press, 1968. 303 pp.
By economic advisor to Castro government.

2157. Burks, David D., "Economic

prospects for Cuba," *Current History*, Feb. 1962. pp. 77-82.

2158. "Caótica situación económica en Cuba," *Economía*, (Miami), Feb. 1965. pp. 1, 4.

2159. Chrisler, Donald, "Cuba in 1965, Agricultural Situation and Food Supply," *Foreign Agriculture*, (Washington), Year 4, No. 9, Feb. 28, 1966. pp. 6-7.

2160. Cuba, Academia de Ciencias, *Economía y Organización*, Havana, 1966. 82 pp. Mimeographed.

2161. Cuba, Partido Unido de la Revolución Socialista, *Más sobre nuestra economía*, Havana, 1964. 71 pp.

2162. *The Cuban Economy*, Washington: Joint Publications Research Service, Aug. 2, 1962. 60 pp.

2163. *Cuban Economic Highlights in 1961*, Washington: Joint Publications Research Service, Jan. 29, 1962. 15 pp.

2164. García, José, *Cuba y su futuro*, Miami: Colegio de Economistas de Cuba en el Exilio, 1964. 331 pp.

2165. González G. Arrese, Ramón, *Independencia económica de Cuba; plan de desarrollo económico y social*, Madrid, 1961. 53 pp.

2166. Haupt, H. G., "Die wirtschaftliche Enturicklung der Republik Kuba [the economic development of the Republic of Cuba], *Wirtschaftswissenschaft*, (Berlin), Feb. 1963. pp. 246-268.

2167. Illán González, José M., *Cuba: Facts and Figures of an Economy in Ruins*, Miami: AIP, 1964. 157 pp.

Former Undersecretary of the Treasury, 1959-1960. "Cuba was in 'take off' stage in 1958."

2168. Kruijer, Gerardus Johannes, *Cuba, Voorbeeld en uitdaging*, Amsterdam: Polak and Van Gennep, 1968. 134 pp. General economic study.

2169. Lamberg, Robert F., "Die Wirtschaftlichen Schwierigkeiten Kubas," *Neue Zürcher Zeitung*, (Zurich), Sept. 11-12, 1963. Economic problems.

2170. Mesa Lago, Carmelo, "Deficiencias en el sistema estadístico de Cuba Socialista," *Problemas del Comunismo*, (Santiago, Chile), Sept.-Oct. 1965. pp. 35-43.

2171. Mesa Lago, Carmelo, *Tres aspectos del desastre económico en Cuba comunista*, Miami: AIP, 1965. 6 pp.

2172. Mijares, José A., *Proyecto para la reconstrucción completa de Cuba*, Miami, 1961. 113 pp. By exiled businessman.

2173. Navarro, Agustín, "La economía cubana," *Espejo*, (Mexico), Oct. 15, 1960. pp. 17-21.

2174. Noyola, Juan F., "Aspectos económicos de la revolución cubana," *Investigación económica*, (Mexico), No. 82, 1961. pp. 331-359.

2175. Pazos, Felipe, "Comentarios a dos artículos sobre la revolución cubana," *Trimestre Económico*, (Mexico), Jan.-Mar. 1962. pp. 1-18. Replies to Paul Baran.

2176. Pazos, Felipe, *Insufficient Development and Economic Pauperization in Cuba*, Washington:

Joint Publications Research Service, July 18, 1962. 15 pp.

2177. Phillips, Joseph D., "Economic Pressures in the Cuban Situation," *Business Review*, Oct. 1960. pp. 6-8.

2178. Presenti, Antonio, *Lecciones de Economía Política*, Havana: Publicaciones Económicas, 1965. 419 pp.

2179. Ramirez Gómez, Ramón, *Cuba, despertar de América; ensayo económico-social*, Mexico: UNAM, 1961. 267 pp.

2180. "Reunión nacional de producción," *Bohemia*, (Havana), Sept. 3, 1961. pp. 54-65.

2181. Seers, Dudley, ed., *Cuba, the Economic and Social Revolution*, Chapel Hill: University of North Carolina Press, 1964. 432 pp.
Education, agrarian reform, sugar production.

2182. Selucky, Radoslav, "Spotlight on Cuba," *East Europe*, (New York), Oct. 1964. pp. 17-22.
Czech official compares Cuba's economy before and after 1959.

2183. Semevskiy, B. N., "Basic National-economic Problems of the Republic of Cuba," *Soviet Geography*, (Moscow), Feb. 1966. pp. 36-43.

2184. Serebrvskaja, M. A., "O dvuh étapah nacionalizacii promyšlennosti na Kube," [On the two stages of nationalization of industry in Cuba], *Učenye Zapiski Kafedr Obščestvennyh Goroda Leningrada*, (Leningrad), No. 4, 1962. pp. 146-158.

2185. Shelton, Raúl M., "La influencia de los factores geopolíticos sobre la economía cubana," *Cuba Nueva*, (Coral Gables), Feb. 1, 1963. pp. 25-30.

2186. *Social and Economic Developments in Cuba*, Washington: Joint Publications Research Service, Oct. 19, 1961. 59 pp.

2187. Stanciu, N., "Dezvoltarea economici nationale a Republicii Cuba," [The development of the Cuban Republic's national economy], *Probleme Economice*, (Bucharest), Jan. 1964. pp. 118-122.

2188. Venezuela, Universidad Central, Instituto de Investigaciones Económicas, *La Economía Cubana*, Caracas, 1961. 139 pp.

2189. Viator (pseud.), "Cuba Revisited After Ten Years of Castro," *Foreign Affairs*, Jan. 1970. pp. 312-321.

D. ECONOMIC POLICY
(See also Research Tools)

1. Documents

2190. Boti, Regino, *La reforma agraria y la industrialización*, Havana: Delegación del Gobierno en el Capitolio Nacional, 1959. 35 pp.

2191. Castro, Fidel, "Abastecimiento y regulación," *Obra Revolucionaria*, (Havana), No. 7, 1962. pp. 7-21.
On food rationing.

2192. Castro, Fidel, "Ante el Primer Congreso Regional de Plantaciones Agrícolas," *Revolución*, Mar. 7, 1961. pp. 2-5.
Economic and social policy.

2193. Castro, Fidel, "Apreciaciones y conclusiones del Primer Ministro,"

Obra Revolucionaria, (Havana), No. 31, 1961. pp. 9-47.
Aug. 27, 1961 speech on future economic plans.

2194. Castro, Fidel, "Comentarios Económicos," *Revolución*, June 18, 1959. pp. 1-9, 16, 18.
Announcing economic plans.

2195. Castro, Fidel, "Cuba habla para los trabajadores y campesinos de América," *Obra Revolucionaria*, (Havana), No. 17, 1960. pp. 5-21.
Aug. 9, 1960 speech on nationalization policy.

2196. Castro, Fidel, "Discurso del 26 de Julio de 1970," *Ediciones COR*, (Havana), No. 11, 1970. 39 pp.
General economic problems.

2197. Castro, Fidel, "Discurso en el IV Aniversario de los Comités de Defensa de la Revolución," *Política Internacional* (Havana), No. 7, 1964. pp. 249-267.
Sept. 28, 1964. On rationing.

2198. Castro, Fidel, *Discurso en la inauguración de las obras de Gran Tierra, en Baracoa, Oriente*, Havana: Instituto del Libro, 1967. 23 pp.
July 27, 1967. "By 1975 Cuba will no longer be an underdeveloped country."

2199. Castro, Fidel, "Discurso en la Primera Reunión Nacional de Producción," *Obra Revolucionaria*, (Havana), No. 30, 1961. pp. 7-12.
Aug. 26, 1961 speech.

2200. Castro, Fidel, "Un discurso explicativo y dos leyes revolucionarias," *Obra Revolucionaria*, (Havana), No. 27, 1961. pp. 7-18.
Statement of Aug. 8, 1961 announcing exchange controls.

2201. Castro, Fidel, *Dos discursos en la escalinata universitaria*, Havana: Comisión de Orientación Revolucionaria, 1963. 47 pp.
Nov. 26 and 27, 1963. On future socio-economic plans.

2202. Castro, Fidel, *Dos millones de quintales de café en 1970*, Santiago de Cuba: Editora Política del PCC de Oriente, 1965. 46 pp.
Nov. 24, 1965 speech on economic plans.

2203. Castro, Fidel, "Esta generación está realizando un gran esfuerzo," *El Mundo*, (Havana), Mar. 15, 1968. pp. 4-8.
Proclaims complete nationalization of small and medium sized businesses. Speech of Mar. 13, 1968.

2204. Castro, Fidel, "Estamos defendiendo el honor del país," *Bohemia*, (Havana), Feb. 13, 1970. pp. 57-59.
Feb. 9, 1970 speech informing the people about the development of the sugar harvest.

2205. Castro, Fidel, "Estamos haciendo una gran revolución social," *Revolución*, Oct. 17, 1960. pp. 8-11, 16.
Explains economic and social policies.

2206. Castro, Fidel, "Este año tendremos que duplicar la producción," *Revolución*, Jan. 12, 1960. pp. 1, 2, 11, 15.
Speech.

2207. Castro, Fidel, "Expone Fidel planes económicos de 1962," *Revolución*. Oct. 21, 1961. pp. 1, 6, 10.

2208. Castro, Fidel, "Hay que derrotar al enemigo en la economía,"

Revolución, May 7, 1963. pp. 1, 5. Declaration from USSR.

2209. Castro, Fidel, *Informe económico sobre Cuba,* Havana: Sección de Divulgación de la Dirección de Cultura del Ejército Rebelde, 1959. 97 pp.
Made on Sept. 17, 1959.

2210. Castro, Fidel, "Liquidación del monocultivo en 1961," *Revolución,* Dec. 21, 1960. pp. 3, 4, 5, 6.

2211. Castro, Fidel, "The 10-million Ton Sugar Harvest is a Historic Battle," *Granma,* (Havana), Nov. 2, 1969. pp. 1-5.

2212. Castro, Fidel, "Orden de refinar a la Esso y a la Shell," *Revolución,* July 1, 1969. pp. 1, 6.
"Or be nationalized."

2213. Castro, Fidel, "Recibimiento a los once pescadores secuestrados," *Ediciones COR,* (Havana), No. 9, 1970. pp. 5-28.
May 19, 1970 speech. Announces 10-million ton sugar harvest will not be achieved.

2214. Castro, Fidel, "Sobre la zafra de 1970," *Ediciones COR,* (Havana), No. 9, 1970. pp. 33-79.
May 20, 1970 speech on problems of sugar harvest.

2215. Castro, Fidel, "Speech at the Ministry of the Revolutionary Armed Forces," *Granma,* (Havana), Nov. 16, 1969. pp. 1-3.
On its role in sugar harvest.

2216. Castro, Fidel, "This Sugar Harvest Begins Today," *Granma,* (Havana), July 20, 1969. pp. 1-5.
The 1970 harvest.

2217. Castro, Fidel, "Without Socialism there Cannot Be Any Development in An Underdeveloped Country," *Granma,* (Havana), Dec. 28, 1970. pp. 6-10.

2218. Castro, Raúl, *La anarquía de la producción capitalista frente a la planificación de la producción socialista,* Havana: Imprenta Nacional, 1961. 32 pp.

2219. Cuba, Comisión Nacional Cubana de la Unesco, *Desarrollo económico y planificación,* Havana: Imprenta Nacional, 1961. 63 pp.

2220. Cuba, Instituto Nacional de Reforma Agraria, *Elementos de planificación,* Havana, 1965. 379 pp.

2221. Cuba, Junta Central de Planificación, *Manual de análisis de procesos económicos para planificación,* Havana, 1961. 79 pp.
Mimeographed.

2222. Cuba, Junta Central de Planificación, *Principales indicadores de la actividad económica,* Havana, 1964. 127 pp.

2223. Cuba, Leyes, *Principal Provisions of Cuban Tax Law,* Washington: Joint Publications Research Service, Mar. 9, 1962. 40 pp.

2224. Cuba, Ministerio de Educación, *Aspectos de la economía política cubana en la época actual,* Havana: Editorial Nacional, 1965. 127 pp.

2225. Cuba, Ministerio de Hacienda, *El balance de la economía nacional,* Havana, 1965. 27 pp.

2226. Cuba, Ministerio de Hacienda, *Informe del Ministro de Hacienda del Gobierno Revolucionario al Consejo de Ministros,* Havana: Editorial Echevarría, 1959. 64 pp.

2227. Cuba, Ministerio de Hacienda, *Nueva etapa en el desarrollo de la economía política marxista,* Havana, 1965. 142 pp.
Mimeographed.

2228. Cuba, Ministerio de Hacienda, *Reglamento sobre la empresa productiva estatal socialista,* Havana, 1965. 26 pp. Mimeographed.

2229. Cuba, Ministerio de Industrias, *Instrucción revolucionaria,* Havana, 1962. 123 pp.

2230. Cuba, Ministerio de Industrias, *Tareas fundamentales,* Havana, 1965. 34 pp.

2231. Cuba, Ministerio del Trabajo, *Proyecto de reglamento para la organización de la emulación socialista, octubre 1962,* Havana: Editorial CTC-R, 1962. 50 pp.

2232. Cuba, National Institute for Savings and Housing, *Revolutionary Reform of Gambling,* Havana, 1959. 31 pp.

2233. Cuba, Partido Unido de la Revolución Socialista, *La emulación socialista,* Havana, 1962. 39 pp.

2234. Cuba, Partido Unido de la Revolución Socialista, *El plan económico y las proporciones entre las ramas de la producción,* Havana, 1963. 44 pp.

2235. Cuba, Presidencia, *5000 premios a los mejores,* Havana: Ediciones Combatientes. Ejército de Oriente, 1965. 52 pp. Castro and Dorticós speak on material incentives.

2236. Dorticós, Osvaldo, "Tareas importantes de nuestros organismos económicos," *Cuba Socialista,* (Havana), Mar. 1966. pp. 26-42.

2237. Escalante, Aníbal, *Economía y planificación,* Havana: Imprenta Nacional, 1961. 24 pp.

2238. Guevara, Ernesto, "The Cuban Economy: Its Past and Its Present Importance," *Internation-*

al Affairs, (London), Oct. 1964. pp. 589-599.

2239. Guevara, Ernesto, "Ernesto Guevara on Cuba's Economic Problems," *New Times,* (Moscow), Oct. 1963. pp. 12-13.

2240. Guevara, Ernesto, *Hay que defender a la patria con el fusil sin descuidar la producción,* Havana: Imprenta Nacional, 1961. 31 pp.

2241. Guevara, Ernesto, *El papel de la ayuda exterior en el desarrollo de Cuba,* Havana: Imprenta Nacional, 1961. 28 pp.

2242. Guevara, Ernesto, "Posición de Cuba en la Conferencia Mundial de Comercio y Desarrollo," *Cuba Socialista,* (Havana), May 1964. pp. 1-24.

2243. Guevara, Ernesto, *El socialismo es el resultado de hechos económicos y de hechos de conciencia,* Havana: Imprenta Nacional, 1961. 48 pp.

2244. Fernández, Marcelo, "Planificación y control de la circulación monetaria," *Cuba Socialista,* (Havana), May 1964. pp. 78-79.

2245. López-Fresquet, Rufo, *Exposición lógica de la política económica del Gobierno Revolucionario,* Havana, 1959. 8 pp. By Treasury Minister.

2246. Noyola, Juan, *La planificación en la construcción del socialismo,* Havana: Ministerio de Educación, 1962. 32 pp. Conference of Oct. 9, 1962.

2247. Núñez Jímenez, Antonio, "Avances sociales y económicos de la revolución cubana," *Revolución,* Oct. 25, 1962. pp. 2-4.

2248. Núñez Jímenez, Antonio, and

Agustín Souchy, *Cooperativismo y colectivismo,* Havana: Editorial Lex, 1960. 343 pp.
Marxist debates an anarchist.

2249. Pazos, Felipe and Regino Boti, "Tesis económica del Movimiento 26 de Julio," *Lunes de Revolución,* (Havana), May 18, 1959. pp. 40-47.

2250. Rodríguez, Carlos R., "El nuevo camino de la agricultura cubana," *Cuba Socialista,* (Havana), Nov. 1963. pp. 71-98.

2251. Rodríguez, Carlos Rafael, *La revolución cubana en su aspecto económico,* Havana: Capitolio Nacional, 33 pp.
Mimeographed.

2252. Sánchez Roca, Mariano, ed., *Leyes fiscales vigentes,* Havana: Ed. Lex, 1959. 376 pp.
Text of revolutionary tax decrees. Annotated.

2253. Torras, Jacinto, "Comercio exterior y desarrollo económico," *Boletín Bibliográfico,* (Caracas), Jan.-Apr. 1961. pp. 99-111.
By high Foreign Ministry official.

2. Commentaries

2254. Alienes, Julián, *El desarrollo económico de Cuba,* Havana: Editorial Lex, 1955. 57 pp.

2255. Alienes y Urosa, Julián, "Tesis sobre el desarrollo económico," *Trimestre Económico,* (Mexico), Vol. 19, 1952. pp. 1-44.

2256. Altshuler, José, "La enseñanza tecnológica universitaria y nuestro desarrollo económico," *Cuba Socialista,* (Havana), April 1962. pp. 13-24.

2257. Anónimo, "Economía y planifi-

cación," *Cuba,* (Havana), Jan. 1962. pp. 62-71.

2258. Anónimo, *Manual para el adiestramiento; introducción en la práctica de la planificación de la economía nacional,* Havana, 1961. 295 pp.
Mimeographed.

2259. Arico, José, "Problemas del desarrollo económico de Cuba," *Pasado y Presente,* (Córdova, Arg.), Apr./Sept. 1964. pp. 49-53.

2260. Basora, Adrian A., "Communist economic development: the Cuban model," *ASTE Bulletin,* Summer 1966. pp. 5-18.

2261. Behr, Edward, "How Is Nationalization Going?" *Current,* (New York), Aug. 1963. pp. 46-49.

2262. Bettelheim, C., "La planificación de la economía cubana," *Comercio Exterior,* (Mexico), Mar. 1963. pp. 152-155.

2263. Boti, Regino, "Algunos aspectos del desarrollo económico de Cuba," *Revista Bimestre Cubana,* (Havana), July-Dec. 1958. pp. 249-282.

2264. Boti, Regino, "El plan de desarrollo económico de 1962," *Cuba Socialista,* (Havana), Dec. 1961. pp. 19-32.

2265. Boti, Regino, "El plan de la economía nacional de Cuba para 1963," *Cuba Socialista,* (Havana), April 1963. pp. 24-40.

2266. Castro, Vicente de, *Economía planificada,* Havana, 1959. 8 pp.

2267. Chediak Ahuayda, Felix, "Legislación cubana sobre desarrollo económico," *Universidad de San Carlos,* (Guatemala), Apr.-June 1957. pp. 105-135.

2268. Chonchol, Jacques, *Programa nacional de producción,* Havana: INRA, 1960. 154 pp.
By Chilean advisor to INRA.

2269. Daei Lillo, José, *Algunos aspectos de la planificación económica,* Santiago de Cuba, 1961. 26 pp.

2270. De Santis, Sergio, "Il dibattio sulla gestione socialista a Cuba," *Critica Marxista,* (Rome), Sept.-Dec. 1965. pp. 284-327.

2271. Dumont, René, *Cuba, socialisme et développement,* Paris: Eds. Du Seuil, 1964. 189 pp.
French economic adviser to revolutionary government. Relates frustrations.

2272. Duquesne y de Zaldo, Carlos, "El proceso de desarrollo económico de Cuba algunas consideraciones en torno al mismo," *Contabilidad y finanzas,* (Havana), Mar. 1958, pp. 97-138; July 1958, pp. 1-26; Aug. 1958. pp. 59-78.

2273. Editorial, "Emulación socialista," *Hoy,* (Havana), Oct. 4, 1962. pp. 6-7.

2274. Escalante, César, "Informe sobre la emulación," *Hoy,* (Havana), Oct. 18, 1964. pp. 5-6.

2275. Fernández Borges, Octavio, *Las inversiones directas,* Havana: Capitolio Nacional, 1961. 15 pp.

2276. Figueras, Miguel A., "Aspectos y problemas del desarrollo económico cubano," *Económica,* (Havana), Feb. 1965. pp. 20-30.

2277. García, Francisco, "La economía cubana," *Panorama Económico,* (Santiago de Chile), Oct. 1963. pp. 149-152+.

2278. García, Francisco, and Juan Noyola, "Principales objectivos de nuestro plan económico hasta 1965," *Cuba Socialista,* (Havana), Sept. 1962. pp. 1-17.

2279. García Vázquez, Francisco, *Aspectos del planeamiento y de la vivienda en Cuba,* Buenos Aires: Jorge Alvarez Editor, 1968. 121 pp.

2280. Garrián de Laubresse, G., "Les nationalisations cubaines," *Annuaire Français de Droit International,* (Paris), No. 7, 1961. pp. 215-226.

2281. Guevara, Ernesto, *Condiciones para el desarrollo económico latinoamericano,* Uruguay: El Siglo Ilustrado, 1966. 134 pp.

2282. Hába, Z., "Vznik socialistického sektora na Kube" [the establishment of a socialist sector in Cuba], *Ekonomický Časopis,* (Bratislava), May-June 1963. pp. 237-251.

2283. Infante, Joaquín, "Características del funcionamiento de la empresa autofinanciada," *Cuba Socialista,* (Havana), June 1964. pp. 25-50.

2284. Lataste, Albán, "1964: Año de la economía," *Cuba Socialista,* (Havana), Feb. 1964. pp. 13-31.

2285. León, Raúl, "Algunas cuestiones relativas a la formación de los precios en la economía cubana," *Comercio Exterior,* (Havana), May 1963. pp. 3-18.

2286. Lincoln, Freeman, "What Has Happened to Cuban Business?" *Fortune,* Sept. 1959. pp. 110-113.

2287. Listov, Vadim, "Ernesto Guevara on Cuba's Economic Prospects," *New Times,* (Moscow), July 4, 1962. pp. 12-14.

2288. Martínez, Alberto, "El Plan de la economía nacional para 1964,"

Cuba Socialista, (Havana), Mar. 1964. pp. 1-22.

2289. Martínez Saénz, Joaquín, *Por la independencia económica de Cuba,* Havana: Ed. Cenit, 1959. 310 pp.
Batista's Treasury Minister's support of the early Castro revolution.

2290. Mesa Lago, Carmelo, *Moscú-Pekin-Habana: Cuba se alínea con la URSS en la pugna entre incentivos materiales y morales,* Miami: Agencia de Informaciones Periodísticas, 1965. 7 pp.

2291. Mora Becerra, Alberto, "En torno a la cuestión del funcionamiento de la ley del valor en la economía cubana en los momentos actuales," *Comercio Exterior,* (Havana), June 1963. pp. 2-10.

2292. Noyola, Juan and Francisco García, "Principales objectivos de nuestro plan de desarrollo económico hasta 1965," *Cuba Socialista,* (Havana), Sept. 1962. pp. 1-17.

2293. Noyola, Juan, "La revolución cubana y sus efectos en el desarrollo económico," *El Trimistre Económico,* (Mexico), July-Sept. 1961. pp. 403-425.

2294. O'Connor, James, "On Cuban Political Economy," *Political Science Quarterly,* June 1964. pp. 233-247.

2295. Oltganu, O., *Creations of State Sector in Cuba's Economy,* Washington: Joint Publications Research Service, Nov. 14, 1962. 20 pp.

2296. Orozco Yera, Rodolfo, *Economía de las empresas cubanas,* Havana, 1964. 278 pp.
Mimeographed.

2297. Piñeiro, Andrés V., "Del Moncada a la Declaración de la Habana," *INRA,* (Havana), Nov. 1960. pp. 4-8.
On socialization of economy.

2298. "The Revolutionary Offensive," *Granma,* (Havana), Mar. 31, 1968. p. 2.
Socializing the economy.

2299. Ricardi, Antonio, "Visión económica de Cuba," *Humanismo,* (Havana), Jan.-Apr. 1959. pp. 158-187.

2300. Rodríguez Martín, Raúl, "El desarrollo económico cubano," *Contabilidad y Finanzas,* (Havana), June 1959, pp. 277-284; July 1959. pp. 13-14.

2301. Slonskio, Stefan, *Kuba, revolucja a relnictwo,* [Cuba: revolution and agriculture], Warsaw, 1963. 106 pp.

2302. *Socialist Emulation in Cuba,* Washington: Joint Publications Research Service, Oct. 3, 1962. 46 pp.

2303. Universidad Popular, Havana, *Economía y planificación; séptimo ciclo,* Havana, 1961. 2 vols.

2304. Velasco, Carmen, *Preliminary Scheme of Draft of Economic Regionalization of Cuba,* Washington: Joint Publications Research Service, Aug. 31, 1965. 17 pp.

2305. White, Byron, "El triunvirato de Cuba planificada," *Revista de Ciencias Sociales,* (Puerto Rico), June 1961. pp. 203-214.

E. AGRICULTURE

2306. Akulai, V. E., "Revoliutsionnye organizatsii Kuby vo glave bor'by za sozdanie natsional'noi assotsiatsii melkikh zemledel'tsev, dekabr' 1960-mai 1961 g.," [Cuban revolutionary organizations in the vanguard of the struggle for the establishment of an association of small farmers, Dec. 1960-May 1961], *Uch. zap. Kishinevskogo un.*, (Moscow), 1964. pp. 143-159.

2307. Anónimo, "El algodón en Cuba," *Revista Geográfica*, (Havana), No. 30, 1960. pp. 39-50.

2308. Anónimo, "Algunas experiencias de la zafra cafetalera," *Cuba Socialista*, (Havana), Feb. 1965. pp. 129-133.

2309. Anónimo, "Arroz: un esfuerzo colosal," *CUBA Internacional*, (Havana), Oct. 1969. pp. 30-37.

2310. Anónimo, "Problemas de la producción tabacalera," *Cuba Socialista*, (Havana), Mar. 1965. pp. 119-132.

2311. Anonymous, *Cuban Agriculture under Castro*, London: Polemic Press, 1963. 24 pp. 1959-1963.

2312. Arredondo, Alberto, *Cuba: Agriculture and Planning 1963-1964*, Coral Gables: University of Miami Press, 1965. 325 pp.

2313. Arredondo, Alberto, "Problemas del arroz en Cuba," *Este & Oeste*, (Paris), Feb. 15-28, 1966. pp. 7-8.

2314. Asociación Nacional de Hacendados de Cuba, *Actas del comité ejecutivo 760 al 783. Actas del consejo de directores 1 al 15, 1959*, Havana, 1960. 1 vol. Mimeographed.

2315. Blazas, Henrikas, "Private Farming Gains Recognition Under Communism," *International Peasant Union Bulletin*, (New York), Nov. 1964, Jan. 1965. pp. 5-9.

2316. Blume, Helmut, "Agrarlandschaft und Agrarreform in Kuba," *Geographische Zeitschrift*, (West Germany), Mar. 1968. pp. 1-17.

2317. Buch, Wilbur F., "Cuba's Agriculture," *Foreign Agriculture*, (Washington), No. 5, 1968. pp. 2-4.

2318. Castillo Rodón, Ernesto, *300 preguntas y respuestas sobre el problema agrario*, Havana: Editorial La Milagrosa, 1960. 96 pp.

2319. Castro, Fidel, *Discurso en la inauguración de la Escuela de Instrucción Revolucionaria para obreros de las granjas del pueblo*, Havana: Imprenta Nacional, 1961. 24 pp.
Oct. 30, 1961 speech. On role of revolutionary cadres in agriculture.

2320. Castro, Fidel, "Hay que concentrar en la agricultura las energías fundamentales de la nación," *Bohemia*, (Havana), Feb. 19, 1965. pp. 78-81.
Interview.

2321. Castro, Fidel, *Plenaria y aniversario*, Havana: Imprenta Nacional, 1961. 47 pp.
Speech of May 17, 1961 on agricultural production.

2322. Castro, Fidel, "Victory in This Valley Will Mean Victory Throughout Our Entire Countryside," *Granma*, (Havana), Feb. 5, 1967. 8 pp. supplement.
Jan. 28 speech.
Agricultural progress.

2323. Cuba, Instituto Nacional de Reforma Agraria, *Un año de producción agropecuaria estatal, 1964*, Havana, 1964. 99 pp.

2324. Cuba, Instituto Nacional de Reforma Agraria, *Costos de pro-*

ducción de los principales cultivos de Cuba, Havana, 1961. 35 pp.

2325. Cuba, Instituto Nacional de Reforma Agraria, *Memoria de la primera Reunión Nacional de Investigaciones Agrícolas,* Havana, 1964. 60 pp.
Mar. 23-24, 1963.

2326. Cuba, Instituto Nacional de Reforma Agraria, *Una norma cubana: tabaco. Proyecto de condiciones de acopio, beneficio y entrega,* Havana, 1964. 85 pp.

2327. Cuba, Leyes, *Compilación legal sobre el café,* Havana: Editorial Librería Martí, 1953. 850 pp.

2328. Dorticós, Eduardo, "Problemas de la estadística en el sector agropecuario," *Cuba Socialista,* (Havana), July 1964. pp. 44-63.

2329. Duyos, Oscar, "Los problemas actuales del acopio y los precios de compra de los productos agrícolas," *Cuba Socialista,* (Havana), May 1964. pp. 66-78.

2330. Ferragut, Casto, *Desarrollo y diversificación de la producción agro-pecuaria,* Havana: Editado por la Delegación del Gobierno en el Capitolio Nacional, 1959. 55 pp.

2331. Francia Mestre, Rafael, "La Reunión Nacional de Producción Agrícola," *Cuba Socialista,* (Havana), July 1963. pp. 45-50.

2332. García, Gaspar, *Biografía del tabaco habano,* Santa Clara: Universidad Central, 1959. 213 pp.

2333. *General Statutes of Agriculture and Live-Stock Societies in Cuba,* Washington: Joint Publications Research Service, June 14, 1962. 12 pp.

2334. Gutelman, Michel, *L'Agricul-*

ture socialisée è Cuba; enseignement et perspectives, Paris: F. Maspero, 1967. 229 pp.
One of the best.

2335. Jímenez, Saul, "Another Step Forward Emerging from Underdevelopment," *Granma,* (Havana), May 25, 1969. p. 5.
Use of herbicides.

2336. Listov, Vadim, "Cuba's Agricultural Societies," *New Times,* (Moscow), Sept. 26, 1962. pp. 26-28.

2337. Mears, Leon Glenn, *Agriculture and Food Situation in Cuba,* Washington: Department of Agriculture, 1962. 22 pp.

2338. Olmova, Gabriela, *Fundamentos económicos de los precios de los productos agrícolas en el socialismo,* Havana: Ministerio de Hacienda, 1965. 4 vols.

2339. Regalado, A., "Las funciones de la ANAP," *Cuba Socialista,* (Havana), June 1964, pp. 9-24; Oct. 1964. pp. 57-71.

2340. Rodríguez, Carlos Rafael, "El nuevo camino de la agricultura cubana," *Cuba Socialista,* (Havana), Nov. 1963. pp. 71-98.

2341. Sánchez, Rafael, "El plan arroz de Oriente," *Bohemia,* (Havana), Dec. 12, 1969. pp. 28-35.

2342. Santana, Roberto, "Papel y línea de desarrollo de la agricultura cubana," *Boletín de la Escuela de Geografía,* (Havana), July 1964. pp. 15-19.

2343. Santos Ríos, Eduardo, "Tecnificar nuestra agricultura es hacerla más productiva," *Cuba Socialista,* (Havana), May 1962. pp. 50-66.

2344. United States, Department of Agriculture, *A Survey of Agricul-*

ture in Cuba, Washington, June 1969. 30 pp.

2345. Vallier, Jacques, "L'agriculture, sector prioritaire de l'économie cubaine," *Problèmes économiques*, (Paris), 1968, pp. 6-13.

2346. Vistinetoki, Max, "Los frutos de la siembra de octubre," *Cuba Socialista*, (Havana), Nov. 1963. pp. 99-114.

1. Sugar
(See also Relations with the United States)

a. History

2347. Alienes y Urosa, Julián, "Ensayo sobre la economía de la caña de azúcar en Cuba," *Trimestre Económico*, (Mexico), Vol. 16, 1949. pp. 432-457.

2348. *Anuario Azucarero de Cuba 1937-1958. Censo de la industria azucarera de Cuba y manual estadístico nacional e internacional*, Havana: Cuba Económica y Financiera, 1938-1959. 21 vols.

2349. Asociación de Técnicos Azucareros de Cuba, *Memoria, 1927-1958*, Havana: Cultural, 1927-1960. 32 vols.

2350. Castillo, Rubén, "La sexta zafra en Oriente," *Bohemia*, (Havana), Jan. 28, 1966. pp. 30-37.

2351. Cepero Bonilla, Raúl, *Política azucarera, (1952-1958)*, Mexico: Editora Futuro, s.a., 1958. 221 pp.

2352. Cuba, Academia de Ciencias, *Cronología de la industria azucarera*, Havana, 1963. 144 pp.

2353. Cuba, Ministerio de la Industria Azucarera, *Desarrollo de la industria azucarera en el mundo, 1958*, Havana, 1967. 87 pp.

2354. Cuba, Ministerio de la Industria Azucarera, *Orden Nacional 50 años de trabajo en la Industria Azucarera. Memorias 1966*, Havana, 1966. 213 pp.

2355. Duquesne y de Zaldo, Carlos, *El proceso de desarrollo y la coyuntura cubana*, Havana: Banco de Fomento Agrícola e Industrial de Cuba, 1957. 58 pp.
Impact of sugar prices on economic development.

2356. Ely, Roland T., *Cuando reinaba su majestad el azúcar*, Buenos Aires: Editorial Sudamericana, 1963. 875 pp.
Social history of sugar industry.

2357. Fuertes, José, "La lucha por la mecanización del corte y el alza de la caña en Camagüey," *Cuba Socialista*, (Havana), Feb. 1964. pp. 147-150.

2358. Guerra y Sánchez, Ramiro, *Sugar and Society in the Caribbean: An Economic History of Cuban Agriculture*, New Haven: Yale University Press, 1964. 218 pp.
First published in Havana in 1927. Calls for reform.

2359. Mörner, Magnus, "Sockerön före Castro," [Sugar island before Castro], *Ekonomisk Revy*, (Stockholm), Nov. 1962. pp. 628-637.

2360. Pedrosa Puertas, Rafael, *Cinco siglos de industria azucarera cubana*, Havana, 1967. 47 pp.

2361. Pérez, Luis Marino, *El convenio internacional del azúcar, 1954 a 1959*, Havana: Cárdenas y Cía, 1959. 32 pp.

2362. Pérez, Luis Marino, *La situación del mercado azucarero mundial*, Havana: Editorial Cenit, 1957. 120 pp.

1953-1957.

2363. Pérez Cisneros, Enrique, *Cuba y el mercado azucarero mundial,* Havana: Ucar, García, 1957. 134 pp.

2364. Ponvert, Katherine (Steele), *Cuban Chronicle; the Story of Central Hormiguero,* Fredericksburg, Va., 1961. 100 pp.
Life in a sugar plantation.

2365. Valdés, Nelson P., "La diplomacia del azúcar: Estados Unidos y Cuba," *Aportes* (Paris), October 1970, pp. 98-119.

b. Documents

2366. Castro, Fidel, *Cada central azucarero; una fortaleza!* Havana: Ministerio de Relaciones Exteriores, 1960. 37 pp.
Mar. 27, 1960 speech. "Sugar mills will be defended against exile air attacks."

2367. Castro, Fidel, "Discurso pronunciado en la sesión de clausura del I Foro Azucarero Nacional," *Política Internacional,* (Havana), No. 7, 1964. pp. 225-248.
Reviews achievements and problems of sugar industry.

2368. Castro, Fidel, "Con esfuerzos como estos se está escribiendo la historia de nuestra patria," *Bohemia,* (Havana), June 11, 1965. pp. 58-71.
June 7, 1965 speech on sugar production achievements.

2369. Castro, Fidel, *Ganar la batalla de la zafra es ganar la batalla de la economía,* Havana: Comisión de Orientación Revolucionaria, 1964. 24 pp.

2370. Castro, Fidel "En 1967 habrá una zafra de siete millones y me-

dio," *El Mundo,* (Havana), May 29, 1965. pp. 5, 6.

2371. Castro, Fidel, "Intentaremos producir más azúcar para vender a bajo precio en E. U.," *Diario de la Marina,* (Havana), Mar. 1, 1959. p. 1, 9B.

2372. Castro, Fidel, "Nace la sexta zafra," *Cuba,* (Havana), Jan. 1966. pp. 20-21.
Statement on 1965 sugar harvest.

2373. Castro, Fidel, "Todo indica que no va a quedar una caña en pie," *El Mundo,* (Havana), Mar. 4, 1965. pp. 1, 5.

2374. Castro, Fidel, "Total la mecanización de nuestra zafra en 2 años," *Revolución,* (Havana), June 5, 1963. pp. 1-6.

2375. Castro, Raúl, *Cooperativas cañeras,* Havana, 1961. 16 pp.
Speech of Apr. 12, 1961.

2376. Castro, Raúl, *A librar la batalla de la III zafra del pueblo,* Havana: Editorial CTC-R, 1963. 15 pp.
Jan. 22, 1963 speech.

2377. Cuba, Fórum Azucarero Nacional, *Agricultura e investigaciones agrícolas. Organización de la cosecha de la caña,* Havana: INRA, 1964. 13 vols.
Mimeographed. Tables, illustrations, diagrams. Thorough study by 200 analysts of the entire process of sugar production.

2378. Cuba, Instituto Nacional de Reforma Agraria, *Reglamento general de cooperativas cañeras,* Havana, 1960. 19 pp.

2379. Cuba, Leyes, *Azúcar: su legislación y su jurisprudencia,* Havana: Editorial Lex, 1948. 4 vols.

2380. Cuba, Ministerio del Azúcar, *Desarrollo de la industria azucare-*

ra en el mundo, Havana, 1966. 118 pp.
Mimeographed.

2381. Cuba, Ministerio del Azúcar, *Memorias del trabajo voluntario V zafra del pueblo,* Havana: MINAZ-SNTIA, 1965. 56 pp.

2382. Cuba, Ministerio del Industria Azúcar, *Resumen zafra 1967,* Havana, 1967. 61 pp.

2383. Cuba, Ministerio de Relaciones Exteriores, *La posición del azúcar cubano en los Estados Unidos de América,* Havana, 1960. 32 pp.
Also in English.

2384. Cuba, Ministerio del Trabajo, *Reglamento de la Emulación Especial de la VI Zafra del Pueblo,* Havana, 1966. 28 pp.

2385. Dorticós, Osvaldo, "La zafra: compromiso nacional," *Verde Olivo,* (Havana), May 26, 1963. pp. 45-47.

2386. Guevara, Ernesto, *Segunda zafra del pueblo,* Havana: Imprenta Nacional, 1962. 24 pp.
On "voluntary labor."

2387. Martínez Sánchez, Augusto Ramiro, *Discurso pronunciado en el acto de clausura de las 6 plenarias azucareras,* Havana: FINTA, 1960. 13 pp.
Mar. 27, 1960 speech.

2388. Rodríguez, Carlos Rafael, *Plenaria nacional azucarera,* Havana, 1962. 32 pp.

2389. Rodríguez, Carlos R., *Speech at Sugar Workers Assembly,* Washington: Joint Publications Research Service, Aug. 30, 1962. 23 pp.

2390. United States, Congress, House, Agriculture Committee, *Extension of Sugar Act of 1948,*

Hearings, Washington, 1960. 151 pp.

2391. United States, Congress, Senate, Committee on Finance, *Temporary Adjustment of Sugar Quotas,* Washington, July 1, 1960. 2 pp.

c. Commentaries

2392. Aguirre, Severo, "First Anniversary of the Sugar Cane Cooperatives," *CUBA,* (Havana), Jan. 1962. pp. 9-15.

2393. Alvarez Díaz, José R., *Castro y el azucár: 1959-1965,* Miami: Movimiento Unidad Revolucionario, 1965. 69 pp.

2394. Anónimo, *Fabricación del uzúcar,* Havana: Editora Pedagógica, 1965. 63 pp.

2395. Anónimo, "A ganar la batalla de la IV Zafra del Pueblo," *Cuba Socialista,* (Havana), Feb. 30, 1964. pp. 107-111.

2396. Anónimo, *Perspectivas de industrialización y del desarrollo de las investigaciones de los derivados de la caña. Informe preliminar,* Havana, 1967. 30 pp.
Mimeographed.

2397. Anónimo, "La quinta zafra del pueblo," *Cuba Socialista,* (Havana), Jan. 1965. pp. 123-131.

2398. Bernardo, Gerardo, *Desaparecerán los trapiches?,* Havana, 1964. 16 pp.
Modernization of sugar mills.

2399. Bernardo, Gerardo, *El primer fórum azucarero nacional,* Havana: Academia de Ciencias de Cuba, 1965. 55 pp.

2400. Borrego Díaz, Orlando, "Problemas que plantea a la industria una zafra de diez millones de toneladas de azúcar," *Cuba Socialista*, (Havana), Apr. 1965. pp. 10-30.

2401. Cuba, Academia de Ciencias, *Azúcar; información temática de actualidad*, Havana, 1964. 4 vols.

2402. Cuba, Academia de Ciencias, *Selección de trabajos*, Havana: INRA, 1965. 153 pp.
On sugar production.

2403. Cuba, Partido Unido de la Revolución Socialista, *Sobre la zafra y el azúcar*, Havana: COR, 1965. 48 pp.
Selections from *Hoy*.

2404. Cepero Bonilla, Raúl, "La conferencia Azucarera de Ginebra," *Cuba Socialista*, (Havana), Mar. 1962. pp. 47-62.

2405. Cepero Bonilla, Raúl, *La revolución cubana y los mercados de azúcar*, Havana: BANFAIC, 1959. 35 pp.

2406. Editorial, "Consumo y tipos de azucares en el mercado mundial," *Bohemia*, Nov. 21, 1969. pp. 38-42.

2407. Garófalo, José M., "Puerto de azúcar," *CUBA Internacional*, (Havana), Feb. 1970. pp. 3-13.
Shipping sugar.

2408. Herrera, Raúl, "Problemas que plantea a la agricultura una zafra de 10 millones de toneladas," *Cuba Socialista*, (Havana), Mar. 1965. pp. 1-23.

2409. Kamenetskiy, A. V., *Loose Storage and Transportation of Unrefined Sugar in Cuba*, Washington: Joint Publications Research Service, Jan. 11, 1963. 6 pp.

2410. Karol, K. S., "Cuba's 10 Million Ton National Gamble," *Le Monde*, (Paris), April 1970, pg. 3.

2411. Menéndez Cruz, Alfredo, "Algunas experiencias de la zafra de 1963," *Cuba Socialista*, (Havana), July 1963. pp. 11-28.

2412. Menéndez Cruz, Alfredo, "Balance de la zafra de 1961," *Cuba Socialista*, (Havana), Sept. 1961. pp. 34-46.

2413. Menéndez Cruz, Alfredo, "Problemas de la industria azucarera," *Cuba Socialista*, (Havana), Aug. 1962. pp. 1-17.
Also in English.

2414. Menéndez Cruz, Alfredo, "La transformación de las cooperativas cañeras en granjas cañeras," *Cuba Socialista*, (Havana), Oct. 1962. pp. 31-43.

2415. O'Connor, James, "Cuba: Salvation through Sugar," *Nation*, Oct. 12, 1963. pp. 212-214+.

2416. Perdomo, E. Manuel and Orlando Camijo, "El mercado azucarero y su avance," *Comercio Exterior*, (Havana), May 1963. pp. 33-39.

2417. Pérez, Luis Marino, *Fuentes de información sobre los mercados azucareros*, Havana: Cárdenas, 1960. 16 pp.

2418. Regalado, Antero, "Los pequeños agricultores y el plan azucarero para 1970," *Cuba Socialista*, (Havana), Aug. 1965. pp. 36-50.

2419. Risquet Valdés, Jorge, "Algunas experiencias de las brigadas de corte y alza mecanizada de la caña en Oriente," *Cuba Socialista*, (Havana), June 1964. pp. 65-83.

2420. Sierra, Angel J., *Azúcar comunista; otra conspiración comunista contra el mundo libre*, Miami:

The Royal Palm Printers, 1967. 166 pp.

2. Stockraising

2421. Aquirre, Severo, "Problemas fundamentales de la producción pecuaria," *Cuba Socialista*, (Havana), May 1963. pp. 31-49.

2422. Alvarez Díaz, José, *La destrucción de la ganadería cubana*, Miami: Universidad de Miami, 1965. 46 pp.

2423. Cuba, Instituto Nacional de Reforma Agraria, *Encuentro técnico cubano-soviético sobre ganadería*, Havana, 1963. 19 pp.

2424. Cuba, Instituto Nacional de Reforma Agraria, *Encuentro técnico cubano-soviético sobre ganado porcino*, Havana, 1962. 10 pp.
Apr. 19, 1962.

2425. Cuba, Instituto Nacional de Reforma Agraria, *Razas de ganado para Cuba*, Havana, 1966. 32 pp.

2426. Delgado, Ada, "La ganadería más allá del Cordón," *Bohemia*, (Havana), Dec. 13, 1968. pp. 28-31.

2427. "Discusión del discurso de Fidel Castro sobre la ganadería," *Cuba Socialista*, Feb. 1962. pp. 132-138.

2428. Eguirrola, Agustín, *Razas de ganado para Cuba*, Havana: INRA, 1962. 44 pp.

2429. Johnson, Beatrice, "Cattle and Dairy Farms in Cuba," *New World Review*, (New York), May 1965. pp. 50-53.

2430. Torres, Felipe, "Algunas cuestiones sobre el desarrollo de la ganadería en Camagüey," *Cuba Socialista*, (Havana), Apr. 1962. pp. 39-47.

2431. Vlasov, P. G., *Livestock Raising in Cuba*, Washington: Joint Publications Research Service, Nov. 14, 1962. 10 pp.
Russian authority.

F. AGRARIAN REFORM

1. Documents

2432. Castro, Fidel, "Agricultores pequeños, sí; burgueses rurales, no," *Revolución*, Aug. 10, 1963. pp. 1-4, 8.

2433. Castro, Fidel, *Aniversario de la ley de Reforma Agraria*, Havana: Imprenta Nacional, 1960. 48 pp.
May 27, 1960 speech.

2434. Castro, Fidel, "Anunció F. Castro la repartición de tierra al campesino," *Diario de la Marina*, (Havana), Feb. 3, 1959. pp. 1A, 3B.
First post-triumph statement on agrarian reform.

2435. Castro, Fidel, "Discurso de Fidel en la clausura del forum de la Reforma Agraria," *Revolución*, July 14, 1959. pp. 2, 6, 8.

2436. Castro, Fidel, *Cuba's Agrarian Reform*, Toronto: Fair Play for Cuba Committee, 1963. 16 pp.
Aug. 18, 1962 speech.

2437. Castro, Fidel, "Nueva fase de la Reforma Agraria," *Revolución*, Mar. 19, 1960. pp. 1, 17.

2438. Castro, Fidel, "Vamos a llevar a cabo la segunda y última Reforma Agraria," *Revolución*, Oct. 5, 1963. pp. 2-6.

2439. Castro, Raúl, "La Reforma Agraria en Cuba," *Cuba*, (Havana), July-Sept. 1960. pp. 9-40.

2440. Castro, Raúl, *La Reforma Agraria es la ley fundamental de la revolución*, Havana: Editado por la Delegación del Gobierno en el Capitolio Nacional, 1959. 30 pp.

2441. Conferencia Regional de Plantaciones de América Latina, *La revolución agraria á Cuba socialiste, acords adoptes,* Havana: Editorial en Marcha, 1961. 70 pp.

2442. Cuba, Delegación del Gobierno en el Capitolio Nacional, *Debates sobre la Reforma Agraria,* Havana, 1959. 5 vols.

2443. Cuba, Fórum Nacional Sobre Reforma Agraria, Havana, 1959, *Sesiones,* Havana, 1960. 636 pp.
Agrarian reform law and proceedings June 28-July 12, 1959.

2444. Cuba, Instituto Nacional de Reforma Agraria, "Carta del INRA a Fidel Castro: Balance y compromisos," *Cuba Socialista,* (Havana), Mar. 1965. pp. 127-132.

2445. Cuba, Instituto Nacional de Reforma Agraria, *Cooperativas: orientación y reglamento,* Havana, 1960. 64 pp.

2446. Cuba, Instituto Nacional de Reforma Agraria, *Granjas del pueblo y cooperativas cañeras,* Havana, 1961. 16 pp.

2447. Cuba, Instituto Nacional de Reforma Agraria, *Granjas estatales; sistema de contabilidad,* Havana, 1964. 823 pp.

2448. Cuba, Instituto Nacional de Reforma Agraria, *Informe económico financiero 1964,* Havana, 1965. 89 pp.

2449. Cuba, Instituto Nacional de Reforma Agraria, *Metas y orientaciones sobre la ganadería en granjas del pueblo y cooperativas cañeras,* Havana, 1961. 16 pp.

2450. Cuba, Instituto Nacional de

Reforma Agraria, *Reglamento general de cooperativas cañeras,* Havana, 1960. 19 pp.

2451. Cuba, Instituto Nacional de Reforma Agraria, *Reunión nacional,* Havana: Editorial Excelsior, 1961. 32 pp.
Sept. 9, 1961.

2452. Cuba, Instituto Nacional de Reforma Agraria, *Zonas de desarrollo agrario: Municipios que comprenden, delegados provinciales, jefes de zonas y abogados de las mismas,* Havana, 1959. 9 pp.
Mimeographed.

2453. Cuba, Leyes, *Ley Constitucional de la Reforma Agraria de 17 de mayo de 1959,* Havana: Editorial Lex, 1960. 41 pp.

2454. Cuba, Movimiento Revolucionario 26 de Julio, *El 26 de Julio le habla de la Reforma Agraria,* Havana: Talleres de la Casa del 26, 1959. 20 pp.

2455. Cuba, Movimiento Revolucionario 26 de Julio, *¿Que es la Reforma Agraria?,* Havana: Imprenta de la Marina de Guerra Revolucionaria, 1959. 16 pp.

2456. Cuba, Partido Socialista Popular, *Ley de Reforma Agraria,* Havana, 1959. 15 pp.
Stand of the Communist Party.

2457. Cuba, Presidencia, *Exposición y divulgación de la ley de Reforma Agraria,* Havana: Editado por la Delegación del Gobierno en el Capitolio Nacional, 1959. 72 pp.

2458. Havana, Oficina del Historiador de la Ciudad, *La Reforma Agraria, obra magna de la revolución en Cuba republicana,* Havana, 1960. 481 pp.
Speeches by Fidel and Raúl Cas-

tro, Osvaldo Dorticós and Antonio Núñez Jiménez.

2459. López Castillo, Raúl, *La ley de
Reforma Agraria; con explicacio-
nes prácticas y formularios de es-
critos y acta notarial,* Havana:
Editorial Lex, 1959. 117 pp.

2460. Núñez Jiménez, Antonio, *Un
año de liberación agraria,* Havana: INRA, 1960. 88 pp.
By INRA head.

2461. Núñez Jiménez, Antonio, "Dos
años de Reforma Agraria," *Bohemia,* (Havana), May 28, 1961. pp.
35-51.

2462. Núñez Jiménez, Antonio, *La
ley de Reforma Agraria en su
aplicación,* Havana: Capitolio Nacional, 1959. 68 pp.
Mimeographed.
Speech of July 5, 1959.

2463. Núñez Jiménez, Antonio, *Hacia la Reforma Agraria,* Havana:
Ed. Tierra Nueva, 1959. 188 pp.

2464. Núñez Jiménez, Antonio, "El
INRA, propósitos y realizaciones,"
Cruz del Sur, (Caracas), Feb.-
Mar. 1960. pp. 58-67.

2465. Núñez Jiménez, Antonio, *Patria o muerte!,* Havana: Imprenta
del INRA, 1961. 494 pp.
By INRA head.

2466. Núñez Jiménez, Antonio, *La
Reforma Agraria en la revolución
Cubana,* Havana: Ministerio de
Relaciones Exteriores, 1960. 71
pp.

2467. Núñez Jiménez, Antonio, "Revolución agraria en Cuba," *INRA,*
(Havana), June 1961. pp. 4-13.

2468. Otero, Lisandro, *Cuba: Z.D.A.,*
Havana: Ediciones R., 1960. 176
pp.

Series of reports on development
of agricultural reform.

2469. Rodríguez, Carlos Rafael, *4
años de Reforma Agraria,* Havana: INRA, Depto. de Enseñanza y Divulgación, 1963. 39 pp.
Also in English.

2470. Veitía, Pablo E., *Presente y
futuro del agro cubano, (un estudio y un plan de Reforma Agraria),* Havana: Editorial Lex, 1959.
140 pp.

2. Commentaries

2471. Aguirre, Severo, "Achievements of Agrarian Reform: Letter
from Havana," *World Marxist Review,* (Toronto), Aug. 1960. pp.
89-91.

2472. Aguirre, Severo, "Ante el tercer aniversario de la Reforma A-
graria," *Cuba Socialista,* (Havana), May 1962. pp. 39-49.

2473. Aguirre, Severo, *La revolución
agraria,* Havana: Comisión Nacional de Escuelas de Instrucción
Revolucionaria, 1961. 37 pp.

2474. Alonso Avila, Antonio, "Five
Years of Communist Agrarian Reform," *Defensa Institucional Cubana,* (Mexico), June 1964. pp.
12-17.

2475. Aranda, Sergio, *La revolución
agraria en Cuba,* Mexico: Siglo
XXI, 1968. 240 pp.

2476. Blume, Helmut, "Agrarlandschaft und Agrarreform in Kuba,"
Geographische Zeitschrift, March
1968. pp. 1-17.

2477. Chonchol, Jacques, "Análisis
crítico de la Reforma Agraria Cubana," *El Trimestre Económico,*
(Mexico), Jan.-Mar. 1963. pp.
69-143.

2478. Colegio Nacional de Ingenieros Agrónomos y Azucareros de Cuba en el Exilio, *Cuba: un fracaso más de la política agraria comunista*, Miami, 1961. 16 pp.

2479. Delgado, Oscar, ed., *Reformas agrarias en la América Latina*, Mexico: Fondo de Cultura Económica, 1965. 760 pp.
Chapter on Cuba.

2480. Dumont, René and Julien Coleou, *La Réforme Agraire à Cuba*, Paris: Presses Universitaires de France, 1962. 148 pp.
Outlines a new plan.

2481. Durán, Marco Antonio, "La Reforma Agraria en Cuba," *Trimestre Económico*, (Mexico), July-Sept. 1960. pp. 410-469.

2482. Gastón, Melchor W., et al., *¿Por qué la Reforma Agraria?* Havana: Agrupación Católica Universitaria, 1959. 64 pp.

2483. Goldenberg, Boris, "La revolución agraria cubana," *Cuadernos*, (Paris), Feb. 1962. pp. 48-56.

2484. Gutelman, Michel, "L'agriculture cubaine: la réforme agraire et les problèmes nouveaux," *Etudes Rurales*, (Paris), Jan.-Mar. 1963. pp. 62-83; Oct.-Dec. 1965. pp. 5-31.

2485. Gutiérrez, Raúl, "Survey de Bohemia: El pueblo opina sobre el gobierno revolucionario y la Reforma Agraria," *Bohemia*, (Havana), June 21, 1959. pp. 8-14 (supplement).

2486. Le Riverend, Julio, "Orígenes de la propiedad agraria en Cuba," *Lunes de Revolución*, (Havana), July 26, 1959. pp. 14-15.

2487. Maldonado Martínez, J. A., *La Reforma Agraria en Cuba*, Mexico: Universidad Nacional Autónoma, 1960. 155 pp.
Law thesis.

2488. Martínez Amengual, Gumersindo, *Presencia de la reforma agraria en América*, Havana: Casa de las Américas, 1962. 230 pp.

2489. Martínez Piedra, Alberto, *Land Reform in Cuba, 1933-1958*, Washington, 1962. 352 pp.
Georgetown University Ph.D. Thesis.

2490. Matthews, Thomas, "The Agrarian Reform in Cuba and Puerto Rico," *Revista de Ciencias Sociales*, (Puerto Rico), Mar. 1960. pp. 107-124.

2491. Millán, Arnaldo, "Las cooperativas campesinas de crédito y servicios en Las Villas," *Cuba Socialista*, (Havana), May 1963. pp. 50-55.

2492. Núñez Jiménez, Antonio, *La liberación de las islas*, Havana: Editorial Lex, 1959. 623 pp.
Land tenure, agrarian reform.

2493. O'Connor, James, "Agrarian Reforms in Cuba, 1959-1963," *Science and Society*, (New York), Spring, 1968. pp. 169-217.

2494. Pino-Santos, Oscar, *La estructura económica de Cuba y la Reforma Agraria*, Havana: Editorial Tierra Nueva, 1959. 110 pp.
Useful description.

2495. Pino-Santos, Oscar, "La Reforma Agraria y el desarrollo económico de Cuba," *Lunes de Revolución*, (Havana), May 18, 1959. pp. 2-33.

2496. Queral Mayo, Eduardo, *Ruta al campo; un cuarto de caballería de tierras y libertad*, Havana: Impr. Cooperativa Obrera de Publicidad, 1959. 187 pp.

Agrarian Reform.

2497. Regalado, Antero, "El camino de la cooperación agraria en Cuba," *Cuba Socialista*, (Havana), June 1963. pp. 42-60.

2498. Regalado, Antero, "Credits for Small Farmers in Cuba," *World Marxist Review*, (Toronto), Mar. 1965. pp. 29-32.

2499. San Martín, Rafael, *Reforma Agraria; la revolución cubana y su temática más apasionante: tierra, hambre, dolor y esperanza*, Buenos Aires: Eds. Agroamérica, 1960. 139 pp.

2500. Veitía, Pablo E., *Presente y futuro del agro cubano: un estudio y un plan de Reforma Agraria*, Havana: Editorial Lex, 1959. 140 pp.

G. INDUSTRY

2501. Anónimo, "El desarrollo industrial de Cuba," *Cuba Socialista*, (Havana), May 1966. pp. 122-127.

2502. Castiñeiras, Juan M., "La industria ligera en la etapa actual," *Cuba Socialista*, (Havana), June 1964. pp. 1-17.

2503. Castro, Fidel, "Estamos creando las bases para la industrialización," *Verde Olivo*, (Havana), Oct. 13, 1963. pp. 4-7.
Oct. 2, 1963 speech to the 7th Congress of Architects.

2504. Cuba, Asociación Nacional de Industriales de Cuba, *Boletin*, Havana, 1952-1959.
Irregular.

2505. Cuba, Asociación Nacional de Industriales de Cuba, *Informe y plan de desarrollo industrial*, Havana, 1959. 60 pp.

2506. Cuba, Cámara de Comercio, *Investigaciones de mercados industriales*, Havana, 1967. 46 pp.

2507. Cuba, Consejo Nacional de Economía, *La estimulación industrial en Cuba*, Havana, 1956. 142 pp.

2508. Cuba, Ministerio de Industrias, *Ciclo de conferencias sobre planificación industrial*, Havana, 1961. 214 pp.

2509. Cuba, Ministerio de Industrias, *Plan de trabajo para 1966*, Havana, 1966. 24 pp.

2510. Cuba, Presidencia, *Discurso en el acto inaugural de la exposición "La Industria al Servicio de la Agricultura,"* Havana: Editora Política, 1967. 23 pp.

2511. García Valls, Francisco, *La industria revolucionaria*, Havana: MINFAR, 1961. 31 pp.

2512. Guevara, Ernesto, "La industrialización en Cuba," *Tiempos Nuevos*, (Moscow), Dec. 9, 1964. pp. 16-17.

2513. Guevara, Ernesto, "Tareas industriales de la revolución en los años venideros," *Cuba Socialista*, (Havana), Mar. 1962. pp. 28-46.

2514. Havana, Universidad, Asociación de Estudiantes de Medicina, *Operación industria*, Havana, 1959. 30 pp.
Exposition of Cuban products.

2515. López Sanabria, Hugo, *Clasificación industrial de las actividades económicas de Cuba*, Havana: Tribunal de Cuentas, 1955. 138 pp.

2516. Nolff, Max, "El desarrollo industrial de Cuba," *Panorama Económico*, (Santiago de Chile), Nov. 1963, pp. 183-188; May 1964. pp. 32-35.

2517. O'Connor, James, "Industrial Organizations in the Old and New Cubas," *Science and Society*, (New York), Spring 1966. pp. 149-190.

2518. Pazos, Felipe, "Dificultades y posibilidades de una política de industrialización," *Humanismo*, (Mexico), No. 24, Oct. 1954. pp. 135-149.

2519. Shulgin, V. N., *Pulp and Paper Industry in Cuba*, Washington: Joint Publications Research Service, Aug. 13, 1962. 8 pp.

2520. Vázquez, José, "Cuba construye su industria química," *Bohemia*, (Havana), June 11, 1965. pp. 38-41.

2521. Véliz, Claudio, "The New Cuban Industrial Policy," *The World Today*, (London), Sept. 1963. pp. 371-374.

H. TRADE

1. Foreign

2522. Álvarez Díaz, José R., *El precio de comerciar con Cuba comunista; análisis de una economía en bancarrota*, Miami: Movimiento Unidad Revolucionaria, 1965. 39 pp.

2523. Anónimo, "Cuba y la conferencia de comercio y desarrollo," *Comercio Exterior*, (Havana), July-Sept. 1963. pp. 49-53.

2524. Anónimo, "La experiencia de Cuba en comercio exterior," *Comercio Exterior*, (Havana), Apr.-June 1964. pp. 50-118.

2525. Ball, George, "Trading relations between the free world and Cuba," *Department of State Bulletin*, (Washington, D.C.), Oct. 22, 1962. pp. 591-595.

2526. Browne, G. A., "Cuba achieves record trade [1957]," *Foreign Trade*, (Canada), July 19, 1958. pp. 16-18.

2527. Cepero Bonilla, Raúl, *Cuba y el mundo: la independencia económica se conquista con la diversificación de los mercados exteriores*, Havana: Editorial Echevarría, 1960. 5 pp.

2528. Club de Rotarios y Leones, *Estado actual de las relaciones comerciales cubanoamericanas. Exposición de datos históricos y estadísticos*, Havana, 1955. 72 pp.

2529. Cuba, Banco Nacional, "El comercio exterior de Cuba en 1958," *Revista del Banco Nacional de Cuba*, (Havana), June 1959. pp. 767-781.

2530. Cuba, Banco Nacional, "Convenios bilaterales que rigen el comercio exterior de Cuba," *Revista del Banco Nacional de Cuba*, (Havana), Dec. 1958. pp. 791-799.

2531. Cuba, Cámara de Comercio, *Informaciones sobre el comercio exterior de Cuba*, Havana, 1966. 37 pp.

2532. Cuba, Cámara de Comercio, *La abolición de las formalidades consulares*, Havana, 1967. 15 pp.

2533. Cuba, Cámara de Comercio, *Términos Comerciales. Trade Terms. Tablas sinópticas anotadas. Annotated Synoptic Tables.* Havana, 1966. 132 pp.

2534. Cuba, Cámara de Comercio, *La valoración aduanal de mercancías importadas*, Havana, 1967. 22 pp.

2535. Cuba, Junta Central de Planificación, Dirección de Estadística, *Comercio exterior de Cuba, 1959*, Havana, 1961. 3 vols.

2536. Cuba, Leyes, *Código de comercio vigente en la República de Cuba*, Havana: J. Montero, 1961. 620 pp.

2537. Cuba, Ministerio de Comercio Exterior, *Comercio exterior de Cuba*, Havana, 1902-1959. Irregular.

2538. Cuba, Ministerio de Comercio Exterior, *Comercio exterior de Cuba; importaciones*, Havana, 1964, 1 vol.

2539. Cuba, Ministerio de Comercio Exterior, *Mercados en breve*, Havana: Editorial Nacional de Cuba, 1966. 273 pp.

2540. Cuba, Ministerio de las Fuerzas Armadas Revolucionarias, *Exportación de azúcar en relación con: países de destino, puertos de salida, puertos de destino, banderas, rutas marítimas*, Havana, 1960. 42 pp. Mimeographed.

2541. Cuba, Ministerio de Hacienda, *Balanzas de comercio, balanzas de pagos e ingreso nacional; 10 años (1949-1958)*, Havana, 1960, XIV. 121 pp.

2542. Cuba, Ministerio de Hacienda, *Convenios bilaterales de pago y su* Mimeographed.
to. de Publicaciones, 1963. 67 pp. *importancia. Regulaciones sobre divisas y su misión*, Havana: Dep-Mimeographed.

2543. Cuba, Ministerio de Relaciones Exteriores, *Desarrollo del comercio exterior en Cuba*, Havana, 1966. 56 pp.

2544. "Cuba: panorama de la reciente evolución del comercio exterior de Cuba," *Comercio Exterior*, (Havana), October 1964. p. 722.

2545. "Cuba y la conferencia de comercio y desarrollo," *Comercio Exterior*, (Havana), July-Sept. 1963. pp. 49-53.

2546. "Cuba's 1966-1968 Trade with Soviet Block," *Rynki Zagraniczne*, (Warsaw), September 4, 1969. pp. 1-2.

2547. "Entrevista con Carlos Rafael Rodríguez," *Caretas*, (Lima), April 28-May 8, 1969. pp. 14-16, 19.

2548. Escarpenter y Fargas, Claudio, *La economía del tráfico marítimo internacional de Cuba*, Havana: Editorial Echevarría, 1958. 210 pp.

2549. Freyre, Jorge, *La supeditación del comercio exterior de Cuba al Bloque Soviético*, Paris: Cuadernos, 1961. 20 pp.

2550. García Valls, Francisco, "La voz de Cuba en la reunión de la CEPAL," *Politica*, (Mexico), June 1, 1965. pp. 1-5.

2551. González Noriega, Julio, "Las inversiones desde el punto de vista del comercio exterior," *Comercio Exterior*, (Havana), January-March, 1964. pp. 71-89.

2552. Lamberg, Robert F., "The Cuban Economy and the Soviet Bloc, 1963-1968," *Studies on the Soviet Union*, (Munich), No. 2, 1968. pp. 116-126.

2553. Lambert, Don E., "Oil, Castro and Communism," *World Oil*, (Caracas), June 1962. pp. 116-120, 130.

2554. Lavergue, Néstor, *El intercam-*

bio mercantil en el socialismo, Havana: Revista Comercio Exterior, 1964. 255 pp.

2555. León, Raúl, "El reciente acuerdo comercial cubano-uruguayo," Cuba Socialista, (Havana), Sept. 1963. pp. 48-54.

2556. León, Raúl, "La planificación del comercio exterior," Cuba Socialista, (Havana), No. 28, 1963. pp. 1-22.

2557. Mora Becerra, Alberto, "Algunas cuestiones en torno al comercio exterior," Comercio Exterior, (Havana), Mar. 1963. pp. 5-7.

2558. Mora Becerra, Alberto, La nueva orientación del comercio exterior cubano, Havana: MINFAR, 1961. 30 pp.

2559. Perdomo, Manuel, "El mercado azucarero y su avance," Comercio Exterior, (Havana), May 1963. pp. 33-39.

2560. Pick, Hella, "More British Ships Trade with Cuba," Manchester Guardian, (London), Apr. 19, 1963. p. 11.

2561. Prybyla, Jan S., "Communist China's Economic Relations with Cuba," Business and Society, (New York), Autumn 1965. pp. 3-7.

2562. Reymer, Jack, "Spanish Capitalism and Cuban Trade," Weekly People, (New York), Feb. 8, 1964. p. 4.

2563. Roa, Raúl, "Cuba no podrá ser eliminada por Estados Unidos del comercio latinoamericano," Bohemia, (Havana), Oct. 19, 1962. pp. 36-37+.

2564. Torras, Jacinto, "Cuba y la Asociación Latinoamericana de Libre Comercio," Cuba Socialista, (Havana), Nov. 1962. pp. 17-27.

2565. Torras, Jacinto, "Las relaciones comerciales y económicas entre Cuba y los Estados Unidos de América," Comercio Exterior, (Havana), July-Sept. 1963. pp. 5-12.

2566. United States, Department of Agriculture, Economic Research Service, Cuba Shifts Trade in Farm Products to Soviet Bloc, Washington, Mar. 1962. 6 pp.

2567. United States, Department of Commerce, Bureau of International Commerce, United States Trade with Cuba, 1960-1963, Washington, 1964. 4 pp.

2568. United States, Department of Commerce, Bureau of International Commerce, World Trade with Cuba, 1961-62, Washington, 1964. 4 pp.

2569. United States Congress, House, Committee on Interstate and Foreign Commerce, Trade with Cuba, Hearings, Washington, 1961. 78 pp.

2570. Vizcaíno, Juan F., "Cuba, comunismo y comercio exterior," Política, (Caracas), June-Aug. 1964. pp. 33-40.

2571. Vizcaíno, Juan F., The Tariff Situation in Cuba: 1927-1958, Miami: Cuban Economic Research Project, 1965. 260 pp.

2572. Wylie, Kathryn and Gae Bennett, "What Has Happened to Our Trade with Cuba," Foreign Agriculture, (Washington, D.C.), Dec. 1961. pp. 8-10.

2573. Zhuikov, G., "Capitalist Trade with Cuba," New Times, (Moscow), Apr. 15, 1964. pp. 16-17.

2. Domestic

2574. Cuba, Cámara de Comercio, *Control sobre la calidad de los productos,* Havana, 1966. 62 pp.

2575. Cuba, Cámara de Comercio, *Memoria,* Havana, 1901-1959. Yearly.

2576. Cuba, Leyes, *Código de comercio y legislación mercantil complementaria,* Havana: Cultural, 1957. 1160 pp.

2577. Cuba, Leyes, *Curso de legislación mercantil,* Havana: Editorial Lex, 1959. 1090 pp.

2578. Cuba, Ministerio de Comercio Interior, *Balance del trabajo y nuevas tareas,* Havana, 1965. 32 pp

2579. Cuba, Ministerio de Comercio Interior, *Organización de mercados de abastos. Plan de organización,* Havana, 1964. 10 pp.

2580. León, Raúl, "Algunas cuestiones relativas a la formación de los precios en la econmía cubana, *Comercio Exterior,* (Havana), May 1963. pp. 3-18.

2581. Luzardo, Manuel, *Intervenciones de nuestro compañero Ministro del Comercio Interior,* Havana: Eds. de la Dirección de Divulgación, 1965. 118 pp.

I. LABOR

2582. Anónimo, "Los trabajadores en el paraíso comunista del Caribe," *Cuba Nueva,* (Coral Gables), Nov. 15, 1962. pp. 16-19.

2583. "Ataques comunistas a la CTC," *Revolución,* (Havana), Aug. 26, 1959. pp. 1, 19.

2584. Borochowicz, Elly, "Cuba—retrospect and prospect," *AFL-CIO Free Trade Union News,* Feb. 1963. pp. 4-5.

2585. Castro, Fidel, "Discurso ante la convención de consejos de técnicos asesores," *Obra Revolucionaria,* (Havana), No. 7, 1961. pp. 7-25.
Feb. 13. On unemployment.

2586. Castro, Fidel, "La llamada hoy no es a las armas: la llamada es al trabajo," *Revolución,* (Havana), June 28, 1963. pp. 1, 2, 3.
June 27, 1963 speech on labor.

2587. Córdova, Efrén, *Derecho laboral cubano,* Havana: Editorial Lex, 1957. 410 pp.

2588. Corporaciones Económicas de Cuba, *Cuba y la OIT,* Miami, 1968, 66 pp.
"Cuba should be expelled from international labor organizations."

2589. Cuba, Central de Trabajadores, *Presupuesto de acción sindical para 1963,* Havana, 1963, 257 pp.

2590. Cuba, Consejo Nacional de Economía, *El empleo, el sub-empleo y el desempleo en Cuba,* Havana, 1958. 31 pp.

2591. Cuba, Partido Comunista, *Temas para centros de trabajo,* Havana: Comisión de Trabajo Ideológico, 1965. 43 pp.

2592. Cuban Economic Research Project, *Labor Conditions in Communist Cuba,* Miami: University of Miami Press, 1963. 158 pp.
Good scholarly survey.

2593. Frente Obrero Revolucionario Democrático Cubano, *Cuba, cómo se construye la esclavitud proletaria,* Miami, 1964. 40 pp.

2594. Garaudy, Roger, "La classe ouvrière, le Parti et l'État dans la révolution cubaine," *Cashiers du Communisme,* (Paris), June 1962. pp. 65-82.

2595. Gilly, Adolfo, *Inside the Cuban Revolution,* New York: Monthly Review Press, 1964. 88 pp.
"Workers have little power."

2596. Gómez, Teófilo, *El derecho del salario,* Havana: Editorial Lex, 1957. 167 pp.

2597. Iglesias, Abelardo, "La situación de los trabajadores en Cuba," *Avance Criollo,* (Miami), June 1, 1962. pp. 35, 54.

2598. Inter-American Regional Organization of Workers, *Trade Unions and People of Cuba Against Despotism,* Mexico: ORIT, 1961. 64 pp.

2599. *Labor and Social Security in Cuba,* Washington: Joint Publications Research Service, Oct. 4, 1962. 48 pp.

2600. Mármol, Guillermo, "El proceso laboral en la Cuba comunista," *Política,* (Caracas), June-Aug. 1964. pp. 11-32.

2601. Martinez Sánchez, Augusto, "La implantación del nuevo sistema salarial en las industrias de Cuba," *Cuba Socialista,* (Havana), Oct. 1963. pp. 8-22.

2602. Masó, Calixto, "El movimiento obrero cubano," *Panoramas,* (Mexico), May-June, 1964. pp. 69-94.

2603. Masó, Calixto, "Los sindicatos y el proceso revolucionario," *Combate,* (San José, Costa Rica), July-Aug. 1962. pp. 17-24.

2604. Mesa Lago, Carmelo, *Cuba socialista intenta subvertir la Organización Internacional del Trabajo,* Miami: Agencia de Informaciones Periodísticas, 1965. 7 pp.

2605. Mesa Lago, Carmelo, "Economic Significance of Unpaid Labor in Socialist Cuba," *Industrial and Labor Relations Review,* (New York), Apr. 1969. pp. 339-357.

2606. Mesa Lago, Carmelo, "Labor + Coercion + Unpaid Hours = Socialist Voluntary Work," *AIP,* (Miami), Sept. 1964, (special report). 14 pp.

2607. Mesa Lago, Carmelo, *The Labor Sector and Socialist Distribution in Cuba,* New York: Frederick A. Praeger, 1968. 250 pp.
Theories vs fact.

2608. Organización Regional Interamericana de Trabajadores, *The Cuban Trade Union Movement Under the Regime of Dr. Castro,* Mexico: ORIT, 1960. 51 pp.

2609. *Profsoiuzy Kuby; sbornik statei vystuplenii i materialov,* [Cuban trade unions; collected articles, addresses, and materials], Moscow, Profizdat, 1963. 166 pp.

2610. Risquet Valdés, Jorge, *Dos artículos de la revista Cuba Socialista,* Havana: INRA, 1964. 35 pp.
On sugar workers.

2611. Rodríguez, Francisco, "Cuba: the First Stage," *Labour Review,* (London), Spring 1962. pp. 8-32.

2612. United States Bureau of Labor Statistics, *Labor in Cuba,* Washington, 1957. 26 pp.

2613. Maxine Valdés and Nelson P. Valdés, "Cuban Workers and the Revolution," *New Politics,* (New York), Fall 1970. pp. 36-48.

2614. Valdespino, Andrés, "La dictadura contra el proletariado," *Bohemia Libre,* (Miami), Sept. 9, 1962. pp. 58-60, 64.

2615. Ventocilla, Eleodoro, *Cuba*

1967, la situación de los trabajadores, Mexico: Tall. graf. de Impresiones Modernas, 1967. 142 pp. Journalist.

2616. Whittemore, E. P., "Cuba's Unions Come Full Circle," *The New Leader,* (New York), Feb. 5, 1962. pp. 24-25.

2617. Woodward, Ralph L., "Cuba: Urban Labor and Communism," *Caribbean Studies,* (Rio Piedros), Oct. 1963. pp. 17-50.

2618. Zeitlin, Maurice, "Alienation and Revolution," *Social Forces,* Dec. 1966. pp. 224-236.
Labor.

2619. Zeitlin, Maurice, "Economic Insecurity and the Political Attitudes of Cuban Workers," *American Sociological Review,* (Washington), Feb. 1966. pp. 35-51.

2620. Zeitlin, Maurice, "Labor in Cuba," *The Nation,* (New York), Oct. 20, 1962. pp. 238-241.

2621. Zeitlin, Maurice, "Political Generations in the Cuban Working Class," *American Journal of Sociology,* (Chicago), Mar. 1966. pp. 493-508.

2622. Zeitlin, Maurice, *Revolutionary Politics and the Cuban Working Class,* Princeton, New Jersey: Princeton University Press, 1967. 306 pp.
"Workers are the backbone of the revolution."

2623. Zeitlin, Maurice, "Revolutionary Workers and Individual Liberties," *American Journal of Sociology,* (Chicago), May 1967. pp. 619-632.

1. History

2624. Alba, Víctor, *Historia del movimiento obrero en América Latina,* Argentina: Limusa Wiley, 1964. 598 pp.
Chapter on Cuba.

2625. Batista, Eugenio, et al., "Análisis comparativo entre las economías del siglo 19 y el 20," *Exilio* (New York), Summer 1968. pp. 3-74.

2626. Grobart, Fabio, "El movimiento obrero cubano de 1925 a 1933," *Cuba Socialista,* (Havana), Aug. 1966. pp. 88-119.
Traces history of Communist Party.

2627. Nikirov, B. S., "Iz istorii rabočego dviženija na Kube," [The history of the labor movement in Cuba], *Voprosy Istorii,* (Moscow), Sept. 1961. pp. 103-115.
CTC history 1934-1958.

2628. Ordoqui, Joaquín, *Elementos para la historia del movimiento obrero en Cuba,* Havana: Editorial CTC-R, 1960. 39 pp.

2629. Page, Charles A., *The Development of Organized Labor in Cuba,* Unpublished Dissertation: UCLA, 1952.
Useful background material.

2630. Portocarrero, Jesús A., *Cuba, paradigma y destino de América,* Miami: Colonial Press, 1966. 770 pp.
Labor under Batista.

2631. Riera Hernández, Mario, *Historial obrero cubano, 1574-1965,* Miami, Florida: Rema Press, 1965. 303 pp.

2632. Rito, Esteban, *Lucha de clases y movimiento obrero,* Havana: Imprenta Nacional de Cuba, 1961. 339 pp.
History of organized labor.

2633. Rivero Muñiz, José, *El primer partido socialista cubano. Apuntes para la historia del proletariado en Cuba,* Havana: Universidad Central de Las Villas, 1962. 120 pp.

2634. Telleria Toca, Evelio, "Presencia obrera en cien años de lucha," *Bohemia,* (Havana), Oct. 11, 1968. pp. 100-107, 128.

2. Documents—Policy

2635. Almeida, Juan, *Discurso pronunciado en la Plaza de la Revolución con motivo de conmemorarse el primero de mayo,* Havana: Editora Política, 1967. 24 pp.
    May 1, 1967.
    Labor and sugar harvest.

2636. Anónimo, "Las normas de trabajo y la escala salarial," *Nuestra Industria,* (Havana), Oct. 1964. pp. 2-3, 37-47.

2637. Anónimo, "Nuevo régimen salarial," *Bohemia,* (Havana), May 24, 1963. p. 65.

2638. Castro, Fidel "Discurso en la CTC Revolucionaria con motivo de la clausura del X Congreso Obrero Nacional Revolucionario," *Revolución,* (Havana), Nov. 23, 1959. pp. 4, 5, 7-8.
    Fidel preserves communist influence in labor movement by imposing unity.

2639. Castro, Fidel, "La mayor batalla del gobierno: la batalla contra el desempleo," *Diario de la Marina,* (Havana), Feb. 20, 1959. pp. 1, 18A.

2640. Castro, Fidel, "Primer Congreso Obrero Libre," *Revolución,* (Havana), Nov. 20, 1959. pp. 16-18.

Nov. 18, 1959 speech calling for labor unity.

2641. Castro, Fidel, "A los trabajadores hay que enseñarlos a pensar como clase y no como sector," *Revolución,* (Havana), May 30, 1960. pp. 1, 4, 6, 14.

2642. Castro, Fidel, *A los obreros de la construcción,* Havana: MICONS, 1963. 52 pp.

2643. Cuba, Central de Trabajadores, *La lucha contra el burocratismo,* Havana, 1967. 31 0p.

2644. Cuba, Confederación de Trabajadores, *Las tareas del movimiento sindical en la edificación socialista,* Havana: Editorial Vanguardia Obrera, 1961. 159 pp.

2645. Cuba, Ministerio de Bienestar Social, *¿Qué sabe usted del trabajo voluntario?,* Havana, 1960. 18 pp.
    Mimeographed.

2646. Cuba, Ministerio de la Construcción, *Normas de trabajo,* Havana, 1965. 2 vols.

2647. Cuba, Ministerio de Educación, *Plan general de emulación socialista para el MINED y el SINTEC,* Havana, 1963. 45 pp.

2648. Cuba, Ministerio del Trabajo, *Instrucciones para el estudio del salario,* Havana, 1962. 31 pp.

2649. Cuba, Ministerio del Trabajo, *Instrucciones sobre la concertación de los convenios de trabajo,* Havana: Editorial CTC-R, 1962. 24 pp.

2650. Cuba, Ministerio del Trabajo, *Las normas de trabajo: ¿qué son, para qué sirven y cómo se van a aplicar?,* Havana: Editorial CTC-R, 1962. 36 pp.

2651. Cuba, Ministerio del Trabajo,

De la política laboral del Gobierno Revolucionario, Havana, 1962. 90 pp.

2652. Cuba, Ministerio del Trabajo, *Qué es una comisión de reclamaciones y cómo funciona,* Havana, 1961. 64 pp.

2653. Cuba, Ministerio del Trabajo, *¡La revolución cumple!,* Havana: Cooperativa Obrera de Publicaciones, 1959. 47 pp.

2654. Cuba, Presidencia, *Discurso en el homenaje a los trabajadores de la Medicina,* Havana: Ministerio de Salud Pública, 1961. 11 pp.

2655. Cuba, Presidencia, *La responsibilidad de la dirigencia sindical ante la revolución,* Havana: Editorial CTC-R, 1962. 27 pp.
Sept. 7, 1962 speech at the XXVI National Council of the Cuban Confederation of Labor.

2656. Dorticós, Osvaldo, "The Working Class of the New Cuba," *Political Affairs,* (New York), Oct. 1962. pp. 36-40.

2657. Escalona, Pedro, "Salarios y normas: logros de 1963," *Trabajo,* (Havana), Dec. 1963. pp. 2-5.

2658. Guevara, Ernesto, *Cada obrero un estudiante,* Havana: Capitolio Nacional, 1961. 48 pp.

2659. Guevara, Ernesto, *May Day Speech to Labor,* New York: Fair Play for Cuba Committee, 1963. 23 pp.

2660. Guevara, Ernesto, *El papel de la clase obrera en la construcción del socialismo y emulación, parte vital del trabajo de la nación,* Havana: Sindicato Nacional de Trabajadores de la Aviación, 1962. 63 pp.

2661. Guevara, Ernesto, "La victoria de Cuba está en la unión, en el trabajo, en el espíritu de sacrificio de su pueblo," *Bohemia,* (Havana), Apr. 9, 1961. pp. 66-71.

2662. Hart Dávalos, Armando, *El trabajo del dirigente sindical de la enseñanza,* Havana: Ministerio de Educación, Depto. de Publicaciones, 1962. 18 pp.

2663. Hung, Roberto, *Necesidad de los tribunales de trabajo,* Santiago de Cuba: Tip. San Román, 1959. 25 pp.

2664. Martínez Sánchez, Augusto, "La implantación del nuevo sistema salarial en las industrias de Cuba," *Cuba Socialista,* (Havana), Oct. 1963. pp. 8-22.
By labor minister.

2665. Martínez Sánchez, Augusto, *La política laboral de la revolución socialista,* Havana: Editorial CTC-R, 1962. 90 pp.

2666. Martínez Sánchez, Augusto, *La revolución en el campo laboral,* Havana: Capitolio Nacional, 1960. 26 pp.
April 1, 1960 speech.

2667. Peña, Lázaro, *Speech at the 16th National Congress of the CTC-R,* Washington: Joint Publications Research Service, Oct. 8, 1962. 67 pp.

2668. Peña, Lázaro, *Tareas actuales del movimiento sindical en el tránsito hacia el socialismo,* Havana: Editorial CTC-R, 1962. 79 pp.
Sept. 7, 1962 report to the XXVI National Council of the Cuban Confederation of Labor.

2669. Roca, Blas, *Crece la responsabilidad de los sindicatos en la construcción del socialismo,* Havana: Editorial CTC-R, 1962. 23 pp.

2670. Roca, Blas, *Algunos conceptos básicos sobre el movimiento sindical y el camino del socialismo*, Havana: Federación Nacional de la Química Industrial, 1961. 31 pp.

2671. Roca, Blas, *Teoría y acción revolucionaria. Algunos conceptos básicos sobre el movimiento sindical*, Havana, 1961. 46 pp.

2672. Roca, Blas, and Lázaro Peña, *Las funciones y el papel de los sindicatos ante la revolución*, Havana: Editorial Vanguardia Obrera, 1961. 88 pp.

2673. Rodríguez, Carlos Rafael, *La clase obrera y la revolución*, Havana: Editorial Vanguardia Obrera, 1960. 82 pp.

3. Legislation

2674. Altenau, O., "Trudovoe zakonodatel 'stvo revoliutsionnoi Kuby," [Labor legislation of revolutionary Cuba], *Vest. Mosk. un. Ser.*, (Moscow), Jan./Mar. 1961. pp. 61-70.

2675. Besada Ramos, Benito, *Comentarios a la ley de procedimiento laboral*, Havana: Editorial Lex, 1961. 98 pp.

2676. Bustamante, José A., "Our Labor Legislation," *Granma*, (Havana), Oct. 30, 1966. p. 2.

2677. Cuba, Confederación de Trabajadores, *Leyes: orgánica del Ministerio del Trabajo y administración de justicia laboral*, Havana, 1962. 67 pp.

2678. Cuba, Leyes, *Ahora nada se detiene: Ley orgánica del Ministerio del Trabajo*, Havana: CTC-R, 1959. 32 pp.

2679. Cuba, Leyes, *Cinco leyes básicos en materia de trabajo*, Havana: Ministerio del Trabajo, 1960. 245 pp.

2680. Cuba, Leyes, *Leyes orgánica y de justicia laboral, mayo de 1962*, Havana: Impr. de la CTC-R., 1962. 75 pp.

2681. Cuba, Leyes, *Reglamento de los contratos referentes al trabajo y reglas para el despido de empleados y obreros*, Havana: Cía. Editora de Libras y Folletos, 1957. 45 pp.

2682. Cuba, Leyes, *La revolución en el campo laboral*, Havana: Ministerio del Trabajo, 1960. 245 pp.

2683. Cuba, Ministerio del Trabajo, *Documentos para los consejos de trabajo*, Havana, 1964. 79 pp. Contains labor justice and social security laws.

2684. Cuba, Ministerio del Trabajo, "Reglamento para la organización de la emulación," *Gaceta Oficial*, (Havana), May 21, 1964. pp. 447-459.

2685. Cuba, Ministerio del Trabajo, "Regulaciones del trabajo," *Hoy*, (Havana), Aug. 29, 1962. p. 6.

2686. Mesa Lago, Carmelo, *Cuba bajo el comunismo. La ley de justicia laboral; culminación del proceso esclavizador de la clase obrera en Cuba comunista*, Miami: AIP, 1964. 14 pp.

2687. Movimiento Revolucionario 30 de Noviembre, *Tribunales de trabajo; anteproyecto*, Miami, 1963. 54 pp.

2688. Onetti Alvarez, Enrique, *Manual de derecho laboral cubano*, Camagüey, 1960. 237 pp.

2689. Sánchez Roca, Mariano, *Orien-*

taciones prácticas y formularios
para la mejor aplicación de la ley
de procedimiento laboral, Havana: Editorial Lex, 1960. 164 pp.

4. Organization

2690. Acevedo, Arturo, "Las campesinos se organizan revolucionariamente," *INRA,* (Havana), June 1961. pp. 96-97.

2691. Cuba, Central de Trabajadores, *Presupuesto de Acción Sindical para 1963,* Havana, 1963. 257 pp.

2692. Cuba, Confederación de Trabajadores Cubanos, "Declaración de principios y estatutos de la CTC," *El Mundo,* (Havana), July 6, 1966. p. 6.

2693. Cuba, Presidencia, *Movilización de la CTC,* Havana: Imprenta Nacional, 1961. 24 pp.

2694. Cuba, Sindicato Nacional de Trabajadores Gastronómicos, *Ocho conferencias revolucionarias,* Havana, 1959. 191 pp.

2695. Hung, Roberto, *Necesidad de los tribunales de trabajos,* Santiago de Cuba, 1959. 25 pp.

2696. Talavera, Israel, "La organización de las brigadas de trabajo en la agricultura," *Cuba Socialista,* (Havana), Apr. 1964. pp. 38-50.

5. Productivity

2697. Abascal, Jesús, ¿"Normas Bajas?" *Trabajo,* (Havana), Aug. 1964. pp. 28ff.

2698. Becquer, Conrado, *El porqué de la congelación de los salarios; la productividad y los sindicatos en el proceso revolucionario,* Havana: Sindicato de Trabajadores de la CMQ, 1960. 22 pp.

2699. Castro, Fidel, *Actitud frente al trabajo,* Havana: Editado por la Comisión de Orientación Reevolucionaria, 1963. 40 pp.
June 27, 30 and July 5, 1963 speeches on labor productivity.

2700. Cuba, Central de Trabajadores, Comisión Nacional de Emulación, *Modelos para el control de la emulación,* Havana: Editorial CTC-R, 1963. 15 pp.

2701. Cuba, Central de Trabajadores, Consejo Nacional de Emulación, *Emulación socialista,* Havana, 1964. 63 pp.
Exhorts workers to produce more.

2702. Cuba, Central de Trabajadores, *Modelos para el control de la emulación,* Havana, 1963. 15 pp.

2703. Cuba, Federación Nacional Ferroviaria, *Los trabajadores, los sindicatos y la producción,* Havana, 1960. 55 pp.

2704. Cuba, Ministerio del Trabajo, *Productividad del trabajo,* Havana, 1962. 90 pp.
Mimeographed.

2705. Cuba, Partido Unido de la Revolución Socialista, *Más sobre la producción y los sindicatos,* Havana, 1963. 49 pp.

2706. Estrada, Héctor, "Como se eliminó el ausentismo en la granja Rigoberto Corcho," *Granma,* (Havana), July 8, 1966. p. 2.

2707. Editorial, "La selección del trabajador ejemplar," *Cuba Socialista,* (Havana), May 1962. pp. 129-132.

2708. Hart, Armando y Miguel Martín, *Sobre el movimiento de avanzada,* Havana: Comisión de Orientación Revolucionaria del Co-

mité Central del Partido, 1967, 31 pp.
On exemplary workers.

2709. Havana, Universidad, *Plan para la emulación socialista en la Universidad de la Habana*, Havana, 1963. 19 pp.

2710. Hernández, Gregorio, "Producción, defensa y superación acuerdan los trabajadores cubanos," *Bohemia*, (Havana), Sept. 14, 1962. pp. 43-47.

2711. Llano, Eduardo del, *La productividad del trabajo y factores de su aumento*, Havana: Escuelas de Instrucción Revolucionaria del PCC, 1966. 88 pp.

2712. Mesa Lago, Carmelo, *La emulación: una fase más de la explotación comunista*, Miami: Agencia de Informaciones Periodísticas, 1965. 11 pp.

6. Congresses

2713. Cuba, Confederación de Trabajadores, *XI Congreso Nacional CTC Revolucionaria*, Havana: Imprenta Nacional de Cuba, 1961. 152 pp.

2714. Cuba, Confederación de Trabajadores, *Los veinticinco congresos nacionales de industrias y el XI Congreso Nacional de la CTC-R*, Havana, 1961. 24 pp.

2715. Cuba, Congreso Nacional de Obreros de la Construcción, *Informe*, Havana: INRA, 1962. 18 pp.

2716. Cuba, Sindicato Nacional de Trabajadores de la Enseñanza, *Informe general al congreso constituyente del Sindicato Nacional de Trabajadores de la Enseñanza*, Havana, 1962. 109 pp.

2717. Fernández, Carlos, "El XI Congreso Nacional de la CTC-R," *Cuba Socialista*, (Havana), Feb. 1962. pp. 45-55.

2718. García Galló, Gaspar Jorge, *Informe del Ejecutivo Nacional del Sindicato de Trabajadores de la Enseñanza*, Havana, 1962. 34 pp.

2719. Martín, Miguel, "Informe central al XII Congreso de la CTC," *El Mundo*, (Havana), Aug. 26, 1966. pp. 5-7.

J. TRANSPORT AND COMMUNICATIONS

2720. Anónimo, "El transporte en Cuba roja," *Economía*, (Miami), Dec. 1964, pp. 6-7; Feb. 1965. pp. 7-8, 9.

2721. Anónimo, "En transporte: organización es la palabra de orden," *Bohemia*, (Havana), Dec. 13, 1968. pp. 32-37.

2722. Benítez, José A., "Cuba a la cabeza en el desarrollo de las flotas mercantes de América Latina," *Granma*, (Havana), June 21, 1966. p. 2.

2723. Cuba, Academia de Ciencias, *Transporte*, Havana, 1966. 44 pp. Mimeographed.

2724. Cuba, Ministerio de Transportes, *Transporte de carga y expreso. Disposiciones en vigor, sección central de tráfico*, Havana, 1963. 63 pp.

2725. Cuba, Ministerio de Transportes, *La confección del plan de desarrollo económico 1962 en el transporte*, Havana, 1961. 98 pp.

2726. Cuba, Ministerio de Transportes, *Indices técnico-económicos del transporte terrestre*, Havana:

Impr. CTC Revolucionaria, 196?.
173 pp.

2727. Cuba, Santiago, *Los delitos del tránsito, prevención y represión*, Havana: Ediciones INRA, 1965. 20 pp.

2728. Escarpenter, Claudio, *The Economics of International Ocean Transport; The Cuban Case before 1958*, Madison: University of Wisconsin Press, 1965. 208 pp.

2729. Inclán Lavastida, Fernando, *El ferrocarril de La Habana a Güines; causas que determinaron su fundación*, Havana, 1964. 8 pp.

2730. Leal, Avelino, "La integración del transporte automotor," *Bohemia*, (Havana), Nov. 1, 1968. pp. 28-32.

2731. Neumann, Peter, "Eine altertümliche transportschleife in Kuba," *Abhandlungen und Berichte des Stastlichen Museums Für Volherkunde Dresden*, (Berlin), No. 22, 1963. pp. 41-86.

2732. Unidad Revolucionaria, *The Maritime Fifth Column*, Miami: U.R., 1965. 32 pp.
Lists ships, cargoes.

K. NATURAL RESOURCES

2733. Alonso, Dora, "De cara al mar," *Bohemia*, (Havana), June 11, 1965. pp. 4-11.
On fishing industry.

2734. Anderson, Cummer M., *Mineral Industry of Cuba*, Washington: Interior Department, Mines Bureau, 1965. 137 pp.

2735. Anónimo, "La industria pesquera," *Bohemia*, (Havana), Jan. 31, 1969. pp. 36-44.

2736. Anonymous, "What Happened to Oil in Cuba," *Oil and Gas Journal*, (Tulsa), Mar. 19, 1962. pp. 85-88.

2737. Bennett, High H., and Robert V. Allison, *The Soils of Cuba*, Washington: Tropical Plant Research Foundation, 1928. 410 pp.

2738. Buesa, René, *Las pesquerías cubanas*, Havana: Centro de Investigaciones Pesqueras, 1964. 93 pp.

2739. Castro, Fidel, "Barcos soviéticos para pescadores cubanos," *Bohemia*, (Havana), July 27, 1962. pp. 46-47.

2740. Castro, Fidel, "Haremos un pescador nuevo que se aleje de la costa y surque océanos," *Revolución*, (Havana), July 19, 1962. pp. 1, 5.
On fishing industry.

2741. Castro, Fidel, "El puerto pesquero será una obra cubana que pertenecerá al pueblo," *Revolución*, (Havana), Sept. 26, 1962. pp. 1, 10.
On fishing fleet to be supplied by Soviets.

2742. Castro, Fidel, "Tenemos que darle el frente al mar y avanzar en el mar," *Bohemia*, (Havana), June 21, 1963. pp. 60-63.
June 18, 1963 speech on fishing industry.

2743. Compañía Cubana de Electricidad, *Habana. Annual Report. 1949-1956*, New York, 1950-1957. 8 vols.

2744. Cuba, Academia de Ciencias, *Conclusiones de la reunión sobre los problemas de la política forestal en Cuba*, Havana, 1967. 13 pp.

2745. Cuba, Junta Central de Planificación, *Comunidades pesqueras*, Havana, 1960. 116 pp.

2746. Cuba, Laws, *Cuban Oil Laws,* Havana: Editorial Lex, 1958. 119 pp.

2747. Cuba, Leyes, *Legislación sobre la pesca,* Havana: Escuela Gráfica Salesiana "Don Bosco," 1959. 148 pp.

2748. *Cuban Fisheries,* Washington: Joint Publications Research Service, Dec. 31, 1964. 75 pp.

2749. Editorial, "En Cuba: sombrío cuadro petrolero," *Petróleo Interamericano,* (Oklahoma), May 1962. pp. 65-70.

2750. Fleites, Mario, "El plan perspectivo de desarrollo eléctrico," *Tecnología,* (Havana), Dec. 1963. pp. 42-46.

2751. Fuentes, Norberto, "Exploradores del petróleo," *Cuba,* (Havana), Feb. 1965. pp. 38-51.

2752. Pacheco, Judas, "Plan hidráulico de Oriente," *Juventud Rebelde,* (Havana), July 29, 1966. p. 8.

2753. Pérez, Faustino, "Las recursos hidráulicos: factor básico del desarrollo económico," *Cuba Socialista,* (Havana), Feb. 1964. pp. 51-61.

2754. Piñeiro, Andrés, "El Instituto Cubano del Petróleo: su historia, sus éxitos y sus planes," *INRA,* (Havana), Oct. 1960. pp. 84-89.

2755. Ramis Ramos, Héctor, V. L. Zharov and V. A. Sakolov, *Investigaciones atunera cubano-soviéticas,* Havana: Instituto Nacional de la Pesca, 1967. 23 pp.

2756. Rego, Oscar F., "Escuelas de pesca," *Granma,* (Havana), May 27, 1966. p. 8.

2757. Ritzhaupt, Hermann, *Las pesquerías de Cuba y algunas recomendaciones para su intensifica-* ción, Havana: Instituto Nacional de la Pesca, 1965. 110 pp.

2758. Sheldon Knowles, Ruth, "Cuba Steps Up Oil Hunt," *World Petroleum,* Nov. 1962. pp. 58-65.

2759. United States, Department of Interior, Mines Bureau, *Producing Nickel-bearing Iron from Cuban Ores,* Washington, 1960. 24 pp.

L. BUDGET, MONEY, BANKING

2760. Anónimo, "Las cifras del presupuesto," *Economía,* (Miami), Feb. 1965. pp. 1, 2.

2761. Anónimo, "El nuevo frente de finanzas," *Con la Guardia en Alto,* (Havana), Sept. 1963. pp. 30-31.

2762. Castro, Fidel, "El presupuesto de 1960 será el mayor de Cuba," *Revolución,* (Havana), Dec. 18, 1959. pp. 1, 2, 6, 7, 12. Speech of Dec. 17, 1959.

2763. Cepero Bonilla, Raúl, "El canje de billetes: un golpe a la contrarevolución," *Cuba Socialista,* (Havana), Oct. 1961. pp. 43-52.

2764. Cuba, Asamblea Nacional de Gestores del Ahorro, *Primera asamblea nacional,* Havana, 1962. 49 pp.; *Segunda asamblea nacional,* 1963, 74 pp.; *Tercera asamblea nacional,* 1963, 110 pp.

2765. Cuba, Banco Continental Cubano, *Memoria anual, 1959-1960,* Havana: Ponciano, 1960. 20 pp.

2766. Cuba, Banco de Fomento Agrícola e Industrial, *Informe anual sobre operaciones de la División Industrial, 1956-1959,* Havana, 1956-1959, 4 vols.

2767. Cuba, Banco Nacional, *Memoria, 1949-1958,* Havana: Editorial Lex, 1949-1959. 11 vols.

2768. Cuba, Banco Nacional, 3 *trabajos sobre la Campaña del Ahorro Popular,* Havana: Banco Nacional de Cuba, 1961. 13 pp.

2769. Cuba, Leyes, *Legislación bancaria y económica-financiera,* Havana: Banco Nacional de Cuba, 1956. 2 vols.

2770. Cuba, Ministerio de Hacienda, *Contabilidad sin libros; resultados y perspectivas de una experiencia,* Havana: Finanzas al Día, 196-. 11 pp.

2771. Cuba, Ministerio de Hacienda, Dirección de Seguros, *Estados financieros de las compañías de seguros y finanzas, 1949-1958,* Havana, 1951-1959. 10 vols.

2772. Cuba, Ministerio de Hacienda, *Presupuesto estatal 1,* Havana, 1962. 70 pp.

2773. Cuba, Ministerio de Hacienda, *Reglamento para la contabilidad de las inversiones básicas y del costo de los trabajos de construcción y montaje,* Havana, 1962. 38 pp.
Mimeographed.

2774. *Cuban Budget for 1961 and 1962,* Washington: Joint Publications Research Service, Oct. 29, 1962. 5 pp.

2775. Fernández, Marcelo, "Desarrollo y funciones de la banca socialista en Cuba," *Cuba Socialista,* (Havana), Feb. 1964. pp. 32-50.

2776. Fernández Valdés, Enrique, *El cheque sin fondos; necesidad de la reforma del régimen legal del cheque en Cuba,* Havana, 1959. 45 pp.

2777. Guevara, Ernesto, "La banca, el crédito y el socialismo," *Cuba Socialista,* (Havana), Mar. 1964. pp. 23-41.

2778. Havana, Municipio, *Presupuesto . . . 1899/1900-1951/1952,* Havana, 1902-1952. 53 vols.

2779. Leon, Charles P., *The National Bank of Cuba: A Study in Institutional Change,* New York, 1964. 33 pp.
New York State University Ph.D. Thesis.

2780. Martínez Sáenz, Joaquín, *Por la independencia económica de Cuba; mi gestión en el Banco Nacional,* Havana: Editorial Cenit, 1959. 310 pp.

2781. Morray, J. P., "Cuba and Communism," *Monthly Review,* July-Aug. 1961. pp. 3-55.
On Oct. 13, 1960 bank and industry nationalization.

2782. Obolenskiy, N., *Finances of Free Cuba,* Washington: Joint Publications Research Service, Jan. 11, 1963. 23 pp.

2783. Regalado, Antero, "Credits for Small Farmers in Cuba," *World Marxist Review,* (Toronto), Mar. 1965. pp. 29-32.

2784. Vilaseca, Salvador, "El Banco Nacional de Cuba y los sistemas de financiamiento," *Economía,* (Havana), Feb. 1965. pp. 3-19.

2785. Wallich, Henry Christopher, *Monetary Problems of an Export Economy. The Cuban Experience 1914-1947,* Cambridge, Mass.: Harvard University Press, 1960. 357 pp.

M. PUBLIC WORKS

2786. Anonymous, "Ready for the Rain!" *Granma,* (Havana), June 22, 1969. pp. 7-9.
Dams in Cuba.

2787. Calderón, Mirta R., "Para do-

mesticar el agua," *CUBA Internacional*, (Havana), Sept. 1969. pp. 30-39.
Dam building.

2788. Cuba, Fórum de la Energía Eléctrica, *Desarrollo energético de Cuba: presente y futuro,* Havana: Comité Nacional Cubano de la Conferencia Mundial de la Energía, 1965. 12 pp.
Mimeographed.

2789. Cuba, Ministerio de Obras Públicas, *La emulación socialista en la construcción,* Havana, 1961. 65 pp.

2790. Cuba, Ministerio de Obras Públicas, *Obras públicas del gobierno revolucionario,* Havana: Tip. Ponciano, 1959. 32 pp.

2791. Perejrest, S., *Conclusiones del desarollo del riego en Cuba,* Havana: Instituto Nacional de Recursos Hidráulicos, 1963. 97 pp.
Mimeographed.

2792. Sánchez Lalebret, Rafael, "Inaugurada la primera hidroeléctrica cubana," *Bohemia,* (Havana), Mar. 15, 1963. pp. 4-9.

2793. Suárez Moré, Rafael, *Proyecto de un puerto en Isla de Pinos,* Havana: Academia de Ciencias de Cuba, 1967. 32 pp.

N. PRODUCTION

2794. Baez, Luis, "Unidades Militares de Ayuda a la Producción," *Granma,* (Havana), Apr. 14, 1966. p. 8.

2795. Cuba, Partido Unido de la Revolución Socialista, *De nuevo sobre la producción,* Havana, 1964. 72 pp.

2796. Guevara, Ernesto, *Primera Asamblea de Producción de la Gran Habana; el informe del Comandante Ernesto Guevara, Ministro de Industrias,* Havana: Imprenta Nacional, 1961. 15 pp.

2797. Vázquez Méndez, Jesús, *Administración de la Producción,* Havana: Editora Pedagógica, 1966. 505 pp.

O. FOREIGN INVESTMENT

2798. Anónimo, "La verdad sobre el pulpo eléctrico," *Revolución,* (Havana), Aug. 22, 1959. pp. 1, 19.

2799. Anonymous, "The U.S. Investment Stake in Cuba," *Financial World,* (New York), Nov. 14, 1962. pp. 11ff.

2800. Banco Nacional de Cuba, *Why You Should Invest in Cuba,* Havana, 1956. 50 pp.
Data on trade and banking.

2801. Compañía Cubana de Electricidad, *Memoria anual 1949-1958,* New York, 1950-1959. 10 vols.

2802. Cuba, Banco de Desarrollo Económico y Social, *Cuba, Land of Opportunity for Investment,* Havana: Editorial Cenit, s. a., 1958. 24 pp.

2803. Cuba, Leyes, *Legislación bancaria cubana,* Havana: Editorial Lex, 1955. 806 pp.

2804. Friedman, Walfang G. and Richard C. Pugh, eds., *Legal Aspects of Foreign Investment,* Boston: Little, Brown, 1959. 812 pp.
Chapter on Cuba.

2805. González Noriega, Julio, "La inversiones desde el punto de vista del comercio exterior," *Comercio Exterior,* (Havana), Jan.-Mar. 1964.

2806. Great Britain, Board of Trade, *Hints to Businessmen Visiting Cuba,* London, 1961. 20 pp.

2807. Johnson, Leland L., "U.S. Business Interests in Cuba and the Rise of Castro," *World Politics,* (Princeton), Apr. 1965. pp. 440-459.

2808. National Foreign Trade Council, *U.S. Businsess in Cuba,* New York, 1960. 4 pp.

2809. Pino-Santos, Oscar, *El imperialismo norteamericano en la economía de Cuba,* Havana: Editorial Lex, 1960. 97 pp.
Polemic.

2810. U.S., Department of Commerce, Bureau of Foreign Commerce, *Investment in Cuba; Basic Information for United States Businessmen,* Washington, 1956. 200 pp.

2811. Varney, H. L., "Castro's War on Capitalism in Cuba," *American Mercury,* (Torrance, Calif.), June 1960. pp. 3-12.

P. TOURISM

2812. Castro, Fidel, "Hay que desarrollar el turismo," *Revolución,* (Havana), Oct. 21, 1959. pp. 2, 8, 16.
Speech of Oct. 19, 1959.

2813. Castro, Fidel, *Una por una iremos ganando los batallas, ahora ésta, que es la del turismo,* Havana: Imprenta Nacional, 1960. 20 pp.
June 15, 1960 speech.

2814. Cuba, Instituto Cubano de Amistad con los Pueblos, *Manual del guía,* Havana, 1964. 58 pp.

2815. Cuba, Instituto Nacional de la Industria Turística, *Cuba Tourist Guide,* Havana, 1960. 38 pp.

2816. Cuba, Instituto Nacional de la Industria Turística, *Regulations and Organization,* Washington: Joint Publications Research Service, Sept. 25, 1962. 30 pp.

2817. Núñez Pascual, Antonio, "Cuba Primps Hopefully for Tourists," *Atlas,* (New York), June 1965. p. 365.

VI. SOCIETY
(See also History, Background to Revolution, Economy)

2818. Alroy, G. C., "Peasantry in the Cuban Revolution," *Review of Politics,* (Notre Dame, Ind.), Jan. 1967. pp. 87-99.

2819. Amaro Victoria, Nelson, "Mass and Class in the Origins of the Cuban Revolution," *Studies in Comparative International Development,* (St. Louis, Mo.), No. 10, 1969. pp. 223-237.

2820. Casa de las Américas, *Cuba: Transformación del hombre,* Havana, 1961. 232 pp.
Essays by Leo Huberman, Alfredo Palacios, C. W. Mills, Harold Cruse, Carlos Fuentes and others.

2821. Free, Lloyd A., *Attitudes of the Cuban People toward the Castro Regime in the Late Spring of 1960,* Princeton: Institute for International Social Research, 1960. 26 pp.

2822. MacGaffey, Wyatt, et al., *Cuba, Its People, Its Society, Its Culture,* New Haven: HRAF Press, 1962. 392 pp.
Key work to background of revolution. Anchor paperback published 1965 as *Twentieth Century Cuba.*

2823. Nelson, Lowry, *Rural Cuba,* Minneapolis: University of Minnesota Press, 1950. 285 pp.
Indispensable.

2824. O'Connor, James, *The Origins of Socialism in Cuba,* Ithaca: Cornell University Press, 1970. 338 pp.
Extremely useful.

2825. Ortiz, Fernando, *Contrapunteo cubano del tabaco y el azúcar,* Havana: Universidad Central de Las Villas, 1963. 540 pp.

2826. Roca, Blas, "Some Aspects of the Class Struggle in Cuba," *World Marxist Review,* (Toronto), Feb. 1965. pp. 3-8.

2827. Rodríguez, Aníbal C., *La participación social y la revolución cubana,* Havana: Impr. de la Universidad de La Habana, 1961. 19 pp.

2828. Tannenbaum, Frank, "Castro and Social Change," *Political Science Quarterly,* (New York), June 1962. pp. 178-204.

2829. Wood, Dennis B., "Las relaciones revolucionarias de clase y los conflictos políticos en Cuba: 1868-1968," *Revista Lationamericana de Sociología,* (Buenos Aires), Mar. 1969. pp. 40-79.

2830. Yglesias, José, "How Life Has Changed in a Cuban Sugar Mill Town," *New York Times Magazine,* July 23, 1967. pp. 8-9, 27-28, 30, 32-34.

A. SOCIAL WELFARE

2831. Aguilera Martin, René, *Sistema, educación y legislación co-operativa*, Havana: Sociedad Editorial Cooperativa, 1960. 216 pp. Social assistance.

2832. Anónimo, *La seguridad social en Cuba*, Miami: Ediciones F.O.R.D.C., 1965. 79 pp.

2833. Casasús, Juan José Expósito, *Apéndice del Código de Defensa Social*, Havana: Editorial Martí, 1960. 789 pp.

2834. Cuba, Comisión sobre Aportes Estatales a la Seguridad Social, *Bases técnicas para la reforma de los seguros sociales*, Havana: Editorial Lex, 1957. 386 pp.
Pre-revolutionary workers' social insurance and security.

2835. Cuba, Consejo Nacional de Economía, *El problema de los seguros sociales en Cuba*, Havana, 1955. 2 vols.

2836. Cuba, Instituto Nacional de Ahorro y Vivienda, *De la renta de lotería al INAV de hoy*, Havana, 1961. 31 pp.

2837. Cuba, Leyes, "Ley de Seguridad Social," *Gaceta Oficial*, (Havana), May 24, 1963. pp. 17-23.

2838. Cuba, Ministerio de Bienestar Social, *Asistencia social en Cuba*, Havana, 1960. 38 pp.
New programs.

2839. Cuba, Ministerio del Interior, Consejo Superior de Defensa Social, *Legislación vigente*, Havana, 1967. 66 pp.

2840. Cuba, Ministerio del Trabajo, *Resolución No. 5798 de 27 de agosto de 1962. Proyecto ley de seguridad social*, Havana, 1962. 6 pp.

2841. Cuba, Ministerio de Salubridad y Asistencia Social, *Asistencia social en Cuba*, Havana: 1960. 38 pp.
History and revolutionary reforms.

2842. Cuba, Ministry of Labor, *Labor and Social Security in Cuba*, Havana, 1962. 48 pp.

2843. "A discusión el proyecto de ley de seguridad social," *Bohemia*, (Havana), Sept. 28, 1962. pp. 28-34.

2844. Echevarría Salvat, Oscar A., *Democracia y bienestar*, Havana: Universidad Católica Santo Tomás de Villanueva, 1960. 199 pp.

2845. Frente Obrero Revolucionario Democrático Cubano, *La seguridad social en Cuba*, Miami, 1965. 79 pp.

2846. Mesa Lago, Carmelo, "El derecho laboral y la seguridad social del futuro," *Cuba Nueva*, (Coral Gables), Dec. 1, 1962. pp. 21-30.

2847. Mesa Lago, Carmelo, "Una nueva etapa de la seguridad social cubana," *Seguridad Social*, (Mexico), Jan.-Feb. 1961. pp. 55-85.

2848. Mesa Lago, Carmelo, *Planificación de la seguridad social*, Madrid: Organización Iberoamericana de Seguridad Social, 1959. 250 pp.
Includes text of Jan. 1959 decrees.

2849. Mesa Lago, Carmelo, *Planificación de la seguridad social*, Havana: Editorial Martí, 1960. 295 pp.

2850. Mesa Lago, Carmelo, "¿Seguridad social o inseguridad socialista?" *Cuba Nueva*, (Coral Gables), Sept. 15, 1962. pp. 18-26.

2851. "New Legislation on Social Security," *Bulletin of the International Social Security Association*, (Geneva), July 1963. pp. 196-198.

2852. "New Reforms in Social Security in Cuba," *Industry and Labor*, (Geneva), June 1, 1961. pp. 368-369.

2853. Núñez, Pastorita, *La obra revolucionaria del Instituto Nacional de Ahorro y Viviendas*, Havana: Capitolio Nacional, 1960. 21 pp.

2854. Oficina Internacional del Trabajo, *Informe del gobierno de Cuba sobre la ley de seguridad social de 1963*, Geneva, 1963. 51 pp.

2855. Pérez Serantes, Mons., "La práctica de la justicia social," *Diario de la Marina*, (Havana), Jan. 13, 1959. pp. 1, 18A.

2856. Tellería, Evelio, "Ahora las playas sí son del pueblo," *Granma*, (Havana), Aug. 14, 1966. p. 9.

B. HEALTH

2857. Agramonte, Armando, "La obra revolucionaria en el campo de la salud pública," *Bohemia*, (Havana), Mar. 1, 1963. pp. 16-21.

2858. Aguiar Sequeira, Joao Baptista, "La salud y la medicina en la Cuba comunista; ¿tenemos razón?," *Defensa Institucional Cubana*, (Mexico), 1964. pp. 4-10.

2859. Bernal, Alfonso, *Psicología y enfermedad*, Havana: Imprenta Universidad de La Habana, 1959. 266 pp.

2860. Bogoyarlenskiy, N. A., *Cuba and Soviet Medicine*, Washington: Joint Publications Research Service, 1963. 8 pp.

2861. Calvó, Rafael, *Indices de infestación por vermes intestinales de Cuba*, Havana: Labaratorio Om, 1959. 27 pp.

2862. Castro, Fidel, "Discurso pronunciado el 10 de septiembre de 1964 en el acto de graduación de 250 nuevos médicos," *Política Internacional*, (Havana), No. 7, 1964. pp. 205-222. Reviews health programs.

2863. Castro, Fidel, "La revolución ha llevado el servicio dental a las zonas rurales," *El Mundo*, (Havana), June 19, 1965. pp. 1, 7. June 18 speech. Summary of health programs.

2864. Cuba, Congreso Médico Nacional, *Medicina; estomatología*, Havana, 1963. 144 pp.

2865. Cuba, Congreso Médico Nacional, *Programa*, Havana, 1966. 460 pp.

2866. Cuba, Congreso Médico Nacional, *Resúmenes*, Havana, 1966. 255 pp.

2867. Cuba, Leyes, *Ley y reglamento orgánico del Ministerio de Salud Pública*, Havana, 1964. 16 pp.

2868. Cuba, Ministerio de Relaciones Exteriores, *Cuba: salud pública y socialismo*, Havana, 1965. 36 pp.

2869. Cuba, Ministerio de Salubridad y Asistencia Hospitalaria, *Análisis y proyecciones*, Havana: Editorial Echeverría, 1959. 37 pp.

2870. Cuba, Ministerio de Salud Pública, *Actualidad tisiológica*, Havana, 1963. 314 pp.

2871. Cuba, Ministerio de Salud Pública, *Cómo debemos alimentarnos*, Havana: Depto. de Investigaciones Nutricionales y Metabólicas, 1960. 11 pp.

2872. Cuba, Ministerio de Salud Pública, *Compilación de trabajos realizados,* Havana: Ministerio de Salud Pública, 1963. 64 pp.
On rural medicine.

2873. Cuba, Ministerio de Salud Pública, *Decree Number 7,* Washington: Joint Publications Research Service, July 3, 1962. 24 pp.

2874. Cuba, Ministerio de Salud Pública, *Desarrollo económico y salud en Cuba revolucionaria,* Havana: Imprenta Nacional, 1961. 168 pp.
Also English edition.

2875. Cuba, Ministerio de Salud Pública, *Estado actual y programa de control de la sífilis en Cuba,* Havana, 1961. 3 pp.

2876. Cuba, Ministerio de Salud Pública, *Informe del Dr. José R. Machado Ventura,* Havana, 1962. 16 pp.
Report to the XVI Assembly of Health held in Minneapolis.

2877. Cuba, Ministerio de Salud Pública, *Informe a la Oficina Sanitaria Panamericana,* Havana, 1962. 16 pp.

2878. Cuba, Ministerio de Salud Pública, *La lepra en Cuba; estado actual y programa de control,* Havana, 1963. 20 pp.

2879. Cuba, Ministerio de Salud Pública, *El MINSAP y los CDR en las tareas de salud,* Havana, 1964. 140 pp.

2880. Cuba, Ministerio de Salud Pública, *Orientaciones para la lucha antituberculosa en Cuba,* Havana, 1963. 354 pp.

2881. Cuba, Ministerio de Salud Pública, *Reglamento de salud pública para los círculos infantiles,* Havana, 1965. 16 pp.

2882. Cubillas, Vicente, *Public Health. A Society which Protects Man,* Havana: Ministry of Foreign Relations, 1968. 5 pp.

2883. Díaz, Roberto, "Cuba, territorio libre de poliomelitis," *Cuba,* (Havana), Apr. 1962. pp. 62-64.

2884. Font, Carlos, "Hacia la salud pública socialista," *Cuba Socialista,* (Havana), July 1965. pp. 33-50.

2885. Font, Carlos, "La salud del pueblo, preocupación básica de la revolución," *Cuba Socialista,* (Havana), Apr. 1963. pp. 41-60.

2886. Furmenko, I. P., *Public Health in Cuba,* Washington: Joint Publications Research Service, Feb. 26, 1964. 8 pp.

2887. González Prendes, Miguel Ángel, *Historia de la lepra en Cuba,* Havana: Museo Histórico de las Ciencias Médicas, 1963. 415 pp.

2888. Grazhul, V. S., *Public Health in Socialist Cuba,* Washington: Joint Publications Research Service, Dec. 26, 1962. 7 pp.

2889. Guevara, Ernesto, *Para ser médico revolucionario o para ser revolucionario lo primero que hay que tener es revolución,* Havana: Colegio Médico Nacional, 1960. 8 pp.

2890. Havana, Municipio, Departamento de Relaciones Públicas, *Resumen estadístico general de los servicios prestados en las distintas dependencias del Depto. de Sanidad durante 1959,* Havana, 1959. 35 pp.

2891. Hernández, Roberto, "La atención médica en Cuba hasta 1958," *Journal of Inter-American Affairs,*

(Coral Gables, Fla.), October 1969. pp. 533-557.

2892. Levchenkov, B. D., *Forensic Medicine of Revolutionary Cuba,* Washington: Joint Publications Research Service, Oct. 28, 1964. 5 pp.

2893. Murua Chevesich, Hugo and Antonio Granda Ibarra, *Manual de seguridad a higiene del trabajo,* Havana: Ministerio de Industrias, 1965. 669 pp.

2894. Ordóñez Carceller, Cosme, Roberto Plasencia Le Riverend and Antonio Granda Ibarra, *Medicina preventiva,* Havana: Editora Pedagógica, 1965. 430 pp.

2895. Pruna, Ruth D. Goodgall da, "Medical Science in Cuba Today," *Scientific World,* (London), No. 4, 1963. pp. 20-22.

2896. Roca, Blas, *Médico cubano, cual es tu porvenir,* Havana: Imprenta Nacional de Cuba, 1961. 63 pp.

2897. Roig de Leuchsenring, Emilio, *Médicos y medicina en Cuba,* Havana: Museo Histórico de Ciencias Médicas, 1965. 269 pp.

2898. Sánchez Lalebret, Rafael, "Anualmente se graduarán dos mil médicos," *Bohemia,* (Havana), Sept. 14, 1962. pp. 36-39+.

C. LIVING CONDITIONS

2899. Acha, Eduardo de, *Arrendamientos urbanos,* Havana: Jesús Montero, 1959. 469 pp.
Landlord-tenant relations, rent controls, leases and subleases by farmers. Pre-1959.

2900. Anónimo, "Toda familia tiene derecho a una vivienda decorosa,"

INRA, (Havana), Nov. 1960. pp. 9-11.

2901. Arrinda, Alberto, "El problema de la vivienda en Cuba," *Cuba Socialista,* (Havana), Dec. 1964. pp. 11-21.

2902. Augier, Angel, "Presencia urbana en la vida y la obra de Nicolás Guillén," *Universidad de La Habana,* (Havana), Jan./Feb. 1963. pp. 13-26.

2903. Baez, Luis, "El milagro de la reforma urbana," *Bohemia,* (Havana), Jan. 29, 1961. pp. 84-87.

2904. Carmado, José F., "El problema de la vivienda y la Ley de Reforma Urbana," *Cuba Socialista,* (Havana), Oct. 1962. pp. 1-9.

2905. Castro, Fidel, "Elimina el vicio y da viviendas al pueblo: INAV dos objetivos," *Revolución,* (Havana), Feb. 22, 1960. pp. 23, 27.

2906. Castro, Fidel, "El Estado no va a sustituir al propietario sino va a convertir en propietario al pueblo," *Diario de la Marina,* (Havana), Mar. 13, 1959. pp. 1, 2A.

2907. Castro, Fidel, "El ideal nuestro es hacer una casa para cada familia," *Revolución* (Havana), Apr. 30, 1960. pp. 13, 16.

2908. Castro, Fidel, "Se prohibirá por el gobierno la construcción de casas para alquilar," *Diario de la Marina,* (Havana), May 10, 1959. pp. 1, 2A.

2909. Cuba, Confederación de Trabajadores, *El trabajo unido de todos,* Havana, 1961. 39 pp.
Workers can own houses if they build them.

2910. Cuba, Instituto Nacional de Ahorro y Viviendas, *Como obte-*

ner su casa a través del INAV, Havana, 1961. 18 pp.

2911. Cuba, Instituto Nacional de Ahorro y Viviendas, *Respuestas a las preguntas que usted se hace con respecto a las casas del INAV,* Havana, 1961. 6 pp.

2912. Cuba, Instituto Nacional de Reforma Agraria, *Vivienda construida en solo 5 días,* Havana, 1961. 16 pp.

2913. Cuba, Instituto Nacional de Reforma Urbana, *Viviendas campesinas, suplemento estadístico,* Havana, 1961. 18 pp.

2914. Cuba, Leyes, *Instituto Nacional de Ahorro y Viviendas: texto completo,* Havana: Imprenta Económico en General, 1959. 15 pp.

2915. Cuba, Leyes, *Ley de alquileres; texto oficial, (Mar. 25, 1959),* Havana: Editorial Selesta, 1959. 17 pp.

2916. Cuba, Leyes, *Ley de alquileres,* Havana: Editorial Selecta, 1959. 32 pp.
Law No. 449 (Oct. 9, 1959).

2917. Cuba, Leyes, *Leyes de alquileres,* Havana: Editorial Lex, 1959. 49 pp.
Law No. 135 of March 10, 1959.

2918. Cuba, Ministerio de Relaciones Exteriores, *La revolución cubana y el campesinado,* Havana, 1966. 34 pp.

2919. Cuba, National Institute of Savings and Housing, *Housing in Revolutionary Cuba,* Havana, 1961. 17 pp.

2920. Editorial, "La vivienda en la Cuba comunista," *Cuba Nueva,* (Coral Gables), Nov. 15, 1962. pp. 5-7.

2921. Efimov, A. V., and I. P. Gri-

gulevich, eds., *Kuba: istorikoetnograficheskie ocherki,* Moscow: Akademii Nauk SSSR, 1961. 598 pp.
Section on housing.

2922. Fernández Caubí, Luis, *Cuba, sociedad cerrada,* Miami: Editorial AIP, 1968. 47 pp.

2923. Fernández Constanzo, Enrique, *Aspectos contables de la Reforma Urbana,* Havana, 1960. 15 pp.
Mimeographed.

2924. Fórum Nacional sobre la Vivienda Campesina, *Sesiones,* Havana: Capitolio Nacional, 1959. 9 vols.

2925. García Vásquez, Francisco, *Aspectos del planeamiento y de la vivienda en Cuba,* Buenos Aires: J. Alvarez, 1968. 121 pp.

2926. Hernández, Gregorio, "Las viviendas en Cuba," *Bohemia,* (Havana), Oct. 12, 1962. pp. 94-98.

2927. Listov, V., "Working-Class Havana," *New Times,* (Moscow), May 1, 1964. pp. 22-23.

2928. López Castillo, Raúl, *Ley de alquileres y su reglamento,* Havana, 1959. 88 pp.
Discussion of urban reform laws.

2929. MacGaffey, Wyatt, "Social Structure and Mobility in Cuba," *Anthropological Quarterly,* Apr. 1961. pp. 94-109.

2930. Matar, José, "Lucha a fondo contra los defectos del frente de abastecimientos," *Con la Guardia en Alto,* (Havana), May 1963. pp. 32-38, 78.
Rationing.

2931. Mears, Leon, G., "The Food Situation in Cuba—Where Shortages Plague the Castro Government," *Foreign Agriculture,* (Washington), June 1962. pp. 7-8.

2932. Merino Brito, Eloy G., *Leyes de alquileres,* Havana: Editorial Selecta, 1959. 149 pp.
Series of comments.

2933. Murray, Marjorie K., "The Food Situation in Cuba," *Monthly Review,* (New York), June 1962. pp. 81-83.

2934. Padrón, Pedro L., "Hábitos de consumo de la población," *Granma,* (Havana), Apr. 6, 1966. p. 8.

2935. Pérez de la Riva, Juan, "La population de Cuba et ses problèmes," *Population,* (Paris), Jan.-Feb. 1967. pp. 99-110.

2936. *Regulations on Food Rationing in Cuba,* Washington: Joint Publications Research Service, Apr. 6, 1962. 14 pp.

2937. Sánchez Boudy, José, "La revolución cubana y la clase media," *Alma Latina,* (San Juan), Aug. 5, 1961, p. 27; Aug. 12, 1961, p. 5; Aug. 26, 1961, p. 5.

2938. Sánchez Roca, Mariano, *Estudio y orientaciones sobre la Ley Constitucional de Reforma Urbana,* Havana: Editorial Lex, 1960. 102 pp.

2939. Santos Fernández, Juan, *La vida rural,* Havana, 1960. 49 pp.
Health conditions.

2940. Suárez Ortega, Alberto, ed., *El procedimiento sumario hipotecario y su nulidad,* Havana: J. Montero, 1959. 330 pp.
Landlord-tenant relations under the urban reform laws.

2941. U. S. Department of Commerce, Foreign Commerce Bureau, *Living Conditions in Cuba,* Washington, Nov. 1958. 7 pp.

2942. Yglesias, José, *In the Fist of the Revolution; Life in a Cuban Country Town,* New York: Pantheon Books, 1968. 307 pp.

2943. Zamora, Cristóbal A., "Un mundo de ensueño," *INRA,* (Havana), Nov. 1960. pp. 48-53.
Former country residences of rich Cubans.

2944. Zerquera Leiva, Gabriel, *Informe técnico del viaje de estudios a la URSS,* Havana: MICONS, 1963. 24 pp.
On housing methods.

D. RACE RELATIONS

2945. Aguiro, Sixto Gastón, *Racismo y mestizaje en Cuba,* Havana: Editorial Lid, 1959. 256 pp.

2946. Arredondo, Alberto, *El negro en Cuba,* Havana: Editorial Alfa 1939. 174 pp.

2947. Barnet, Miguel, *Biografía de un cimarrón,* Havana: Instituto del Libro, 1967. 239 pp.

2948. Betancourt, Juan René, *Doctrina negra. La única teoría certera contra la discriminación racial en Cuba,* Havana: P. Fernández, 1955. 80 pp.

2949. Betancourt, Juan René, *El negro: ciudadano del futuro,* Havana: Cárdenas y Cía, 1959. 248 pp.

2950. Cabrera Torres, Ramón S., *Hacia la rehabilitación económica del cubano negro . . . ,* Havana, 1959. 16 pp.

2951. Carneado, J. F., "La discriminación racial en Cuba no volverá jamás," *Cuba Socialista,* (Havana), Jan. 1962. pp. 54-67.

2952. Castro, Fidel, "Son propios del

fascismo el odio y el prejuicio racial," *Revolución* (Havana), Mar. 25, 1960. pp. 1, 6.

2953. Clytus, John, *Black Man In Red Cuba*. Coral Gables: University of Miami Press, 1970. 158 pp. On "racism."

2954. Cuba, Ministerio de Relaciones Exteriores, *Cuba; Country Free of Segregation*, Havana, 1965. 1 vol.

2955. Depreste, René, "El que no tiene de congo," *Unión*, (Havana), Apr.-June 1965. pp. 66-78. Race.

2956. Gendler, Everett, "Havana: An Eyewitness Report," *Israel Horizons*, Dec. 1968. pp. 9-13. Jewish colony.

2957. Gendler, Everett, "Holy Days in Havana," *Conservative Judaism*, (New York), Winter 1969. pp. 15-24. Jews in Cuba.

2958. Godey, G. J., "Fernando Ortiz, las razas y los negros," *Journal of Inter-American Affairs*, (Coral Gables, Fla.), Apr. 1966. pp. 236-244.

2959. Grigulevich, I. R., "Etnograficheskaia i antropalogicheskaia nauka na Kube posle revaliutsii" [Post revolutionary ethnographical and anthropological studies in Cuba], *Sov. etn.*, (Moscow), Nov.-Dec. 1963. pp. 124-137.

2960. Haward, Charles P., "The Afro-Cubans," *Freedomways*, (New York), No. 3, 1964. pp. 375-382.

2961. *Kuba, istoriko-étnograficheskie ocherki*, Moscow: Izdatel'stvo Akademii Nauk SSSR, 1961. 600 pp. Anthology by Soviet writers.

2962. Labra y Cadrana, Rafael María de, *La brutalidad de los negros*, Havana: Universidad de La Habana, 1961. 45 pp.

2963. López, Evaristo, "The Bitter Little Island," *Réalités*, (Paris), Mar. 1963. pp. 24-29. Black exile lawyer.

2964. Marcos Vegueri, Pascual B., *El negro en Cuba*, Havana, 1955. 30 pp. History of discrimination.

2965. Marianao, Municipio, *Contra la discriminación racial*, Marianao: Municipio de Marianao, 1959. 6 pp.

2966. Martí, Jorge L., "La cuestión racial en la evolución constitucional cubana," *Política*, (Caracas), Apr. 1964. pp. 61-78.

2967. Martínez Guayanés, Anuncia, "Contribuciones étnicas a la sociedad cubana," *Universidad de La Habana*, (Havana), May-June 1962. pp. 31-90.

2968. More, Carlos, "Le peuple noir a-t-il sa place dans la rèvolution cubaine?" *Présence Africaine*, (Paris), Fourth Trimester 1964. pp. 177-230.

2969. Neumann, Peter, "Probleme der Ethnologie und Folklore Kubas," *Ethnographisch-Archäologische Zeitschrift*, (Berlin), No. 5, 1964. pp. 166-169.

2970. North, Joseph, "Negro and White in Cuba," *Political Affairs*, (New York), July 1963. pp. 34-45.

2971. Pereira, Manuel, "Chinatown," *CUBA Internacional*, (Havana), Jan. 1970. pp. 48-57. In Havana.

2972. Ring, Harry, *How Cuba Up-*

rooted Race Discrimination, New York: Pioneer, 1961. 15 pp.
By Trotskyist.

2973. Tejeiro, Guillermo, *Historia ilustrada de la colonia china en Cuba,* Havana: Editorial "Hércules," 1947. 130 pp.

E. YOUTH

2974. Anónimo, "Breve reseña del reciente Congreso Nacional de la Asociación de Jóvenes Rebeldes," *Cuba Socialista,* (Havana), May 1962. pp. 135-138.

2975. Anónimo, *La juventud en la revolución,* Havana, 1964. 160 pp.

2976. Anónimo, "Unión de Jóvenes Comunistas, Cuarto CLAE y XII Congreso de la CTC," *Juventud Rebelde,* (Havana), July 19, 1966. p. 2.

2977. Behar, Carina, "Problemas sociales de la protección familiar del menor en Cuba," *Revista de Servicio Social,* (Havana), Jan./Mar. 1956. pp. 20-25.

2978. Castro, Fidel, "IV aniversario de la integración del movimiento juvenil cubano," *Obra Revolucionaria,* (Havana), No. 26, 1964. pp. 5-24.
On merger of youth groups.

2979. Cuba, Congreso Latinoamericano de Juventudes, *Resoluciones,* Havana: Unión Internacional de Estudiantes, 1960. 81 pp.

2980. Cuba, Ministerio de Educación, *Conferencia Latinoamericana sobre la infancia y la juventud en el desarrollo nacional,* Santiago de Chile, 1965. *Informe de Cuba,* Havana, 1965. 58 pp.

2981. Cuba, Ministerio de Educación, *Nuevo carácter de la Unión de Pioneros de Cuba,* Havana, 1967. 29 pp.

2982. Cuba, Organizaciones Revolucionarias Integradas, Asociación de Jóvenes Rebeldes, *El libro de la juventud,* Havana, 1961. 100 pp.

2983. Cuba, Organizaciones Revolucionarias Integradas, *La revolución y los niños,* Havana: Imprenta Nacional de Cuba, 1961. 14 pp.

2984. Cuba, Organizaciones Revolucionarias Integradas, Unión de Pioneros Rebeldes, *Estudio trabajo y felicidad para los niños,* Havana: Capitolio Nacional, 1961. 8 pp.

2985. Cuba, Partido Comunista, Unión de Jóvenes Comunistas, *Carta de organización,* Havana, 196?. 55 pp.

2986. Cuba, Partido Comunista, Unión de Jóvenes Comunistas, *III Pleno Nacional de la UJC,* Havana, 1967. 5 vols.

2987. Cuba, Partido Comunista, Unión de Jóvenes Comunistas, *Sobre el movimiento brigadista y la UJC,* Havana, 1967. 32 pp.

2988. Cuba, Partido Comunista, *La Unión de Pioneros de Cuba,* Havana, 1966. 14 pp.
CP children's organization.

2989. Cuba, Partido Comunista, Unión de Pioneros, *Metas de adelanto pioneril,* Havana, 1967. 187 pp.

2990. Cuba, Partido Unido de la Revolución Socialista, *La juventud en la revolución,* Havana, 1964. 160 pp.

2991. Cuba, Unión de Jóvenes Comunistas, *Estatutos,* Havana: Impr. Nacional, 1962. 30 pp.

2992. González, Ernesto, *The Youngest Island in the World,* Havana: Ministerio de Relaciones Exteriores, 1968. 8 pp.
On Isle of Pines.

2993. González, Víctor, "El trabajo de la Unión de Jóvenes Comunistas en el campo," *Cuba Socialista,* (Havana), Apr. 1965. pp. 45-63.

2994. Green, Gil, "Cuba's Accent on Youth," *New World Review,* (New York), Fourth Quarter, 1969. pp. 96-101.

2995. Guerra, Aldo, "Plenaria de los Jóvenes Rebeldes," *INRA,* (Havana), Nov. 1960. pp. 22-23.

2996. Hart, Armando, "Nuestro partido tiene gran confianza en la juventud," *El Mundo,* (Havana), Oct. 22, 1966. pp. 1, 9.
Youth and revolution.

2997. Iglesias, José, "Cuban Report: Their Hippies, Their Squares," *New York Times Magazine,* Jan. 12, 1969. p. 25+.

2998. Junco, Sergio (pseud.), *Yanqui no! Castro no! Cuba sí!,* New York: Young Peoples Socialist League, 1962. 12 pp.
Cuban Trotskyist.

2999. Khuzemi, I. K., and V. K. Mashkin, *Vstrecha s iunost'iu ostrova muzhestva,* [A meeting with the young people of the island of courage], Moscow: Mal. gvardiia, 1964. 78 pp.

3000. Llana, Maria E., "Los Pioneros Rebeldes," *INRA,* (Havana), May 1961. pp. 72-75.

3001. Marin, M., "Las brigadas técnicas juveniles," *Granma,* (Havana), June 23, 1966. p. 2.

3002. Martín, Miguel, "Novyi etap v deiatel'nosti Soiuza molodykh kommunistov Kuby," [New phase in the work of the League of Young Cuban Communists], *Molodai kommunist,* (Moscow), Dec. 1964. pp. 101-105.

3003. Mella, Julio A., *La lucha revolucionaria contra el imperialismo,* Havana: Editora Popular de Cuba, 1960. 106 pp.
Role of youth.

3004. Navarro Alfonso, Bienvenido, *Excursión de pioneros,* Havana: Cary, Llinás, 1961. 16 pp.
CP children's organization.

3005. Pardo, Ana, "Los Círculos Infantiles," *INRA,* (Havana), Apr. 1961. pp. 4-9.
Children nurseries.

3006. Quintela, Carlos, *La juventud cubana y la revolución,* Havana, 1962. 27 pp.

3007. Rivero, Adolfo, *La Unión de Jóvenes Comunistas,* Havana, 1962. 33 pp.

3008. Rodríguez, Miguel, "El entrenamiento del hombre nuevo," *Juventud Rebelde,* (Havana), Oct. 15, 1966. p. 3.
Youth-military.

3009. Sutherland, Elizabeth, *The Youngest Revolution; a Personal Report on Cuba,* New York: Dial Press, 1969. 277 pp.
Youth and women.

3010. Torroella, Gustavo, *Estudio de la juventud cubana,* Havana: Comisión Nacional de la Unesco, 1963. 156 pp.
1,070 students interviewed; mostly 16-18 year olds.

3011. Torroella, Gustavo, "Ideals and Values of Young People in Cuba," *International Journal of Adult and Youth Education,* (Paris), No. 2, 1964. pp. 107-113.

3012. Valdés, Maxine, "Generation Gap: Cuban Style," *Dissent*, (New York), Jan.-Feb. 1970. pp. 57-58.

F. STUDENTS

3013. Cuba, Federación Estudiantil Universitaria, *Carta abierta a los estudiantes norteamericanos*, Havana, 1960. 54 pp.
Denounces U.S. policy.

3014. Cuba, Federación Estudiantil Universitaria, *Historia de una lucha*, Havana, 1967. 106 pp.
Summary history of FEU.

3015. Cuba, Presidencia, *Carta a los estudiantes chilenos*, Havana: INRA, 1960. 12 pp.
Letter of Osvaldo Dorticós.
"The revolution has not been betrayed."

3016. Cuban Student Directorate, *Those Who Rebel and Those Who Submit*, Miami, 1964. 27 pp.

3017. Dorticós, Francisco, "Cuba Proposes Students' Creation of a Continental Organization for Revolutionary Struggle," *Granma*, (Havana), Aug., 7, 1966. p. 7.

3018. Emmerson, Donald K., ed., *Students and Politics in Developing Nations*, New York: Frederick A. Praeger, 1968. 444 pp.
Chapter on Cuba.

3019. Hart, Armando, "El imperialismo no ha podido neutralizar la fuerza estudiantil," *Juventud Rebelde*, (Havana), Aug. 12, 1966. pp: 4-5.
Aug. 11, 1966 speech to OCLAE.

3020. Suchlicki, Jaime, "El estudiantado de la Universidad de la Habana en la política cubana, 1956-1957," *Journal of Inter-American Affairs*, (Coral Gables, Fla.), Jan. 1967. pp. 145-167.

3021. Suchliki, Jaime, "Stirrings of Cuban Nationalism: the Student Generation of 1930," *Journal of Inter-American Affairs*, (Coral Gables, Fla.), July 1968. pp. 350-368.

3022. Unión Internacional de Estudiantes, *Reunión del comité ejecutivo de la UIE*, Habana: Publicado por la Unión Internacinal de Estudiantes y la Federación Estudiantil Universitaria, 1961. 102 pp.

G. WOMEN

3023. Acevedo, Arturo, "La mujer de hoy en nuestros campos," *INRA*, (Havana), Apr. 1961. pp. 54-59.

3024. Berezhnaia, Nataliia, "Velikie zhenshchiny malen'koi strany: interv'iu s Violetoi Kasal' i Sesiliei Garsiia," [Great women of a small country, interview with Violeta Casal and Cecilia García], *Zhenshching mira*, (Moscow), 1960. pp. 15-17.

3025. Berezhnaia, N., "Zhenshchiny Kuby," [The women of Cuba], *Novae vremia*, (Moscow), June 1963. pp. 6-7.

3026. Castro, Fidel, "Aquí, como los hombres, luchan las mujeres," *Obra Revolucionaria*, (Havana), No. 25, 1960. pp. 9-15.
Sept. 23, 1960 speech on the formation of the Federation of Cuban Women.

3027. Castro, Fidel, "Desaparece con la revolución la discriminación de la mujer," *Bohemia*, (Havana), Feb. 26, 1965. pp. 36-45.

Feb. 19, 1965 speech to Cuban Federation of Women.

3028. Castro, Fidel, "Discurso pronunciado en el acto de clausura de la V Plenaria Nacional de la Federación de Mujeres Cubanas," *Política Internacional*, (Havana), No. 16, 1966. pp. 263-280.
Dec. 10, 1966. On importance of revolutionary women.

3029. Cruzada Femenina Cubana, *Informe al VIII congreso de la Confederación Internacional Obrera de Sindicatos Libres*, Miami, 1965. 41 pp.
Mimeographed. On women's status in the island.

3030. Cuba, Federación de Mujeres Cubanas, *Acceso de la mujer cubana a la educación*, Havana: Instituto del Libro, 1967. 54 pp.

3031. Cuba, Federación de Mujeres Cubanas, *Cuarta Plenaria Nacional*, Havana, 1966. 150 pp.

3032. Cuba, Federación de Mujeres Cubanas, *V Plenaria Nacional*, Havana, 1967. 47 pp.
Presentations by Fidel Castro, Armando Hart, and Vilma Espin.

3033. Cuba, Partido Unido de la Revolución Socialista, *La mujer y la revolución*, Havana: Comisión de Trabajo Ideológico, 1965. 43 pp.
Selections from *Hoy*.

3034. Espín, Vilma, *Informe de Cuba en el Primer Congreso Latinomericano de Mujeres*, Havana, 1959. 43 pp.

3035. Espín, Vilma, "La mujer en la revolución cubana," *Cuba*, (Havana), Jan. 1962. pp. 1-8.

3036. Ferré, Mariano, "La Federación de Mujeres Cubanas en su quinto aniversario," *Bohemia*, (Havana), Aug. 27, 1965. pp. 58-61.

3037. Hernández, Melba, *La delegada permanente de Cuba a la Comisión Interamericana de Mujeres*, Havana, 1960. 13 pp.

3038. Perera, Hilda, "Women in a New Social Context in Cuba," *International Journal of Adult and Youth Education*, (Paris), No. 3, 1962. pp. 144-149.

3039. *Reports on Cuban Women's Federation*, Washington: Joint Publications Research Service, Oct. 29, 1962. 45 pp.

3040. Restano Castro, Aurelia, comp., *Las mujeres, en la revolución cubana*, Havana: Capitolio Nacional, 1960. 27 pp.

3041. Silverio, M., "Women Behind Castro," *Coronet*, (New York), Apr. 1959. pp. 162-168+.

3042. Suárez, María, *El dolor de ser mujer*, Havana, 1960. 306 pp.
Women's liberation.

3043. Torre, Silvio de la, *Mujer y sociedad*, Havana: Editora Universitaria, 1965. 252 pp.

3044. *Women and the Cuban Revolution*. New York: Pathfinder Press, 1970. 15 pp.

3045. Zell, Rosa Hilda, "Mosaico en rojo y negro; presencia femenina en el 26 de Julio de 1953," *Lunes de Revolución*, (Havana), July 26, 1959. pp. 8-11.

H. FAMILY

3046. Moline Lopez, Ramón, "La nueva ley matrimonial en Cuba," *Información Democrática*, (Miami), Apr. 1964. pp. 10-11.

3047. Rodríguez, Aníbal C., "Sobre la familia cubana," *Universidad de La Habana,* (Havana), May-June 1962. pp. 7-29.

3048. Santa Cruz y Mallén, Francisco Xavier de, *Historia de familias cubanas,* Havana: 1940-1950. 6 vols.

I. CRIME

3049. Cuba, Instituto Nacional de Ahorro y Viviendas, *Revolutionary Reform of Gambling,* Havana, 1959. 31 pp.

3050. Cuba, Santiago, "La lucha contra la delinquencia," *Cuba Socialista,* (Havana), Dec. 1964. pp. 22-42.

J. JUSTICE

3051. Acción Cubana Institucionalista, *Cuba ante el mundo: destrucción comunista del derecho y la Justica,* Miami, 1960. 158 pp.

3052. Agencia de Informaciones Periodísticas, *Cuba: terror y muerte; una exposición objectiva del inhumano presidio política y el genocidio en Cuba comunista,* Miami: Ed. AIP, 1964. 82 pp.

3053. Alabau Trelles, Francisco, *La revolución y el poder judicial,* Havana: Imprenta Económica, 1959. 111 pp.

3054. Alonso Avila, Antonio, *Violación de los derechos humanos por la legislación comunista de Castro,* Miami: La Voz de Cuba, 1962. 72 pp.

3055. Anónimo, "Acerca de los Tribunales Populares," *Cuba Socialista,* (Havana), Aug. 1963. pp. 40-54.

3056. Anonymous, "The Reeducation of Minors and Adults," *Granma,* (Havana), May 25, 1969. pp. 7-9.

3057. Castro, Fidel, "Discurso en la concentración en respaldo al Gobierno Revolucionario," *Revolución,* (Havana), Mar. 25, 1959. pp. 24-27.
Calls for popular support of revolutionary justice.

3058. Castro, Fidel, "Mientras más egoístas y más antirrevolucionarios se muestren los intereses enemigos de la revolución, más drásticas van a ser las medidas revolucionarias," *Diario de la Marina,* (Havana), Mar. 3, 1959. pp. 1, 2A, 17A.
Speech denouncing acquittal of forty-three airmen; demanded their re-trial.

3059. Castro, Fidel, "Próximo el cese de los tribunales de la revolución," *Diario de la Marina,* (Havana), May 12, 1959. pp. 1A, 14A, 9B.
On revolutionary justice.

3060. Colegio de Abogados de la Habana en el Exilio, *El caso de Cuba ante el derecho internacional,* Miami, 1967. 223 pp.

3061. Conte Agüero, Luis, *¡Paredón!,* Miami: Tacuba, 1962. 196 pp.
Lists those executed by revolutionary government from 1959-1961.

3062. Cuba, Leyes, *Legislación vigente de aplicación para los tribunales revolucionarios,* Havana: Capitolio Nacional, 1959. 58 pp.

3063. Cuba, Leyes, *Ley de enjuiciamiento criminal, vigente en la República de Cuba,* Havana: Instituto del Libro, 1967. 349 pp.

3064. Cuba, Ministerio del Interior, *De inadaptados sociales: a hombres útiles a la patria,* Havana, 1964. 28 pp.

3065. Cuba, Ministerio del Interior, *Sobre la reeducación penal,* Havana, 1964. 46 pp.

3066. Díaz-Versón, Salvador, *Caníbales del siglo XX,* Miami: Editora Libertad, 1962. 123 pp.
Lists Cubans "killed by Castro," 1959-1962.

3067. Directorio Magisterial Revolucionario, *Denunciamos imperdonable crimen comunista en Cuba,* Miami, 1963. 12 pp.

3068. Directorio Revolucionario Estudiantil, *El gobierno de Castro y los derechos humanos,* New York: La Voz de Cuba, 92 pp.
Report to the Inter-American Commission on Human Rights.

3069. Illás Cuza, A. L., *Cuba ante el mundo; destrucción comunista del derecho y la justicia,* Mexico, 1960. 158 pp.

3070. International Commission of Jurists, *Cuba and the Rule of Law,* Geneva, 1962. 267 pp.
Summary of social and political developments, 1959-1962, from a legal viewpoint.

3071. Martínez Arizala, Aurelio, *A Red Inferno in the Caribbean,* San Juan: "Gente Pub," 1964. 310 pp.
On "monstrous crimes."

3072. Martino, J., and N. Weyl, *I Was Castro's Prisoner: An American Tells His Story,* New York: Devin-Adair Co., 1963. 280 pp.

3073. Massó, José Luis, *¿Que pasa en Cuba?,* Madrid: Frente Revolucionario Democrático, 1961. 114 pp.

"Crime and terror under communism."

3074. *Message of the Cuban Political Prisoners to the Free Men and Countries of the World,* Miami, 1964. 20 pp.
Signed "Isle of Pines, Oct. 1964."

3075. Morell Romero, José, "El poder judicial en Cuba bajo el régimen comunista," *Estudios sobre el Comunismo,* (Santiago dc Chile), July-Sept. 1962. pp. 103-106.

3076. Organización de Estados Americanos, Comisión Interamericana de los Derechos Humanos, *Informe sobre la situación de los presos políticos y sus familiares en Cuba,* Washington, 1963. 74 pp.
Also in English.

3077. Pan American Union, Inter-American Commission on Human Rights, *Informe sobre la situación de los derechos humanos en la República de Cuba,* Washington, 1962. 9 pp.

3078. Quijada, Francisco, *Cuba bajo el terror,* Caracas, 1962. 80 pp.
Journalist's observations of "police state."

3079. Rodríguez Quesada, Carlos, *David Salvador, Castro's Prisoner,* New York: Labor Committee to Release Imprisoned Trade Unionists and Democratic Socialists, 1961. 23 pp.

3080. Unidad Revolucionaria, *A Disgrace to the Americas: Communist Cuba,* Miami, 1963. 25 pp.
Human rights violation.

3081. Wieck, David, "Freedom and Power," *Liberation,* (New York), Jan. 1966. pp. 28-33.
Freedom in Cuba?

VII. EDUCATION
(See also Research Tools, Revolution—General)

3082. Anónimo, "El país de los cuatro mil embajadores; primera plenaria de becados en el extranjero," *Cuba*, (Havana), 1963. pp. 6-13.

3083. Anonymous, "More Revolution in Education," *Granma*, (Havana), Apr. 14, 1968. pp. 8-9.

3084. Castro, Fidel, "La batalla más grande la tienen que librar los maestros, más educadores que soldados," *Diario de la Marina*, (Havana), Apr. 14, 1959. pp. 1A, 14A.

3085. Castro, Fidel, *Discurso a los escolares en Ciudad Libertad*, Havana: Oficina del Premierato, 1959. 20 pp.
Speech of Sept. 14, 1959. "Military barracks will become schools."

3086. Castro, Fidel, "Discurso en la clausura del Encuentro Nacional de Monitores," *El Mundo*, (Havana), Sept. 18, 1966. pp. 5-8.
On compulsory education.

3087. Castro, Fidel, "Discurso en la graduación de profesores alumnos del Instituto Pedagógico Makarenko," *Política Internacional*, (Havana), No. 16, 1966. pp. 253-259.
Dec. 3, 1966. On educational philosophy of revolution.

3088. Castro, Fidel, "Discurso pronunciado en la escuela para maestros 'Manuel Ascunde Dome-

nech,'" *Política Internacional*, (Havana), No. 15, 1966. pp. 111-121.
July 18, 1966. Outline of educational policy.

3089. Castro, Fidel, "Educación y revolución," *Obra Revolucionaria*, (Havana), No. 19, 1961. pp. 9-56.

3090. Castro, Fidel, "Muchas monjas y hermanos de colegios privados han manifestados sus deseos de continuar ejerciendo el magisterio," *Revolución*, (Havana), May 12, 1961. pp. 1, 8.

3091. Castro, Fidel, *El trabajo ha de ser el gran pedagogo de la juventud*, Havana: Comisión de Orientación Revolucionaria, 1964. 31 pp.
Dec. 2, 1964 speech. "Education and work should go hand in hand."

3092. Castro, Fidel, "Vincularemos enseñanza y producción," *Revolución*, (Havana), Jan. 18, 1962. pp. 2, 3, 4.

3093. Conference on the Development of Higher Education in Africa. Malagasy Republic, 1962. Delegation of Cuba, *Exposición del observador de Cuba sobre la experiencias relacionadas con la aplicación de la reforma de la enseñanza superior cubana*, Havana: Comisión Nacional Cubana de la UNESCO, 1962. 15 pp.

3094. Conferencia Internacional de Instrucción Pública, Geneva (Switzerland), 1967, *Informe a la XXX Conferencia Internacional de Instrucción Pública convocada por la OIE y la UNESCO*, Havana: Ministerio de Educación, 1967. 89 pp.

3095. Corrales González, Manuel, *Cuba en la XI Conferencia General de la UNESCO*, Havana, 1961. 8 pp.
Progress report on literacy campaigns.

3096. Cuba, Comisión Nacional Cubana de la Unesco, *Cuba y la Conferencia de Educación y Desarrollo Económico y Social*, Santiago de Chile, 1962. 180 pp.

3097. Cuba, Comisión Nacional Cubana de la Unesco, *Informe del secretario permanente en ocasión de la XI conferencia general de la Unesco*, Havana, 1962. 62 pp.

3098. Cuba, Ministerio de Educación, *Escuela Nacional. Información y motivos de discusión para los colectivos técnicos preparados por la Dirección de Educación Primaria del Ministerio de Educación*, Havana: Editora Pedagógica, 1966-1967.
Seventeen pamphlets.

3099. Cuba, Ministerio de Educación, *Informe a la XXVII conferencia internacional de instrucción pública convocada por la OIE y la UNESCO*, Havana: Editorial Nacional de Cuba, 1964. 142 pp.

3100. Cuba, Ministerio de Educación, *Informe de Cuba a la Conferencia sobre Educación y Desarrollo Económico y Social convocada por la UNESCO, la CEPAL y la OEA del 4 al 19 de marzo de 1962 en Santiago de Chile*, Havana, 1962. 78 pp.

3101. Cuba, Ministerio de Educación, *Informe de Cuba a la XIV Reunión de la Conferencia General de la UNESCO*, Havana, 1966. 39 pp.

3102. Cuba, Ministerio de Educación, *Informe del Ministro de Educación de Cuba*, Havana, 1961. 30 pp.

3103. Cuba, Ministerio de Educación, *Informe de la República de Cuba a la XII Reunión de la Conferencia General de la Unesco, 1962*, Havana, 1963. 52 pp.
Education achievements, 1961-1962.

3104. Cuba, Ministerio de Educación, *Informes sobre los planes y cursos que desarrollan actualmente los organismos encargados de la formación y superación del personal docente*, Havana, 1963. 32 pp.
Reports on plans to create new teachers.

3105. Cuba, Ministerio de Educación, *Mensaje educacional al pueblo de Cuba*, Havana, 1960. 122 pp.
Collection of addresses on educational reform.

3106. Cuba, Ministerio de Educación, *Plan INRA-MINED 1965-1966*, Havana, 1965. 78 pp.

3107. Cuba, Ministerio de Educación, *Por la calidad de la enseñanza*, Havana, 1965. 124 pp.
Diaries, speeches.

3108. Cuba, Ministerio de Educación, *Primer seminario de unidad del sistema nacional de educación*, Havana, 1965. 8 pp.
Basic policy document.

3109. Cuba, Ministerio de Educación, *Programa: plan de estudios-evaluación del escolar, curso: 1962-63,* Habana: Editora del Ministerio de Educación, 1962. 175 pp.

3110. Cuba, Ministerio de Educación, *Report of the Republic of Cuba to the XII meeting of the General Conference of UNESCO, 1962,* Havana, 1963. 83 pp.

3111. Cuba, Ministerio de Educación, *Segundo Congreso de Consejos Municipales de Educación,* Havana, 1961. 128 pp.

3112. Cuba, Ministerio de Educación, *. . . y toda Cuba es una gran escuela,* Habana, 1964. 111 pp.
The organization of the educational system in 1963-64.

3113. Cuba, Ministerio de Educación, *Vanguardias de la educación en el curso 1963-64,* Havana, 1965. 78 pp.

3114. Cuba, Ministerio de Relaciones Exteriores, *Cuba: una gran escuela,* Havana, 1965. 27 pp.

3115. Cuba, Ministry of Foreign Affairs, Department of Cultural Affairs, "1961: The Year of Education," *Cultural Bulletin,* June 1961. pp. 1-8.

3116. Cuba, Universidad Popular, *Educación y revolución,* Havana: Imprenta Nacional de Cuba, 1961. 319 pp.
Collection of lectures by prominent educators and revolutionaries.

3117. Dessau, Adalberto, *Problemas importantes de la educación socialista,* Habana: Ediciones del ISE., 1963. 48 pp.

3118. Directorio Magisterial Revolucionario, *Cuba: anécdotas de la enseñanza comunista,* Miami, 1965. 22 pp.

3119. Directorio Magisterial Revolucionario, *La educación y la subversión marxistaleninista en Cuba,* Miami, 1963. 42 pp.

3120. Directorio Magisterial Revolucionario, *Exposición a la Conferencia sobre Educación y Desarrollo Económico y Social en América Latina, Santiago de Chile,* Miami, 1962. 12 pp.
Refutes Cuba's UNESCO report.

3121. Directorio Magisterial Revolucionario, *La farsa de la educación en Cuba comunista,* Miami, 1963. 32 pp.

3122. Elías de Ballesteros, Emilia, *La globalización de la enseñanza, instrumento educador de la escuela nueva,* Habana: Cultural, 1959. 223 pp.

3123. Fagen, Richard R., *Cuba: the Political Content of Adult Education,* Stanford: Hoover, 1964. 77 pp.
Lists courses and texts.

3124. García Galló, Gaspar, *Conferencias sobre educación,* Habana: Ministerio de Educación, 1962. 68 pp.
Education official outlines duties of teachers.

3125. García Galló, Gaspar, "Educar: tarea decisiva de la revolución," *Escuela y Revolución en Cuba,* (Havana), Feb.-Mar. 1963. pp. 2-15.

3126. García Galló, Gaspar, *Los fundamentos de nuestra educación socialista,* Havana: SINTEC, 1963. 30 pp.

Speech of November 28, 1962, by an Education Ministry official.

3127. García Galló, Gaspar, *Los organismos populares de la educación y la enseñanza elemental*, Havana: Consejo Nacional de Educación, 1965. 119 pp.

3128. García Suárez, Pedro, "El maestro en la mar: cada barco una escuela," *Bohemia*, (Havana), Apr. 2, 1961. pp. 4-7.

3129. García Tudurí, Mercedes, "Resumen de la historia de la educación en Cuba," *Exilio*, (New York), Winter 1969-Spring 1970. pp. 108-142.

3130. Gómez Fuentes, Virgilio, *Realizaciones de la revolución*, Havana: Imprenta Nacional, 1961. 71 pp.
Educational achievements.

3131. Hardin, Henry N., *Evaluating Cuban Education*, Coral Gables: University of Miami Press, 1965. 95 pp.
Scholarly.

3132. Hart, Armando, "El desarrollo de la educación en el período revolucionario," *Cuba Socialista*, (Havana), Jan. 1963. pp. 20-39.

3133. Hart, Armando, *Education Since the Revolution*, New York: Fair Play for Cuba Committee, 1963. 10 pp.

3134. Hart, Armando, "Política educacional," *Humanismo*, (Havana), Jan.-Apr. 1959. pp. 358-362.

3135. Hart, Armando, "La Revolución y los problemas de la educación," *Cuba Socialista*, (Havana), Dec. 1961. pp. 33-58.

3136. Lu Ting-Yi, *Es necesario combinar la enseñanza con el trabajo productivo*, Havana: Editora Política, 1964. 38 pp.

3137. Organización Latinoamericana de Solidaridad, *Cuba: Una educación de masas para las masas*, Havana: Instituto del Libro, 1967. 66 pp.
Summary of programs.
Bibliography.

3138. Pardo, Ana, "Hombres recogerá quien siembre escuelas," *INRA*. (Havana), Nov. 1960. pp. 14-17.

3139. Popkin, Ray, "Castro's 'Crash' Program in Education," *Saturday Review*, (New York), Mar. 21, 1964. pp. 64-65+.

3140. Rego, Oscar F., "La educación en Cuba," *Granma*, (Havana), Jan. 19, 1966. p. 2.

3141. Rego, Oscar F., "Más de cien años de lucha en la educación," *Bohemia*, (Havana), Jan. 2, 1969. pp. 102-111.

3142. Rego, Oscar F., "La revolución en el frente educacional," *Bohemia*, (Havana), July 26, 1963. pp. 83-95.

3143. Roca, Blas, *En la clausura del ciclo educación y revolución de la Universidad Popular*, Havana: Impr. Nacional, 1961. 56 pp.

3144. Roucek, Joseph S., "Changes in Cuban Education since Castro," *Phi Delta Kappan*, (Bloomington, Indiana), Jan. 1964. pp. 193-197.

3145. Roucek, Joseph S., "Pro-Communist Revolution in Cuban Education," *Journal of Inter-American Studies*, (Coral Gables, Florida), July 1964. pp. 323-336.

3146. Sosa, Jesualdo, *La educación y el niño en América Latina*, Havana, 1965. 86 pp.
Compares Cuba and Mexico.

3147. Soto, Lionel, *Política y pedagogía en el movimiento tecnológico,* Havana: Consejo del plan de la enseñanza tecnológica, 1967. 47 pp.

3148. Torroella, Gustavo, "Cuba: avanzada educacional mundial," *Bohemia,* (Havana), Jan. 20, 1967, pp. 106+; Jan. 27, 1967. pp. 22+.

3149. Torroella, Gustavo, "¿A dónde va la nueva educación?" *Bohemia,* (Havana), Nov. 11, 1966, p. 106+; Nov. 18, 1966, p. 24+; Nov. 25, 1966. p. 20+.

3150. United Nations, *International Yearbook of Education,* Geneva, 1959-.
Annual section on Cuba.

A. LEGISLATION AND FINANCING

3151. Cuba, Leyes, *Nuevo ordenamiento legal de la enseñanza,* Havana, 1960. 735 pp.

3152. Cuba, Ministerio de Educación, *Compilación sobre legislación aplicable a educación,* Las Villas, 1964. 1 vol.
Decrees and laws related to education.

3153. Cuba, Ministerio de Educación, *El financiamiento de la educación en Cuba antes y después de la revolución,* Havana, 1966. 5 pp.

3154. Cuba, Ministerio de Educación, *Reforma integral de la enseñanza,* Havana, 1959, 62 pp.

3155. Ferrer, Raúl, "La ley de nacionalización de la enseñanza," *Cuba Socialista,* Sept. 1961. pp. 47-65.

B. TEACHERS

3156. Alfonso, Carmen, "Forjando nuevo tipo de maestro," *Juventud Rebelde,* (Havana), Aug. 5, 1966. p. 10.

3157. Anónimo, "La formación emergente del maestro en Cuba," *Bohemia,* (Havana), Feb. 28, 1964. pp. 7-11.

3158. Cuba, Ministerio de Educación, *Cómo se forma un maestro en Cuba socialista,* Havana, 1965. 27 pp.

3159. Cuba, Ministerio de Educación, *Graduación de 1,200 maestros voluntarios,* Havana, 1961. 48 pp.

3160. Cuba, Ministerio de Educación, *... Y me hice maestro, que es hacerme creador; graduación de los primeros 1,600 maestros voluntarios,* Habana, 1960. 16 pp.
Government drive to attract people into teaching.

3161. Directorio Magisterial Revolucionario, *Las escuelas formadoras de maestros y su destrucción por los comunistas cubanos,* Miami, 1965. 14 pp.

3162. Directorio Magisterial Revolucionario, *Los mártires del magisterio,* Miami, 1965. 24 pp.
Teachers who died fighting against Castro.

3163. Directorio Magisterial Revolucionario, *Sugerencias a los maestros para la reconstrucción nacional de Cuba,* Miami, 1964. 77 pp.

3164. García Galló, Gaspar, *Naturaleza y función de la organización de los trabajadores de la enseñanza*, Habana, 1963. 86 pp.
Round table discussion on teachers' role.

3165. Prieto, Abel, "How primary School Teachers Begin Learning their Profession," *Granma*, (Havana), Aug. 7, 1966. p. 2.

C. TEACHING METHODS

3166. Cuba, Ministerio de Educación, *Técnicas escolares modernas*, Habana, 1959. 37 pp.

3167. Unesco, *Informe sobre los métodos y los medios utilizados en Cuba para eliminar el analfabetismo*, Havana: Editora Pedagógica, 1965. 79 pp.
Praises Cuban methods of ending illiteracy.

D. LITERACY CAMPAIGN

3168. Anónimo, "El año del adoctrinamiento en Cuba," *Revista Interamericana de Educación*, (Bogotá), May-June 1962. pp. 169-172.

3169. Anónimo, *Cuba: guerrillas contra la ignorancia*, Lima: Ediciones Futuro, 1961. 127 pp.
Literacy brigades.

3170. Anónimo, "Cuba, territorio libre de analfabetismo," *Cuba*, (Havana), Jan. 1962. pp. 17-23.

3171. Castro, Fidel, "La alfabetización," *Casa de las Américas*, Havana), Nov.-Dec. 1961. pp. 3-37.
On literacy drive during 1961.

3172. Castro, Fidel, "Aprenderán a leer más de un millón de cubanos," *Revolución*, (Havana), May 15, 1961. pp. 1, 4, 5, 6.

3173. Castro, Fidel, "Eradicaremos el analfabetismo," *Revolución*, (Havana), Oct. 11, 1960. pp. 3, 4, 5, 12.
"By the end of 1961."

3174. Cuba, Ministerio de Educación, *Alfabetización, nacionalización de la enseñanzo*, Havana, 1961. 71 pp.
Literacy campaign aids nationalization of Cuba.

3175. Cuba, Ministerio de Educación, *¡Hemos cumplido!*, Havana: Imprenta Nacional, 1961. 24 pp.
"Cuba is free from illiteracy."

3176. García Galló, Gaspar "La lucha contra el analfabetismo en Cuba," *Cuba Socialista*, (Havana), Oct. 1961. pp. 69-81.

3177. Hart, Armando, *Informe del Ministro de Educación de Cuba sobre lucha contra el analfabetismo y tareas de la sociedad y los estudiantes*, Habana, 1961. 30 pp.
Policy statement on illiteracy and duties of citizens.

3178. Hart, Armando, "On the National Campaign against Illiteracy in Cuba," *World Student News*, (Leiden, Netherlands), No. 4, 1962. pp. 26-28.

3179. Jesualdo (pseud.), "Cuba, territorio libre de analfabetismo," *Casa de las Américas*, (Havana), Nov.-Dec. 1961. pp. 38-49.

3180. Núñez Machín, Ana, "Breve recuento de la campaña de alfabetización," *INRA*, (Havana), Jan. 1962. pp. 4-9.

3181. Olema García, Duara, *Maestra voluntaria*, Havana: Casa de las Américas, 1962. 148 pp.

Novel on the 1961 literacy campaign.

3182. Rodríguez, José, "Impresiones de un alfabetizador," *Casa de las Américas,* (Havana), Nov.-Dec. 1961. pp. 50-57.

3183. Unión Internacional de Estudiantes, *Seminario internacional sobre analfabetismo,* Habana, 1961. 111 pp.
On problems of illiteracy.

E. TEXTBOOKS, GUIDELINES

3184. Anónimo, "Orientaciones a los alfabetizadores," *Revolución,* (Havana), Aug. 22, 1961. p. 10.

3185. Anónimo, *Temas sobre la revolución para los alfabetizadores,* Havana: Ejército de Alfabetizadores, 1961. 141 pp.

3186. Cuba, Comisión Nacional de Alfabetización, *Orientación para el brigadista,* Havana: Imprenta Nacional de Cuba, 1961. 12 pp.

3187. Cuba, Ministerio de Educación, *Lecturas de español para institutos de administración, institutos tecnológicos industriales, institutos tecnológicos agropecuarios,* Havana, 1965. 207 pp.

3188. Cuba, Ministerio de Educación, *Manual para alfabetizador,* Havana, 1961. 98 pp.

3189. Cuba, Ministerio de Educación, *Técnicas de orientación de grupo,* Habana, 1962. 47 pp.

3190. Cuba, Partido Unido de la Revolución Socialista, *Problemas teóricos sobre pedagogía,* Havana, 1965. 238 pp.

F. PRIVATE SCHOOLS

3191. Directorio Magisterial Revolu-

cionario, *Destrucción de la escuela privada cubana,* Miami, 1965. 20 pp.

3192. Rego, Oscar, "Saludan los dueños y directores de escuelas privadas la nacionalización de la enseñanza," *Bohemia,* (Havana), June 4, 1961. pp. 14-16.

G. PRE-PRIMARY EDUCATION

3193. García Mendiondo, Silva, *La expresión entre niños prescolares,* Havana: Instituto del Libro, 1967. 159 pp.

H. PRIMARY EDUCATION

3194. Cuba, Ministerio de Educación, *Los círculos de interés en la educación primaria,* Havana, 1965. 85 pp.

3195. Cuba, Ministerio de Educación, *La educación primaria en las montañas,* Havana: Editorial Nacional de Cuba, 1965. 191 pp.

3196. Cuba, Ministerio de Educación, *Programa de educación física para las escuelas primarias,* La Habana: Editora Pedagógica, 1966. 190 pp.

3197. Cuba, Ministerio de Educación, *Programas para la escuela primaria,* La Habana: Editora Pedagógica, 1966. 155 pp.

3198. Directorio Magisterial Revolucionario, "La educación primaria en Cuba antes y después del advenimiento del regimen comunista," *Cuba Nueva,* (Coral Gables), Oct. 15, 1962. pp. 21-26.

3199. Directorio Magisterial Revolucionario, *La destrucción de la enseñanza primaria en Cuba,* Miami: Editorial AIP, 1965. 28 pp.

3200. Guerra, Ramiro, "Estado de la enseñanza primaria en 1956-1957," *Diario de la Marina*, (Havana), Mar. 12, 1959. p. 4A.

3201. Lemus, Luis Arturo, *Organización y supervisión de la escuela primaria*, Habana: Cultural, 1962. 403 pp.
Organization of primary education.

3202. Soy del Pozo, Juan Pedro, *Tabla y calendario agrícola para las escuelas primarias*, Havana: Editora Pedagógica, 1966. 14 pp.

I. SECONDARY EDUCATION

3203. Cuba, Ministerio de Educación, *Programa de actividades para los Consejos Estudiantiles de Curso: Escuela Secundaria Básica*, Habana: Depto. de Organizaciones Circum-Escolares, 1962. 76 pp.

3204. Cuba, Ministerio de Educación, *Programa de actividades: Instituto Pre-Universitario*, Habana, 1962. 73 pp.

3205. Cuba, Ministerio de Educación, *Programas de secundaria básica*, Havana, 1962. 256 pp.

3206. Cuba, Ministerio de Educación, *¿Y qué puedo estudiar ahora?*, Habana, 1962. 48 pp.
Possibilities open to secondary school students.

3207. Directorio Magisterial Revolucionario, *El comunismo y la destrucción de la enseñanza secundaria*, Miami, 1965. 40 pp.

3208. Marban Escobar, Edilberto, "Cómo se apoderó el comunismo de la enseñanza secundaria en Cuba," *Cuba Nueva*, (Coral Gables), Oct. 1, 1962. pp. 9-15.

3209. Rego, Oscar F., "Alfabetización, seguimiento, batalla del 6° grado," *Bohemia*, (Havana), Dec. 18, 1964. pp. 30-33.

3210. Salazar, José, *Escuela secundaria*, Havana: Instituto Nacional de Reforma Agraria, 1960. 95 pp.
Plan for uniform system.

J. UNIVERSITY EDUCATION

3211. Anónimo, "Fases de la reforma universitaria," *Vida Universitaria*, (Havana), 1962-1963, editorials, monthly.

3212. Bello, Enrique, "La reforma universitaria en Cuba," *Boletín de la Universidad de Chile*, (Santiago, Chile), Aug. 1962. pp. 18-29.

3213. Boza Domínguez, Luis, *La situación universitaria en Cuba*, Santiago de Chile: Editorial del Pacífico, 1961. 200 pp.
Anti-Castro.

3214. Castro, Fidel, "The Mission of the Universities is Not to Train Just Technicians, but Revolutionary Technicians," *Granma*, (Havana), Dec. 25, 1966. pp. 9-12.
Dec. 18, 1966 speech.

3215. Castro, Raúl, *Universidad, gobierno y pueblo deben ser la misma cosa*, Marianao: Municipio de Marianao, 1960. 23 pp.
Speech of February 23, 1960.

3216. Cuba, Ministerio de Educación, *Conclusions del primer seminario de evaluación anual de las universidades cubanas*, Havana, 1965. 159 pp.

3217. Cuba, Ministerio de Educación, *La reforma de la enseñanza en Cuba*, Havana, 1962. 115 pp.

3218. Directorio Magisterial Revolu-

cionario, ¿Debe mantenerse la autonomía universitaria?, Miami, 1965. 76 pp.
Answer is negative.

3219. Directorio Magisterial Revolucionario, La destrucción de la enseñanza universitaria, Miami: Editorial AIP, 1965. 32 pp.

3220. Directorio Revolucionario Estudiantil, Como cayó la Universidad, Mexico, 1965. 18 pp.

3221. Duch, Juan "Habla Juan Marinello," Política, (Mexico), Aug. 1, 1962. pp. 32-34.
Interview with Dean of Havana University.

3222. Juventud Socialista Universitaria, Un plan revolucionario de reforma universitaria, Havana: Impr. del Cerro, 1959. 22 pp.

3223. Marinello, Juan, Dos discursos sobre la reforma universitaria, Havana: Impr. de la Universidad de la Havana, 1962. 26 pp.

3224. Marinello, Juan, Revolución y universidad, Havana: Gobierno Provisional Revolucionario, 1960. 27 pp.

3225. Portuondo, José Antonio, Tres temas de a reforma universitaria, Santiago de Cuba: Universidad de Oriente, 1959. 42 pp.

3226. Portuondo, Juan Miguel, Como los comunistas se apoderaron de la Universidad de La Habana, Miami, 1962. 54 pp.
Former professor of medicine.

3227. Puig y Pupo, José Ramón Rolando, Apuntes sobre la Escuela de Derecho y la Universidad de La Habana, Habana: Talleres Tipográficos de la Universidad de La Habana, 1959, 78 pp.

3228. Rodríguez, Carlos R., "La re-

forma universitaria," Cuba Socialista (Havana), Feb. 1962. pp. 22-44.
Also English edition.

3229. Santiago de Cuba, Universidad de Oriente, Leyes y estatutos de la Universidad de Oriente, Santiago de Cuba, 1959. 124 pp.

3230. Santiago de Cuba, Universidad de Oriente, La reforma universitaria, 10 de enero de 1962, Santiago de Cuba, 1962. 44 pp.

3231. Santiago de Cuba, Universidad de Oriente, La voz de la Universidad Oriente, Santiago de Cuba, 1959. 109 pp.
University and duties in the revolution.

3232. Havana, Universidad de La Habana, Acuerdos de la Comisión Mixta para la Reforma Universitaria, 15 de octubre de 1959, Havana, 1959. 60 pp.

3233. Havana, Universidad de La Habana, Crítica y reforma universitaria, Havana, 1959. 382 pp.

3234. Havana, Universidad de La Habana, Proyecto de Estatutos de la Universidad de La Habana, Havana, 1960. 110 pp.

3235. Havana, Universidad de La Habana, La Reforma Universitaria en la Facultad de Ciencias Sociales y Derecho Público, Havana: González y Cía, 1959. 67 pp.

3236. Havana, Universidad de La Habana, La Universidad hacia una nueva etapa, Havana, 1960. 30 pp.
Contains statements by university authorities and the University Federation of Students on university reform.

3237. Havana, Universidad de la Ha-

bana, *Universidad de la Habana,* Havana, 1966. 113 pp.
Description in Spanish, French and English.

3238. *University Reform Provisions,* Washington: Joint Publications Research Service, Feb. 19, 1962. 39 pp.

3239. Various, "La reforma de la enseñanza superior en Cuba," *Universidad de la Habana,* Jan.-Feb. 1962. pp. 27-141.

K. WORKER-PEASANT EDUCATION

3240. Aguilera, René, *Sistema, educación y legislación cooperativa,* Havana: Editorial Neptuno, 1960. 216 pp.
On rural education cooperatives.

3241. Alvisa, Heriberta, "Tres investigaciones en educación obrera y campesina," *Psicología y Educación,* (Havana), Oct.-Dec. 1964. pp. 30-37.
Adult education program.

3242. Borjas, Manuel, "En las zonas montañosas de Oriente," *Con la Guardia en Alto* (Havana), Sept. 1963. pp. 24-29.
Education in remote areas.

3243. Castro, Fidel, *Discurso en la graduación de maestras en el Instituto Makarenko para alumnas campesinas,* Havana: Comisión de Orientación Revolucionaria, 1963. 16 pp.
Dec. 6, 1963. On rural education.

3244. Castro, Fidel, "Discurso pronunciado en el acto inaugural del Primer Congreso Nacional de Educación Rural," *Revolución,* (Havana), Aug. 28, 1959. pp. 1, 17-18.

3245. Castro, Fidel, *Discurso sobre la batalla que libran los trabajadores para alcanzar el 6to grado,* Havana: Comisión de Orientación Revolucionaria, 1964. 23 pp.
Nov. 20, 1964. On educational progress.

3246. Cuba, Ministerio de Educación, *La escuela al campo,* Havana, 1967. 23 pp.

3247. Cuba, Ministerio de Educación, *Las cooperativas escolares,* La Habana, 1959. 16 pp.
The organization of primary and secondary schools in rural areas.

3248. Cuba, Ministerio de Educación, *Orientaciones para el curso secundario de superación obrera y campesina,* La Habana: Editorial Nacional de Cuba, 1963. 30 pp.

3249. Cuba, Ministerio de Educación, *El seguimiento: Organización y programas,* Habana, 1962. 56 pp.
Continuing rural education.

3250. Ferrer, Raúl, "Avance de la educación obrera y campesina en Cuba," *Cuba Socialista,* (Havana), July 1963. pp. 29-44.

3251. Periú, Maria de los Angeles, "Experiencias de la educación obrera y campesinas en Cuba," *Cuba Socialista,* (Havana), Feb. 1965. pp. 18-38.

3252. Rego, Oscar F., "La escuela al campo," *Bohemia,* (Havana), Jan. 31, 1969. pp. 24-27.

L. TECHNICAL EDUCATION

3253. Dorticós, Osvaldo, "En el proceso de construcción económica y cultural, la revolución exige técnicos y profesionales de alta calidad científica, y de alta calidad revolucionaria," *Bohemia,* (Havana), Oct. 1, 1965. pp. 50-53.

3254. González, Enrique, "Intermediate-level Technicians," *Granma,* June 29, 1969. p. 6.

3255. Hart, Armando, "La educación ante la revolución científico-técnica," *Cuba Socialista,* (Havana), Apr. 1964. pp. 1-21.

3256. Hart, Armando, "La enseñanza técnica profesional de nivel medio y universitario," *Cuba Socialista,* (Havana), May 1964. pp. 25-41.

3257. Montané, Jesús, "Avanzamos hacia la revolución técnica a paso de vencedores," *Bohemia,* (Havana), May 21, 1965. pp. 36-39.

3258. Moré Benítez, J.B., "La revolución técnica y la escuela universitaria de Ciencias Políticas," *Cuba Socialista,* (Havana), Sept. 1964. pp. 64-77.

M. MILITARY EDUCATION

3259. Castro, Raúl, *Discurso pronunciado con motivo de la graduación de los estudiantes integrantes de la marcha del II frente "Frank País,"* Habana: Editora Política, 1966. 14 pp.

3260. Martínez, Ángel, *El instructor revolucionario,* Habana: MINFAR, Depto. de Instrucción, 1961. 21 pp.

N. PHYSICAL EDUCATION

3261. Cambó Arcos, Rafael P., *Organización deportiva,* Havana: Instituto Nacional de Deportes, 1963. 78 pp.
Role of sports in the educational system.

3262. Castro, Fidel, "Millions of Us Have Lived the Triumph of Our Athletes," *Granma,* (Havana), Mar. 29, 1970. pp. 1-3.

3263. Cuba, Ministerio de Educación, *Educación Física,* Havana: Instituto del Libro, 1967. 190 pp.

3264. Cuba, Ministerio de Educación, *Programa de educación física para las escuelas secundarias básicas,* Habana, 1960. 22 pp.

3265. García Galló, Gaspar, *La educación física y el deporte y la recreación como un principio fundamental de la educación socialista,* Havana: SINTEC, 1963. 39 pp.

3266. Ubeda, Luis, "Todo el pueblo debe hacer deportes," *INRA,* (Havana), Jan. 1962. pp. 34-39.

O. SCHOOLS OF REVOLUTIONARY INSTRUCTION
(See also Politics)

3267. Castro, Fidel, *Se enseña haciendo y se hace enseñando,* Havana: Dirección Nacional de Escuelas de Instrucción Revolucionaria, 1962. 38 pp.
Dec. 20, 1961 speech to the schools of Revolutionary Instruction on Marxism-Leninism.

3268. Castro, Fidel, "Si no hay educación revolucionaria no habrá partido revolucionario," *Revolución,* (Havana), June 30, 1962. pp. 2, 4, 5.
Speech on role of revolutionary instructors.

3269. Cuba, Escuela Nacional de Instrucción Revolucionaria "Carlos Rodríguez Careaga," *Memorias,* Habana, 1964. 52 pp.

The fifth session of the school for communist cadres.

3270. Soto, Lionel, *Las escuelas de Instrucción Revolucionarias en el ciclo político-técnico,* Havana: Editorial EIR, 1965. 30 pp.

Advocates Communist cadres.

VIII. CULTURE

3271. Arcocha, Juan, "A marchar intelectuales," *Revolución*, (Havana), April 13, 1960. pp. 1, 14.

3272. Augier, Angel, "Los escritores ante la revolución," *El Mundo*, (Havana), Nov. 19, 1967. p. 4.

3273. Augier, Angel, "Órbita de Juan Marinello," *Bohemia*, (Havana), Nov. 1, 1968. pp. 34-45.

3274. Cabrera Infante, Guillermo, *Declaraciones del novelista cubano*, 1968. 6 pp.
About his defection.

3275. Cabrera Infante, Guillermo, "Los escritores latino-americanos en el exilio," *Letras Nacionales*, (Bogotá), May-June 1968, No. 20. pp. 61-70.
Cuban intellectuals and the revolution.

3276. Carbonell, Walterio, *Cómo surgió la cultura nacional*, Havana: Ediciones Yaka, 1961. 131 pp.

3277. Carpentier, Alejo, "La actualidad cultural de Cuba," *Sur*, (Buenos Aires), Mar.-Apr. 1965. pp. 61-67.

3278. Carpentier, Alejo, "Intervención ante el Congreso de Escritores y Artistas," *ISLAS*, (Santa Clara), Jan.-June 1962. pp. 89-100.
Position paper on intellectuals' role in the revolution.

3279. Castro, Fidel, *Palabras a los intelectuales*, Havana: Consejo Nacional de Cultura, 1961. 32 pp.
June 30, 1961 speech.

3280. Castro, Fidel, "Revolution and Culture," *Granma*, (Havana), Jan. 21, 1968. pp. 2-5.
Speech at closing session of Cultural Congress of Havana on Jan. 21, 1968.

3281. Congreso Nacional de Escritores y Artistas de Cuba, *Memoria*, Havana: Ediciones Unión, 1961. 135 pp.
18 to 22 August 1961.

3282. Coulthard, G. R., "Cuban Literary Prizes for 1963," *Caribbean Studies* (Puerto Rico), Jan. 1965. pp. 48-55.

3283. Cuba, Academia de Ciencias, *Reunión de expertos sobre las relaciones culturales entre Africa y América Latina*, Havana, 1966. 10 pp.

3284. Cuba, Comisión Nacional Cubana de la Unesco, *Cuba: educación y cultura*, La Habana; 1963. 66 pp.
Also in English.

3285. Cuba, Congreso Cultural de la Habana, *Seminario preparatorio. Reunión de intelectuales de todo el mundo sobre problemas de Asia, Africa y América Latina*, Havana, 1967. 79 pp.
Oct. 25-Nov. 2, 1967.

3286. Cuba, Congreso Nacional de

Cultura, *Memorias*, Havana, 1962. 157 pp.
Dec. 14-16, 1962.

3287. Cuba, Congreso Nacional de Escritores y Artistas, *Memoria del Congreso,* Havana: Ediciones Unión, 1961. 135 pp.

3288. Cuba, Consejo Nacional de Cultura, *Anteproyecto del plan de cultura de 1963,* Havana, 1963. 23 pp.

3289. Cuba, Consejo Nacional de Cultura, *Reglamento de la escuela de activistas de cultura,* Havana, 1967. 14 pp.

3290. Cuba, Federación Estudiantil Universitaria, Havana, *Operación cultura,* Havana: Universidad de la Havana, 1959. 163 pp.

3291. Cuba, Ministerio de Estado, *Anuario cultural,* Havana, 1944-1959. 15 vols.

3292. Cuba, Ministerio de Relaciones Exteriores, *The Revolution and Cultural Problems in Cuba,* Havana, 1962. 76 pp.

3293. Cuba, Presidencia, *Discurso en el Primer Congreso de Escritores y Artistas,* Havana: Consejo Provincial de Cultura, 1961. 23 pp.

3294. Cuba, Presidencia, *Discurso pronunciado por . . . en la clausura del Seminario previo al Congreso Cultural de la Havana.* Havana: Consejo Nacional de Cultura, 1967. 47 pp.
Nov. 2, 1967.

3295. Daltón, Roque, *El intelectual y la sociedad,* Mexico: Siglo XX Editores, 1969. 151 pp.

3296. "Debate sobre la política cultural de la República que seguirá el gobierno," *Diario de la Marina,* (Havana), Feb. 2, 1959. pp. 1, 6A.

3297. Desnoes, Edmundo, "Erinnerungen. eines Zurückgebliebenen," *Kursbuch 18,* Oct. 1969, pp. 63-79.

3298. Fernández, Alvaro, "Primer Congreso Nacional de Cultura," *Cuba,* (Havana), No. 10, 1963. pp. 74-81.

3299. Fernández Retamar, Roberto, et al., "Carta abierta de los intelectuales cubanos al poeta Pablo Neruda," *Política,* (Mexico), Aug. 1, 1966. pp. 37-40.

3300. Fernández Retamar, Roberto, *Ensayo de otro mundo,* Havana: Instituto del Libro, 1967. 188 pp.

3301. Fernández Retamar, Roberto, "Hacia una intelectualidad revolucionaria en Cuba," *Casa de las Américas,* (Havana), Jan.-Feb. 1967. pp. 4-18.

3302. Fernández Retamar, Roberto, *Papelería,* Havana: Universidad Central de Las Villas, 1962. 300 pp.
Nationalism, "comandantes y licensiados," poetry and revolution, culture; writers and artists in a revolutionary society.

3303. Fernández Retamar, Roberto, "Presentación de los estatutos," *Lunes de Revolución,* (Havana), Aug. 28, 1961. pp. 28-31.
Document on writers' and artists' duties.

3304. Fornet, Ambrosio, "Entrevista con Lisandro Otero," *La Gaceta de Cuba,* (Havana), Mar. 15, 1963. pp. 4-5.
Otero is cultural czar.

3305. Fox, Arturo A., "Sobre la libertad intelectual en Cuba," *Hispania,* Sept. 1965. pp. 584-585.

3306. García Buchaca, Edith, "Cultura y clases sociales," *Cuba Socialista,* (Havana), Nov. 1963. pp. 115-124.

3307. García Buchaca, Edith, "El Primer Congreso de Escritores y Artistas Cubanos," *Cuba Socialista* (Havana), Oct. 1961. pp. 82-91.

3308. García Buchaca, Edith, "Las transformaciones culturales de la revolución cubana," *Cuba Socialista,* (Havana), Jan. 1964. pp. 28-54.

3309. Gil de Lamadrid, José, "La Casa de las Américas; la cultura en su puesto de combate," *Bohemia,* (Havana), Mar. 1963. pp. 70-73+.

3310. Guillén, Nicolás, "Informe al Congreso de Escritores y Artistas," *ISLAS,* (Santa Clara), Jan.-June. 1962. pp. 67-87.

3311. Havana, Consejo Provincial de Cultura, *La cultura para el pueblo,* Havana, 1961. 4 pp.

3312. Luis, Carlos M., "Los intelectuales y las milicias," *Revolución,* (Havana), Apr. 15, 1960. p. 12.

3313. Maldonado-Denis, Manuel, "The Situation of Cuba's Intellectuals," *Christian Century,* Jan. 17, 1968.

3314. "Manifiesto de los intelectuales cubanos," *Marcha,* (Montevideo), Dec. 4, 1959. p. 9.

3315. Marinello, Juan, *Contemporáneos noticia y memoria,* Las Villas: Editora del Consejo Nacional de Universidades, Universidad Central de Las Villas, 1964. 325 pp.

3316. Marinello, Juan, "Libertad y responsibilidad," *ISLAS,* (Santa Clara), Jan.-June 1962. pp. 103-106.

3317. Marinello, Juan, "Los trabajadores de la cultura deben defender la sociedad que los liberta," *Bohemia,* (Havana), Aug. 27, 1965. pp. 104-105.

3318. Masó, Fausto, "Los escritores cubanos y el castrismo," *Política,* (Caracas), Dec. 1963. pp. 49-57.

3319. Masó, Fausto, "Literatura y revolución en Cuba," *Mundo Nuevo,* (Buenos Aires), Feb. 1969. pp. 50-54.

3320. Menocal y Cueto, Raimundo, *Origen y desarrollo del pensamiento cubano,* Havana: Editorial Lex, 1945-47. 2 vols.

3321. Neruda, Pablo, "Carta de Neruda a los cubanos," *Política,* (Mexico), Aug. 15, 1966. p. 41.

3322. Núñez, Carlos, "El papel del intelectual en los movimientos de liberación nacional," *Casa de las Américas,* (Havana), Mar.-Apr. 1966. pp. 83-99.

3323. Organization of American States, Special Consultative Committee on Security, *Congreso Cultural de La Habana,* Washington, 1968. 112 pp. "Subversive, not cultural."

3324. Otero, Lisandro, et al., "Conversación sobre el arte y la literatura," *Casa de las Américas,* (Havana), Jan.-Apr. 1964. pp. 130-138.

3325. Piñera Llera, Humberto, "Cultura y revolución en Cuba," *Sur,* (Buenos Aires), Mar.-Apr. 1965. pp. 68-78.

3326. Pogolotti, Graziela, *Examen de conciencia,* Havana: Ediciones Unión, 1965. 154 pp.

3327. Pogolotti, Marcelo, *Época y conciencia,* Mexico: Editorial Cultura, 1961. 377 pp.

3328. Portuondo, José A., "Cuba, nación 'para sí,'" *Cuadernos Americanos,* (Mexico), Nov.-Dec. 1961. pp. 147-172.
Cultural nationalism.

3329. Portuondo, José A., "The Cuban Revolution and the Intellectuals," *New World Review,* (New York), Vol. 32, No. 9, Oct. 1964. pp. 37-44.

3330. Portuondo, José A., *Estética y Revolución,* Havana: Ediciones Unión-Ensayo, 1963. 108 pp.
Articles written from 1954 to 1963.

3331. Portuondo, José A., "Los intelectuales y la revolución," *Cuba Socialista,* (Havana), June 1961. pp. 51-64.

3332. Roig de Leuchsenring, Emilio, *El grupo minorista de intelectuales y artistas habaneros,* Havana: Oficina del Historiador de la Ciudad de La Habana, 1961. 47 pp.
Precursors.

3333. Schleifer, Marc, "Conversations in Havana," *Monthly Review,* (New York), Apr. 1964. pp. 651-656.

3334. Susanina, Sofía, *La cultura es patrimonio del pueblo,* Havana: Ediciones con la Guardia en Alto, 1966. 24 pp.

3335. Torriente, Leopoldo de la, "La política cultural y los escritores y artistas cubanos," *Cuadernos Americanos,* (Mexico), Sept.-Oct. 1963. pp. 78-89.

3336. Torriente, Leopoldo de la, "La revolución y la cultura cubana," *Cuadernos Americanos,* (Mexico), July-Aug. 1960. pp. 13-26.

A. ESSAYS

3337. Arrufat, Antón, *Mi antagonista y otras observaciones,* Havana: Ediciones R., 1963. 98 pp.

3338. Bueno, Salvador, ed., *Los mejores ensayistas cubanos,* Lima: Imprenta Torres Aguirre, 1959. 126 pp.
By Enrique E. Varona, Fernando Ortiz, José A. Ramos, Jorge Mañach, Juan Marinello, Raúl Roa, José A. Portuondo.

3339. Casal, Julián del, *Crónicas habaneras,* Havana: Universidad Central de Las Villas, Dirección de Publicaciones, 1963. 303 pp.

3340. Castellanos, Francisco José, *Ensayos y diálogos,* Havana: Comisión Nacional Cubana de la Unesco, 1961. 276 pp.

3341. Delmonte, Domingo, *Humanismo y humanitarismo; ensayos críticos y literarios,* Havana: Editorial Lex, 1960. 146 pp.

3342. Desnoes, Edmundo, *Punto de vista,* Havana: Instituto del Libro, 1967. 135 pp.

3343. Entralgo, Elías, *Lecturas y estudios,* Havana: Comisión Nacional Cubana de la Unesco, 1962. 356 pp.

3344. Feijóo, Samuel, *Azar de lecturas, crítica,* Santa Clara: Universidad Central de Las Villas, Departamento de Estudios Hispánicos, 1961. 378 pp.

3345. Fornet, Ambrosio, *En blanco y negro,* Havana: Instituto del Libro, 1967. 203 pp.

3346. García Buchaca, Edith, *La teoría de la superestructura, la literatura y el arte,* Havana: Consejo Nacional de Cultura, 1961. 54 pp.

3347. Griñán Peralta, Leonardo, *En-*

sayos y conferencias, Santiago de Cuba: Editora del Consejo Nacional de Universidades, Universidad de Oriente, 1964. 165 pp.

3348. Lezama Lima, José, *Órbita. Ensayo preliminar, selección y notas de Armando Alvarez Bravo*, Havana: Ediciones Unión, 1966. 392 pp.

3349. Marinello, Juan, *Meditación americana; cinco ensayos*, Buenos Aires: Procyon, 1959. 219 pp.

3350. Menéndez Serpa, Gabriel José, *Crónicas, Pensamientos*, Havana, 1960. 110 pp.

3351. Portuondo, José Antonio, "Crítica de la época," *Cuba Socialista*, (Havana), Nov. 1963. pp. 133-143.
Cultural criticism.

3352. Portuondo, José Antonio, *Crítica de la época y otros ensayos*, Havana: Editora del Consejo Nacional de Universidades, Universidad Central de Las Villas, 1965. 311 pp.

3353. Rodríguez Feo, José, *Notas críticas*, Havana: Ediciones Unión, 1962. 173 pp.

3354. Salper, Roberta, "Literature and Revolution in Cuba," *Monthly Review*, (New York), October 1970. pp. 15-30.

B. LITERATURE

1. Novels

3355. Abascal, Jesús, *Staccato*, Havana: Ediciones Unión, 1967. 60 pp.

3356. Acosta, Leonardo, *Paisaje del hombre*, Havana: Instituto del Libro, 1967. 101 pp.

3357. Agostini, Víctor, *Dos viajes*, Havana: Ediciones R., 1965. 287 pp.

3358. Agüero, Luis, *La vida en dos*, Havana: Casa de las Américas, 1967. 268 pp.

3359. Aguililla, Araceli C. de, *Primeros recuerdos, novela*, Havana: Ediciones Unión, 1963. 199 pp.

3360. Alfonso, Miguel, *Clarivel, novela de amor y dolor*, Havana, 1962. 78 pp.

3361. Alonso, Dora, *Ponolani*, Havana: Ediciones Granma, 1966. 132 pp.

3362. Alonso, Dora, *Tierra inerme*, Havana: Casa de la Américas, 1961. 202 pp.

3363. Aparicio Nogales, Raúl, *Frutos del azote*, Buenos Aires: Editorial Palestra, 1961. 128 pp.
1933-1959.

3364. Arango, Ángel, *El planeta negro*, Havana: Ediciones Granma, 1966. 74 pp.

3365. Arango, Ángel, *Robotomaquia*, Havana: Instituto del Libro, 1967. 74 pp.

3366. Arenal, Humberto, *El sol a plomo*, Mexico: Ediciones Nuevo Mundo, 1959. 32 pp.

3367. Arenal, Humberto, *La vuelta en redondo*, Havana: Ediciones R., 1962. 103 pp.

3368. Arenal, Humberto, *Los animales sagrados*, Havana: Instituto del Libro, 1967. 142 pp.

3369. Arenas, Reinaldo, *Celestino antes del alba*, Havana: Ediciones Unión, 1967. 219 pp.

3370. Arcocha, Juan, *A Candle in the Wind*, New York: L. Stuart, 1967, 187 pp.
Family conflicts in revolutionary process.

3371. Arteaga, Rolando, *El acróbata,* Havana, 1962. 53 pp.

3372. Augier, Angel, *Isla en el tacto,* Havana: Ediciones Unión, 1965. 110 pp.

3373. Barnet, Miguel, *La sagrada familia,* Havana: Casa de las Américas, 1967. 216 pp.

3374. Becali, Ramón, *Los dioses mendigos,* Havana, 1965. 192 pp.

3375. Becerra, José, *La novena estación, novela basada en hechos reales de la revolución,* Havana: Imprenta El Siglo XX, 1959. 133 pp.
Batista police brutality.

3376. Benit, Euardo, *Birín; novela,* Havana: Universidad Central de Las Villas, 1962. 185 pp.

3377. Blas, Sergio Gil, *Dos hombres,* Havana: La Milagrosa, 1961. 156 pp.

3378. Bravo, Celia, *Necesito su amor,* Havana: Distribuidora Antillana de Libreria, 1961. 123 pp.

3379. Bravo, Humberto, *Milicias de aurora,* Havana: Tierra Nueva, 1961. 91 pp.

3380. Cabrera Infante, Guillermo, *Tres tristes tigres,* Barcelona: Editorial Seix Barral, 1967. 451 pp.
Novel.

3381. Camus, Emilio Fernández, *Caminos llenos de borrascas,* Madrid, 1962. 247 pp.

3382. Carpentier, Alejo, *El acoso; novela,* Buenos Aires: Editorial Losada, 1956. 111 pp.

3383. Carpentier, Alejo, *El reino de este mundo,* Lima: Editora Latinoamericana, 1958. 172 pp.

3384. Carpentier, Alejo, *El siglo de las luces,* Havana: Ediciones R., 1965. 423 pp.

English version published as *Explosion in a Cathedral,* (1963).

3385. Carpentier, Alejo, *Guerra del tiempo; tres relatos y una novela,* Mexico: Compañía General de Ediciones, 1959. 275 pp.

3386. Carpentier, Alejo, *Los pasos perdidos,* Mexico: Cía. General de Ediciones, 1959. 288 pp.

3387. Cobo Sausa, Manuel, *El cielo será nuestro,* Medellín: Libros de America, 1965. 298 pp.
About Cuban exiles.

3388. Collazo, Miguel, *El libro fantástico de Oaj,* Havana: Ediciones Unión, 1966. 107 pp.

3389. Correa, Arnaldo, *Asesinato por anticipado,* Havana: Ediciones Granma, 1966. 132 pp.

3390. Correa, Arnaldo, *El primer hombre a Marte,* Havana: Ediciones Granma, 1967. 131 pp.

3391. Denning, Richard, *This is My Night,* Derby: Monarch Books, 1961. 139 pp.

3392. Desnoes, Edmundo, *El cataclismo,* Havana: Ediciones R., 1965. 293 pp.

3393. Desnoes, Edmundo, *Inconsolable Memories,* New York: New American Library, 1967. 155 pp.

3394. Desnoes, Edmundo, *No hay problema,* Havana: Burgay y Cía, 1961. 225 pp.
Relates bourgeois mentality in revolutionary process.

3395. Díaz, Jesús, *Los años duros,* Havana: Casa de las Américas, 1966. 105 pp.

3396. Eguren, Gustavo, *La robla,* Havana: Ediciones Unión, 1967. 202 pp.

3397. Fernández, David, *La onda de*

David, Havana: Instituto del Libro, 1967. 148 pp.

3398. Fernández, Pablo Armando, *Los niños se despiden,* Havana: Casa de las Américas, 1968. 547 pp.
Social clash among Cuban, Spaniards, and Americans.

3399. Gallardo, Cecilio, *Su egoísmo lo mató, novela guajira,* Bejucal, Cuba: Impr. Bravo, 1963. 163 pp.

3400. Gámez, Tana de, *The Yoke and the Star; A Novel of the Cuban Revolution,* Indianapolis: Bobbs-Merrill, 1966. 309 pp.

3401. García, Lorenzo, *Antología de la novela cubana,* Havana: Dirección General de Cultura, 1960. 508 pp.

3402. Gavrikov, Yuri, comp., *Kubinskaya novela XX veka,* Moscow, 1965. 513 pp.

3403. González, Dagoberto, *Delirio de amor,* Havana, 1966. 109 pp.

3404. González, José R., *La noche ancha,* Havana: Ediciones La Tertulia, 1960. 239 pp.

3405. González del Cascorro, Raúl, *Concentración Pública,* Havana: Ediciones Union, 1964. 123 pp.

3406. González del Cascorro, Raúl, *La semilla,* Havana: Ediciones R, 1965. 116 pp.

3407. Herrera, Mariano, *Después de la zeta,* Havana: Ediciones Revolución, 1964. 118 pp.

3408. Hurtado, Oscar, *Carta de un juez,* Havana: Ediciones R, 1963. 92 pp.

3409. Ibarguengoitia, Jorge, *Los relampagos de Agosto,* Havana: Casa de las Américas, 1965. 116 pp.

3410. Juárez, Bel, *En las lomas de El Purial,* Havana: Ediciones R, 1962. 114 pp.

3411. Labrador, Enrique, *La sangre hambrienta,* Havana: Cruzada Latinoamericana de Difusión Cultural, 1959. 205 pp.

3412. Leante, César, *Padres e hijos,* Havana: Ediciones Unión, 1967. 124 pp.

3413. Lezama Lima, José, *Paradiso,* Havana: Ediciones Unión, 1966. 617 pp.

3414. Linares, Manuel, *Los Fernández,* Barcelona: Editorial Maucci, 1965. 410 pp.
On Cuban rural life.

3415. López, César, *Circulando el cuadrado,* Havana: Ediciones R, 1963. 113 pp.

3416. López-Nussa, Leonel, *Tabaco,* Havana: Universidad Central de Las Villas, 1963. 257 pp.

3417. Lorenzo Fuentes, José, *El sol ese enemigo,* Havana: Ediciones R, 1962. 111 pp.

3418. Lorenzo Fuentes, José, *El vendedor de días,* Havana: Ediciones Unión, 1967. 69 pp.

3419. Loveira, Carlos, *Juan Criollo,* Havana, Consejo Nacional de Cultura, 1962. 441 pp.

3420. Meza y Suárez, Ramón, *El duelo de mi vecino,* Havana: Publicación de la Comisión Nacional Cubana de la UNESCO, 1961. 160 pp.
Novel.

3421. Monreal Almela, Manuel, *El fin de la esperanza,* Havana: Editora Revolucionaria Bayo Libros, 1963. 171 pp.

3422. Monreal Almela, Manuel, *Los novios,* Havana: Impr. Marón, 1963. 223 pp.

3423. Navarro, Noel, *Los caminos de la noche,* Havana: Ediciones Granma, 1967. 202 pp.

3424. Navarro, Noel, *Los días de nuestra angustia,* Havana: Ediciones R, 1962, 383 pp.

3425. Otero, Lisandro, *Pasión de Urbino,* Havana: Instituto del Libro, 1967. 88 pp.

3426. Otero, Lisandro, *La situación,* Havana: Casa de las Américas, 1963. 317 pp.

3427. Perera, Hilda, *Mañana es 26,* Havana: Lázaro Hermanos, 1960. 227 pp.

3428. Piñeiro, Abelardo, *El descanso,* Havana: Ediciones Unión, 1962. 20 pp.

3429. Pogolotti, Marcelo, *El caserón del Cerro,* Havana: Universidad Central de Las Villas, 1961. 237 pp.

3430. Sánchez Torrentó, Eugenio, *Francisco Manduley, la historia de un pescador de ranas,* Coral Gables: Service Offset Printers, 1965. 70 pp.

3431. Sarusky, Jaime, *La búsqueda,* Havana: Ediciones R, 1961. 206 pp.

3432. Sardiñas Llennart, José, *Azar del júbilo,* Havana: Ediciones Belic, 1965. 28 pp.

3433. Soler Puig, José, *Bertillón 166,* Havana: Casa de las Américas, 1960. 244 pp.

3434. Soler Puig, José, *En el año de enero,* Havana: Ediciones Unión, 1963. 238 pp.
"Liborio" views the revolution.

3435. Suardíaz, Luis, *Haber vivido,* Havana: Ediciones Unión, 1966. 154 pp.

3436. Tully, Andrew, *A Race of Rebels,* New York: Simon and Schuster, 1960. 250 pp.
Background to revolution.

3437. Vieta, Ezequiel, *Pailock el prestidigitador,* Havana: Ediciones Granma, 1966. 112 pp.

3438. Vieta, Ezequiel, *Vivir en Candonga,* Havana: Ediciones Unión, 1966. 157 pp.

2. Short Stories

3439. Abascal, Jesús, *Soroche y otros cuentos,* Havana: Ediciones El Puente, 1963. 72 pp.

3440. Agostini, Víctor, *Bibijaguas,* Havana: Ediciones Unión, 1963. 119 pp.

3441. Agüero, Luis, *De aquí para allá,* Havana: Ediciones R, 1962. 125 pp.

3442. Alonso, Dora, *En busca de la gaviota negra,* Havana: Editora Juvenil, 1966. 143 pp.

3443. Anónimo, ed., *Cuentos, antología,* Havana: Ediciones Unión, 1967. 76 pp.

3444. Anonymous, ed., *Cuban Short Stories 1959-1966,* Havana: Book Institute, 1967. 229 pp.

3445. Arrufat, Antón and Fausto Masó, *Nuevos cuentistas cubanos,* Havana: Casa de las Américas, 1961. 253 pp.
Short stories by Victor Agostini, Jorge Guerra, Oscar Hurtado, Jorge Rigol, Servando Cabrera, Calvert Casey and others.

3446. Bayo, Armando, *Cuentos del ancho camino (selección),* Havana, 1965. 127 pp.

3447. Bayo, Armando, *La rosa de los vientos,* Havana, 1965. 239 pp.

3448. Benítez, Antonio, *Tute de*

reyes, Havana: Casa de las Américas, 1967. 120 pp.

3449. Brene, José Ramón, *Matías Pérez, el ingenioso criollo,* Havana: Editora Pedagógica, 1966. 15 pp.

3450. Brenes, María, *Diez cuentos para un libro,* New York: Las Américas Publishing, 1963. 99 pp.

3451. Bueno, Salvador, ed., *Los mejores cuentos cubanos,* Lima: Imprenta Torres Aguirre, 1959-1960. 2 vols.

3452. Buzzi, David, *Los desnudos,* Havana: Ediciones Unión, 1967. 277 pp.

3453. Cabrera, Lydia, *Cuentos negros de Cuba,* Havana: Ediciones Nuevo Mundo, 1961. 150 pp.
Short stories coming from black Cuban folklore.

3454. Cabrera Infante, Guillermo, *Así en la paz como en la guerra,* Havana: Ediciones R, 1960. 201 pp.
Short stories dealing with life during the Batista regime (1952-58).

3455. Cabrera Infante, Guillermo, *Tres tristes tigres,* Barcelona: Seix Barral, 1967. 451 pp.

3456. Carballido Rey, José M., *El gallo pinto y otros cuentos,* Havana: Ediciones Unión, 1965. 115 pp.

3457. Carpentier, Alejo, *Tientos y diferencias,* Havana: Ediciones Unión, 1966. 110 pp.

3458. Casey, Calvert, *El Negro,* Havana: Ediciones R, 1962. 124 pp.

3459. Cohen, J. M., ed., *Writers in the New Cuba,* London: Penguin Books, 1967. 191 pp.
Anthology.

3460. Cuba, Ministerio de Educación, *Selección de cuentos cubanos,* Havana, 1962. 143 pp.

3461. Cuevas, Guillermo, *Ni un sí, ni un no; cuentos y cosas,* Havana: Ediciones El Puente, 1962. 93 pp.

3462. Daranas, Manuel A., *Tres cuentos,* Havana, 1967. 14 pp.

3463. Díaz Llanillo, Esther, *El castigo,* Havana: Ediciones Revolución, 1966. 89 pp.

3464. Díaz Martínez, Manuel, *El país de Ofelia,* Havana: Ediciones Revolución, 1965. 104 pp.

3465. Díaz Martínez, Manuel, *La tierra de Saud,* Havana: Ediciones Unión, 1967. 54 pp.

3466. Feijóo, Samuel, *Cuentos populares cubanos,* Havana: Universidad Central de Las Villas, 1960-1962. 2 vols.

3467. Fernández, Angel Luis, *La nueva noche,* Havana: Ediciones El Puente, 1964. 58 pp.

3468. Fernández, Arístides, *Cuentos,* Havana: Instituto Municipal de Cultura, 1959. 178 pp.
Short stories.

3469. Ferrer, Surama, *Cuatro cuentos,* Havana: Caballo de Fuego, 1961. 22 pp.

3470. Friol, Roberto, *En la cabaña del Tío Tom,* Havana: Biblioteca Nacional José Martí, Departamento Colección Cubana, 1967. 55 pp.

3471. Gallegos Mancera, Eduardo, *Cartas de la prisión, Hector Mujica: cuentos de lucha,* Havana: Ediciones Venceremos, 1965. 86 pp.

3472. Gómez, José Jorge, *La corteza y la savia,* Havana: Ediciones Presencia, 1959. 139 pp.

3473. González de Cascorro, Raúl, *Gente de Playa Girón,* Havana: Casa de las Américas, 1962. 110 pp.

3474. Granados, Manuel, *Adire y el tiempo roto,* Havana: Casa de las Américas, 1967. 350 pp.

3475. Guillén, Nicolás, *El Gran Zoo,* Havana: Instituto del Libro, 1967. 85 pp.

3476. Havana, Consejo Provincial de Cultura, *El cuento, panorama general,* Havana: Imprenta CTC-R, 1964. 44 pp.

3477. Hernández Catá, Alfonso, *Cuentos,* Havana: Academia de Ciencias de Cuba, 1966. 136 pp.

3478. Herrero, Juan Luis, *Tigres en el Vedado,* Havana: Instituto del Libro, 1967. 80 pp.

3479. Jorge Cardoso, Onelio, *El caballo de coral,* Moscow: Editorial Artístico Literaria, 1962. 157 pp.

3480. Jorge Cardoso, Onelio, *Cuentos completos,* Havana: Ediciones Unión, 1965. 259 pp.

3481. Jorge Cardoso, Onelio, *Iba caminando,* Havana: Ediciones Granma, 1966. 121 pp.

3482. Jorge Cardoso, Onelio, *El perro,* Havana, 1964. 18 pp.

3483. Labrador, Enrique, *Conejito ulán,* Havana: Ediciones La Tertulia, 1963. 34 pp.

3484. Labrador, Enrique, *El gallo en el espejo,* Lima: Torres Aguirre, 1959. 129 pp.

3485. Llana, María, *La reja,* Havana: Ediciones R, 1965. 109 pp.

3486. Llópis, Rogelio, *El fabulista,* Havana: Ediciones R, 1963. 131 pp.

3487. Llópis, Rogelio, *La guerra y los basiliscos,* Havana: Ediciones Unión, 1962. 97 pp.

3488. Novás Calvo, Lino, *El otro cayo,* Mexico: Ediciones Nuevo Mundo, 1959. 184 pp.

3489. Otero, José Manuel, *Cuatro cuentos,* Havana: Ediciones Belic, 1965. 38 pp.

3490. Otero, José Manuel, *El paisaje nunca es el mismo,* Havana: Ediciones Unión, 1963. 93 pp.

3491. Perera, Hilda, *Cuentos de Adli y Luas,* Havana: Dirección General de Cultura, 1960. 67 pp.

3492. Perera, Hilda, *Cuentos de Apolo,* Havana: Lázaro Hermanos, 1960. 109 pp.

3493. Piñera, Virgilio, *Presiones y diamantes,* Havana: Ediciones Unión, 1967. 105 pp.

3494. Pita Rodríguez, Felix, *Cuentos completos,* Havana: Ediciones Unión, 1963. 169 pp.

3495. Roa, Raúl, *Escaramuza en las vísperas y otros engendros,* Havana: Editora Universitaria, 1966. 411 pp.

3496. Rodríguez Feo, José, comp., *Aquí once cubanos cuentan,* Montevideo: Arca, 1967. 169 pp.

3497. Rodríguez Feo, José, ed., *Cuentos de horror y de misterio,* Havana: Instituto del Libro, 1967. 433 pp.

3498. Sáez, Luis M., *El iniciado,* Havana: Instituto del Libro, 1967. 36 pp.

3499. Sarusky, Jaime, *Rebelión en la octava casa,* Havana: Instituto del Libro, 1967. 153 pp.

3500. Serpa, Enrique, *Aletas de tiburón,* Havana: Ediciones La Tertulia, 1963. 23 pp.

3501. Tamayo, Evora, *La vieja y la*

mar, Havana: Ediciones R, 1965. 147 pp.

3502. Valle, Gerardo del, *¼ Fambá y 19 cuentos más,* Havana: Ediciones Unión, 1967. 210 pp.

3503. Viana, Renato, *Los que por tí murieron,* Miami, 1961. 64 pp.

3504. Viera Trejo, Bernardo, *Militante del odio,* Miami: Editorial AIP, 1964. 153 pp.

3. Criticism

3505. Abella, Rosa, "Bibliografía de la novela publicada en Cuba, y en el extranjero por cubanos, desde 1959 hasta 1965," *Revista Iberoamericana,* (Pittsburgh), July-Dec. 1966, Vol. XXXII, No. 62. pp. 313-318.

3506. Agüero, Luis, "Saldo y promesa," *Casa de las Américas,* (Havana), Jan.-Apr. 1964. pp. 60-67.
Discusses new Cuban novels.

3507. Anónimo, *Introducción a la literatura cubana,* Havana: Consejo Nacional de Cultura, 1967. 8 pp.

3508. Bělič, Oldřich, *O kubánské literatuře,* Prague: Nakl. politické literatury, 1964. 247 pp.

3509. Bueno, Salvador, *Historia de la literatura cubana,* Havana: Editora del Ministerio de Educación, 1963. 464 pp.
Excellent survey.

3510. Campos, Julieta, "La novela de la revolución cubana," *Revista de la Universidad de Mexico,* May 1961. pp. 6-7.

3511. Carballo, Emmanuel, "Cuba: por decreto no se puede crear una literatura socialista," *Siempre,* (Mexico), Mar. 16, 1966. p. 13.

3512. Díaz, Filiberto, "Cuba y su literatura," *Mundo Nuevo* (Buenos Aires), Sept.-Oct. 1969. pp. 83-86.

3513. Fornet, Ambrosio, "La nueva narrativa y sus antecedentes," *Casa de las Américas,* (Havana), Jan.-Apr. 1964. pp. 3-10.

3514. Henríquez Ureña, Max, *Panorama histórico de la literatura cubana,* Havana: Ed. Revolucionaria, 1967. 2 vols.

3515. Lax, Judith Heckelman, *Themes and Techniques in the Socially Oriented Cuban Novel, 1933-1952,* Syracuse, New York, 1961. 242 pp.
Syracuse University Ph.D. Thesis.

3516. Lazo, Raimundo, *La literatura cubana,* Havana: Editora Universitaria, 1967. 251 pp.
History to 1966.

3517. Leal, Rine, *En primera persona, 1954-1966,* Havana: Instituto del Libro, 1967. 369 pp.

3518. Llopis, Rogelio, "Puntos de vista acerca de la nueva literatura cubana," *La Gaceta de Cuba,* (Havana), Oct. 1964. pp. 10-11.

3519. Menton, Seymour, "La novela de la revolución cubana," *Cuadernos Americanos,* (Mexico), Jan.-Feb. 1964. pp. 231-241.

3520. Pogolotti, Marcelo, *La República de Cuba al través de sus escritores,* Havana: Ed. Lex, 1958. 208 pp.

3521. Portuondo, José A., *Bosquejo histórico de las letras cubanas,* Havana: Ministerio de Relaciones Exteriores, 1960. 81 pp.
Traces development of social novels.

3522. Various, "Ecrivains de Cuba," *Les lettres nouvelles,* (Paris), Dec. 1967-Jan. 1968. pp. 1-343.

3523. Vitier, Medardo, *Valoraciones,* Havana: Universidad Central de Las Villas, 1960-1961. 2 vols. Literary criticism.

4. Poetry

a. General

3524. Aguilar Derpich, Juan, *Canto de bronce,* Havana: Cooperativa Periodística Luz-Hilo, 1963. 62 pp.

3525. Alfonso, Antonio, *Orto en ocaso,* Havana: La Milagrosa, 1959. 126 pp.

3526. Alfonso, Domingo, *Sueño en el papel,* Havana: Ediciones de la Organización Nacional de Bibliotecas Ambulantes y Populares, 1959. 64 pp.

3527. Almagro, Luis F., *Los apasionados,* Havana: F. Vaillant, 1961. 22 pp.

3528. Álvarez Baragaño, José, *Poemas escogidos,* Havana: Ediciones Unión, 1963. 143 pp.

3529. Anónimo, *Poesía del mundo,* Havana: Ministerio de Educación, Dirección de Cultura, 1961.

3530. Anónimo, *5 poetas jóvenes,* Havana: Ediciones Belic, 1965. 46 pp.

3531. Anonymous, *Cuban poetry 1959-1966,* Havana: Book Institute, 1967. 788 pp.

3532. Antón, Héctor, *En busca de la poesía pura,* Havana: Ucar, García Imprenta, 1960. 157 pp.

3533. Arozarena, Marcelino, *Canción negra sin color,* Havana: Ediciones Unión, 1966. 71 pp.

3534. Arrufat, Antón, *En claro,* Havana: Ediciones La Tertulia, 1962. 71 pp.

3535. Augier, Ángel I., *Breve antología,* Havana: Universidad Central de Las Villas, Dirección de Publicaciones, 1963. 125 pp.

3536. Barnet, Miguel, *La piedra fina y el pavorreal,* Havana: Ediciones Unión, 1963. 61 pp.

3537. Barros, Silvia, *Veintisiete pulgadas de vacío,* Havana: Imprenta Arquimbau, 1961. 43 pp.

3538. Branly, Roberto, *Apuntes y Poemas,* Havana: Ediciones Unión, 1966. 64 pp.

3539. Brito Burón, Estrella, *Quiéreme las manos,* Havana, 1964. 115 pp.

3540. Cañizares, Dulcila, *Déjame donde estoy,* Havana: Ediciones Unión, 1966. 57 pp.

3541. Casal, Julián, *Prosas, poesías,* Havana: Consejo Nacional de Cultura, 1963-1964. 4 vols.

3542. Casaus, Víctor, *Todos los días del mundo,* Havana: Ediciones La Tertulia, 1966. 66 pp.

3543. Cuza Male, Belkis, *Tiempos de sol,* Havana: Ediciones El Puente, 1963. 91 pp.

3544. Diego, Eliseo, *El oscuro esplendor,* Havana: Ediciones Belic, 1966. 52 pp.

3545. Escardó, Rolando, *Libro de Rolando; poesía,* Havana: Ediciones R, 1961. 183 pp.

3546. Ecardó, Rolando, *Las ráfagas,* Havana: Universidad Central de Las Villas, 1961. 134 pp.

3547. Feijoó, Samuel, *Azar de lecturas,* Santa Clara: Universidad

Central de los Villas, 1961. 378 pp. illus.

3548. Feijóo, Samuel, *Los trovadores del pueblo,* Havana: Universidad Central de Las Villas, 1960.

3549. Feria, Lina de, *Casa que no existía,* Havana: Instituto del Libro, 1967. 52 pp.

3550. Fernández, David, *Días y hombres,* Havana: Ediciones Unión, 1966. 43 pp.

3551. Fernández, Pablo Armando, *Himnos,* Havana: Ediciones La Tertulia, 1962. 19 pp.

3552. Fernández, Pablo Armando, *Toda la poesía,* Havana: Ediciones R, 1961. 222 pp.

3553. Fernández Retamar, Roberto, *Buena suerte viviendo,* Mexico: Alacena/Era, 1967. 86 pp.

3554. Fernández Retamar, Roberto, *Con las mismas manos,* Havana: Ediciones Unión, 1962. 210 pp.

3555. Fernández Retamar, Roberto, *En su lugar, la poesía,* Havana: Ediciones La Tertulia, 1959. 14 pp.

3556. Fernández Retamar, Roberto, *Historia antigua,* Havana: Ediciones La Tertulia, 1965. 49 pp.

3557. Fernández Retamar, Roberto, *Poesía joven de Cuba,* Lima: Imprenta Torres Aguirre, 1959. 127 pp.
Anthology.

3558. Fernández Retamar, Roberto, *Poesía reunida 1948-1965,* Havana: Ediciones Unión, 1966. 328 pp.

3559. Fernández Retamar, Roberto, *Vuelta de la antigua esperanza,* Havana: Ucar, García, 1959. 25 pp.

3560. Ferrer, Margarita, *Cuba en verso, décimas de anticipo y un romance fantástico,* (1958-1964), Havana, 1965. 52 pp.

3561. Geada, Rita, *Cuando cantan las pisadas,* Buenos Aires: Editorial Américalee, 1967. 125 pp.

3562. González Concepción, Felipe, *Altar de mis ensueños,* Havana, 1966. 94 pp.

3563. Guillén, Nicolás, *Antología poética,* Rio de Janeiro: Leitura, 1961. 147 pp.
In Portuguese.

3564. Guillén, Nicolás, *Balada,* Havana: Movimiento por la Paz y la Soberanía de los Pueblos, 1962. 4 pp.

3565. Guillén, Nicolás, *Buenos días, Fidel,* Mexico: Gráfica Horizonte, 1959. 13 pp.

3566. Guillén, Nicolás, *Elegía a Jesús Menéndez,* Havana: Imprenta Nacional. 1962. 46 pp.

3567. Guillén, Nicolás, *Poesías,* Havana: Comisión Nacional Cubana de la Unesco, 1962. 14 pp.

3568. Guillén, Nicolás, *¿Puedes?,* Havana: La Tertulia, 1960. 13 pp.

3569. Guillén, Nicolás, *Sus mejores poemas,* Lima: Torres Aguirre, 1959. 124 pp.

3570. Hurtado, Oscar, *Paseo del Malecón,* Havana: Ediciones R, 1965. 19 pp.

3571. Hurtado, Oscar, *La seiba,* Havana: Ediciones R, 1961. 69 pp.

3572. Iznaga, Alcides, *La roca y la espuma,* Havana: Editora Universitaria, 1965. 294 pp.

3573. Jamís, Fayad, *Cuerpos,* Havana: Ediciones Unión, 1966. 252 pp.

3574. Jiménez López, José, *Mis o-*

bras versos y poesías, Havana, 1963. 10 pp.

3575. Lezama Lima, José, *Antología de la poesía cubana,* Havana: Consejo Nacional de Cultura, 1965. 3 vols.

3576. López, César, *Silencio en voz de muerte,* Havana: Ediciones Unión, 1963. 65 pp.

3577. Luis, Raúl, *Los días nombrados,* Havana: Consejo Nacional de Cultura, 1966. 10 pp.

3578. Mario, José, *Muerte del amor por la soledad,* Havana: Ediciones El Puente, 1964. 52 pp.

3579. Mario, José, *La torcida raíz de tanto daño,* Havana: Ediciones El Puente, 1963. 9 pp.

3580. Martínez Furé, Rogelio, *Poesía yoruba,* Havana: Ediciones El Puente, 1963. 169 pp.

3581. Menéndez, Aldo, *Helena,* Havana: Ediciones La Tertulia, 1965. 27 pp.

3582. Michelena, Margot, *Remembranzas,* Havana, 1963. 78 pp.

3583. Navarro Luna, Manuel, *Poemas,* Havana: Ediciones Unión, 1963. 206 pp.

3584. Nogueras, Luis Rogelio, *Cabeza de zanahoria,* Havana: Instituto del Libro, 1967. 61 pp.

3585. Olivera, Otto, *Cuba en su poesía,* Mexico: Ediciones De Andrea, 1965. 217 pp.

3586. Oraá, Pedro de, *La voz a tierra,* Havana: Ediciones Unión, 1965. 78 pp.

3587. Oviedo, José Miguel, ed., *Antología de la poesía cubana,* Lima: Ediciones Paradiso, 1968. 197 pp.

3588. Padilla, Heberto, *La hora,* Havana: Ediciones La Tertulia, 1964. 15 pp.

3589. Pedroso, Regino, *Poemas, antología,* Havana: Ediciones Unión, 1966. 299 pp.

3590. Peralta, Ileana, *Temperamentales,* Havana, 1963. 66 pp.

3591. Pérez Díaz, Bernardo, *Mis hermanos los versos,* Havana, 1964. 40 pp.

3592. Piñeiro, Abelardo, *En mi barrio,* Havana: Ediciones La Tertulia, 1962. 14 pp.

3593. Pita Rodríguez, Félix, *Las noches,* Havana, 1964. 34 pp.

3594. Rigali, Rolando, *De pie frente a mí, yo,* Havana: Impr. Arquimbau, 1963. 139 pp.

3595. Rivero, Juan Felipe, *Poéticas prácticas,* Havana, 1965. 75 pp.

3596. Rivero, Isel, *Tundra, poema a dos voces,* New York: Las Américas Publishing, 1963. 91 pp.

3597. Riverón Hernández, Francisco, *Todo el amor,* Havana, 1963. 109 pp.

3598. Rodríguez Rivera, Guillermo, *Cambio de impresiones,* Havana: Ediciones La Tertulia, 1966. 51 pp.

3599. Rubiera, Rafael, *Sin fecha,* Madruga, Cuba: JUCEI Municipal de Madruga, 1963. 127 pp.

3600. Ruiz-Sierra Fernández, Oscar, *Pensando en Cuba,* Río Piedras, Puerto Rico: Graficart, 1967. 99 pp.
By exile.

3601. Sariol, Juan F., *Juguetería de ensueños y otros poemas,* Manzanillo: Editorial El Arte, 1966. 145 pp.

3602. Smith, Octavio, *Estos barrios,* Havana: Ediciones La Tertulia, 1966. 86 pp.

3603. Ulloa, Néstor, *Canto al hom-*

bre de América, Matanzas, 1966. 8 pp.

3604. Various, "En Cuba ahora," *Pájaro casacabel,* (Mexico), Jan.-July 1967. pp. 1-48.

3605. Various, *La primavera de Cuba; versos y cuentos de escritores cubanos,* Kiev: Editorial Juventud, 1962. 252 pp.

3606. Vidal, Manuel, *Tratado de amor,* Havana: Ediciones Belic, 1964. 43 pp.

b. Revolutionary

3607. Alcides, Rafael, *Himnos de montaña,* Havana: Capitolio Nacional, 1961. 108 pp.

3608. Álvarez Baragaño, José, *Himno a las milicias,* Havana: Editorial Guerrero, 1961. 36 pp.

3609. Álvarez, Baragaño, José, *Poesía, revolución del ser,* Havana: Ediciones R, 1960. 96 pp.

3610. Anónimo, *La poesía social en Cuba,* Havana, 1966. 48 pp.

3611. Araújo, Leocada, comp., *Para la niñez cubana, poesías revolucionarias en la Cuba que triunfa,* Havana: BANFAIC, 1959. 32 pp.

3612. Bayo, Alberto, *Fidel te espera en la Sierra,* Havana: Ed. Bayo Libros, 1965. 287 pp.

3613. Cuba, Comités de Defensa de la Revolución, *Pueblo en verso,* Havana: Ediciones Con la Guardia en Alto, 1966. 126 pp.

3614. Cuba, Consejo Nacional de Cultura, *Exposición, zafra y poesía,* Camagüey, 1966. 30 pp.

3615. Fajardo, Adela, *Versos para escolares,* Havana: Imprenta Reyes, 1961. 8 pp.

3616. Guillén, Nicolás, *La paloma de*

vuelo popular, Buenos Aires: Editorial Losada, 1959. 157 pp.

3617. Guillén, Nicolás, *Prosa de prisa, crónica,* Havana: Universidad Central de Las Villas, 1962. 343 pp.

3618. Jamís, Fayad, *Por esta libertad,* Havana: Casa de las Américas, 1962. 68 pp.

3619. Núñez, Ana, *Sangre resurrecta; poesía revolucionaria,* Havana: Imprenta CTC-R, 1961. 29 pp.

3620. Orta, Jesús, *Cartilla y farol, poemas militantes,* Havana: Ejército de Alfabetizadores, 1962. 41 pp. For literacy campaign.

3621. Orta, Jesús, *De Hatuey a Fidel,* Havana: Edición de la Delegación del Gobierno Revolucionario 1960. 87 pp.

3622. Orta, Jesús, *Musa popular revolucionaria,* Havana: Gobierno Provincial Revolucionario, 1960. 240 pp.

3623. Orta, Jesús, *El pulso del tiempo,* Havana: Ediciones Granma, 1966. 268 pp.

3624. Padilla, Heberto, *El justo tiempo humano,* Havana: Ediciones Unión, 1962. 133 pp.

3625. Pita Rodríguez, Félix, *Las crónicas, poesía bajo consigna,* Havana: Ediciones La Tertulia, 1961. 96 pp.

3626. Pujals, Marta *Recopilación de poesías revolucionarias,* Havana, 1966. 22 pp.

3627. Rodíguez Santos, Justo, *La epopeya del Moncada, poesía de la historia: 1953-1963,* Havana: Ediciones Unión, 1963. 160 pp.

3628. Rubiera, Rafael, *Sonetos de trinchera y otros poemas,* Havana:

Ediciones del Consejo Provincial de Cultura, 1962. 39 pp.

3629. Various, *Para el 26 de Julio,* Havana: Ediciones Unión, 1962. 223 pp.

3630. Valdés, Estrella, *Poemas revolucionarios,* Havana: Imprenta Nacional, 1961. 32 pp.

3631. Valdés, José I., *16 poemas revolucionarios,* Havana: Gobierno Provincial Revolucionario, 1960. 33 pp.

c. Criticism

3632. Anónimo, *La poesía social en Cuba,* Havana: Impr. Revolucionaria, 1965. 48 pp.
Deals with rural life.

3633. Cuadra Landrove, Angel, ed., *Ensayo histórico-literario; la poesía cubana frente al comunismo,* Miami: Unidad Nacional Revolucionaria, 1969. 63 pp.

3634. Cuba, Consejo Provincial de Cultura, *La poesía, panorama general,* Havana: Imprenta CTC-R, 1964. 28 pp.

3635. López Morales, Humberto, ed., *Poesía cubana contemporánea; un ensayo de antología,* Cádiz: Colección Arrecife, 1963. 148 pp.

3636. Mario, José, "Novísima poesía cubana," *Mundo Nuevo,* (Paris), Aug. 1969. pp. 63-69.

3637. Triana, José, "La poesía actual," *Casa de las Américas,* (Havana), Jan.-Apr. 1964. pp. 34-48.

5. Plays

3638. Alfonso, Francisco, *Yerba, hedionda,* Havana: La Milagrosa, 1959. 79 pp.

3639. Álvarez, María, *La víctima,* Havana: La Milagrosa, 1959. 84 pp.

3640. Anónimo, *Tres obras dramáticas de Cuba revolucionaria,* Havana: Municipio de Marianao, Gobierno Revolucionario, 1961. 48 pp.

3641. Arrufat, Antón, *Todos los domingos,* Havana: Ediciones R, 1965. 91 pp.

3642. Bravo, Humberto, *Monólogo del miliciano y la miliciana,* Havana: Capitolio Nacional, 1961. 12 pp.

3643. Brene, José Ramón, *El gallo de San Isidro,* Havana: Ediciones R, 1964. 161 pp.

3644. Brene, José Ramón, *Santa Camila de la Habana Vieja y Pasado a la criolla,* Havana: Ediciones El Puente, 1963. 97 pp.

3645. Cuba, Comités de Defensa de la Revolución, *Teatro,* Havana: Ediciones con la Guardia en Alto, 1965. 45 pp.

3646. Cuba, Consejo Nacional de Cultura, *Obras de repertorio,* Havana: Talleres de la CTC-R, 1961.
Eight plays.

3647. Piñera, Virgilio, *Aire frío,* Havana: La Milagrosa, 1959. 164 pp.

3648. Piñera, Virgilio, *Teatro completo,* Havana: Ediciones R, 1960. 485 pp.

3649. Pita, Santiago, *El príncipe jardinero y fingido Cloridano,* Havana: Consejo Nacional de Cultura, 1963. 113 pp.

3650. Quintero, Héctor, *Contigo pan y cebolla,* Havana: Ediciones R, 1965. 139 pp.

3651. Reguera Saumell, Manuel, *Re-*

cuerdos de *Tulipa,* Havana: Ediciones R, 1965. 113 pp.

3652. Rodríguez, Benicio, *Realengo 20; el drama del campesino cubano y los ladrones de tierras,* Havana: Editorial La Milagrosa, 1959. 96 pp.

3653. Triana, José, *El parque de la fraternidad,* Havana: Ediciones Unión, 1962. 109 pp.

3654. Triana, José, *La noche de los asesinos,* Havana: Casa de las Américas, 1965. 110 pp.

C. FINE ARTS

1. Music

3655. Ardévol, José, *Música y revolución,* Havana: Ediciones Unión, 1966. 223 pp.
Authoritative.

3656. Carpentier, Alejo, *La música en Cuba,* Havana: Imprenta Económica Integral, 1961. 205 pp.

3657. Cuba, Comités de Defensa de la Revolución, *Himno de los Comités de Defensa de la Revolución,* Havana, 1961. 1 p.

3658. Cuba, Consejo Nacional de Cultura, *Cuentos y décimas, concurso 1965. Zafra azucarera,* Havana, 1966. 38 pp.

3659. Cuba, Consejo Nacional de Cultura, *Himnos y marchas revolucionarias,* Havana: Ediciones del Consejo Nacional de Cultura, 1962. 37 pp.

3660. Cuba, Ministerio de las Fuerzas Armadas, *Himnos y canciones,* Havana, 1962. 40 pp.

3661. Feijóo, Samuel, *La décima popular,* Havana: Imprenta Nacional, 1961. 179 pp.

3662. Guay, V., "Cuban Music and the Revolution," *Music Journal,* Sept. 1969, pp. 72-73+.

3663. Hart, Armando, *Discurso al Sindicato de Artistas y la Unión Sindical de Músicos,* Havana, 1960. 22 pp.
Oct. 24, 1960.

3664. León, Argeliers, *Música folklórica cubana,* Havana: Biblioteca Nacional José Martí, 1964. 148 pp.

3665. León, Argeliers and María Teresa Linares de León, *Música guajira,* Havana: Ediciones del CNC, 1965. 12 pp.

3666. Orta, Jesús, *Marcha triunfal del ejército rebelde y poemas clandestinos y audaces,* Havana, 1959. 46 pp.

3667. Sociedad Cubana de Autores Musicales, *Descarga musical,* Havana, 1964. 52 pp.

2. Art

3668. Autores varios,, *Pintura contemporánea en Cuba,* Havana, 1960. 13 pp.

3669. Cuba, Consejo Nacional de Cultura, *Artes plásticas y desarrollo social,* Havana, 1964. 19 pp.

3670. Cuba, Biblioteca Nacional José Martí, *Dibujos y publicaciones de Marcelo Pogolotti desde octubre de 1964,* Havana, 1964. 16 pp.

3671. Hurtado, Oscar, "Pintores cubanos," *Bohemia,* (Havana), Jan. 8, 1965. pp. 74-76.

3672. *Kubanische revolutionare graphik,* Dresden: VEB Verlag der Kunst, 1962. 92 pp.

3673. Marinello, Juan, *Conversación con nuestros pintores abstractos,*

Santiago de Cuba: Universidad de Oriente, 1960. 84 pp.
PSP defends socialist realism.

3674. Rodríguez, Alberto, *Las artes gráficas*, Santiago de Cuba: Universidad de Oriente, 1963. 100 pp.

3675. Schleifer, Marc, "Letter from Havana," *The Nation*, Apr. 27, 1964. pp. 442-445.
Art and the Revolution.

3676. Sutherland, Elizabeth, "Letter from Havana," *The Nation*, Nov. 4, 1961. pp. 359-361.
Art controversy.

3. Theater

3677. Anónimo, "Panorama del teatro cubano," *Cuba en la Unesco*, (Havana), Feb. 1965. pp. 3-175.

3678. Arrufat, Antón, "An Interview on the Theater in Cuba and in Latin America," *Odyssey Review*, (NY), Dec. 1962. pp. 248-263.

3679. Badia, N., "Cuba," *World Theatre*, Jan. 1965. p. 60.

3680. Barletta, Leónidas, "Sobre un teatro del pueblo," *Casa de las Américas*, (Havana), Jan./Feb. 1962. pp. 87-107.

3681. Blanco Fernández, José, *Teatro revolucionario*, Havana, 1966. 62 pp.

3682. Cid Pérez, José, ed., *Teatro cubano contemporáneo*, Madrid: Aguilar, 1959. 430 pp.
Anthology.

3683. Casa de las Américas, ed., *Teatro cubano*, Havana: Casa de las Américas, 1961.
Four plays by Fornés, Parrado, Estorino and Arrufat.

3684. Cuba, Consejo Provincial de Cultura, *El teatro, panorama general*, Havana: Impr. CTC-R, 1964. 21 pp.

3685. "Cuba," *World Theatre*, May-July 1966. pp. 308-309.

3686. Dauster, F., "Cuban Drama Today," *Modern Drama*, Sept. 1966. pp. 153-164.

3687. Felipe, Carlos, *Teatro cubano*, Havana: Ucar, García, s. a., 1960. 245 pp.

3688. Ferrer, Rolando, *Teatro*, Havana: Ediciones Unión, 1963. 173 pp.

3689. González, Nati, "Centro Dramático de Las Villas," *Granma*, (Havana), May 4, 1966. p. 8.
Theater.

3690. González, Nati, *Teatro cubano contemporáneo*, Havana, 1958. 267 pp.
Covers 1927-1958.

3691. González, Nati, *Teatro cubano: 1927-1961*, Havana: Ministerio de Relaciones Exteriores, 1961. 181 pp.

3692. Leal, Rine, "El teatro en un acto en Cuba," *Unión*, (Havana), Jan.-Apr. 1963. pp. 52-75.

3693. Leal, Rine, ed., *Teatro cubano en un acto*, Havana: Ediciones R, 1963. 354 pp.

3694. Parrado, Gloria, *Teatro*, Havana: Ediciones Unión, 1966. 64 pp.

3695. Piñera, Virgilio, et al., "El teatro actual," *Casa de las Américas*, (Havana), Jan.-Apr. 1964. pp. 95-107.

3696. Robreño, Eduardo, *Historia del teatro popular cubano*, Havana: Oficina del Historiador de la Ciudad, 1961. 93 pp.

3697. Vieta, Ezequiel, *Teatro*, Havana: Ediciones Belic, 1966. 60 pp.

4. Movies

3698. Agramonte, Arturo, *Cronología del cine cubano,* Havana: Ediciones ICAIC, 1966. 172 pp. Movies from 1894-1963.

3699. Colina, José de la, "El cine en Cuba," *Casa de las Américas,* (Havana), Jan.-Apr. 1964. pp. 126-129.

3700. Guevara, Alfredo, "El cine cubano tiene 10 años," *Bohemia,* (Havana), Jan. 31, 1969. pp. 68-69.

3701. Rodríguez, Mario, "El cine cubano busca su auténtico carácter," *INRA,* (Havana), Apr. 1961. pp. 10-15.

3702. Sutherland, Elizabeth, "Cinema of Revolution—90 Miles from Home," *Film Quarterly,* (Berkeley, Calif.), Winter 1961-1962. pp. 42-48.

D. ARCHITECTURE

3703. Congreso de la Unión Internacional de Arquitectos, *La Arquitectura en los países en vías de desarrollo: Cuba,* Havana, 1963. 118 pp.

3704. Cuba, Colegio Nacional de Arquitectos, *Estatutos,* Havana, 1963. 11 pp.

3705. Cuba, Congreso de los Constructores, *Memorias,* Havana: Dirección de Divulgación del MICONS, 1965. 183 pp.

3706. Rowntree, Diana, "The New Architecture of Castro's Cuba," *Architectural Forum,* (New York), Apr. 1964. pp. 122-125.

E. SCHOLARLY DISCIPLINES

1. History Revisionism

3707. Barrero Pérez, Juan G., *La cubanía aniquilada por la enmienda Platt,* Sancti Spíritus, Cuba, 1958. 245 pp.

3708. Carbonell, Walterio, "Visión de la Isla: El marxismo y la historia de Cuba," *Bohemia,* (Havana), Feb. 26, 1965, pp. 26-28; Mar. 5, 1965. pp. 26-29.

3709. Chain, Carlos (Capitán), "La formación de la nación cubana," *Verde Olivo,* (Havana), Feb. 5, 1967. pp. 15-17, 55-56.

3710. Corbitt, Duvon C., "Cuban Revisionist Interpretations of Cuba's Struggle for Independence," *Hispanic American Historical Review,* Aug. 1963. pp. 395-404.

3711. Entralgo, Elías, *Lecciones de historia de Cuba,* Havana: Archivo Nacional, 1960-1961. 3 vols.

3712. García, Pedro, "Emilio Roig de Leuchsenring," *Bohemia,* (Havana), Apr. 26, 1963. pp. 18-20. Cuba's main revisionist historian.

3713. Havana, Oficina del Historiador de la Ciudad, *Revaloración de la historia de Cuba por los Congresos Nacionales de Historia,* Havana, 1959. 282 pp.

3714. Portuondo, José A., "Hacia una nueva historia de Cuba," *Cuba Socialista,* (Havana), Aug. 1963. pp. 24-39.

3715. Roig de Leuchsenring, Emilio, *Los Estados Unidos contra Cuba republicana,* Havana, 1960. 299 pp.

3716. Smith, Robert F., "Twentieth Century Cuban Historiography,"

Hispanic American Historical Review, Feb. 1964. pp. 44-73.

2. Philosophy

3717. García Galló, Gaspar, *Nuestra moral socialista,* Havana: Ed. del Ministerio de Educación, 1964. 88 pp.

3718. Oltuski, Enrique, "Filosofía revolucionaria," *Lunes de Revolución,* (Havana), July 26, 1959. pp. 6-8.

3719. Piñera Llera, Humberto, *Panorama de la filosofía cubana,* Washington: Unión Panamericana, 1960. 128 pp.

3. Social and Physical Sciences

3720. Blanco de la Carrera, Fernando, Mario Ramos and Román Rodríguez, *La importancia del estudio de las ciencias,* Havana: Ministerio de Educación, 1964. 33 pp.

3721. Cuba, Academia de Ciencias, *Conferencia de las academias de ciencias de los países socialistas,* Havana, 1967. 1113 pp.

3722. Cuba, Academia de Ciencias, *Primera Reunión de Información Científica y Técnica. Memoria,* Havana: Instituto de Documentación e Información, 1966. 88 pp. Mimeographed.

3723. Cuba, Instituto Nacional de Reforma Agraria, *Resultados del encuentro técnico agrícola soviético-cubano, celebrado del 5 al 23 de abril de 1962,* Havana, 1962. 40 pp.

3724. Hartman, Heinz, "Sociology in Cuba," *American Sociological Review,* (Washington, D.C.), Aug. 1963. pp. 624-628.

3725. Le Roy Gálvez, Luis Felipe, *La Facultad de Ciencias de la Universidad de La Habana en el centenario de su creación,* Havana, 1963. 32 pp. Biographical data.

3726. Ricard, Marta, "Esquema del desarrollo de la enseñanza de los estudios sociales en Cuba revolucionaria," *Escuela y Revolución en Cuba,* (Havana), Feb.-Mar. 1963. pp. 90-93.

3727. Havana, Universidad de la Habana, *La investigación científica: un panorama,* Havana, 1963. 60 pp.

F. FOLKLORE

3728. Alvarado, Américo S., *7 leyendas matanceras,* Matanzas: Seminario Vanguardia, 1960. 82 pp.

3729. Alzola, Concepción Teresa, *Folklore del niño cubano,* Havana: Universidad Central de Las Villas, 1961-1962. 2 vols.

3730. Cabrera, Lydia, *La sociedad secreta Abakúa narrada por viejos adeptos,* Havana: Ediciones C.R., 1959. 296 pp. Voodoo.

3731. Cardoso, Onelio Jorge, ed., *El pueblo cuenta,* Havana: Imprenta Nacional, 1961. 69 pp.

3732. Cardoso, Onelio Jorge, *Gente de pueblo,* Las Villas: Universidad Central, Biblioteca de Investigaciones Folklóricas, 1963. 198 pp. Present day folklore.

3733. Cuba, Academica de Ciencias, *Prosa oral: Anecdotario pinero,* Havana, 1967. 32 pp.

3734. Cuba, Consejo Nacional de Cultura, *La Trova Cubana, (Iconografía),* Havana: Ediciones de

la Coordinación Provincial, 1966.
106 pp.

3735. Díaz Fabelo, Teodoro, *Olarum*,
Havana: Editora Departamento de
Folklore, T.N.C., 1960. 117 pp.

3736. Feijóo, Samuel, "Breve análisis
sobre el guajiro actual," *ISLAS*,
(Santa Clara), Jan.-June 1965. pp.
37-40.

3737. Feijóo, Samuel, ed., *Diario
abierto; temas folklóricos cubanos*,
Havana: Universidad Central de
Las Villas, 1960. 301 pp.

3738. Feijóo, Samuel, *Mitos y leyen-
das en Las Villas*, Santa Clara:
Editora del Consejo Nacional de
Universidades, 1965. 252 pp.

3739. Feijóo, Samuel, *Sabiduría guajira*, Havana: Editora Universitaria, 1965. 359 pp.

3740. Franco Ferrán, José Luciano,
Folklore criollo y afrocubano,
Havana: Junta Nacional de Ar-
queología y Etnología, 1959. 99
pp.

3741. Iglesia y Santos, Alvaro de la,
Tradiciones cubanas, Lima: Impr.
Torres, Aguirre, 1959. 2 vols.

3742. Lorenzo Fuentes, José, *Magua-
raya arriba*, Havana: Universidad de Las Villas, Dirección de
Publicaciones, 1963. 117 pp.

3743. Menéndez Alberdi, Adolfo,
*Azúcar; viejo tema poético y folk-
lórico cubano*, Havana, 1967. 19
pp.

3744. Mesa, Blanca Mercedes and
Antonia María Trista, *Cuentos,
relatos y refranes pineros*, Havana: Academia de Ciencias de
Cuba, 1967. 51 pp.

3745. Millares Vázquez, Ángel, *Car-
naval de La Habana, desarrollo
histórico*, Havana: JUCEI Municipal, 1964. 14 pp.

3746. Ortiz, Fernando, *La africanía
de la música folklórica de Cuba*,
Havana: Editora Universitaria,
1965. 486 pp.
Scholarly monograph.

3747. Yanes, Leoncio, *Donde canta
el tocoloro*, Havana: Universidad
Central de Las Villas, 1963. 172
pp.

G. HUMOR

3748. Agencia de Informaciones Periodísticas, *La realidad cubana
vista por los caricaturistas de
América*, Miami, 1965. 6 pp.

3749. Boan, Angel, *Dos años tras la
cortina de chicle*, Havana: Luz-
Hilo, 1961. 175 pp.
Ridicules U.S. efforts to isolate
Cuba.

3750. Cardi, Juan Ángel F., *Brevísi-
ma pero muy documentada historia de la prensa*, Havana: Ediciones Palante, 1966. 34 pp.

3751. Cardi, Juan Ángel F., *El amor
es cosa de dos*, Havana, 1966. 62
pp.

3752. Chago, pseud., *El humor otro*,
Havana: Ediciones R, 1963. 185
pp.
Cartoonist.

3753. Desnoes, Edmundo, "El humo-
rismo en Cuba," *Casa de las Américas*, (Havana), Jan.-Apr. 1964.
pp. 113-121.

3754. Desnoes, Edmundo, "Humor
ahora," *CUBA Internacional*,
(Havana), Jan. 1970. pp. 18-24.

3755. Fresquet, Fresquito, (pseud.),
De tonto que soy, Havana: Edicio-
res Belic, 1964. 28 pp.
Humor.

3756. Nuez, René de la, *Allí fumé*, Havana: Ediciones Unión, 1966. 28 pp.
Critique of revolutionary bureaucracy.

3757. Nuez, René de la, *Cuba sí, dibujos humorísticos*, Havana: Ediciones R, 1963. 127 pp.

3758. Palante, *Un, dos, tres*, Havana, 1966. 31 pp.

3759. Wilson, Luis, *Criollitas de Wilson*, Havana, 1966. 63 pp.

H. MASS MEDIA

3760. Anónimo, *La crisis publicitaria en Cuba*, Havana, 1960. 41 pp.

3761. Backer, Jack E., 'The 'Prestige Press' and News Management in the Cuban Crisis," *Journalism Quarterly*, (Minneapolis, Minn.), Spring 1964. pp. 264-265.

3762. Bernstein, Victor and Jesse Gordon, "The Press and the Bay of Pigs," *The Columbia University Forum*, (New York) Fall 1967. pp. 4-13.

3763. Bueno Montoya, M., "La prensa cubana en el régimen de Fidel Castro," *Nuestro Tiempo*, (Madrid), Mar. 1961. pp. 315-328.

3764. Castro, Fidel, "Jamás será interferida por el Gobierno de Cuba la libertad de la Prensa," *Diario de la Marina*, (Havana), Apr. 24, 1959. pp. 1, 2A.

3765. Castro, Fidel, *The Press Has the Great Task of Orienting the People*, Havana: Ministerio de Relaciones Exteriores, 1961. 36 pp.

3766. Castro, Fidel, César Escalante and Isidoro Malmierca, *Sobre la propaganda. Fragmentos selec-* cionados de distintas intervenciones, Havana: Partido Comunista de Cuba, 1965. 30 pp.

3767. Congreso Interamericano de Locutores, *La verdad de Cuba en las antenas del mundo*, Havana: Ministerio de Relaciones Exteriores, 1959. 30 pp.

3768. Cuba, Ministerio del Trabajo, *Reglamento para la organización de la emulación en la prensa revolucionaria*, Havana, 1964. 30 pp.

3769. "Cuban Revolt Story Was Underplayed," *Editor and Publisher*, Feb. 21, 1959. p. 56+.

3770. "Cuban Story Called Failure of Journalism," *Editor and Publisher*, (New York), Jan. 3, 1959. p. 48.

3771. Dewart, Leslie, "Cuba and the Wayward Press," *The Canadian Forum*, (Toronto), June 1961. pp. 54-56.

3772. Escalante, César, *Algunos problemas en torno a la propaganda revolucionaria*, Havana: Imprenta Nacional, 1961. 16 pp.

3773. Escalante, Cesár, "Lo fundamental en la propaganda revolucionaria," *Cuba Socialista*, (Havana), Sept. 1963. pp. 18-31.

3774. Fernández, Francisco, "La prensa y la opinión pública en Cuba," in Palgunov, Nikolai, ed., *La prensa y la opinión pública*, Havana: Editorial Nacional de Cuba, 1962. pp. 125-188.

3775. Fina, Francisco, *La prensa en Santiago de las Vegas*, Santiago de las Vegas: Editorial Anteña, 1961. 15 pp.

3776. Francis, Michael J., "The U.S. Press and Castro: A Study in Declining Relations," *Journalism*

Quarterly, (Minneapolis, Minn.), Summer 1967. pp. 257-266. 1959-1961.

3777. Havana, Colegio Provincial de Periodistas, *Fórmula para la costeabilidad de un salario de $300 mensuales para los periodistas,* Havana: Ed. Adelaida, 1959. 23 pp.

3778. Lewis, Howard L., "The Cuban Revolt Story: AP, UPI and 3 Papers," *Journalism Quarterly,* (Minneapolis, Minn.), Autumn 1960. pp. 573-578.

3779. Marrero, Juan, "Prensa Latina Was Born in the Sierra," *Granma,* (Havana), June 22, 1969. p. 11.

3780. Newman, Alfred, "Operation Truth: a Cuban Diary," *Reporter,* (Milwaukee, Wisc.), Feb. 19, 1959. pp. 27-32.

3781. Portuondo, José A., *"La Aurora" y los comienzos de la prensa y de la organización obrera en Cuba,* Havana: Imprenta Nacional de Cuba, 1961. 115 pp.

3782. *Reporting on Cuba,* Havana: Books Institute, 1967. 115 pp.

3783. Roca, Blas, *"Bohemia" contrarevolucionaria y pro-imperialista,* Havana: Partido Socialista Popular, 1959. 2 pp.

3784. *Visión sobre Cuba,* Havana, 1959. 56 pp.

I. PUBLISHING

3785. Cuba, Biblioteca Nacional, *Movimiento editorial en Cuba: 1959-1960,* Havana, 1961. 44 pp.

3786. "Libros: casi dos para cada uno," *CUBA Internacional,* (Havana), July 1969. pp. 4-9. Book publishing since 1965.

3787. Pereira, Manuel, "Para multiplicar los libros," *CUBA Internacional,* Mar. 1970. pp. 56-57. Bookstores that trade, not sell.

J. STAMPS

3788. Arredondo, Alberto, *Estafa internacional: utiliza el régimen comunista de La Habana la filatelia en un negocio sucio de 112 millones de dólares,* Miami: AIP. 9 pp.

3789. Cuba, Ministerio de Comunicaciones, *Album para sellos de Cuba,* Havana: Publicaciones Filatélicas, 1963. 64 pp.

3790. Cuba, Ministerio de Comunicaciones, *Breviario del correo en Cuba,* Havana, 29 pp.

3791. Cuba, Ministerio de Comunicaciones, *Catálogo abreviado de los sellos de correos de Cuba Revolucionaria,* Havana: Empresa Comercial Filatélica, 1965. 37 pp.

3792. Cuba, Ministerio de Comunicaciones, *Reglamento de los servicios de Correos, giros postales y telégrafos,* Havana, 1965. 25 pp.

3793. Cuba, Ministerio de Comunicaciones, *La revolución cubana y sus sellos de correos,* Havana, 1962. 12 pp.

IX. RELIGION

3794. Agüero, Sixto Gastón, *El materialismo explica el espiritismo y la santería,* Havana: Orbe, 1961. 92 pp.
Communist analyzes "spiritualism."

3795. Aldeaseca, Jaime de, *Mientras el mundo gira,* Havana: Impr. Ucar, García, 1960. 217 pp.
Catholic TV sermons.

3796. Anónimo, *Pasión de Cristo en Cuba; testimonio de un sacerdote,* Santiago de Chile: Departamento de Publicaciones del Secretariado de Difusión, 1962. 76 pp.

3797. Anonymous, "Bishops: Cuba Pastoral Letter," *Catholic Messenger,* Aug. 18, 1960. p. 12.

3798. Anonymous,"Cuba: the Church Attempts a Rapprochement," *Latin America,* (London), Feb. 23, 1968. pp. 57-58.

3799. Aparicio Laurencio, Angel, *Donde está el cadáver se reúnen los buitres,* Santiago de Chile, 1963. 206 pp.
Chronicle of religious persecution.

3800. Arango, Dario Padre, S.J., *¡Respondednos camaradas!,* Medellín, Colombia, 1961. 16 pp.
Religious persecution.

3801. Arce Martínez, Sergio, *La misión de la Iglesia en una sociedad socialista,* Havana, 1965. 34 pp.
Theological analysis.

3802. Barrios, Pablo L., *Manifiesto a los católicos y nuestros mensajes,* Havana, 1961. 41 pp.

3803. Benítez, Antonio, "Los nuevos aires de San Carlos," *CUBA Internacional,* Feb. 1970. pp. 26-35.
Church and revolution.

3804. Castro, Fidel, "Prestaron los católicos de Cuba su cooperación decidida a la causa de la libertad," *Diario de la Marina,* (Havana), Jan. 7, 1959. pp. 1, 2-A.

3805. Castro, Fidel, "Revolución es destrucción de todos los privilegios y de todo lo pasado," *Revolución,* (Havana), Dec. 17, 1960. pp. 1, 10, 13.
Church policy.

3806. Castro, Fidel, "Traicionar al pobre es traicionar a Cristo," *Revolución,* (Havana), Aug. 11, 1960. pp. 1, 6, 12.
Reply to church criticism.

3807. Cepeda, Rafael, "La conducta cristiana en una sociedad revolucionaria: testimonio desde Cuba," *CIDOC Informa,* (Mexico), Mar. 16, 1966. pp. 101-105.

3808. Contreras, Orlando, "Opina Obispo cubano," *CUBA Internacional,* Aug. 1969. pp. 22-25.

3809. "Cuba and the Church," *Commonweal,* (New York), Mar. 13, 1964. pp. 716-719.

3810. Cuba, Santiago, "El clero reaccionario y la revolución cubana," *Cuba Socialista,* (Havana), June 1962. pp. 8-29.

3811. Dewart, Leslie, *Christianity and Revolution; The Lesson of Cuba,* New York: Herder and Herder, 1963. 320 pp.

3812. Díaz, Evelio (Bishop), *Message by a Catholic Bishop About the Cuban Land Reform,* Havana, 1959. 3 pp.
Favors it.

3813. Directorio Revolucionario Estudiantil, *La persecución de la Iglesia Católica en Cuba,* Quito, Ecuador, 1963. 32 pp.

3814. Editorial, "Bishops of Cuba, Pastoral Letter," *Catholic Messenger,* Aug. 18, 1960. p. 12.

3815. Foyaca, Manuel, *La Iglesia Católica frente al comunismo,* Havana: Editorial Lex, 1960. 336 pp.
Defends church.

3816. Gall, Norman, "Castro and the Church," *The New Leader,* (New York), Sept. 14, 1964. pp. 3-5.

3817. Galland, Valdo, "Impressions of the Protestant Churches in Cuba," *Motive,* (Nashville, Tenn.), Feb. 1965. pp. 41-45.

3818. González Acevedo, Alberto, *El mundo de los fantasmas,* Havana: Editorial Nacional de Cuba, 1963. 32 pp.
Denounces spiritualism and superstition.

3819. Harris, W. Donald, "Churchman Reports on Recent Visit to Cuba," *Presbyterian Life,* (Philadelphia), Apr. 1, 1963. pp. 29-31.

3820. Labelle, Yvan, "The Church in Socialist Cuba," *CIF Reports,* (Cuernavaca), Apr. 1, 1965. pp. 48-50.

3821. Landono, Fernando, "La Santa Sede y Cuba," *Revista Javeriana,* (Bogotá), Vol. 57, No. 283, Apr. 1962. pp. 263-268.

3822. Listov, V., "Bitaia karta imperilizma," [the trumped card of imperialism], *Nauka i religiia,* (Moscow), June 1963. pp. 36-38.
Communism—religion.

3823. Menéndez, Mario, "La Iglesia y la revolución cubana," *Bohemia,* (Havana), Nov. 4, 1966. pp. 18-26.

3824. Morán, Braulio, (pseud.) and Leslie Dewart, "Cuba and the Church; an Exchange of Views," *The Commonweal,* (New York), Mar. 13, 1964. pp. 716-719.

3825. Nitya, Eddu, *La suprema revelación. Precedida de oda a la revolución, las siete reglas del perfecto espiritista, Fidel ante la humanidad,* Havana: Tip. Ideas, 1961. 8 pp.

3826. Olba Benito, Miguel Angel, "La persecución religiosa a la obra misionera en la Cuba comunista," *Defensa Institucional Cubana,* (Mexico), Feb. 1964. pp. 25-29.

3827. "Pastoral Letter of the Cuban Hierarchy," *Tablet,* (London), Aug. 20, 1960. p. 772.

3828. Pérez Serantes, Mons., "Pastoral sobre el castigo a criminales de guerra," *Diario de la Marina,* (Havana), Feb. 1, 1959. pp. 1, 6B.
Archbishop of Santiago de Cuba.

3829. Pérez Varela, Angel, *Notas para la historia del Santuario de la Virgen de Regla,* Havana, 1967. 96 pp.

3830. Piedra, A. M., "Cuban Case: History Repeats Itself," *Catholic Educational Review,* (Washington, D.C.), Apr. 1967. pp. 252-258.

3831. Roca, Blas, "La lucha ideológica contra las sectas religiosas," *Cuba Socialista*, (Havana), June 1963. pp. 28-41.

3832. Roca, Blas, *Veneno en "La Quincena,"* 13 *artículos sobre la campaña contrarrevolucionaria de la jerarquía católica*, Havana, 1961. 71 pp.

3833. Ruiz, Pedro Pablo, *El espiritismo en Cuba*, Havana: Editorial Más Allá, 1958-1959. 3 vols.

3834. San Martín, Hernán, "La santería cubana," *Anales de la Universidad de Chile*, (Santiago de Chile), Nov.-Dec. 1961. pp. 150-156.

3835. Sociedad Bíblica de Cuba, *Día de la Biblia. Ofrendas 1965*, Havana, 1966. 18 pp.

3836. Tyseira, Oscar, *Cuba marxista vista por un católico*, Buenos Aires: J. Alvarez, 1964. 197 pp.
Also a Peronista.

3837. Valdespino, Andrés, "La Iglesia no rompe con Castro para no abandonar a los fieles," *Bohemia Libre*, (Miami), Feb. 18, 1962. pp. 43-45, 61, 63.

3838. Various, *Castro, el anticristo de la Sierra Maestra*, Ciudad Trujillo, 1960. 58 pp.
Nine "professional opinions."

3839. Velasco, Margarita, "La iglesia católica en Cuba," *Punto Final*, (Chile), Feb. 25, 1969. pp. 14-17.

INDEX OF AUTHORS